THE MARKETPLACE MINISTRY HANDBOOK

THE MARKETPLACE MINISTRY HANDBOOK

A Manual for Work, Money and Business

Edited by

R. Paul Stevens & Robert Banks

REGENT COLLEGE PUBLISHING
Vancouver, British Columbia

The Marketplace Ministry Handbook
Copyright © 2005 by R. Paul Stevens & Robert Banks
All rights reserved.

Published 2005 by Regent College Publishing
5800 University Boulevard, Vancouver, BC V6T 2E4 Canada
Web: www.regentpublishing.com
E-mail: info@regentpublishing.com

Views expressed in works published by Regent College Publishing are those of
the author and do not necessarily represent the official position of Regent College
<www.regent-college.edu>.

All Scripture quotations, unless otherwise indicated, are taken from the Holy
Bible, New International Version®. NIV®. Copyright 1973, 1978, 1984 by
International Bible Society. Used by permission of Zondervan Publishing House.
All rights reserved.

Library and Archives Canada Cataloguing in Publication Data

   The marketplace ministry handbook : a manual for work, money and business
/ edited by R. Paul Stevens & Robert Banks.

Includes bibliographical references and index.
ISBN 1-57383-294-4

   1. Work—Religious aspects—Christianity. I. Banks, Robert J. II. Stevens, R.
Paul (Robert Paul), 1937-

BT738.5.M37 2005   261.8'5   C2004-906041-4

CONTENTS

HOW TO USE THIS GUIDE FOR ALL ITS WORTH

"Marketplace Ministry" seems an oxymoron, like fried ice or black light. The marketplace is the location for exchanging goods, services and values, whether in e-commerce, a village marketplace, the mall, the professional office, the multinational corporation or the local retail store down the street. This exchange involves money, power, competition, careers, compensation, and sometimes whisteblowing. "Ministry," in contrast, brings to most people's minds the kind of things we do in church: singing hymns or worship songs, teaching the Bible and nurturing people's spiritual lives. What do they have to do with each other?

From the Christian perspective, which is the undergirding philosophy of this manual, ministry is not just something we do in church. Nor it is merely overtly religious activity such as bringing church-like ministries into the marketplace. It is all the ways we serve God and God's purposes in the world, as well as the church. And one of the main places we serve God and our neighbour is in the workplace.

Most people spend about 88,000 hours of their lifetime in the workplace, and even more if one is a farmer or a professional. The same people, if they are dedicated Christians may only spend about 4000 hours in church services and religious meetings. Unfortunately there is often little connection between the two, between Sunday and Monday. This manual is about bridging the gap, namely exploring how to be full-time ministers of God in the world as well as the church. To do this we must think Christianly about life—loving God with our minds by thinking coherently and reflecting on the realities we face nine to five from the perspective of biblical revelation. But there is more to the articles than mere thought. They are also concerned with how we live in the realities of complex and ambiguous situations we face in the work world. So the authors in this manual do theology "from below" drawing out the implicit meaning in everyone's attitude to and handling of work. But they also do theology "from above" by applying the great truths in Scripture to the realities of life. Theology brings together both thought and action, both study and behaviour. So Christian theology is always applied theology. The Puritan William Perkins once said that "theology is the science of living blessedly forever." That is what the manual seeks to empower with special focus on the realities of the work-a-day world.

Not surprisingly there is an article on "Business Ethics." But there are also articles, just to name a few, on money, compromise, credit, workplace dress-code, homemaking, management, organizational culture, profit, talents and retirement.

They are written by a wide variety of people who have thought and lived deeply on their subject: academics, homemakers, business leaders, professionals and a tradesperson, all men and women that make up the richly endowed people of God.

You can read this manual from front to back. But, as the articles are listed alphabetically, you might want to start with your own questions and look up the article on that subject. Occasionally you may look for an article and find a pointer to a related one, indicated by "See...." At the end of each article is a section called "References and Resources." This is not only a list of books and articles on which the author has drawn, but indicates some resources that you can pursue for further study.

As the two editors of this volume we are delighted to see these thoughtful and seminal articles to be circulated widely as we have spent most of our lives as educators, pastors, and workers, attempting to bridge the Sunday-Monday gap, exploring a down-to-earth spirituality and empowering the whole people of God for service and life in the home, workplace, society and the church. These articles were originally part of a larger volume, *The Complete Book of Everyday Christianity*. Enjoy this manual and grow in faith, hope and love in what can make marketplace involvement truly a ministry.

R. Paul Stevens and Robert Banks

LIST OF ARTICLES

LIST OF CONTRIBUTORS

DR. DAVID AUGSBURGER, professor of pastoral counseling, Fuller Theological Seminary: **Conflict Resolution**

DR. STUART BARTON BABBAGE, author: **Retirement**

ROBERT BANKS, theological educator, former director, Macquarie Christian Studies Centre, Sydney, Australia: **Commuting; Compromise; Gossip; Mobility; Ownership, Private; Part-Time Employment; Service, Workplace; Shiftwork; Stress, Workplace; Work Ethic, Protestant; Workplace**

WILLIAM DIEHL, consultant, author: **Competency; Conflict, Workplace; Firing; Negotiating; Office Politics; Promotion**

DONALD E. FLOW, president, Flow Automotive Companies: **Profit**

DR. CRAIG GAY, associate professor of interdisciplinary studies, Regent College: **Consumerism**

DR. DAVID GILL, teacher and writer, adjunct professor, New College Berkeley, Fuller Theological Seminary and San Jose State University: **Power, Workplace; System; Technology**

ROBERT GIRARD, pastor, author: **Failure**

PETE HAMMOND, director, InterVarsity Marketplace: **Accountability, Relational**

DR. ALEXANDER D. HILL, president, InterVarsity Christian Fellowship, USA: **Business Ethics**

DR. PATRICK LATTORE, director of corporate and foundation relations, Children's Hospital Los Angeles Foundation; adjunct assistant professor of leadership, Fuller Theological Seminary: **Leadership**

KATHRYN LOCKHART, homemaker, humorist: **Dress Code, Workplace**

DR. PAUL MARSHALL, senior fellow, Center for Religious Freedom, Freedom House, Washington, D.C.: **Power**

DR. MICHEL MESTRE, professor, Faculty of Business and Economics, Trinity Western University: **Unemployment**

HAL MILLER, software engineer: **Success**

PETER MOGAN, lawyer: **Contracts**

RUTH OLIVER, Volunteer Bureau, Vancouver: **Volunteer Work**

DR. RICHARD W. POLLAY, professor of marketing, University of British Columbia: **Advertising**

GORDON PREECE, chaplain and lecturer in ethics and lay ministry, Ridley College, Melbourne, Australia: **Work**

DR. PETER QUEK, senior pastor, Scarborough Chinese Baptist Church: **Competition**

DR. JOHN E. RICHARDSON, associate professor of management, Pepperdine University: **Discrimination, Workplace; Whistle-Blowing**

GERRY SCHOBERG, registrar, Regent College: **Structures; System**

JOHN SCHREIDER, professor of theology, Calvin College: **Money**

R. PAUL STEVENS, professor of applied theology, Regent College: **Advertising; Ambition; Calling/Vocation; Career; Credit Card; Drivenness; Global Village; Insurance; Investment; Organization; Organizational Culture and Change; Organizational Values; Principalities and Powers; Professions/Professionalism; Stewardship; Structures; Trades; Unemployment; Vocational Guidance; Wealth**

JOHN R. SUTHERLAND, professor of management and business ethics, Trinity Western University: **Credit; Debt; Strikes; Unions**

DAN WILLIAMS, pastor, author: **Committees; Planning**

DR. WALTER WRIGHT, JR., director, DePree Center, Fuller Theological Seminary: **Accountability, Workplace; Integrity; Loyalty, Workplace; Management**

SCOTT YOUNG, campus minister, UCLA: **Networking**

ACCOUNTABILITY, RELATIONAL

It used to be popular to say, "No one is an island," reflecting a cultural understanding of connectedness and responsibility between people. But it is different today. Simon and Garfunkel's plaintive 1960s folksong preached, "I am a rock; I am an island," reflecting the extreme of our society's rugged individualism. It is in this environment that accountability has almost disappeared and loneliness has become dominant.

Designed for Accountability

Rugged individualism goes against God's design for human society. We were designed to be interconnected and complementary to each other. Even though the word *accountability* does not occur in most Bible translations, the concept is foundational. Male and female were designed to "become one flesh" (Genesis 2:24). People of faith are to answer to one another (Acts 15:1-4; James 5:14-20).

A very clear picture of accountability is presented by Paul in his letter to the Corinthian church. Here he uses the image of a builder to describe all people of faith. He then describes how what we build will be measured and the quality or lack of it will bring either reward or loss. He clearly explains how responsible we are to God for all we are and do (1 Cor. 3:10-23).

Meaning of Accountability

What does accountability actually mean? Some contemporary definitions include the following:

Reckoning. Computation. A statement explaining one's conduct. *(Webster's Dictionary)*

Accounting denotes certain theories, behavioral assumptions, measurement rules and procedures for collecting and reporting useful information concerning the activities and objectives of an organization. *(Encyclopedia Britannica)*

Accountability looks back to some deed done or attitude held. Obligation looks forward to moral demands that need to be met in relationships. (Cole, pp. 734-35)

Our cultural understanding suggests that accountability is best designed when it encourages desirable performance. This process is served by the disciplines of bookkeeping or the classifying of data and activities in order to measure them against agreed-upon standards and expectations.

But in the community of faith it is much more. Accountability for believers is more dynamic. It is organic in nature and expressed through relationships, networks and systems. It is developed through visibility as in commissioning or storytelling,

Accountability and Commitment

Peter Block, in his excellent book *The Empowered Manager,* calls attention to the difference between commitment and sacrifice. When responsibility is imposed from outside and not owned by the person responsible, it requires sacrifice. The individual must sacrifice his or her personal vision to pursue a vision owned by someone else. This is neither satisfying nor motivating. Responsibility is assigned by someone else, and accountability is measured by someone else. On the other hand, ownership of responsibility leads to commitment. When the individual owns responsibility for the purpose, accountability flows from personal commitment. This is the highest form of motivation. The individual is accountable to himself or herself to fulfill the accepted responsibility as an expression of his or her own personal vision.

Accountability and Power

This distinction becomes painfully important in organizational settings where responsibility is given (and accepted), where accountability is expected, but the authority or resources necessary to fulfill the responsibility are not provided. This is the classic definition of powerlessness and leads to a significant loss of motivation and performance. It is critically important that the appropriate authority and resources be available to enable the person to fulfill the responsibility. Otherwise accountability is personally frustrating and organizationally meaningless.

In an organizational setting it is important to distinguish between accountability for results and accountability for tactics or strategies. Responsibility is best shared when it focuses on results and allows the individual to invest himself or herself in the determination of the best way to achieve those results in line with the organization's mission and values. If too much specificity is involved in this, there is little responsibility given and thus little accountability. The assumption here is that responsibility can and should be shared, recognizing that this does not release those drawn into its exercise from responsibility and accountability.

Whether in business or volunteer church work, accountability structures need to be clearly defined. This can be one to one in spiritual friendships, through small groups, by means of performance reviews and through formal accountability groups, such as those outlined in David Watson's book *Covenant Discipleship.*

Accountability at its best is the ownership of responsibility for results with self-evaluation and self-correction as one moves toward the accomplishment of a purpose or the living of a vision. It assumes personal integrity and organizational trust and loyalty.

See also ORGANIZATION; ORGANIZATIONAL CULTURE AND CHANGE; ORGANIZATIONAL VALUES

References and Resources

P. Block, *The Empowered Manager* (San Francisco: Jossey-Bass, 1987); D. L. Watson, *Covenant Discipleship: Christian Formation Through Mutual Accountability* (Nashville: Discipleship Resources, 1991).

—Walter Wright Jr.

ADVERTISING

Years ago Marshall McLuhan said, "Ours is the first age in which many thousands of our best trained minds made it a full-time business to get inside the collective public mind . . . to manipulate, exploit, and control" (p. v). Given its pervasive and persuasive character, advertising is without doubt one of the most formative influences in popular culture, shaping values and behavior and telling people how and why to live. It is estimated that the average North American is subjected to over one thousand advertisements daily in one or other of the media (television, radio, magazines, newspapers, billboards, direct mail) covering everything from perfume to automobiles, from fast food to insurance.

Advertising is simply any paid form of nonpersonal presentation to promote products, services or ideas, sometimes, but not always, in a way attractive to the person the advertiser wishes to influence. In a market economy, advertising can supply information needed for the people to make an informed choice. But on the other hand, advertising is frequently used to persuade people or even seduce them to believe that what they want is what they need and that consuming a particular product will in some way change them. In other words, advertising tinkers with identity and values.

Not a Recent Invention

While many people think advertising was invented on Madison Avenue in New York City during the post-World War II boom, advertising is as old as civilization. Ironically one of the oldest pieces of advertising from antiquity that can be viewed today is an inscription of a woman in the pavements of ancient Ephesus (modern Turkey) advertising the nearby brothel. But even before this, in ancient Egypt (3200 B.C.) the names of kings were stenciled on temples, and runaway slaves were "advertised" on papyrus. Advertising took a giant step forward with the invention of movable type and the printing of the Gutenburg Bible (A.D. 1450). It could then be endlessly repeated and mass-produced. Not long after this, an English newspaper advertised prayer books for sale, a forerunner of the newspaper ad. While it can be argued that people have always been trying to persuade others to do, buy or experience something—from town criers to preachers—it is unquestionable that rapid industrialization, urbanization, the proliferation of media and now the information superhighway have

17

escalated advertising to a central role in culture formation, perhaps even in spiritual formation, since it is a major player in establishing values and defining meaning-giving experiences.

As a form of communication, advertising has some good intended effects, some recognized by commentators on the Third World scene, where advertising has found almost virgin territory. Besides sometimes giving people information to make choices when there is more than one product or service offered, advertising is often used to promote desirable social aims, such as savings and investment, family planning, health-promoting products (such as antimalarial drugs), lifestyles that will reduce AIDS and fertilizers that will enhance crop production (MacBride, p. 154). Advertising helps the media to be autonomous from politics—not a small matter in some countries. But when we consider the overall impact, it is less clear to most observers that the effects of a highly commercialized culture are beneficial. Nowhere is this more evident than in the West.

The Not-So-Subtle Message

The intended effect of advertising is not merely to make a sale but to awaken or produce predispositions to buy an advertised product or service (Britt, p. 195). To advertise "Coke Is It" is not simply to sell a brand, but to have us think of branded, packaged goods when thirsty, not just plain water. It also alters our perceptions so that when we experience that branded beverage, we will see it a certain way, associating fizziness with youthfulness and joy. The total effect of advertising is to preoccupy society with material goods and services as the path to happiness and the solution to virtually all problems and needs. Commercial persuasion appears to program not only our shopping patterns but also the larger domain of our social roles, language, goals, values and the sources of meaning in our culture.

Advertising does this very effectively for several reasons. It is (1) pervasive, appearing in many modes and media; (2) repetitive, reinforcing the same and similar ideas relentlessly; (3) professionally developed, with all of the attendant research sophistications to improve the probabilities of attention, comprehension, retention and/or behavioral impact; and (4) delivered to an audience that is increasingly detached from traditional sources of cultural influence like families, churches or schools. A stunning example of the deceptiveness of advertising is the story of American cigarette ads in the 1960s. Backed by massive television budgets, they implied that filtered brands were good for our health. Smoking rates among teenagers continued to grow even after the famous report of the surgeon general in 1964.

Unintended Consequences

Not surprisingly, such an intrusive and all-pervasive system of communication has been negatively critiqued by academics and social scientists who are concerned with the effects of advertising on role-modeling, child development, social behavior and even religious belief. A Yale psychologist confessed, "Advertising makes me miserable" by an intensified pursuit of goals that would not have been imagined save for advertising (Dollard, p. 307). People are induced to keep productive in order to keep consuming, to work in order to buy because we are always in need of more. This has the serious (unintended) side effect of displacing feelings from people to objects and an alienating effect in which the self is perceived not as a child of God or as a person in community, but as an exchange commodity. Life is trivialized, not dignified, when someone becomes evangelistic about mundane material objects like mayonnaise.

Nowhere may interpersonal relations be more affected than in the home as the roles of both women and children as consumers get expanded and redefined. Advertising has become an insolent usurper of parental function, "degrading parents to mere intermediaries between their children and the market" (Henry, p. 76). Relations with neighbors, the proverbial Joneses we strive to keep up with, are increasingly based on envy, emulation and competition. Advertising works on the tension-arousal and tension-reduction (with the use of the product) process. In the case of the poor and marginalized, the inaccessibility of the products being offered "may create in some viewers feelings of frustration sufficient to make them engage in antisocial acts" (Myers, p. 176).

Advertising, for almost as long as it has existed, has used some sort of sexual sell, sometimes promising seductive capacities, sometimes more simply attracting our attention with sexual stimuli, even if irrelevant to the product or the selling point. While less graphic than pornography, advertising is more of a tease than a whore, for sexual stimulation is moderated and channeled. Nevertheless, the overall effect represents a challenge to standards of decency, a devaluing of women and a revaluing of the body. Erik Barnouw notes that we now see women caressing their bodies in showers with a frequency and reverence of attention that makes "self-love a consecrated ritual" (p. 98).

Advertising also affects the credibility of language. S. I. Hayakawa notes that "it has become almost impossible to say anything with enthusiasm or joy or conviction without running into the danger of sounding as if you were selling something" (p. 268). Advertising is a symbol-manipulating occupation. For example, "Christmas and Easter have been so strenuously exploited commercially that they almost lose their religious significance" (Hayakawa, p. 269). Because virtually all citizens seem to recognize this tendency of ad language to distort, advertising seems to turn us into a community of cynics, and we doubt the advertisers, the media and authority in all its forms. Thus we may also distrust other received wisdoms from political authorities, community elders, religious leaders and teachers of all kinds. But without trustworthy communication, there is no communion, no community, only an aggregation of increasingly isolated individuals, alone in the mass.

Religious Significance

Some anthropologists view advertising in terms of rituals and symbols—incantations to give meaning to material objects and artifacts. Advertising defines the meaning of life and offers transcendence in the context of everyday life. Our commercial-religious education begins early with jingles, slogans and catch phrases, the total commercial catechism, so that children learn the "rite words in the rote order." So direct exhortations are employed, literally a series of commandments, a secular litany that Jacques Barzun identified as "the revealed religion of the twentieth century" (p. 53). "You get only one chance at this life; therefore get all the gusto you can!" is a theological claim and a moral injunction. Toward this end advertising appeals to the traditional seven deadly sins: greed, lust, sloth, pride, envy and gluttony, with anger only infrequently exploited or encouraged. Since these words are frowned upon in the advertising community, they must be given a different spin. Lust becomes the desire to be sexually attractive. Sloth becomes the desire for leisure. Greed becomes the desire to enjoy the good things of this life. Pride becomes the desire for social status (Mayer, p. 128). In this way advertising cultivates what Paul called "the works of the flesh" (Galatians 5:17-23; Galatians 6:8 NRSV). Morality is subverted; values are revised; ultimate meaning is redefined.

The Ethics of Persuasion

All this happens largely without the viewer knowing it. Those who defend the present state of the advertising art claim that the most far-reaching advertising campaign cannot force someone to buy something he or she does not want. The citizen is supposedly immune to persuasion. But advertising is by definition intrusive, so intrusive that the real message communicated on television or in magazines is often the commercials. This successful commanding of attention makes the attempt to concentrate on the remaining content of media "like trying to do your algebra homework in Times Square on New Year's Eve" (Hayakawa, p. 165).

Such intrusion, first into our consciousness and then into our inner voices, distracts us from the serenity of solitude and thereby inhibits self-awareness. The repetitive, fantastic, one-sided and often exhortative rhetorical styles of advertising combine to blur the distinction between reality and fantasy, producing a state of uncritical consciousness, passivity and relative powerlessness. Nonwants becomes wants; wants become needs. Advertising would never have taken hold the way it has without the American (and ultimately the Western) psyche having undergone a change in the direction of viewing itself therapeutically. We need help; advertising offers it. Not only this, but morals and values get adapted to the message: indulge, buy, now and here. As Barnouw observes, "The viewer's self-respect requires a rejection of most commercials on the conscious level, along with some ridicule. Beneath the ridicule the commercial does its work" (p. 83).

It does this work in ways that are ethically questionable. Advertising is advocative through giving incomplete information, half-truths or careful deceptions, by being insistent, exhortative and emphatic. It appeals essentially to emotions, seducing people to indulge themselves now rather than defer gratification, reducing life to the here and now, if not the moment. It reinforces social stereotypes, aggravates sexism, racism and ageism. In idealizing the "good life" advertising makes us perpetually dissatisfied. Can it be resisted?

Battling Seduction

The myth of immunity to advertising's inducements is clearly a delusion for some or perhaps many or even most of the public, including Christians. So the first thing we need to do is admit that we live in an advertising environment. Then what?

First, Christian organizations and churches need to repent of their own seductive advertising. The end never justifies the means. Keeping the televangelist on the air does not justify half-truths and appeals to the flesh. Many relief organizations use rhetorical devices and selected "truths" to get money for their great cause. A good first step would be for Christian organizations to establish an ethical code for their own advertising to be published along with their financial statements.

Second, the church or groups of people can lobby or use legitimate channels of political expression to press for the closer regulation of advertising. Some obscene ads have been effectively banned by consumers boycotting certain suppliers, although an unintended side effect is sometimes more publicity for the product itself, as happened with some of the Calvin Klein ads (Faltermayer, p. 64).

Third, Christians working in the advertising industry need the prayerful support of their church as they are stewards of the culture and shapers of morals. There is no place in the world where it is easy to work as a Christian (even the church), but there is no place so demonized that a Christian might not be called to work there. The well-known novelist and apologist Dorothy Sayers worked for many years in advertising and turned the experience to good literary and theological effect.

Fourth, individually we can become more critical of advertising, reflecting on what we see and hear and discussing the intended and unintended consequences as families and groups of friends. One of the most important facets of Christian education in the family is to learn how to more than survive in the world. This will normally involve limiting time watching television, deliberately excluding commercials where possible and discussing the values implicit in advertising.

Fifth, in place of the seven deadly sins, which are often cultivated by the advertising industry, we should cultivate the seven cardinal virtues—wisdom, justice, temperance, courage, faith, hope and love (see Organizational Values; Values). Spiritual conflict is a fact of life in this world, but if we live in the Spirit and are firmly rooted in a genuine community of the Spirit we can battle the world, the flesh and the devil victoriously. Paul said, "Live by the Spirit, and you will not gratify the desires of the sinful nature" (Galatians 5:16 NRSV).

Sixth, the recovery of solitude, sabbath and spiritual disciplines are crucial to regaining and keeping our true identity. Most people in the Western world need

The Old Testament is rich in examples of both unholy and holy ambition. These are often given to us without comment, leaving us to read between the lines for their positive or negative effects. Joseph's dreams were not simply an expression of a subconscious superiority complex; they were a part of his having a legitimate vision of greatness under God. Though at first Joseph wrongly used his dreams as weapons against his brothers (Genesis 37:1-11) and only later learned to let God be the architect of their fulfillment, his dreams were a powerful motivating factor in his life. Jacob, in contrast, was rightly ambitious to have the Lord's blessing but resorted to stealing and subterfuge to get it (Genesis 25:19-34; Genesis 27:1-40), thus fulfilling his prophetic name (which means "heel-grabber"). Gideon had the holy ambition of wanting to save Israel, Joshua of conquering the land, Nehemiah of restoring the kingdom and Paul of planting a self-propagating church in every major center of the Roman Empire.

Unfortunately passages like Matthew 6:33 that encourage holy ambition are usually applied exclusively to Christian service roles in the church and evangelistic activity in the world rather than to the promotion of kingdom values in the home, workplace and community. Having an ambition to provide extraordinary service to customers and to provide fair compensation packages to employees can be as holy as desiring to plant a new church in a presently unreached area. Indeed, selfish ambition may be easily disguised in a Christian service career and praised as godly zeal.

Any consideration of ambition must take into account the function of personality. More important, however, is the way ambition becomes an expression of our spirituality and therefore an important dimension of self-knowledge and self-discipline in everyday life.

Bad and Good Ambition

As a work of the flesh, selfish ambition is present when we define ourselves by our achievements, rather than by our character. For many men, and increasingly for women, the choice of career represents an "idealized fantasy of who one is or might become . . . the medium through which these dreams are enacted and judged" (Ochberg, p. 3). Defining our identity by achievement is, in the end, self-defeating as it leads either to a frenzied, driven life spurred by diminishing returns of past successes or to despair when we realize we can never become that wished-for self. Because our motives are so mixed, the search for a satisfying and challenging career is less like fitting a peg into its slot and more like compressing an unruly spring into a container and wondering how long it will stay (Ochberg, p. 4).

At the root of this spiritual pathology is the autonomous self trying to find meaning in life by its own action rather than as a child of God. Symptoms of this selfish ambition are relentless striving with an inability to rest, discouragement at the lack of recognition obtained for one's hard work, predatory competition (even in Christian leadership), use of the present situation (and people) as a stepping stone and an "endless itchiness for other possibilities" (Schnase, p. 17). The Bible leaves little room for exalting human achievement and constantly points us in the direction of exulting in God's achievements. But our motives are always mixed, and a theology of grace accepts humanness just as it is. At the same time it points to something better. Because ambition is not uniformly evil, it is a risk worth taking.

Life without ambition would be largely passive and complacent, victim to the latest manipulating persuader or discouraging turn, rather than directed toward a goal. As a redeemed passion, ambition gives force to a life direction of seeking God's purposes in family, workplace, church and community. Ambitious people take initiative and are future oriented and consistently motivated: "Ambition gives color to our dreams and places before us an appetite for the possibilities of life. Ambition gives us strength of character to turn aspirations into reality through muscle and sweat, mind and imagination" (Schnase, p. 14). Ambition can be redeemed through *orthopathy*, that is, the conversion of our passions to line up with God's *pathos*, what God cares about. A truly Christian conversion is concerned not only with orthopraxy (true and right action) but also with orthopraxy (true and right affections).

Converting the Passions

As the Galatians 5:16-26 passage makes plain, simple trust in Jesus does not immediately eliminate the battle within. Ambition is a reflection of this inner struggle.

Ongoing reconquest. After initial conversion the Christian normally experiences an ongoing reconquest of the person through walking and living in the Spirit (Galatians 5:15, 25) and maintaining a crucified perspective on our fallen human nature (the flesh; Galatians 2:3; Galatians 5:24; Galatians 6:14). The latter is not self-crucifixion, mortifying one's bodily life, or self-hatred but fully and continuously agreeing with God's judgment on our autonomous self-justifying life. Since such a life puts God to death and crucifies Christ in our hearts, it is worthy of death. Negatively, walking according to the Spirit means not setting the mind on or doing the deeds of the flesh (Romans 8:5; Galatians 5:19-21) nor doing the deeds of the flesh, but putting these desires and deeds to death by the Spirit (Romans 8:13; Galatians 5:16-18, 24-26). Also, the one who walks by the Spirit does not boast in human achievement (Phil. 3:3-6), human wisdom (1 Cor. 2:1-6) or righteousness (Romans 2:17-19; Galatians 2:15-21). Thus, walking according to the Spirit means a renunciation of the desires and deeds of the flesh, including the temptation to define our identity and self-worth by "getting ahead." In a positive statement, walking according to the Spirit implies that the Christian "keeps in step" (Galatians 5:25) with what the Spirit is already doing. This involves setting one's mind on the things of the Spirit (Romans 8:5) and allowing the Spirit to produce character fruits (Romans 12-14; Galatians 5:19-21) and to empower works of holiness (Romans 12:9-21; compare Isaiah 58).

Inside godly ambition. Several life patterns in the New Testament surround and illuminate the process of the conversion of our ambitions: self-control, contentment, faithfulness, neighbor love and praise. *Self-control* is bringing one's whole self into harmony so that we are in charge of our own life—thoughts, feelings, appetites, drives and bodily needs. Some people claim they want Christ to take control of their lives, but this may be something less than the full dignity of being a self-controlled child of God. Self-control is the fruit of the Spirit (Galatians 5:23), a byproduct of a life lived in harmony with God's purposes and for God's glory. Ironically we are most likely to be freed from compulsive ambition and addictions when we give up trying to accomplish the conversion of our passions by self-justifying self-discipline and focus on following Jesus and glorifying God.

Contentment is not antithetical to godly ambition, but it is incompatible with selfish ambition. Ambition and contentment must coexist peacefully in the Christian soul (Shelley, p. 3). Paul was able to confess that he had "learned the secret of being content in any and every situation" (Phil. 4:12). He gained this through trust in God (Phil. 4:13) and the practice of continuous thanksgiving (Phil. 4:6). Paul claims he had "learned" contentment; it was not something automatically gained through conversion or by an ecstatic Spirit-filling. It is sometimes argued that we should be content with what we have but not content with what we are. This seems to shortchange the full conversion of our passions, a conversion involving the pruning of unworthy ambitions to encourage godly ambitions. This is best done in the company of other believers who can hold us accountable and, when necessary, name the lie in our stories. In this way we can be released from the slavery to more, better and bigger.

Faithfulness feeds the godly ambition and is complementary (Galatians 5:22). Eugene Peterson described the faithful life as a "long obedience in the same direction," a life neither passively quiet nor frantically busy. In the marketplace ambition can be good if it is used for the common good and is harmonized with the advancement of others (Troop, p. 25), a life pattern I call *neighbor love*. In 1 Cor. 3-4 Paul raises the crucial question of evaluation, or *God's praise,* in the context of a congregation that compared its leaders and prided itself on spiritual advancement. He argues that "each will be rewarded according to his own labor" (1 Cor. 3:8), stressing that any difference in work will be for God to reward and judge at the final judgment (1 Cor. 3:10-15; compare Matthew 25:21). No one else is capable of finally evaluating a servant of God: "Even the servant's own self-evaluation means nothing. Only one opinion matters—that of the Lord" (Kuck, p. 179), a factor that is relevant not only for Christian service workers but Christians tempted to unholy ambition in the workplace or political realm.

Self-control, contentment, faithfulness, neighbor love and praise all contribute to the redemption of ambition, for they liberate ambition from paralyzing self-centeredness. J. S. Bach had it right. He wrote over every manuscript what we can write over balance sheets, sermons and shopping lists: "SDG," which means *soli Deo gloria* (to God alone be the glory). Coupled with this should be the statement by the playwright Anton Chekhov: "One would need to be a God to decide which are the failures and which are the successes in life" (Kuck, p. 174).

See also CALLING; CAREER; DRIVENNESS; SUCCESS; WORK

References and Resources
W. Barclay, *Flesh and Spirit: An Examination of Galatians 5:19-23* (London: SCM, 1962); J. Epstein, *Ambition: The Secret Passion* (New York: Dutton, 1980); D. Kuck, "Paul and Pastoral Ambition: A Reflection on 1 Cor. 3-4," *Currents in Theology and Mission* 19, no. 3 (1992) 174-83; R. L. Ochberg, *Middle-Aged Sons and the Meaning of Work* (Ann Arbor, Mich.: U.M.I. Research Press, 1979); R. Schnase, *Ambition in Ministry: Our Spiritual Struggle with Success, Achievement and Competition* (Nashville: Abingdon, 1993); M. Shelley, "From the Editors," *Leadership* 11, no. 3 (1990) 3; J. Troop, "High Hopes," *Christianity Today* 30, no. 14 (1986) 24-25.

—R. Paul Stevens

BUSINESS ETHICS

Business is often compared to a poker game. Both, it is argued, require nondisclosure and distrust in order to succeed, with only the naive showing their true intentions. Mark Twain's observation that "an ethical man is a Christian holding four aces" reflects a notion still in vogue today—that ethics and competitive environments like business or winner-takes-all games rarely mix.

A Separate Business Ethic?

The poker metaphor serves to legitimize business behavior that would be considered immoral in the personal realm—bluffing, deception and contributing to another's harm. All of these behaviors are justified in the name of their "real world" contexts.

Advocates of dual morality, that is, applying one set of ethics in the marketplace and another in the home and church, expect employees to lay aside personal values and to focus solely on generating corporate profits. Everything possible, except perhaps breaking the law, must be done to enhance the bottom line. Subordinates have no right to interject personal values, such as environmental protection, fairness to fellow workers or contempt for dishonest sales techniques, into corporate matters. A century ago businessman Dan Drew, founder of Drew Seminary, smartly summed up this philosophy: "Sentiment is all right up in the part of the city where your home is. But downtown, no. Down there the dog that snaps the quickest gets the bone. I never took any stock in a man who mixed up business with anything else" (quoted in Steiner and Steiner, p. 333).

A soul mate of Drew was oil baron John D. Rockefeller. Influenced by his devout Baptist mother, he developed on the one hand a strong personal religious ethic. His shrewd father taught him on the other hand to win at any cost in business, once boasting, "I cheat my boys every chance I get. I want to make them sharp." Rockefeller resolved this contradiction by compartmentalizing his life into two separate realms.

Ruthless in business, he gave kickbacks to railroads, violently suppressed labor unrest and bribed competitors' employees to give him inside information. However, in his personal life he donated nearly half a billion dollars to a countless variety of worthy causes. One writer concludes that "Rockefeller was a conscientious Christian who struggled to end the livelihood of his every rival" (Steiner and Steiner, p. 27).

Such a segmented ethical system is inherently unchristian because it ignores the twin doctrines of creation and sovereignty. The apostle Paul argues that no realm of life is beyond the lordship of Christ. Indeed, all things were created "through him," "in him" and "for him." His authority sustains the created order, extending over "thrones, or dominions, or principalities, or powers" (Col. 1:16 KJV).

As such, Christ has power over all beings and institutions. No human activity—including the practice of business—falls outside of his lordship. To argue otherwise is to denigrate his authority. The sacred-secular split embodied by Drew and Rockefeller must be rejected because Christian ethics cannot be relegated to part-time status, applied only on evenings and weekends. On the contrary, Martin Luther correctly asserted that Christian vocation is best expressed in life's most common experiences.

It must also be noted that business is no mere poker game but a major social institution. To compare it to a game is to trivialize its importance. Further, not all of its so-called players understand the unwritten dog-eat-dog rules. Many, including immigrants, family members, the elderly and the young, do not have their guards up and are easy prey. Finally, to argue that employees must turn off their consciences when they enter their workstations is to ignore the lessons of Nuremberg and My Lai (Konrad, pp. 195-97).

God's Character and Human Nature

How then should Christians, having rejected dual morality, behave in the workplace? Simply put, we are called to imitate God. But what does this mean? Three divine characteristics repeatedly emphasized in Scripture are holiness, justice and love. Of course, such imitation is easier said than done. Despite our noblest intentions, we regularly exaggerate, break promises and hide our errors. Why? We do so because we are sinners whose moral grip is weak and whose moral vision is clouded. This is particularly problematic in the hothouse of the marketplace where financial stakes are high, career destinies are decided and the temptation to rationalize is strong.

Even as sinners, however, we generally aspire for wholeness and regret when we fall short. Our consciences, though less reliable than originally designed, are still operative. Personal redemption and the guidance of the Holy Spirit also contribute significantly to our efforts.

Holiness in Business

During the Middle Ages *holiness* was construed to mean separation from ordinary life in order to pursue otherworldly contemplation. Hence business—perhaps the most fleshy of all human enterprises— was viewed as being "dirty," even antithetical to holiness. Fortunately, this is not an accurate definition of biblical holiness.

Holiness has three primary attributes: zeal for God, purity and accountability. The first attribute, zeal for God, requires that all human concerns—material goods, career goals and personal relationships—be considered of secondary importance. As Jesus observed, only one master can be primary (Matthew 6:24). Does this mean that God is opposed to business success? No, the crucial point is that holiness is fundamentally about priorities. As long as business is a means of honoring God rather than an end in itself, the concept of holiness is not violated. What holiness prevents is making business, or any other human activity, an idol.

The second attribute of holiness is purity. Ethical purity reflects God's moral perfection and separation from anything impure. Jesus beckons his followers to "be perfect . . . as your heavenly Father is perfect" (Matthew 5:48), and Paul encourages believers to be "holy and blameless" (Ephes. 5:27). In business such purity means being morally different from one's peers. This includes, but is by no means limited to, purity in communication (not skewing financial reports, not manipulating contract language and not using innuendo to undercut others) and purity in sexuality (not making lewd comments, not engaging in flirting and not participating in sexual discrimination).

The third attribute of holiness is accountability. Scripture abounds with illustrations of righteousness being rewarded and of sin being punished. The analogy may be rough, but accountability is not solely a theological concept. It is an economic principle as well. For while the market neither credits righteousness nor sanctions sin per se, it does tend to reward companies that keep promises and are honest while punishing enterprises that regularly miss deadlines and produce substandard products.

Many false perceptions of holiness exist. J. I. Packer writes, "Partial views abound. Any lifestyle based on these half-truths ends up looking grotesque rather than glorious; one-sided human development always does" (p. 163). Three such misguided views of holiness are legalism, judgmentalism and withdrawal. Legalism reduces holiness to rule keeping. Like the Pharisees of Jesus' day, legalistic managers tend to be procedurally rigid, emphasizing policies and petty rules over employee welfare. Judgmentalists justify themselves by pointing out even greater moral lapses in others, having long memories of subordinates' errors. Ironically, they are doomed to lives of hypocrisy because of their inability to measure up to their own standards. Finally, those who define holiness as withdrawal from society are guilty of confusing moral separation, which Scripture endorses, and physical separation, which it generally does not. Judging from the company Jesus and Paul kept, they would feel quite comfortable mingling with today's stockbrokers, IRS agents and sales representatives.

Justice in Business

On his conversion to Judaism, entertainer Sammy Davis Jr. commented, "Christianity preaches love your neighbor while Judaism preaches justice. I think that justice is the big thing we need." Fortunately, he was only partially correct. Christianity also emphasizes justice. Four key concepts are procedural rights, substantive rights, meritorious justice and contractual justice.

Procedural rights focus on fair processes. Scripture requires a decision-maker to be impartial, having neither preexisting biases nor any conflict of interests. Nepotism is a classic violation of this principle. Another example occurs when a corporate board member fails to disclose her personal financial interest in another company with which the board is negotiating. Procedural justice also mandates that adequate evidence be marshaled and that each person affected by a decision be afforded the opportunity to tell his or her side of the story. Thus, auditors must be thorough and able to authenticate all findings. In like manner, supervisors should hesitate before dismissing employees for theft, disloyalty or incompetence solely on the word of a coworker or circumstantial information. In the New Testament both Jesus and Stephen were denied such simple due process (Matthew 26:60; Acts 6:13).

Substantive rights are ones such as the right to own property, to physical safety, to prompt payment for work completed and to be told the truth. Hence employees must steal neither time nor material, because such behavior violates their employer's property rights. Likewise, employers must neither deceive nor discriminate against their employees, because this would infringe on their right to be told the truth and to be treated with dignity. When parties fail to respect substantive rights, the government is often called in to remedy the harm (Romans 13:1-7).

Meritorious justice links the concepts of cause and effect. Good choices (for example, working hard or selecting trustworthy business partners) bring success, while bad choices (for example, hiring a mediocre manager or expanding too rapidly) produce failure. Merit earns its own rewards. Proverbs concurs: "He who works his land will have abundant food, but the one who chases fantasies will have his fill of poverty" (Proverbs 28:19). Similarly, Jesus states, "With the measure you use, it will be measured to you" (Matthew 7:2), and Paul advises: "A man reaps what he sows" (Galatians 6:7).

Contractual justice recognizes that individuals may agree to take on additional duties vis-à-vis each other. This may be as simple as a seller and buyer transferring title to a house or as sophisticated as the merging of two multinational corporations. Each party's performance is conditioned on the performance of the other. Examples of such expanded duties include business partners who agree to divide their earnings. By contrast, neighbors assume no such obligations. Likewise, while employers pay their workers and retain the right to bring disciplinary action against them for poor performance, friends possess no such rights. The difference is that contractual justice permits the creation of additional duties. Similarly, God's covenant with Israel extended extraordinary rights to Abraham's progeny but also imposed additional responsibilities. Compliance was rewarded by peace and prosperity; breaches were met with severe sanctions (Leviticus 26:3-39).

As central as justice is to the core of Christian ethics, it must, however, never be separated from holiness and love. Isolated, it becomes harsh, permitting no second chances for those who fail. None of us cherishes working for a company that fires staff for minor breaches of corporate policy or that reacts in knee-jerk fashion with a lawsuit for every noncompliance by a supplier or dealer. Of course, the problem is not with justice or holiness, but with us. We stumble over their high standards due to our moral imperfections (Romans 7:1-25). A third characteristic—love—is therefore vital to complete our picture of Christian business ethics.

Love in Business

Many consider love to be the apex of Christian ethics. Paul identified it as the greatest human virtue, and Martin Luther thought it best described the essence of God's character (Bloesch, p. 42). Jesus ranks love for God first and love for neighbor second. It is important to note that his definition includes both holiness (making God our highest priority) and justice (always taking the interests of others into account).

Love's primary contribution to the holiness-justice-love mix is its emphasis on relationships. By way of example, imagine an embezzler who now regrets what she has done. While holiness causes her to feel unclean and justice creates a fear of getting caught, love produces a sense of grief over the harm caused to others. Breaching relationships causes such pain.

While it is tempting to define *love* as a "soft" virtue, concluding that it has no place in the rough and tumble of the marketplace, we need only note that business history is littered with companies ruined by fractured relationships. Indeed, commercial ventures depend more upon cooperation than competition. To be successful, partners must get along with each other; supervisors must engender loyalty among their subordinates; and suppliers must be brought into a supportive network.

Love has three primary characteristics: empathy, mercy and self-sacrifice. *Empathy* is the capacity to celebrate others' joys and shoulder their burdens, that is, to sincerely feel what others feel. Of course, it would strain credibility to argue that modern capitalism operates primarily on the basis of empathetic love. Backs are scratched to mutual advantage, and perhaps achieving reciprocal respect is the best that can be expected. Christian empathy goes far beyond this, however, encouraging corporate executives to demonstrate concern for the less fortunate, to take personal interest in the fate of deathly ill associates and to sympathize with sales staff who miss quotas due to unexpected personal problems.

Mercy is empathy with legs. It takes the initiative in forgiving, redeeming and healing. Christian mercy seeks reconciliation, even to the extent of loving one's enemy (Matthew 5:38-44). Other ethical systems refuse to go so far. Aristotle and Confucius, for example, taught that the duty to love is conditioned on the other person's response. The Christian position demands much more, requiring us to live not according to the golden rule but beyond it (Bloesch, p. 33).

Self-sacrifice means that love willingly sacrifices the very rights that justice bestows. For example, an employee motivated by love may voluntarily relinquish her office in order to accommodate a disabled peer. Or a spouse may consent to move so that his wife's career is enhanced. Saint Francis of Assisi was so sacrificial in giving his clothes to the poor that his disciples had difficulty keeping him dressed. Sacrificial love frightens us because it appears to be a blank check with no limits. While soldiers who jump on hand grenades to save the lives of their comrades and Jesus' sacrificial death are admired, business leaders understandably balk at such extreme vulnerability.

Are there any limits to such love? Clergyman Joseph Fletcher, author of *Situation Ethics,* thinks not. He contends that love is Christianity's sole ethical principle and that holiness concepts (for example, zeal for the truth, ethical purity and concern for right and wrong) are to be cast aside when they impede love. Fletcher's approach provides minimal guidance as to what actions should be taken in a morally unclear situation. Does love really provide moral cover for falsifying a document in order to protect a fellow worker? Does an executive's concern for shareholder wealth and employee job security justify his bribing government officials? For Fletcher, "altruistic sinning" is the order of the day. This emasculated definition of love not only ignores holiness but flouts justice as well. What good are the rights of property ownership and due process if they can be willy-nilly disregarded in the name of love? Justice prohibits such behavior by providing a base line set of rights—dignity being primary—that can neither be given or taken away in the name of love.

Love places limits upon itself. Is it really loving to lie for a peer who is using drugs? Serving as a doormat in such situations may actually cause more long-term harm to the person being "helped." King David's slavish devotion to his son Absalom resulted in a selfish, and ultimately self-destructive, personality (2 Samuel 15). Biblical self-love calls us to love our neighbor as ourselves (Luke 10:27). The ethical rule of thumb regarding self-love is an inverted golden rule: if we would feel ethically uncomfortable asking another to do a particular act, then we ought not consent to do it for others. Christian self-love does not condone abuse or servility. Rather, incorporating the concepts of holiness, justice and love, it produces healthy reciprocal relationships.

Holiness, Justice and Love in Business

A balanced view requires that holiness, justice and love be respected equally. Without holiness, love degenerates into permissiveness. Nearly anything can be justified in the name of love—defamation, price fixing, industrial espionage. Conversely, holiness without love produces unforgiving perfectionism. Who would want to work for a supervisor who embodies such an ethic? But holy love produces the highest and purest form of integrity and compassion.

Likewise, love without justice lapses into favoritism and a short-term perspective. Imagine an employee being given a day off with full compensation without regard to the perception of partiality by other staff. Justice without love is equally unacceptable. To twist the facts of the prior example, what do we think of supervisors who always go by the book, never acknowledging exceptional individual circumstances? Such a harsh approach leaves us feeling cold. Only when combined do justice and love form "tough love," a disciplined balancing of long-term interests.

Finally, holiness without justice drifts toward withdrawal from the marketplace and a privatized form of religion. Conversely, justice without holiness results in an amoral form of procedural fairness that lacks moral substance. Decision-makers become absorbed in procedural details (for example, time lines, required signatures, waivers) and fail to focus on the deeper rights and duties involved. Only through holy justice can ethical integrity and procedural justice both be ensured.

The ultimate goal is to produce practitioners who imitate God's holy, just, loving character in the marketplace. This is the true character of biblical business ethics.

See also ACCOUNTABILITY, WORKPLACE; BUSINESS; COMPROMISE; INTEGRITY; NEGOTIATING; POWER; WORKPLACE; PRINCIPALITIES AND POWERS; PROFIT; SUCCESS

References and Resources

T. Beauchamp and N. Bowie, *Ethical Theory and Business,* 4th ed. (Englewood Cliffs, N.J.: Prentice-Hall, 1993); D. Bloesch, *Freedom for Obedience: Evangelical Ethics for Contemporary Times* (San Francisco: Harper & Row, 1987); R. Chewning, *Biblical Principles and Business,* vols. 1-4 (Colorado Springs: NavPress, 1989); R. Chewning, J. Eby and S. Roels, *Business Through the Eyes of Faith* (New York: Harper & Row, 1990); J. F. Fletcher, *Situation Ethics: The New Morality* (Philadelphia: Westminster Press, 1966); A. Hill, *Just Business: Christian Ethics in the Marketplace* (Downers Grove, Ill.: InterVarsity Press, 1997); A. Hill, "Colossians, Philemon and the Practice of Business," *Crux* 30, no. 2 (1994) 27-34; A. Konrad, "Business Managers and Moral Sanctuaries," *Journal of Business Ethics,* 1 (1982): 195-200; J. Packer, *Rediscovering Holiness* (Ann Arbor, Mich.: Servant, 1992); L. Smedes, *Mere Morality* (Grand Rapids: Eerdmans, 1983); G. Steiner and J. Steiner, *Business, Government and Society* (New York: Random House, 1983); J. Stott, *Christian Counter-Culture: The Message of the Sermon on the Mount* (Downers Grove, Ill.: InterVarsity Press, 1978); O. Williams and J. Houck, *Full Value: Cases in Christian Business Ethics* (San Francisco: Harper & Row, 1978).

—Alexander D. Hill

CALLING/VOCATION

The English word *vocation* comes from the Latin *vocatio,* which means "calling"; they are the same thing, though this is not obvious to the people who use these words. Experiencing and living by a calling provides a fundamental orientation to everyday life. But most of the world today has strayed from this and defines calling as a self-chosen career, usually a professional one that involves keeping appropriate standards and norms.

The fact that many people speak of their jobs as their "vocation" while pastors and missionaries speak of "being called" shows how inadequately we have grasped the universal call of God to every Christian. As Os Guinness says, calling means that our lives are so lived as a summons of Christ that the expression of our personalities and the exercise of our spiritual gifts and natural talents are given direction and power precisely because they are not done for themselves, our families, our businesses or even humankind but for the Lord, who will hold us accountable for them. A calling in Scripture is neither limited to nor equated with work. Moreover, a calling is to someone, not to something or somewhere. This last statement is sublimely significant but missed in this postvocational world.

Misunderstanding Calling

There are many indications that we are living in a postvocational world, one which views human beings as determining their own occupations and roles. Some difficulties arise from a secular approach, others from a distorted religious understanding.

Secular misunderstanding. In the secular mindset, a calling has been reduced to the occupation a person chooses. But "choosing a vocation" is a misnomer. To speak of a calling invites the question "By whom?" It is certainly not oneself! In line with this, vocational guidance has been reduced to *career selection.* As a secular perversion of calling, careerism invites people to seek financial success, security, access to power and privilege, and the guarantee of leisure, satisfaction and prestige (Donahue, p. 318). Some young people despair of finding a career and wrongly assume they lack a vocation. When people retire or become unemployed, they think they have lost their vocation.

One consequence of reducing a calling to an *occupation* is that work and ministry easily become professionalized, introducing a dangerous distortion. Without a deep sense of calling many people drift into a toxic mix of drivenness expressed in workaholism and the compulsive pursuit of leisure, a debilitating substitute for the freedom of the called life and the experience of sabbath. But if the secular world has missed the meaning of a calling, the people best positioned to teach it seem also to have misunderstood it.

Ecclesiastical misunderstanding. In most churches the average Christian has a job or profession, which he or she chooses. The minister, however, has a calling. The professional ministry has been elevated as the vocation of vocations and the primary work to which a person should give evidence of a call. Martin Luther was eloquent on the tragic results of this two-level view of vocation, stemming as it did from medieval monasticism, though now extending into modern Christianity:

> Monastic vows rest on the false assumption that there is a special calling, *a vocation,* to which superior Christians are invited to observe the counsels of perfection while ordinary Christians fulfill only the commands; but there simply is no special religious vocation since the call of God comes to each at the common tasks. (Bainton, p. 156)

As we will see, this profound misunderstanding is partly responsible for the widespread difficulty of relating Sunday to Monday and translating Christian faith into everyday activities. Unfortunately the Reformation introduced another distortion.

Reformational misunderstanding. Following the Protestant Reformation, a calling became equated exclusively with the personal experience of the providence of God placing us in a "station," or "calling," where we were to serve God as ministers. Called people live in harmony with their gifts and talents, discerning circumstances and accepting their personalities and life situations as God's "call." The Reformers did not universally teach this.

On the basis of 1 Cor. 7:17 ("Each one should retain the place in life that the Lord assigned to him and to which God has called him"), Luther opposed the prevailing idea that in order to serve God fully, a person should leave his or her previous way of life and become a member of the priesthood or of a religious order (Kolden, pp. 382-90). This is the one place where Paul, or any other New Testament writer, seems to use call language for the "place in life" or "station" we occupy (for example, slave, free, married, single, etc.). It is complicated by the fact that in 1 Cor. 7:17 Paul speaks of the situation as that "to which God has called him" and in 1 Cor. 7:20 of "the situation which he was in when God called him." Though such life situations get taken up in God's call and are transformed by it, the call of God comes to us in these situations (1 Cor. 7:20) and is much more than occupation, marital status or social position. Although Paul comes very close to seeing the setting in which one is called as *calling* itself, he never quite makes that jump. At most, *calling* refers to the circumstances in which the calling took place. This does not mean that a person is locked forever in a particular situation: "Rather, Paul means that by calling a person within a given situation, that situation itself is taken up in the call and thus sanctified to him or her" (Fee, 309-10).

This Reformational overemphasis on staying where God has placed us has led to reducing mission, suspecting charismatic gifts and, ironically, downplaying nonclerical ministry. But there is a half-truth in this distortion. The purpose of God is revealed in our personality and life path. Elizabeth O'Connor says, "We ask to know the will of God without guessing that his will is written into our very beings" (O'Connor, pp. 14-15).

Reasons for the Loss of Vocation

Several factors have converged to produce the contemporary postvocational society. First, medieval monasticism, based ultimately on Greek dualism, contributed a two-level approach to Christian living: the ordinary way (in society) and the spiritual way (in the monastery or priesthood). This distinction is now thoroughly embedded in all strands of Christianity, including evangelical Protestantism.

Second, the Protestant Reformation, in part because it was a reaction, failed to liberate the laity fully. In medieval monasticism Christians elected a superior religious

Spirit of God. While it may be appropriate to speak of one's daily work or specific ministry initiatives as included in the calling, the New Testament does not normally do so! This individual call also has three dimensions, which Greg Ogden outlines in these terms: (1) we experience an inner oughtness; (2) it is bigger than ourselves; and (3) it brings great satisfaction and joy (p. 209). You have a sense that you were "born to this."

Corporately, the call of God brings into existence a people that belongs to God (1 Peter 2:9-11) with members belonging to one another. Together we live a community life that bears witness to our true identity and serves God's purposes of humanizing the world until Christ comes again. This call of God is comprehensive (Ephes. 4:1) and embraces work, service in the church, family life, civic and creational responsibilities, mission in the world and personal spirituality. The call of God engages us totally and not merely in the religious sector of our lives.

The general and the particular. The distinction between a general calling to salvation and discipleship and a particular calling to a specific context for discipleship was elaborated by the Puritans. William Perkins, the only Puritan author to describe callings in a systematic way, emphasized calling as "a certain kind of life ordained and imposed on man by God for the common good" (p. 46), though Perkins himself often spoke of callings as though they were simply occupations, some of which were not lawful callings. It seems Perkins fused the two ideas of duties and occupations. In time the Puritan movement lost this synthesis that reflects the biblical balance of calling to salvation expressed in the concrete everyday contexts of our life (family, nation, city, etc.).

In summary, God's call is primarily soteriological rather than occupational— we are called more to someone (God) than to do something. Luther "extended the concept of divine call, vocation, to all worthy occupations" (Bainton, pp. 180-81), but he meant that the Christian is called to be a Christian in whatever situation he or she finds himself or herself, rather than equate vocation with occupation (Kolden, pp. 382-90). Further, there is no authority in the Bible for a special, secondary call from God as a prerequisite to enter the professional ministry. The call to leadership in the church comes from the church! While a special existential call may be given by God in some cases, the primary biblical basis upon which a person may enter pastoral leadership is character (a good reputation and ethical behavior) and God-given gifts of leadership (1 Tim. 3; 1 Peter 5:1-10). There is no status difference between leaders and people, so-called clergy and so-called laity, and only in some areas is there a functional one.

In the same way there is no need to be called through an existential experience to an occupation or other responsibilities in society. God gives motivation and gift; God arranges circumstances and guides. Through God's leading, work, family, civil vocation and neighboring are encompassed in our total response to God's saving and transforming call in Jesus. Misunderstanding on this point has been promoted by the overemphasis of 1 Cor. 7:17, mentioned previously. Focusing on this one text has had several side effects: (1) it minimizes the corporate, people-of-God aspect of vocation, (2) makes too much of the specific place one occupies in society as though the place itself were the calling, and (3) focuses on task, or *doing,* to the exclusion of *being.* Nevertheless, one should regard the various contexts of life—marriage and singleness, workplace, neighborhood, society—as taken up into the call of God and therefore expressed in terms of holiness and service rather than arenas chosen for personal self-fulfillment. Thus vocational guidance is not discerning our call but in the context of our call to discipleship discerning the guidance of God in our lives and learning how to live in every dimension in response to God's call. (For an investigation of the process of making occupational and life decisions in light of the above, *see* Vocational Guidance.)

Living as Called People

Understanding and experiencing calling can bring a deep joy to everyday life. Paraphrasing Os Guinness, I note several fruits of living vocationally rather than simply yielding to careerism, occupationalism or professionalism. First, calling enables us to put work in its proper perspective—neither a curse nor an idol but taken up into God's grand purpose. Second, it contributes to a deep sense of identity that is formed by whose we are rather than what we do. Third, it balances personal with public discipleship by keeping our Christian life from becoming either privatized or politicized. Fourth, it deals constructively with ambition by creating boundaries for human initiative so that we can offer sacrificial service without becoming fanatical or addicted. Fifth, it equips us to live with single-mindedness in the face of multiple needs, competing claims and diversions—the need is not the call. Sixth, it gives us a deep sense of integrity when living under secular pressures by inviting us to live in a counterculture and a countercommunity—the people of God—so we can never become "company people." Seventh, it helps us make sense of the brevity of our lives, realizing that just as David "had served God's purpose in his own generation, [and] fell asleep" (Acts 13:36), we can live a meaningful life even if our vision cannot be fully realized in one short lifetime. Eighth, the biblical approach to calling assures us that every believer is called into full-time ministry—there are no higher and lower forms of Christian discipleship.

See also AMBITION; CAREER; PROFESSIONS/PROFESSIONALISM; SERVICE, WORKPLACE; SUCCESS; TRADES; VOCATIONAL GUIDANCE; WORK

References and Resources

L. T. Almen, "Vocation in a Post-vocational World," *Word and World* 4, no. 2 (1984) 131-40; R. Bainton, *Here I Stand: A Life of Martin Luther* (Nashville: Abingdon, 1978); K. Bockmuehl, "Recovering Vocation Today," *Crux* 24, no. 3 (1988) 25-35; L. Coenen, "Call," in *New International Dictionary of New Testament Theology* (Exeter, U.K.: Paternoster, 1975) 1:271-76; J. A. Donahue, "Careerism and the Ethics of Autonomy: A Theological Response," *Horizons* 15, no. 2 (1988) 316-33; W. Dumbrell, "Creation, Covenant and Work," *Crux* 24, no. 3 (1988) 14-24; D. Falk, "A New Testament Theology of Calling with Reference to the 'Call to the Ministry,' " M.C.S. thesis, Regent College, May 1990; G. D. Fee, *First Corinthians*, New International Commentary on the New Testament (Grand Rapids: Eerdmans, 1987); O. Guinness, "The Recovery of Vocation for Our Time" (unpublished audiotape); M. Kolden, "Luther on Vocation," *Word and World* 3, no. 4 (Fall 1983) 382-90; P. Marshall, "Calling, Work and Rest," *Christian Faith and Practice in the Modern World*, ed. M. A. Noll and D. F. Wells (Grand Rapids: Eerdmans, 1988) 199-217; E. O'Connor, *Eighth Day of Creation: Gifts and Creativity* (Waco, Tex.: Word, 1971); G. Ogden, *The New Reformation: Returning the Ministry to the People of God* (Grand Rapids: Zondervan, 1990); W. Perkins, *The Work of William Perkins* (Appleford, U.K.: Sutton Courtenay, 1969); K. L. Schmidt, "kaléw" in *Theological Dictionary of the New Testament*, ed. G. Kittel, trans. G. W. Bromiley (Grand Rapids: Eerdmans, 1965) 3:487-91.

—R. Paul Stevens

CAREER

A career is an occupation for which people train and in which people expect to earn their living for most of their working years. It is part of one's calling but must not be equated with vocation. A calling, or vocation, is the summons of God to live our whole lives for his glory; a career is part of that but not the whole. A job is work that is simple toil out of necessity. In one sense Joseph could think of himself as having the career of a shepherd (following in his father's path), a job as a slave in Potiphar's house (something he did for survival) and the vocation or calling of saving the lives of God's family of promise and the Egyptians (Genesis 45:5).

In the modern Western world the idea of a career is profoundly challenged on several fronts: (1) The possibility of spending one's whole life doing one kind of work has been eroded except perhaps for the professions. Even there, people make career changes within their profession or into other professions. (2) Often one trains for an occupation but must learn to transfer the skills to other occupations. In-service training and lifelong learning are replacing the idea of up-front education for a lifetime career. (3) The notion of stability and security implied in a career is increasingly threatened by the exponential change taking place in the modern world largely fueled by the technological revolution. Workers in the Western societies are scrambling to stay on top of this change.

In a penetrating reflection, Walter Kiechel III asks three questions about the emerging trend: "Can technology help make service jobs as productive as manufacturing jobs have been, in ways that are high-paying to the worker and enriching to society? How many Americans have the basic education and the flexibility to become technical workers or new-style service workers? How many of us are ready for the changes in the very nature of work that the emerging economy will bring with it?" (p. 52). His last question hints at the coming redefinition of work from repetitive task to intervention in a programmed process, a relocation of the workplace from factory/office to multiple locations including the home, a rescheduling of the workday from regular to adjustable hours and a rethinking of work life from dealing with tangibles to dealing with intangibles.

Change is something Christians should especially welcome because of their conviction of the sovereignty of God, the certainty of our identity as children of God (not just plumbers or university professors) and the biblical insight that Christians live at the intersection of the kingdom of God and fallen human society—always a place of ferment and change. Because Christians have a sense of vocation, they are able to encompass several career changes within the larger purpose of their lives to serve God and God's purposes in the church and the world. The shift in modern society from producing products to offering services provides new career opportunities for Christians who are called to be servants (Matthew 20:26). The challenge to be a lifelong learner fits perfectly the vocation of being a disciple, for the education of a disciple never ends.

With the escalation of information and communication capabilities, and careers associated with them, the deeper questions of what we are communicating will surface. Over a century ago Henry David Thoreau wrote: "We are in great haste to construct a magnetic telegraph from Maine to Texas; but Maine and Texas, it may be, have nothing important to communicate." Speaking to this, Kiechel asks, "Information for what purpose? Knowledge to serve what human aim or itch? Where's the juice?" (p. 48). Followers of Christ will have many opportunities to bring meaning to the secular world as they take their place in so-called secular careers. Pastoral ministry may offer new opportunities to address the soul needs of human beings, though it is debatable whether in the strictest sense the ministry should ever be a career (see Financial Support; Tentmaking). With escalating stress levels, antistress professions (including counselors, therapists and exercise advisers) will take on a new importance. Christians will not be immune to the anxiety-producing dimensions of postmodern society, but they have resources to find rest within the pressures (Matthew 11:28).

As free time becomes more important than pay as the currency in negotiating lifestyle, Christians will need a theology and spirituality of leisure. Sabbath, the threefold rest of God, humankind and creation, is fundamental to gaining perspective on life, to discovering each day and each week why one is working and for whom, and to learning to approach our work as justified by faith rather than performance. Without a spirituality of careers, and sabbath in particular, we could miss the opportunities afforded by information technology and find ourselves deeply enslaved to our own technological creations. Our identities all too easily become attached exclusively to our careers when they should be founded more deeply (and with more freedom and personal health) on our God. Years ago Augustine said that if you want to know who people are, do not ask them what they do for a living. Ask them whom they love.

See also AMBITION; CALLING; SERVICE, WORKPLACE; SUCCESS; VOCATIONAL GUIDANCE

References and Resources

J. A. Bernbaum and S. M. Steer, *Why Work? Careers and Employment from a Biblical Perspective* (Grand Rapids: Baker, 1986); W. Diehl, *Thank God It's Monday* (Philadelphia: Fortress, 1982); R. M. Grant, *Early Christianity and Society* (New York: Harper & Row, 1977); L. Hardy, *The Fabric of This World* (Grand Rapids: Eerdmans, 1990); W. Kiechel III, "How We Will Work in the Year 2000," *Fortune* 127, no. 10 (1993) 39-52; P. Marshall, "Calling, Work and Rest," in *Christian Faith and Practice in the Modern World,* ed. M. Noll and D. Wells (Grand Rapids: Eerdmans, 1988) 199-217; R. Slocum, *Ordinary Christians in a High-Tech World* (Waco, Tex.: Word, 1986); R. P. Stevens, *Disciplines of the Hungry Heart: Christian Living Seven Days a Week* (Wheaton, Ill.: Harold Shaw, 1993); R. P. Stevens, *Liberating the Laity* (Downers Grove, Ill.: InterVarsity Press, 1985).

—R. Paul Stevens

COMMITTEES

The ambivalence of some people with regard to committees can be summed up in the cartoon that shows a minister reading a story to his child, with his paraphrase going like this: "And when the pastor cut down the beanstalk, the giant committee came tumbling down, and the church lived happily ever after." This sentiment was echoed by another pastor who described committees as one thing the devil really loves. Of course the church is only one context in which committees exist. They are present in every sphere of life, for example, workplaces, community organizations, voluntary associations and so on. Committees intersect with two social phenomena: leadership and group or meeting dynamics. Christian hesitations about the appropriateness of committees arise from both spheres.

Leadership often appears to happen in the absence of or in spite of committee work. It is true that the biblical record is weak on the role of the committee in leadership. Leadership is overwhelmingly an individual affair in the Old Testament, being regularly mediated through three types of individuals: prophets, priests or princes. This reality reaches a climax when all three roles are summed up in Jesus. We hardly think of Jesus as setting his plans by committee. In fact, he sometimes had to resist the will of the potential committee represented by his disciples (Matthew 16:21-23). Likewise, when Paul received wisdom from the majority in an ad hoc committee, he chose to ignore it (Acts 21:10-14), though this is an exceptional example. As we will see, the Bible does support the idea of setting and accomplishing goals through groups. In the New Testament especially we see people working in teams: plural eldership, Paul's normal practice of team ministry and shared ministry in local churches.

The other hesitation comes from the actual functioning of committees, especially committee meetings. Because of sin or ignorance, meetings sometimes are very unprofitable and frustrating: time is wasted, conflict goes unresolved, decisions are not reached or implemented, people are not heard, or people are heard too much.

Better, it seems, to forget committees (and especially committee meetings) and just let someone get on with the job at hand.

The Value of Committees

In the end, the deep theological rationale for committees comes less from proof texts in the Bible and more from an overall sense of the biblical plan for salvation. The plan is simply to form a people for God, a body made up of cells, individual people who have all received the Spirit. Spiritual gifts, including any gifts of leadership, are not concentrated comprehensively in individuals, whether prophets, priests or princes. Instead, the metaphor of the body suggests connection, one gift reinforcing and supplementing another, so that the whole body "grows and builds itself up in love, as each part does its work" (Ephes. 4:16).

This idea is the basis for using committees: the whole is greater than the sum of the parts, whether in making decisions or dividing up the tasks of a project. The latter notion is probably generally accepted: using teamwork to conquer an obstacle or exploit an opportunity makes sense. However, we are more comfortable with the model of a coach deploying the players than with the model of the players deploying themselves according to an agreed-upon strategy. Thus, we are back to the idea of a singular leader. For example, we might think of Moses dividing up the job of judging the children of Israel or Nehemiah parceling out the job of rebuilding the wall of Jerusalem. In the end, however, this does not represent committee work. Committees represent a commitment to forming policies, plans or strategies within a group. In other words, leadership is shaped and directed by a group process, in the belief that ten heads are better than one.

There are dangers in committees: an individual's hiding behind the group to avoid personal responsibility or the group lapsing into such complex processes that decisions are never made. As a wit once observed, a committee is a group of people who individually can do nothing but as a group decide that nothing can be done. On the other hand, committees can also be very effective in avoiding dangers: manipulative leaders and foolish plans. The output and impact of a good committee are threefold: good decisions, good relationships and good leadership. The only way to make sure that these results happen is to make sure that good decisions, relationships and leadership are also the basis of every committee.

The Effective Committee

A committee is a species of small group. Like every small group, an effective committee must be based on a strong sense of what it is trying to accomplish. How will the committee know when it is doing (or has finished) its job? To what precise external end is the committee committed? The clearer the sense of purpose, and the more it shapes every meeting agenda, the more satisfying and successful the committee will be. Every committee should give more time to clarifying purpose and procedures than is usually set aside.

The purpose may be set by the group, as in the case of the "nominating committee" in Acts 1:15-26, or it may be mandated by a higher authority, as in the appointment of the Seven to manage charity toward widows in Acts 6:1-6. The latter is instructive in two other ways. First, it shows that the members of the first committee in the church, the apostles, knew they had to protect their agenda from distractions. Every group of elders in a local church today needs to take this to heart. Second, it shows a group moving beyond an advisory or animating role to actually accomplishing the plan that it formulated. A committee may be constituted to advise some external leader or animate some of its members toward action, but the most effective committee is probably the one that seeks to implement its plan together as a group. A plan worked by the owners of the planning is usually worked best.

Setting and accomplishing a purpose require a process of communicating ideas and coming to a consensus about the idea that will prevail. This requires a good base of positive relationships. Committee members need to be committed to one another as much as to their purpose. This bond is strengthened by good group dynamics: honoring the gift of each member, listening to every contribution, submitting to one another and fighting fairly. See Em Griffin's book *Getting Together* (pp. 134-56) for help with conflict resolution. Good dynamics during committee meetings help to forge the sorts of relationships that produce good teamwork when the committee moves into action mode. The story of the "committee of Jerusalem" in Acts 15 provides a healthy model for a group process; note especially the careful listening.

Finally, committees need good leadership if they are to be effective. Leaders must focus on maintaining purpose and maintaining relationships. If one person cannot handle both these functions, then there should be two official leaders: one to manage the agenda and one to facilitate communication. Emphasizing one or the other aspect of committee work leads to imbalance. Most commonly, task supplants relationships. Roberta Hestenes has written a good corrective for this in *Turning Committees into Communities*. Good, balanced leadership during a committee meeting will release good leadership after the meeting. This is what Paul hoped for in Acts 20: he not only reminded the Ephesian elders of their purpose but also took part as they prayed, wept and embraced him.

Even though they sometimes seems to keep minutes and waste hours, committees are here to stay, both in the church and in the wider world. Christians have an excellent opportunity to help them be a true expression of the body of Christ and a positive force for kingdom purposes.

See also CONFLICT RESOLUTION; LEADERSHIP; ORGANIZATION

References and Resources

E. Griffin, *Getting Together* (Downers Grove, Ill.: InterVarsity Press, 1982); R. Hestenes, *Turning Committees into Communities* (Colorado Springs: NavPress, 1991).

—Dan Williams

COMMUTING

Commuting to work by private or public transportation is one of the daily realities of modern life. In previous times people generally worked in their homes or walked a relatively short distance to their place of employment. But with the advent of the train and tram, bus and automobile, along with the spread of suburbia, getting to and from work has become a more complex and time-consuming business.

A generation ago people were congratulating themselves that working hours were fewer, little realizing that in most cases these were taken up by extra time commuting. Now that working hours are expanding again, and freeways are becoming more clogged, there is a danger that commuting hours will also rise. This is especially the case for those who are unemployed and can find work only a long distance from home.

Commuting Times and Patterns

By far the greatest proportion of people commute to work by car. This varies from city to city and depends on climatic conditions, quality of public transportation and provision of cycleways. In most places, 90 percent or more of commuters travel by automobile, and somewhere between 5 percent and 15 percent travel by public transportation, mostly train or bus. Although improvements in public transportation, along with diversification of it and additions to it, in recent years have reclaimed some people from their cars, it is still used by only a small proportion of the commuting population. This is significant enough to ease some congestion on the roads, but not enough to make a wholesale difference in the quality of road or rail commutes.

On the whole, commuting time by car has remained surprisingly stable over the last couple of decades. At present the average length of car trips in the larger cities in North America is roughly equivalent. Older, denser metropolises in the East and Midwest lose what they gain by being more compact through the greater length of time it takes to traverse them. In newer, more sprawling metropolises in the South and West, traffic flows a little faster and so makes up for the longer distances between job and suburb. The majority of car trips, almost 40 percent, take about twenty to thirty minutes, 20 percent around ten to fifteen minutes less, 20 percent around ten to fifteen minutes more, and fewer than 10 percent up to an hour in length. A small but growing proportion of people—whether going by car, bus, train or ferry—travel two hours or more a day to work. There are also those who commute by plane.

Most people who commute by car travel alone. In North America car-pooling is usually defined as two or more passengers, in other countries three or more. Though the ratio of car-poolers to lone travelers varies from city to city, on average it is around one in seven but can vary from half to double that number. Those who travel by van or bus, less so by tram or train, often socialize with fellow commuters, especially in the western states. Such people build a modest level of community through regularly traveling at the same time with each other day after day. This is especially the case where longer distances are involved.

The amount of stress and frustration caused by some forms of commuting, especially traveling by car, is a matter of widespread complaint. Here and there some interesting responses to these expressions of dissatisfaction are beginning to emerge. For example, driving schools are beginning to include in their lessons to new drivers sessions on stress management as well as on how to deal with rudeness. Also, family members and neighbors intentionally or instinctively help those who are drivers among them to debrief at the end of the day, that is, to report on the dangers they have encountered, obstacles they have overcome and fatigue they are experiencing.

The amount of time people spend commuting, the fact that they mostly do it alone and, as roads get busier and trains become fewer, the tiring or frustrating nature of commuting generally raise many questions. These are worth asking in an effort to become more aware of what is at stake and what are the options with respect to commuting: When there is a choice, is it more important to live closer to work, schools and shops in less advantageous surroundings so that families and friends can have more time together, or is quality of location and residence more important? Are there additional ways in which commuting can become a more sociable, community-building activity or even a more reflective, educational one? Is it possible to handle commuting better so that it is less energy-taxing and anxiety-producing and so would give people more chance at the end of the day to socialize or engage in other worthwhile activities?

These are not the only questions. We could ask how we can improve people's capacity to drive safely and courteously on the roads so as to reduce traffic accidents. Or we might consider the impact of commuting long distances on those who find it difficult to find or keep work. Since our adoption of the automobile has led to the deterioration of public transportation, we might consider our responsibility to older, younger, poorer or disabled people who most rely on public transportation to get around. But it is the first, basic, set of questions that will be addressed here.

Commuting Practices and Possibilities

In recent ethical thought much has been made about the importance of developing a range of character-based practices that are genuinely virtuous. Insofar as people seek to acquire good driving habits, they are developing a standard way of operating that will serve them well on the road. But what other practices might be relevant in driving to and from work, ones more related to personal well-being, community building, educational or spiritual development? And what practices might be helpful for those who do not commute by car? Are there specific practices related to being a passenger rather than a driver?

Perhaps the first desirable practice with respect to commuting is that time spent traveling to and from work be decreased as much as is realistically possible. All forms of commuting, but particularly those undertaken by car, add to our already congested, polluted and often accident-ridden transportation situation. If the time people spent commuting could be decreased, morning rush hours of between five miles per hour (in London) and fifteen miles per hour (in many American cities) would be greatly aided. Pollution—in Los Angeles every car puts approximately its own weight into the air as pollutant each year—would lessen. The awful physical, psychological and economic toll of road injuries and deaths would be significantly diminished.

But how do people go about decreasing the amount of time it takes to travel to and from work? Fortunately there is a growing tendency for people to seek work closer to home, but perhaps they should also consider moving home closer to work. It is ironic that many people move to outer suburbs because of less cost and greater safety and then put themselves on the roads at even more expense, especially if they then need a second car, and at greater risk, due to the extra driving.

When decreasing the distance between work and home is not possible, and even when it is, more commitment to car-pooling would make some real contributions. It would help develop community on the commute and so nurture an increasingly scarce yet absolutely basic resource in modern society. Many people can testify to both the short-term and long-term benefits of this. While it challenges our fetish about individual convenience and freedom of choice and requires some accommodation to others' schedules and rhythms, we could do much more in this direction than we attempt at present.

The same case can be made for making the move from commuting by car to traveling by public transportation. People complain that commuting by public transportation usually takes longer. Since someone else is doing the driving, however, the commuter has more time for profitable and sometimes enjoyable personal activities, such as reading, reflecting, meditating, praying, keeping a journal and planning. Sometimes there can be other benefits, such as socializing with a more ethnically diverse, older and poorer range of people. (This, by the way, could help overcome some of the stereotyping and suspicion that so often go on between different racial or class groups who rarely meet.) Another benefit is increased educational possibilities. (One group of daily commuters between two large cities were instrumental in getting a continuing-education organization to conduct daily classes on the train and eventually to add a whole car especially for that purpose.) People are often surprised to find out that a move to commuting by public transportation also generally results in considerable financial savings.

Those who must commute a relatively lengthy period of time can take steps to minimize the degree of effort and anxiety involved in arduous daily travel: for example, making use of flextime arrangements so that travel to and from work can take place at other than rush hours or working a ten-hour day so that an extra day a week can be used for leisure or being at home. When a car audio system is available, and so long as it is not just a tranquilizing substitute for a more radical change in commuting patterns, playing relaxing music can also be helpful, as an increasing number of people are finding. In places where a good and pleasant bicycle-path network is provided, people can bike to work. For a small percentage of people—almost 5 percent of the population—there is also the option of walking. Another possibility, and not only for the 5 percent of people already telecommuting, is searching for ways of doing some work each week from home.

For the remainder, it is helpful to begin looking at the complexities, surprises, frustrations and delays of traveling by private or public transportation as opportunities in the Spirit to grow in patience and self-control, as well as in the creative use of time.

Conclusion

As well as individual changes, there are changes that political and urban authorities can implement to improve the commuting experience. In various cities a number of these are already in operation. They include placing a tax on businesses if a certain percentage of their employees do not car-pool or travel by public transportation, providing more bus and car-pool lanes on freeways, introducing "smart" technology to improve travel conditions and reduce commuting time, and, where they have some likelihood of being effective, proposing new public-transportation initiatives.

Employers and supervisors can also help. As is already happening in some firms and agencies, they can pay employees extra to car-pool or travel by public transportation, since this costs less than providing parking spaces at work. Even churches can make a contribution to commuting by encouraging their members to car-pool as much as possible to meetings, providing vans or buses for those who cannot or can little afford to use public transportation, siting themselves near well-served public-transportation routes, and decentralizing many of their activities to local centers or homes so that people have less distance to travel.

See also WORKPLACE

References and Resources

D. Engwicht, Reclaiming Our Cities and Towns (Philadelphia: New Society, 1993); J. McInnes, *The New Pilgrims: Living as Christians in a Technological Society* (Sydney: Albatross, 1980).

—Robert Banks

COMPETENCY

In their places of work, families, communities and churches, Christians give praise to God by using their time and talents as competently as they possibly can. Their competency is a fundamental service to the world.

The book of Genesis sets the tone. At the end of each day, God looked upon the work he had done and saw that it was good. On the final day of creation "God saw all that he had made, and it was very good" (Genesis 1:31)—*very* good. That is the creation God gave us. And the very first command God gave to humans was "Be fruitful and increase in number; fill the earth and subdue it" (Genesis 1:28). To *subdue* is to bring under one's control, not to destroy. The arena for this service to God is the whole of creation, not just church-related activities.

Our society is so complex and interrelated that we depend on the competency of many others to meet our needs. The airline pilot's competency is far more important to his passengers than whether he is a Lutheran or Roman Catholic. The competency of those schoolteachers who help educate our children is much more important to us than whether they also teach Sunday school. We depend on the competency of our auto mechanics to keep our cars safe; whether they attend church conventions is secondary. We depend on the competence of our surgeon; whether she sings in the choir is incidental. So, too, competency is crucial for farmers, salespeople, bus drivers, custodians, politicians, pastors and lawyers. Each one, by doing his or her job with high competency, serves God by helping to keep creation *very* good.

In criticizing the church for not helping people see the importance of competency in their daily lives, Dorothy L. Sayers wrote, "The church's approach to an intelligent carpenter is usually confined to exhorting him not to be drunk or disorderly in his leisure hours and to come to church on Sundays. What the church should be telling him is this: that the very first demand that his religion makes upon him is that he should make good tables" (pp. 56-57). If our daily work is praise of God and service to God's creation, it is surely spiritual in nature. The term *spirituality of work* was first coined by Pope John Paul II in his encyclical *On Human Work*. In writing for the National Center for the Laity, Gregory Pierce says, "A spirituality of work necessitates orienting ourselves toward the divine through our daily activity of improving and sustaining the world" (p. 26). To see our work as spiritual compels us to execute it with the greatest of competency. No longer can a job be seen simply as a means of earning enough money with which to live.

The emphasis on total quality management in business in recent years is evidence that the American work force is not as competent as it could be. Incompetence can be found in all levels of an organization, from the CEO to the janitor. Total quality management recognizes this fact and addresses it. An example of what can be done to increase competency comes from the American automobile industry. During the 1980s Japanese and German cars got a larger share of the U.S. market due to better design, higher quality and lower prices. The trend was obvious. Either the American auto industry had to become more competent in its design, quality and costs or else it would die. Through massive changes at all levels of the industry, some of which resulted in many jobs' being lost, the carmakers began to reverse the trend. By the mid-1990s, American-built cars were equal to or better than their foreign competitors in design, quality and cost. Aided by the low value of the dollar in relation to the yen and mark, American car prices have become the lowest in the world market. This happened because a total industry became more competent.

Organizational competency is not confined to the for-profit sector of our society. Many human-service agencies operate far below their potential simply because of a philosophy that employees cannot be evaluated with respect to competency. This is the bane of the not-for-profit organizations. It is a serious misunderstanding of the nature of voluntary work. Sometimes, in such organizations, when incompetence is recognized, managers are themselves too incompetent to deal with it. American churches have relied on voluntarism to provide money and assist in the programs and governance of congregations and judicatories. The personal involvement of competent church members is largely responsible for the greater vitality, attendance and feeling of ownership in American churches than in state-supported churches in other countries.

Not only service organizations but also educational institutions need to deal with competency issues. With colleges and universities facing reduced enrollments due to demographic factors, it is the competent educational institution that will survive. Long-time policies that rewarded seniority rather than competency in teaching are being changed in many schools.

Competency in one's daily life is not confined to one's paid job. A society needs competent parents to raise our children and give them values. Surely we serve God and maintain God's "very good" creation as we bring in new lives and, in turn, educate them to use their God-given talents. The challenge has become greater as the number of single-parent families has increased and as the pattern of double wage earners in the traditional family has increased as well. Many parents are overcome with stress as they try to balance the demands of the workplace and the home, with the demands of the paid job usually taking precedence over family needs. As a result, many have an uneasy sense that they are not as competent in their parenting as they should be. Churches need to help people with their priority setting here.

Competency is demanded of us in our community activities. Surveys and polls tell us that Americans are unhappy with the competency of their elected political leaders. Yet, strangely, less than half of those eligible to vote do so, and less than 1 percent of the public ever volunteers to help in political campaigns. Competent citizenship calls for an active role in our political process, for government too can play a major role in keeping creation good. Furthermore, a unique characteristic of American society is the way in which people have volunteered their time and money for human services, the arts and other civic causes. Competent citizens are needed in order to maintain and improve our social fabric—God's creation.

Competency in one's job, family, community and church—this is what is asked of us. To strike the right balance in accordance with the gifts God has given us drives us to meditation, prayer and dependence on the Holy Spirit.

See also AMBITION; DRIVENNESS; PROMOTION; SUCCESS; WORK; WORK ETHIC, PROTESTANT

References and Resources

W. Diehl, *The Monday Connection: A Spirituality of Competence, Affirmation and Support in the Workplace* (New York: Harper & Row, 1991); W. E. Diehl, *Thank God It's Monday,* Laity Exchange Books Series (Philadelphia: Fortress, 1982); W. F. Droel and G. F. A. Pierce, *Confident and Competent* (Notre Dame, Ind.: Ave Maria, 1987); G. F. A. Pierce, "A Spirituality of Work," *Praying,* Sept.-Oct. 1983, p. 26; D. L. Sayers, *Creed or Chaos?* (New York: Harcourt Brace, 1949); E. F. Schumacher, *Good Work* (New York: Harper & Row, 1979); G. Tucker, *The Faith-Work Connection: A Practical Application of Christian Values in the Marketplace* (Toronto: Anglican Book Centre, 1987).

—William E. Diehl

COMPETITION

Competition is a fact of everyday life. Students compete for academic honors by scoring high marks in examinations. Athletes compete in a race, and only the first three runners past the finish line receive prizes of recognition (*see* Sports). Businesses compete for a market share of their products and services. Churches compete for the attention and voluntary support of adherents in the midst of a pluralistic, multireligious society. Nations compete for economic advantage in the global village. But what do we mean by competition? Is it always, or normally, negative? Can we construct a theology of competition?

The negative consequences of competition in society are easily identified, especially in business. Competition in the corporate world forces companies to reengineer in order to survive, often leading to loss of jobs (*see* Firing). Unionized employees negotiate for better compensation, but the prospects for job security are increasingly jeopardized by demands for greater benefits. Consumers benefit from competitive pricing, but sometimes at the expense of small businesses unable to offer the volume discount promised by chain stores in their weekly advertisements.

At the personal level, our children compete in examinations and sports. Students strive for a place at the university based on their academic achievements in high school. Undoubtedly these harsh realities affect our perspective on priorities and purposes in personal life. Should we pursue a "successful life" by embodying an unbridled competitive spirit (*see* Success)?

Beyond Definition?

The word *competition* has a history. As the *Oxford English Dictionary* notes, the root word *compete* derives from the Latin *competo,* which in its original sense means "to fall together, coincide, come together, be convenient or fitting, be due." But by the sixteenth century it took on a stronger sense of engagement with another person, thus "to enter into or be put in rivalry *with,* to vie *with* another *in* any respect." Subsequently, it came to be used "to strive *with* another, *for the attainment of a thing, in* doing something." In order to achieve a certain end or goal, we strive with another person, and in the process we may overcome obstacles or challenges, whether personal or impersonal. But these definitions fail to account for the complex character of human competition as it involves biological, psychological, rational, voluntary and social factors.

A theoretical understanding of competition must consider the human situation. The field of sociobiology, represented by E. O. Wilson, distinguishes two modes of competition, scramble and contest. The former is exploitative, without universal rules of conduct governing the scramble for limited resources. The latter involves a conscious struggle for appropriating specific resources and thus permitting a winner in a contest competition. When a group of boys scramble for coins thrown on the ground, a contest ensures certain rules of behavior and predicts certain agreed-upon outcomes, such as winner-take-all. But an evolutionary model of competition that assumes the commonality of animals and humans competing for survival for limited resources appears to make some sense, but it is incomplete, especially with regard to the ambiguous motivation of human beings.

Competition has a moral character; individuals are able to exercise self-control in limiting or suspending pernicious kinds of aggressive competition. Often this is not done. Examples in the Bible of people striving with one another for personal advancement in unbridled sibling competition include Cain and Abel, Jacob and Esau, and James and John. The story of Joseph is especially illuminating. Joseph's brothers schemed to eliminate him as they competed for parental attention and acceptance. Joseph was both a victim and a victor. But the biblical account suggests that a higher purpose determined the outcome (Genesis 50:20). Whereas the brothers' attempts at destroying Joseph's future seemed obviously malicious, the unintended consequence of Joseph's fortune pointed to a divine drama with significant benefits for the extended family.

Inside Competition

Why is it important for human beings to act in a competitive manner? Psychological explanations point to the need to gain recognition, approval and acceptance. Along this line public demonstrations of competitive behavior are often motivated by a desire to overcome weakness, helplessness and loss of individuality. So Stuart Walker concludes that "competitors think of themselves as being primarily motivated to develop, demonstrate, and enjoy competence" (p. 4). In other words, competitive behavior is largely about winning and about public awareness, regardless of the outcome. Walker has possibly overstated the case, since it is conceivable that an individual might run a race for the sake of proving to himself a level of achievement associated with the sense of excelling in a particular field of sport rather than merely winning public recognition.

The difficulty in determining actual motivations in competitive conduct may be due in part to the ambiguities and complexities of human behavior. There is more to motivation than the individual. Greek ideals exemplified in Aristotle's notion of human good and in Plato's articulation of timeless virtue illustrate the potential of personal actions. Values, standards and ideals are not created in a vacuum but are shaped by social and personal experiences. Therefore, competition and cooperation are not necessarily antithetical in a given society. In fact, anthropologists like Margaret Mead have described the relative significance of both types of behavior in tribal groups. Mead concludes that

> competitive and cooperative behaviour on the part of individual members
> of a society is fundamentally conditioned by the total social emphasis of
> that society, that the goals for which individuals will work are culturally
> determined and are not the response of the organism to an external,
> culturally undefined situation, like a simple scarcity of food. (p. 16)

If we accept the *cultural* dimension without denying the *natural* disposition inherent in human behavior, then we can recognize how competition and cooperation may take place simultaneously. This happens when an athlete competes with others while cooperating with members of his or her own team to challenge their opponents. What is important here is the impact of cultural and structural factors in determining the outcome for a particular group of individuals. While some societies exhibit cooperative characteristics, others appear more competitive (Mead, p. 511).

The Protestant Work Ethic

Not only culture but even religion influences competitive behavior. The classic explanation of competition was given by Max Weber. In *The Protestant Ethic and the Spirit of Capitalism,* Weber accounts for the impact of theological ideas on human behavior and social life. He sees the Reformation as leading ultimately to the emergence of a capitalist economy in Europe. Weber's basic hypothesis revolves around the notion of divine election as a key theological idea that influenced the moral and ethical outlook of Protestant Christians. In particular, he suggested that the believer needed concrete confirmations for his experience of salvation. Therefore, individuals took hold of the opportunities for work, investment and industrious activity in order to produce tangible rewards of achievement that could be interpreted as divine approval. In other words, divine blessing in this life indicated positive assurance of salvation for eternity.

Participation in God's gift of salvation demanded a conscious performance in this world—hard work, prudence, frugal stewardship and productive output. Weber was careful to highlight the affinity between a certain work ethic and the emergence of a successful middle class. While he was not necessarily arguing for a direct cause-effect relationship between the Protestant work ethic and the rise of capitalism in Europe, Weber persuasively demonstrated a strong correlation. His conclusion remains compelling: the emerging culture of capitalism was in a complex but significant way influenced by the religious idea of divine election and by the ethical orientation to competing for success in this world. In the Work Ethic article Weber's thesis is more completely critiqued. What is needed now is to develop a fully biblical approach. Thus far, we have considered the lexical, functional, biological, psychological, cultural and religious factors influencing our concept of competition. But how does the Bible speak of competition? Can we construct a theology of competition? When is competition good, even holy?

Competition in the Old Testament

The Bible is full of competitive activity. The Old Testament stories, ranging from the exodus to the exile, depict the struggle of God's people in the face of religious pluralism and political conflicts. The challenge of maintaining loyalty to the one true God was central to the story of covenant faithfulness. Recognizing the Old Testament drama of divine contention for Israel's allegiance, each narrative uncovers a competitive tension between Yahweh and the diabolical schemes of Satan. The life of Job reveals a cosmic competition in which Satan is granted limited jurisdiction over the circumstances of Job and his family. Israel had to choose, time and again, the one true God and to obey his revealed laws for holy living, to give up popular myths and religious idolatry in favor of the distinct lifestyle demanded by the God of Abraham, Moses and David.

Thus incidents like Aaron and the golden calf and David and Goliath illustrate the danger of competing ideas about God. On both occasions, the people were motivated by fear, helplessness and the need for security. These motivations were largely inspired by an inadequate view of God and an inflated view of the enemy. Moses and David contested for the people's allegiance to God as a prerequisite for competing against their enemies. Narratives such as the exodus and David and Goliath highlight the persevering character of God in demanding total allegiance in the midst of competing forces. In these instances competition in the religious life of Israel issued from this theological understanding.

Competition in the New Testament

In the New Testament Paul uses the metaphor of an athlete engaged in a race (1 Cor. 9; Phil. 3), and Jesus teaches with parables about the danger and potential of competitive behavior (Luke 16:1-8; Luke 19:12-27). The parable of the shrewd manager focuses on the resourcefulness of an employee facing malicious accusations of impropriety and eventual dismissal. By turning his employer's creditors into friends, he transformed hostile circumstances into opportunities for survival. Competitive behavior in this instance was marked by a streetwise motivation to strive for economic security. Jesus commended the shrewd manager for his prudent actions. In the words of Eugene Peterson's translation,

> The master praised the crooked manager! And why? Because he knew
> how to look after himself. Streetwise people are smarter in this regard

than law-abiding citizens. They are on constant alert, looking for angles, surviving by their wits. I want you to be smart in the same way—but for what is right—using every adversity to stimulate you to creative survival, to concentrate your attention on the bare essentials, so you'll live, really live, and not complacently just get by on good behavior.

Not only does Jesus acknowledge the competitive nature of living in the world, but he recommends a streetwise approach to survival that overcomes the destructive potential of competition. For the Christian, this competitive advantage is gained by a circumspect awareness of the issues and the relationships affected by changing circumstances. Sometimes, cooperating with our competitors may produce positive results. In contrast hostile, predatory competition bent on destroying relationships and institutions often leads to unscrupulous actions. When a salesperson exaggerates the value of a product, an unwitting consumer might succumb to deceptive persuasion. However, when the product fails to deliver in performance, the reputations of both salesperson and company are greatly discredited. In the final analysis, competing for consumer confidence is more important than sales profits. Companies and employees succeed in a competitive economy by delivering quality products and services and thus ensuring customer satisfaction.

There is more in the parable of the ten minas (Luke 19:12-27) than stewardship of investments. Jesus deliberately draws attention to the character of each servant who was given a mina. The one who earned ten more was rewarded with responsibility for ten towns. Similarly, the servant who invested the operating capital and earned five more minas was recognized for his achievement. In turn, he also gained additional responsibility for five towns. Finally, the parable focuses on the servant who avoided the risk of investment. Out of fear, he opted to deposit the money in an unsecured and unprofitable place. The master condemned the foolish attitude of this servant and, in an unexpected manner, deprived him of the asset by transferring the money to the servant who gained ten.

While the narrative appears similar to the parable of the talents, what is unique about this parable is the circumstance surrounding the events. The master had to secure authorization from a distant ruler in order to return with legitimate governing powers over the region. The period of absence was marked by protests from the local citizens as well as tensions among the servants over the master's instructions. How should they deal with local resistance to the master's sphere of influence? At the same time, how would they invest the capital entrusted to them in the face of competition? The servants were competing with external uncertainties and with internal challenges. Each servant had equal opportunity to invest, but the social and economic circumstances were not necessarily favorable. High standards of achievement were demanded by the master, thereby increasing the pressure to perform. How do we explain the variable productivity of the servants despite equal capital investment opportunity? What accounts for the difference in results? Why did the master reward the servant with ten minas additional capital taken from the unproductive servant?

Good Competition

As the parable suggests, competition can bring out the best and the worst in each person, depending on the motivations. Jay Newman, in his study of competition in religious life, agrees with Simmel's sociological thesis that competition "not only provides the individual with the occasion for self-realization and self-respect, but simultaneously presents him with an incentive and an opportunity to contribute to social progress" (p. 48). In other words, competition enhances the value of human relationships by cultivating the best from each person. Unlike the destructive potential of conflict, one positive outcome of competition is excellence in character and in performance.

Sports and athletic activities are usually associated with the idea of competition. In a race, every runner aims for first prize. Apart from the first three places, all other contestants are not even recognized. Paul's metaphor of the athlete in the coliseum assumes the competitive spirit. However, he does not appeal to the unbridled side of aggressive competition. In 1 Cor. 9:24-27, Paul compares himself to an athlete in training for the games, not unlike present-day sportsmen preparing for the Olympic marathon races. It seems Paul is urging for a competitive spirit in the Christian's life. But the metaphor of a race and the goal of winning the prize does not preclude the possibility of a marathon. In a race, only one person gets the prize. But the analogy of winning in a competition cannot be applied to the Christian in a simplistic manner. Surely Paul is not suggesting that only one Christian will complete the race and win the prize. Instead, the reference to disciplined training for the express purpose of gaining the reward points to a deep concern in Paul's life that he will not become disqualified at any point in his race toward the end.

Paul maintains a clear vision of the ultimate reason for his Christian endeavor: "Forgetting what is behind and straining toward what is ahead, I press on toward the goal to win the prize for which God has called me heavenward in Christ Jesus" (Phil. 3:13-14). Every Christian, in Paul's estimate, is called to run in a race that has an eschatological purpose more profound and deeper than a hundred-yard sprint. We may assume that Paul exaggerates the point of winning the race in order to make the more important claim that each person "should run in such a way as to get the prize." Therefore Paul views the competition as more of a marathon than a sprint. The difference is that everyone who completes the marathon wins.

A Sprint or a Marathon?

In the context of daily life and organizations, we may choose to regard competition as a race or a marathon. Whereas in a race only a few winners enjoy recognition, everyone who competes in a marathon and finishes actually wins. Charles Handy, a management consultant, suggests that competition "is good news for everyone, but only if everyone can win" (p. 83). He recalls the feedback from several thousand managers in America who were invited to account for the occasions when they did their best: "they did not talk about competition, but about goals that were exciting and challenging, about autonomy and ownership, high visibility and accountability, and an exciting task" (Handy, p. 85). From our earlier discussion about the definitions of competition, we recognize the basic elements in Handy's observations that match Paul's concept of competing in a marathon.

The quality of our goals and the challenges of the tasks before us make for a positive engagement in work and daily life. We compete by pursuing goals of excellence. When work entails a sense of ownership and accountability, each worker is given the opportunity to prove their merits. Organizations that offer incentives and motivate toward realistic goals will cultivate a healthy work force. Whereas monopolies in a market economy tend to take their products and services for granted, and internal monopolies exist through isolating or removing external challenges, people become lazy. Handy observes,

> In tough competitive situations people like to be surrounded by people less competent than themselves because it gives them a better chance of winning. That is not good news for the organization. Nor do people always, or even often, take the risks or make the creative leaps which competition is supposed to encourage. The fear of failing is usually much stronger than the hope of winning, so people play safe. (p. 85)

Competition usually involves a positive effort to aim for a set of goals worthy of the individual or organization in the face of changing circumstances and varying opposition. One may do this with integrity and courage. Competition issues from a basic theological conviction that God calls each person to live out his or her full potential, which is not defined by human evolution but by what Christ has accomplished in each one (Phil. 3:12). Furthermore, competition at the personal and social levels involves risks. The ethic of excellence can transform the destructive character of unbridled, unscrupulous competition into a creative spirit of true competition; of turning races into marathons. The Christian thrives in a competitive environment through a clear vision of the ultimate purpose for living and working.

See also BUSINESS ETHICS; CONFLICT RESOLUTION; INTEGRITY; NEGOTIATING

References and Resources

C. Handy, *Inside Organizations: 21 Ideas for Managers* (London: BBC Books, 1990); J. Newman, *Competition in Religious Life,* editions SR vol. 11 (Waterloo, Ont.: Wilfred Laurier University Press, 1989); M. Mead, ed., *Cooperation and Competition Among Primitive Peoples* (New York: McGraw-Hill, 1937); S. H. Walker, *Winning: The Psychology of Competition* (New York: W. W. Norton, 1980); E. O. Wilson, *Sociobiology: The New Synthesis* (Cambridge, Mass.: Belknap/ Harvard University Press, 1975).

—Peter Quek

COMPROMISE

Compromise is generally regarded as a dirty word. It is something to avoid. To make a compromise, to be compromised, even to accept a compromise, is to settle for second best, at worst to be involved in a shady activity. Therefore ethically inclined, especially Christianly committed, people should steer away from compromise. The difficulty with this view is that there is scarcely any situation in life in which at some point compromise is not required. This is so when a group decision has to be made by a committee, for example, since it is rare for several people to reach complete agreement. Or this is so, as in the case of social services or welfare, when limited resources mean that some have to miss out or get less than others. Or this is so in schools when conflicting opinions between parents and teachers mean that no decision is going to completely satisfy everybody. Even on the home front, juggling the sometimes competing options and demands in two-career families requires compromise—for example, when the whole family must decide to move so that one of its members can take up a job offer or promotion elsewhere. Some Christians, especially those who are very idealistic, are troubled by having to abandon what they feel is God's will for them or in general so that they can adjust to the positions or aspirations of others. Since they are concerned to do God's will, anything less seems a departure from God's ideal plan for them or wider purposes.

This issue becomes particularly acute in connection with our work. It is often thought to be especially connected to certain occupations. Politics, for example, with its adversarial dynamics, is as well "the art of compromise" (a definition Luther would have found quite acceptable). This is why many people regard politics with suspicion, but nothing would take place in politics, even developing and implementing the best policies, without it. And according to the New Testament, politics is a task in which even unbelievers, if doing right, can be servants of God (Romans 13:4). It is not essentially different in the world of commerce, especially in the making of business deals. This is also the case in various professions, especially in law. In a world that is more and more culturally diverse and pluralistic, a whole range of activities inside and outside the workplace require the various parties to make concessions to one another. But making compromises in any of these areas troubles many Christians, leading them to regard themselves as second-rate Christians or to develop a growing skepticism about the relevance of biblical ideals to everyday life.

Approaching the Issue of Compromise

What do we mean by the word *compromise?* Generally we use it in one of two ways. First, it is used for taking a middle way between two courses of action that may be based on different principles or on different possibilities derived from the same principle. Second, it is used for a decision or action that seems to involve a lowering of standards. I want to suggest that a situation such as the first usage has in mind certainly enables us to engage in a positive or legitimate compromise. Regarding the second usage, what sometimes appears to be a lowering of standards in making a decision may not necessarily involve that. But I also want to suggest that depending on the circumstances and the decision, the first situation can lead to a negative or illegitimate compromise as much as the second.

It is also helpful to distinguish compromise from two overlapping ways of operating: between compromising and strategizing and between compromising and negotiating. Strategizing involves working out a long-term, often complex, set of tactics for reaching a desired end. This may involve all kinds of moves and countermoves, unexpected demands and apparent concessions, which initially and for some time may obscure the goal of the exercise. Such strategies are means to an end, temporary positions that are part of the larger game being played. Strategizing is broader than compromising and may involve good or bad strategies as well as good or bad compromises. A subset of strategizing is negotiating. While there may be legitimate and illegitimate, or more and less legitimate, ways of conducting negotiations, compromise is not necessarily involved here, though sometimes it is. A negotiator may make many proposals and responses in coming to an agreement without at any point yielding something basic, only appearing to do so. In the case of both strategizing and negotiating, a person may take into account people's sensitivities, particular circumstances or specific cultural contexts, without which a good agreement—or sometimes any agreement—cannot be reached. So, to the extent that compromising is sometimes confused with appropriate strategizing or negotiating, there need not necessarily be anything negative involved in it.

What then is compromise? Is it, as is commonly thought, betraying one's basic convictions for the sake of expediency, because it is opportunistic to do so, to relieve the pressure one is under or simply as a consequence of moral weakness? Or is it possible to make good compromises that are not a betrayal of principles so much as an appropriate, perhaps under the circumstances the most appropriate, response to them? If this is the case, how can we tell the difference between these two, and what practical steps can people take to ensure that they do not break faith with their own strongest convictions and standards or those of the institution they represent?

Toward a Positive View of Compromise

It is possible to compromise in ways that are positive and defensible from a Christian point of view. As always, the Bible provides a good place to start. There are many biblical stories in which people made decisions that seem to be acceptable to God or to even further God's will even though these did not express all of their basic beliefs or hopes. A clear example is the meeting in Jerusalem between Paul and Barnabas, on the one hand, and the apostles and elders, on the other, to discuss the validity of the Gentile mission. There was considerable debate, and the upshot was an agreement in which the Jewish Christians endorsed Paul's initiative in taking the gospel to the Gentiles and Paul's missionary team accepted the condition that they communicate certain restrictions on the behavior of Gentile Christians that could be interpreted as supportive of idolatry and promiscuity (Acts 15:23-29). Another example in Acts is Paul's apparently contradictory practice of, in one place, circumcising one of his coworkers and, in another place, refusing to do so. The first concerned Timothy, who was half-Jewish; Paul felt there was some ground for placating the scruples some Jewish Christians had about him. The second concerned Titus, a Gentile, whose circumcision, no matter how strongly certain Jewish Christians may have desired it, would have betrayed Paul's basic convictions about Gentile Christians' freedom from keeping Jewish observances.

But elsewhere Paul is quite outspoken about his missionary practice of becoming "all things to all people" (1 Cor. 9:22). When he preaches the gospel, he takes serious account of the religious and cultural convictions of his hearers. If they are Jews or observe the law, he accommodates them and speaks as one who respects the Jewish heritage and law himself. If they are "strong" and do not observe particular holy days or follow regulations concerning food and drink, he begins with the freedom in Christ he experiences in such areas despite being a Jew. On the other hand, if they take the opposite point of view, since he too sometimes feels "weak," he is willing to begin from that and proceed from there. This way of operating is not restricted to Paul's missionary endeavors; it is also his regular pastoral practice. When confronted by viewpoints at some distance from his own, unless they are being advocated in a proud, hardened or manipulative way, as much as possible he seeks some common ground and then articulates his own position and tries to draw people toward it (as with discussions on ascetic sexual and overly charismatic practices in 1 Cor. 7 and 1 Cor. 12-14). Though Paul has often been accused of compromise in the negative sense because he acted in all these ways, it is not difficult to defend him against this charge in the name of a higher consistency.

The Negative Side of Compromise

We also find in the Bible examples of poor or negative compromises that are condemned. In Paul's letters we find the classic case of the behavior of Peter in the controversy between Jewish and Gentile Christians at Antioch. Though Peter has his own strong convictions on what is required of each group, convictions that are virtually identical with Paul's, he bends under pressure from certain people who have come down from Jerusalem and who were probably misinterpreting the position of his fellow apostle James. Peter urges the withdrawal of the Jewish Christians from the Lord's table because of the Gentile Christians' different eating habits (Galatians 2:11-14). At principle here from Paul's point of view was the gospel's full acceptance of the Gentiles even though they did not observe all the regulations of the law of Moses. Though it was not his intention, Peter's position was a compromising one in a seriously negative sense. This is why Paul would not yield so much as an inch.

The story of Peter's rebuke indicates, as we know, that compromise can have serious negative effects. This is so, first and foremost, for the person who makes it. Acting in this way weakens a person's capacity to made good compromises or other good decisions in the future. It is also unfortunate for those affected by the compromise, all of whom, not only the ones allegedly being protected, will suffer from the result. The key then is how to know the difference between good and bad, or better and worse, compromises. At this point our moral terminology can often get in the way. So long as we think only in terms of black and white, only in terms of good and bad, we are limited in our capacity to deal with such situations as discerning when good compromises can be made, what they are, when we are in danger of making a bad compromise or when no compromise should be made at all.

We can be helped here by the language of the Old Testament Wisdom literature, which expands its moral vocabulary to judge actions according to whether they are wise or unwise, fitting or unfitting, appropriate or inappropriate. There are times when it is better not to press for something that is good simply because it would not be wise to do so and we would jeopardize any possibility of its happening later. Or sometimes it may be wise to engage in an action even if it is not what we would most prefer since it is the best that is likely to come out of the situation and is far better than other choices that could be made. Other words than compromise could be used in such cases. Depending on the nature of the decision and the surrounding circumstances, terms like adjustment, accommodation, concession or conciliation could apply, again demonstrating that compromise in the pejorative sense is not necessarily in view.

In such cases the theologian Reinhold Niebuhr tended to talk in terms of our having an attitude of "delayed repentance." That is, we make the best decision we can under the circumstances, which is often the "lesser of two evils," then later ask God to forgive us. But if such a decision is the best compromise we can make in that situation, while we may regret that it could not be otherwise, repentance does not seem called for. Does this not mean that it is the will of God for us in that circumstance? Given the circumstances, what more could be called for? For example, when Jesus is unable to heal in a certain place because people's faith was lacking, was it a compromise on his part? Helpful here is Dietrich Bonhoeffer's distinction between ultimate and penultimate realities, the latter constrained by events, situations and people in this world. Sometimes the latter, to use his words, require us to "sacrifice a fruitless principle to a fruitful compromise" (pp. 79-101). The latter, though not the ultimate, is still derived from it and points toward it.

Learning How to Make Good Compromises

A legitimate or, to use Bonhoeffer's words, fruitful compromise, then, will seek to preserve our basic faith convictions, safeguard loving relationships and retain vision for the future. If it does, this will be an expression of the will of God in its particular time, place and set of circumstances. More specific criteria include the following: Does it generate good or bad effects? Is it likely to lessen evil and wrong? Does it extend justice, particularly to those who require it most? Will it exhibit a proper regard for all persons with a stake in it? Have those involved shown throughout a genuine concern for truth in what is under discussion? Is there a recognition of the choice involved and an avoidance of talk about "having to do it"? Do both the process and the decision display the virtue of patience? Can the decision be altered if circumstances change and another decision becomes possible? Though these criteria are still very general, at least they provide a framework within which a proper decision can be reached and the appropriate compromises, if necessary, made.

What can we do to ensure as far as possible that we are in the best position to judge an issue by these criteria and work toward the best possible compromise? The following considerations are relevant whether we are dealing with issues between husband and spouse or parents and children in the family, with issues arising between friends or neighbors, with issues that we encounter in the workplace or in voluntary associations, with issues that come before us in the church or church-related ministry, or with issues of a social or political kind on which we have to cast a vote. In all these situations we should (1) continue to give first priority to maturing in our relationship with God and others, for good compromises are more likely to proceed from people who are attempting with God's help to become increasingly good. (2) Keep the big picture in mind, never letting go of our ultimate aims and purposes, so that we can preserve a proper perspective on the issues at hand. (3) Consult closely as much as possible with other people so that we have as much wisdom as possible in making decisions involving compromise. (4) Be prepared to give way on minor issues where a major issue is at stake; otherwise, we will tend to confuse the forest for the trees and win or lose small victories at the expense of big ones. (5) Aim at a win-win rather than a win-lose, or lose-win, situation, for which lateral thinking or seeing new possibilities is really required.

If we keep these factors in mind, are serious about bringing such matters to God in prayer and meditation, and have resort to a group of supportive people with whom we can sometimes talk over these issues, we can have every confidence that God will go with us into our decisions and help us discern how best to respond.

See also BUSINESS ETHICS; CONFLICT RESOLUTION; INTEGRITY; NEGOTIATING

References and Resources

D. Bonhoeffer, *Ethics* (New York: Macmillan, 1955); J. Calvin, *The Institutes of the Christian Religion*, ed. J. T. McNeill, 2 vols. (Philadelphia: Westminster, 1960); W. J. Diehl, *The Monday Connection* (New York: Harper Collins, 1991); K. E. Kirk, *Conscience and Its Problems* (London: Longman, 1933); H. R. Niebuhr, *The Responsible Self* (New York: Harper & Row, 1979); W. Temple, *Christian Faith and the Common Life* (London: Allen & Unwin, 1938); H. Thielicke, *Politics,* vol. 2 of *Theological Ethics* (Philadelphia: Fortress, 1969); W. Ury, *Getting to Yes* (Boston: Houghton Mifflin, 1981); H. F. Woodhouse, "Can Compromise Be the Will of God?" *Crucible*, January-March 1982, 22-30.

—Robert Banks

CONFLICT RESOLUTION

Conflict is a natural part of life. Although many people think conflict means open controversy, a truer definition might be the absence of peace—which can be obtained in its most complete sense only from God. Whenever people interact with one another, there is a potential for a difference in opinion or purpose. Most people are able to deal with minor differences. When major conflicts arise, however, many people do not know what to do. They fear conflict, react defensively or have difficulty negotiating just agreements. As a result, valuable relationships are damaged or destroyed, time and money are wasted, and promising businesses and careers fail.

In American culture today, litigation in civil court has become a common substitute for direct personal interaction. As a result, conflicts may be resolved as to substantive issues but are almost never resolved as to personal relationships. A focus on satisfying individual rights has supplanted concern for the good of the whole community. In some other cultures there continues to be reliance on the judges at the gate (Ruth 4:1-12), but in America's increasingly anonymous society the perceived cost-benefit of resolving conflict between individuals amicably has been skewed in favor of keeping the conflict unresolved.

Popular Christian Attitudes Toward Personal Conflict

Some Christians are more vulnerable than other people to conflict, this vulnerability arising from a misunderstanding about what it means to be *Christlike.* For example, some Christians believe they always should "turn the other cheek," without realizing that unless one does so freely, without resentment, this is no true reflection of Christ's peacemaking character. Such actions are like the Pharisees' carrying out the letter rather than the spirit of the law. Further, giving in may be inconsistent with God's Word, which includes also the concepts of justice, restitution and personal accountability. Others imagine that they should carry out God's justice. They may appoint themselves as God's avenging angel, even though Jesus instructed us not to do so (Matthew 7:1-2). Such an attitude is precisely the opposite of how God approaches discipline, which is with a loving and expectant heart (Hebrews 12:1-13). Finally, some Christians spend a great deal of energy on broader matters of peace and justice. Although these are important, such people sometimes pay scant attention to resolving their own interpersonal conflicts, failing to recognize the broader community implications of individual discord.

All these attitudes can lead to confusion, abuse or pent-up anger. In contrast, to seek resolution of disputes according to biblical principles means seeking both personal reconciliation and the just settlement of substantive issues, not only for the purpose of human unity but also to bring praise and honor to God (1 Cor. 10:31). Jesus specifically urged peacemaking among his followers as a personal attitude that brings blessing (Matthew 5:9).

God's Interest in Conflict Resolution

As well as giving us the ultimate model of reconciliation—Jesus Christ (Hebrews 10:10)—the Old and New Testaments are full of direction and action from God on the reconciliation of persons to himself. There are many pictures of unilateral forgiveness and provision for sacrifice as a substitute for judgment. It is obvious that complete, direct, personal reconciliation is one of God's major preoccupations (Hebrews 2:1-4). God's method of resolving conflict serves both as a model for our own behavior and as a reminder of our own utter dependence on God as the source of all good we hope to achieve.

By studying the ultimate conciliator at work, certain guidelines emerge for dealing with conflict in our daily lives:

1. Conflict allows us to grow to be more like Christ (2 Cor. 12:7-10).

2. Peacemaking starts with our own personal attitude, which in turn comes from a focus not on the conflict but on God (1 Peter 3:13-15).

3. It is possible to reconcile oneself unilaterally, but only if the past is forgiven completely (Phil. 4:2-9).

4. Resolving conflict may require different methods at different times and places (1 Samuel 25:26-35; Esther 7:1-6; Proverbs 6:1-5; Acts 16:22-24; Acts 22:22-23, 29).

5. Differences of opinion are inevitable and usually are acceptable (1 Cor. 12).

6. Reconciliation does not necessarily require giving up or giving in, especially when someone is being hurt by ongoing conflict; loving confrontation may be preferable (Galatians 6:1-5).

7. God reconciled all to himself through sacrifice and forgiveness, but we must pass this gift on to others to realize its full benefits (Ephes. 4:29-32).

8. Resolving conflict God's way may require us to accept consequences and to alter our behavior (Ephes. 4:22-32).

9. Justice is God's, not ours (Luke 6:27-39).

Biblical peacemaking involves an active commitment to restore damaged relationships and develop agreements that are just and satisfactory to everyone involved (1 John 3:18). A spirit of forgiveness, open communication and cooperative negotiation clear away the hardness of hearts left by conflict and make possible reconciliation and genuine personal peace. True biblical vulnerability, honesty and forgiveness can restore a person's usefulness, both to God and to others, and lead to complete restoration of relationships (Galatians 6:1-3; Ephes. 4:1-3, 24).

Resolving Conflict as Believers

The Bible contains two basic messages about how believers should seek to resolve conflict in their daily lives. First, as with most things in life, God's Word contains promises, principles and practical steps needed for resolving conflict and reconciling people. Second, it is clear that peacemaking is an essential discipling ministry of the local church, not a task reserved for professional counselors or lawyers.

See it as an opportunity for obedience and witness. Sometimes we wonder why God has allowed a certain conflict to come into our lives. Instead of viewing conflict as a painful burden, Christians can learn to see it as an opportunity to please God and to draw attention to God's wisdom, power and love (1 Cor. 10:31-33). God has promised to use even our conflicts for good (Genesis 50:19-20; Romans 8:28). This perspective allows for a positive and confident response to conflict as we ally ourselves with the most powerful peacemaker in the world.

Examine your own part in the conflict first. This includes not only your actions but also your attitudes, motives, acts and omissions. Because it reveals our sinful attitudes and habits and helps us to see where we need to change, conflict provides an opportunity for us to grow to be more like Christ (Psalm 32:3-5; Psalm 139:23-24; 1 John 1:8-10). This growth takes place when we follow Jesus' command to accept responsibility for our own contributions to a problem before pointing out what others have done wrong (Matthew 7:5).

Look for steps you personally can take. Few things in the Bible are as clear as the steps we are to follow when seeking to resolve conflict, particularly within the body of believers. Each of us is commanded to make the first move when in disagreement with another (Matthew 5:24). One opportunity provided by conflict is to serve others. Sometimes this can be done through acts of kindness and mercy (Proverbs 19:11), but at other times it requires constructive confrontation (Matthew 18:15). Recall that Jesus confronted people not simply by declaring their sins to them but by engaging them in conversation designed to make them arrive at the same conclusion on their own (Matthew 7:12; Luke 5:27-28; John 4:7-26).

Accordingly, if someone is angry with you, go to them immediately (Matthew 5:23-24), even if you believe the other's anger is unjustified. If you are angry with someone else, first ask yourself if the issue really is worth fighting about and check your attitude—are you actually looking forward to the confrontation? If an offense cannot be overlooked, go privately and express your concerns. But do not assume that the other knows or understands your feelings; explain what you are concerned about but also why (Matthew 18:15). Be sure to affirm the relationship and your desire to work things out lovingly before launching into a discussion of the issues (2 Cor. 2:5-8).

Making the first move does not mean that someone else has done something wrong or bad. An otherwise innocent word or act can cause an unexpected negative reaction in another, leading to serious disagreement (James 3:5-7). One can apologize for the trouble such miscommunication has caused simply because one regrets the result. Too often, however, our own sins have played a part either in creating the conflict or in escalating it (James 4:1-3).

Call on the church for help if necessary. Private confrontation is a preferable first step, so long as we can speak the truth in love (Ephes. 4:15). But if after sincere good-faith efforts to work things out you are unable to resolve the issue or mutually forgive each other (Proverbs 19:11; 1 John 3:16-20), then seek out the assistance of a few "witnesses" (Matthew 18:16). These are present not to provide evidence or accuse the parties but to act as supportive advisers to both sides and help restore peace (Phil. 4:3). This can be done informally with a respected relative, friend or other adviser trusted by both parties or more formally with a pastor, church-appointed committee or trained conciliator.

If someone will not listen to you and the witnesses, then, as we are instructed, "tell it to the church" and allow it to decide the matter for the parties (Matthew 18:17) as a matter of church discipline. This is preferable to filing lawsuits in civil court (1 Cor. 6:1-8). Today, as in Paul's time, our churches (and most believers) have abdicated this authority to the legal system, yet the courts do not focus on restoration of personal relationships, only on the disposition of tangible assets and liabilities. The church should model God's view that discipline is an act of love and shepherding (Hebrews 12:6).

Going to court is a possible last resort. Finally, if a party will not listen to the church, then we are commanded to treat the other as an unbeliever (Matthew 18:17). Does this mean that now we are free to sue in court? Yes, but our decision to do so should depend on the nature of the dispute and the consequences to us or others in our care if we do not pursue our claims (Phil. 2:3-4).

Even though Paul's admonition about lawsuits is directed at believers suing believers, it only makes sense to tie God's conflict-resolution principles back to witness through reflection of Christ's character. Christ's approach was to be merciful even while directly confronting a harmful attitude or act. Whatever the choice, our attitude needs to remain one of obedience to and reliance on God, and the aim should be peace with others, even unbelievers (Romans 12:17-18; 1 Cor. 10:31-11:1).

Because Jesus loved and sought out unbelievers even as he tried to both correct and heal them, we can at least attempt to work out differences with unbelievers using the same progression of steps as we would with believers (1 Peter 2:12). Serving an angry lawsuit on an unbeliever, before trying to work out things another way, may not be the defendant's best introduction to God's redemptive plan!

Some believers use the steps in Matthew 18:15-20 as a substitute for civil legal processes but demonstrate the same vengeful zeal and advocacy as if in court. The key to effective use of Matthew 18 is to appreciate it as God's detailed direction to us on how to keep peace on earth—our attitude should be one of caution, prayerfulness and thanksgiving.

See also COMPROMISE; CONFLICT, WORKPLACE; NEGOTIATING

References and Resources
E. Dobson et al., *Mastering Conflict and Controversy* (Portland, Ore.: Multnomah, 1992); R. Fisher and W. Ury, *Getting to Yes: Negotiating Agreement Without Giving In* (2nd ed.; New York: Penguin, 1991); J. Hocker and W. Wilmot, *Interpersonal Conflict* (3rd ed.; Dubuque, Iowa: Wm. C. Brown, 1991); Institute for Christian Conciliation, 1537 Avenue D, Suite 352, Billings, MT 59102, (406) 256-1583;

B. Johnson, *Polarity Management: Identifying and Managing Unsolvable Problems* (Amherst, Mass.: HRD Press, 1992); S. Leonard, *Mediation: The Book—A Step-by-Step Guide for Dispute Resolvers* (Evanston, Ill.: Evanston Publishing, 1994); G. Parsons and S. Leas, *Understanding Your Congregation as a System* (Washington, D.C.: Alban Institute, 1993); K. Sande, *The Peacemaker: A Biblical Guide to Resolving Personal Conflict* (Grand Rapids: Baker, 1991).

—David Augsburger

CONFLICT, WORKPLACE

Conflict is so common in the workplace that one can safely say, "It goes with the territory." But the types of conflict are varied.

Many Kinds of Conflict

The most commonly recognized workplace conflict is between labor and management. The dwindling power of American labor unions has not lessened tensions between those who manage and those who produce, especially in those organizations that have retained a hierarchical structure. Management wants to minimize unit costs; labor wants to maximize compensation and benefits. Finding creative ways to increase productivity can sometimes meet the wants of both groups. But when increased productivity is achieved by fewer persons doing the same amount of work in the same way, the physical and psychological effect on the work force can be devastating.

Pity those persons who daily work at the interface of labor and management: the first-line supervisors. These are the persons who are called upon to see that management's plans or directives are carried out—sometimes against their own convictions. These are the persons who are called upon by the work force to communicate its complaints and wants to a management that is sometimes not interested in listening. To make matters worse, the highest-ranked labor representative, who gets paid on an hourly rate for overtime, can often have more take-home pay than the lowest-ranked management representative, who works the same number of hours but gets no overtime pay because he or she is a salaried employee.

There can be conflicts in the workplace when an employee whose style is collegial works in an organizational culture that is very autocratic. For a long time there has been conflict over dress codes, but that is changing as younger employees keep pushing back the boundaries. Even IBM, whose male executives and sales personnel always wore dark suits, black shoes, white shirts and a conservative tie, is starting to weaken. But observe the dress of most male business travelers at airports; they still are invariably clad in dark suits, black shoes and, perhaps, a colored or striped shirt.

A great source of workplace conflict arises from tensions between work and family. The percentage of parents who are holding down a full-time job continues to climb. Approximately two-thirds of married American women are in the paid work force.

Single parents, most of whom are women, have little choice about work: either enter the work force or be dependent on family or society for support. The need to care for family while holding down a full-time paid job creates tensions that spill over into the workplace. And the demands of the workplace create tensions that spill over into the family. What does a working parent do when a child develops a sudden illness and will not be accepted by the normal caregiver? Or suppose an employee's aged parent falls at home and needs immediate help? Does the employee take a vacation day? call in sick? In either event, the employee's supervisor is confronted with an unexpected staffing problem. Work must be reassigned, and there is resentment among all affected. If the family emergencies happen too frequently, conflict develops.

Most employers have yet to find ways to reduce the work-family tensions that nag so many of their employees. In the case of the birth of a child, U.S. federal law now mandates that employees be allowed to take unpaid leaves of absence. But companies do not look upon such leaves with favor. Early reports show that while mothers will take leaves beyond their employer's normal maternity policies, fathers seldom take any leave. Why? The workplace views an unpaid leave of absence as proof of the father's lack of commitment to the organization.

In short, much of the American workplace is still not "family friendly." When an employee puts the family ahead of the job, there is conflict at the place of work.

Add to the family-work tensions the fact that many people are working longer hours, either by choice or by job demands. In her book *The Overworked American,* Juliet B. Schor deals with the strange fact that although the standard of living of the American worker has increased significantly since the 1950s, the per capita hours worked have gone up instead of down. From 1969 to 1987 the annual hours of paid employment in the American labor force increased 163 hours, equal to four extra weeks of work per year. Schor suggests that our insatiable desire for more material possessions may be the reason we choose to work more hours. A more likely cause, however, is that the drive for greater productivity and the downsizing of the work force in many organizations have put greater demands upon a smaller number of people. Whatever the reason, when the workplace gets more time, the family gets less.

Conflict can break out as coworkers compete for promotions. There is conflict when a boss takes credit for the ideas or contributions of his or her workers (*see* Office Politics). Conflict arises when an employee has been given an unfair performance appraisal (*see* Firing). When senior employees hog all the best weeks for vacations, there is conflict.

Women in the work force bear additional burdens of conflict over those listed above. Women continue to be overrepresented in those jobs that are lower on the pay scale. Retail sales, fast-food outlets, nursing homes, clerical support for managers and professionals, child care and domestic services are all heavily populated by women, and they generally do not pay well. To make matters worse, women generally still receive less pay than men for the same job or one of equal value. It is unjust and makes for conflict in the workplace.

The advancement of women into managerial jobs, law partnerships, directorships and CEO positions has been very slow, despite more than a generation of highly capable women in the work force. To the term *glass ceiling* has been added an even more devastating term for women—the *sticky floor*. Not only is there an invisible barrier preventing women from ever reaching top positions, but many women are glued to jobs at the bottom of the pay scale. With more injustice, there is more conflict.

To top it all off, women at every level of the work force constantly must be alert to sexual harassment or discrimination. It can be intentional and as blatant as being asked to trade sexual favors for job advancement. Or it can be unthinking, as when all the men in a work unit go out for a drink late on Friday afternoon but forget to invite the one female associate of equal rank.

What has been said about women in the work force applies also to African-Americans, Latinos and persons from Asia. Hard as it is to believe, Jews still suffer from discrimination in some sectors of the American work force. Conflict arises as minority persons constantly overhear jokes that demean their race, sex, color or religion.

A Christian Response

What is a Christian to make of so much conflict in the workplace? How is the Christian to deal with so much injustice and conflict? Several fundamental truths about conflict and work will help Christians answer these questions.

First, conflict is a part of life; it is not peculiar to the workplace. The Bible is filled with stories involving conflict. Jesus told his disciples that to follow him could result in conflict of fathers against their children and brothers against brothers (Matthew 10:21). Conflict is a manifestation of humans' self-centeredness, that is, original sin.

Second, the place of work is part of God's creation and is just as much under God's care as the place of worship. What goes on in the place of worship on Sunday is intended to help us deal with the place of work on Monday. Churches can help their members deal with conflict by providing adult-education programs on conflict resolution, personal time management, discrimination and ways to bring about change. Some congregations encourage small groups to meet regularly in order to share conflict issues in their daily lives and receive suggestions and support from other Christians. Many church judicatories have professional mediation resources available to assist in specific conflict situations.

Third, we need to recognize that the place of work is where we respond to God's call in our lives. As baptized Christians, we affirm that God calls all people into ministry. We respond to God's call through faithful ministries in our places of work, our homes, our communities and our church. With the assurance of God's presence, we are confident in facing conflict wherever it is encountered.

Fourth, we use the gifts we have been given by God to deal with conflict in the workplace. Some types of conflict call for reconciliation between parties. Some types of conflict call for education and new ways of doing things. Where conflict is the result of injustice, we may have to immerse ourselves in deeper conflict in order to correct the injustice.

Finally, we need to remember that the place of work does not define us or own us. We are children of God and are owned by God. That is our identity; our identity is not our job. It is difficult to remember this in the heat of daily work, but when we take the time to reflect on our lives, we will know that no matter how much conflict there may be in the workplace, it cannot separate us from a loving God.

See also CONFLICT RESOLUTION; MANAGEMENT; OFFICE POLITICS; POWER, WORKPLACE; STRESS, WORKPLACE

—William Diehl

CONSUMERISM

The word *consumerism* is occasionally used to denote the consumer movement and advocacy on behalf of consumers vis-à-vis the producers of consumer products. The term is also infrequently used to refer to the economic theory that maintains the growth of consumption is always good for an economy. Normally, however, consumerism is lamented as a significant behavioral blemish in modern industrial society. It suggests an inordinate concern—some might say an addiction—with the acquisition, consumption and/or possession of material goods and services. Consumerism implies foolishness, superficiality, triviality and the destruction of personal and social relationships by means of selfishness, individualism, possessiveness and covetousness. The prevalence of consumerism suggests a general contraction of the compass of modern culture.

Interpreting Consumerism

It is often suggested that consumerism is simply the necessary complement, on the side of consumption, to the modern capitalist economy's dramatic expansion of production. Consumerism, from this first perspective, is largely engineered by the producers of products. It is the result of the artificial stimulation, principally by means of manipulative advertising, of an ever-increasing need for mass-produced consumer products. The ready availability of consumer credit in modern society, often financed by manufacturers, buttresses the plausibility of this (principally neo-Marxist) interpretation.

Consumerism has also been interpreted as a principal means of defining class and status boundaries in modern industrial society. Thus an individual might identify himself or herself as a member of a particular group by consuming, as the term *status symbol* suggests, the requisite products and services. As new consumer products and services are constantly being introduced, however, the specific indicators of class and status are constantly changing, in effect forcing individuals to continually consume new and different products. From this second perspective, consumerism does not have to do with greed or manipulation so much as with the ratio of what one thinks one ought to possess relative to others against the backdrop of constantly changing shopping opportunities.

A third interpretation combines the first and second perspectives to suggest that consumerism is simply the behavioral reflection of a fundamentally new kind of culture. Within this new culture need has, in effect, become a new religion, and advertisers and other specialists have become priestly mediators of new, and predominantly materialistic, virtues and values.

Historians point out, however, that many of the features of modern consumer culture, including manipulative advertising and the deliberate stimulation of desire, had already begun to emerge in the eighteenth century and so antedate the modern revolution in production by almost a century. This has led British social historian Colin Campbell to suggest that the roots of modern consumerism may not lie in the advent of modern production techniques so much as in Romanticism's emphasis on heroic individualism and self-creation. Consumerism's relentless "desire to desire," in other words, is not simply foisted on consumers by producers of consumer products but stems ultimately from a romantic ethic in which the individual is bound to realize himself or herself in the experience of novelty and more or less immediate gratification. This ethic has been amusingly summarized in the quip "I shop, therefore I am." It was this romantic ethic, Campbell suggests, that stimulated subsequent developments in production. The emphasis on self-creation by means of the consumption of things and experiences continues to animate much of contemporary culture.

Religious Consumerism

The rise of denominational, and now religious, plurality in modern societies has led to a situation in which we are increasingly encouraged to "shop for," and so to be consumers of, religion itself. The consumption of religion, furthermore, suggests a fundamental change in the meaning of religious belief such that it has increasingly less to do with conviction and more and more to do with personal preference. Many churches and religious organizations have responded to the changing meaning of belief by obligingly repackaging religion to make it conveniently and easily consumable. Such trends have contributed to the emergence of a kind of religious marketplace in which modern consumers are faced with a veritable smorgasbord of religious options.

Christian Reflections on Consumerism

Understood as a preoccupation with the consumption of material goods and services, consumerism has little to commend it from a Christian point of view. In the first instance, it suggests a kind of mindlessness on the part of modern consumers. As essayist Wendell Berry observes in a provocative piece entitled "The Joy of Sales Resistance," the contemporary preoccupation with marketing, salesmanship and consumption could arise only in a society whose members are expected to think and do and provide very little for themselves. More seriously, exorbitant Western consumption habits have undoubtedly contributed to the degradation of the natural environment and the rapid depletion of natural resources. Consumerism has also been blamed for the exacerbation of poverty, both domestically and in the developing world.

As a behavior, consumerism betrays significant confusion about the nature of the human situation. More specifically, it discloses confusion about the dangerous logic of *need*. One of the desert fathers, Saint Neilos the Ascetic (d. 430), is said to have advised his disciples to remain within the limits imposed by our basic needs and to strive with all their power not to exceed them. "For once we are carried a little beyond these limits in our desires for the pleasures of this life," Neilos warned, "there is no criterion by which to check our onward movement, since no bounds can be set to that which exceeds the necessary." Neilos went on to outline the sorts of absurdities that inevitably result from attempting to satisfy material desires beyond the reasonable limits of need, and in so doing he described something very much like late twentieth-century consumer culture. And it is certainly the case that much of the dissatisfaction and disappointment that so pervade modern life owes to the insatiable logic of *need* in consumer culture. The "more is better" attitude of modern consumer culture makes it very difficult to say, "Enough is enough." Of course, from a Christian point of view, the logic of need is insatiable simply because such things as pride, covetousness, lust, gluttony, envy and sloth are unlimited in the fallen situation.

The preoccupation with consumption may also betray a fundamental misunderstanding of one's own identity before God. To identify oneself only by the things one is able to consume is, in effect, to lack a true sense of one's self. This is the point of Jesus' simple, yet penetrating, questions: "What good will it be for a man if he gains the whole world, yet forfeits his soul? Or what can a man give in exchange for his soul?" (Matthew 16:26). To imagine that we can create or sustain ourselves by means of our possessions or consumption habits, Jesus suggests, is tragically mistaken. It is also stupid, for such things have no lasting future. If we stake our identities—our *selves*—to these things, then we will pass away with them.

Yet beyond folly, consumerism also tends toward idolatry. To the extent that we seek security in consumption, we in effect worship another god, thereby arousing the anger and jealousy of the God and Father of our Lord Jesus Christ. Recall, in this connection, the apostle Paul's equation of greed and idolatry (Col. 3:5), as well as the prophetic warning that the fate of idolaters is to become just as worthless as the gods they worship (Jeremiah 13:1-11). Of course, it is not difficult to trace the connection between the fragility and ephemerality of many people's sense of themselves and the essentially restless and ephemeral nature of the gods of consumption.

Responding Christianly to Consumerism

The Christian response to consumerism is already suggested in the theological criticism of this behavior, but it may also help to recall that the original meaning of *consume* is "to burn," "to exhaust" and "to destroy completely." The object of our response to consumerism is to try—with the Lord's gracious help—to avoid destroying ourselves in this behavior and to try to prevent our neighbor from being destroyed by such behavior as well (*see* Simpler Lifestyle). Our first duty, then, as Wendell Berry insists, is to "resist the language, the ideas, and the categories of this ubiquitous sales talk, no matter from whose mouth it issues" (p. xi).

It may also help to juxtapose the modern obsession with acquisition, grasping and possessing with the Christian virtues of gratitude, generosity and hope. Far from encouraging us to accumulate or consume as much as we possibly can, the Scriptures exhort us to view our lives as a gracious gift from God for which we are to be grateful. We are further exhorted to express our gratitude by giving ourselves generously away in the love of God and in the love of our neighbor (1 Tim. 6:18).

Finally, because the plausibility of consumerism depends entirely on the apparent permanence of life in this world, we must continually remind each other—and ourselves—that this world and its lusts are indeed passing away (1 Cor. 7:30-31). "Sell your possessions and give to the poor," Jesus says to us. "Provide purses for yourselves that will not wear out, a treasure in heaven that will not be exhausted, where no thief comes near and no moth destroys" (Luke 12:33).

See also ADVERTISING; MONEY; STEWARDSHIP

References and Resources

W. Berry, "Preface: The Joy of Sales Resistance," to *Sex, Economy, Freedom & Community*, (New York: Pantheon, 1993) xi-xxii; C. Campbell, *The Romantic Ethic and the Spirit of Modern Consumerism* (Oxford: Basil Blackwell, 1987); A. T. During, *How Much Is Enough? The Consumer Society and the Future of the Earth* (London: Earthscan, 1992); J. F. Kavanaugh, *Following Christ in a Consumer Society: The Spirituality of Cultural Resistance* (Maryknoll, N.Y.: Orbis Books, 1991); L. Shames, *The Hunger for More: Searching for Values in an Age of Greed* (New York: Times, 1989); T. Walter, *Need: The New Religion* (Downers Grove, Ill.: InterVarsity Press, 1985).

—Craig M. Gay

CONTRACTS

In a typical day, most of us enter into several contracts, usually without giving them much attention. When we buy a newspaper, get a haircut, take a ride on a bus or make a long-distance telephone call, whether we know it or not we are entering into a contract. Our contracts can be verbal or written. They may be direct or implied, simple or complex. The purchase of a carton of milk at the local grocery store is an example of a simple, implied and verbal contract. A person takes his or her purchase to the counter, the store clerk asks for a sum of money, and the customer tenders the required sum and takes the milk out of the store. It is understood by both the customer and the store owner that there is to be an exchange of money and goods by which the customer will come to own the milk and the store will get to keep the money. A bus ride is a more complex transaction. Posted on the vehicle are lengthy written terms related to payment, risk and proper conduct. By entering into the bus, the passengers are assumed to have read and agreed to all of those written terms. Similarly, if we purchase goods using a credit card, we are expected to have read and accepted all the terms set out in the agreement that accompanies the issue of the credit card.

At another level, the law will imply certain terms and conditions into a sale of goods, such as "merchantability" and "fitness for description." The implied term of merchantability means that if the milk we purchase at the grocery store turns out to be sour, the store will be required to replace the carton or refund the purchase price. The implied term of fitness would give the patron of the hair salon the right to a

remedy if she asked for an auburn tint and ended up with flaming orange hair.

Understanding Contracts

It is no accident that contracts are an everyday feature of our lives. Alongside covenantal forms of interconnecting, the contractual form of transaction is one of the basic forms of human interaction and relationships. Moreover, contract is the building block of our legal and social structures. It is therefore important for the Christian to understand what contracts are all about, how and when to enter into contracts, biblical principles regarding contractual behavior, how to respond when contracts are broken, and under what circumstances and in what relationships the contractual model would be inappropriate.

Black's Law Dictionary defines a contract as "an agreement between two or more persons which creates an obligation to do or not to do a particular thing. Its essentials are competent parties, subject matter, a legal consideration, mutuality of agreement and mutuality of obligation." The above definition alludes to certain basic contract essentials, in the absence of which there would be no enforceable contract at law. Of course, we all enter into agreements that are not intended to be legally enforceable, such as an agreement with a child to read her a story if she helps set the table for dinner. Such an agreement would not be a contract at law because the child could not be considered "competent" as a minor. The first essential to contract is that the parties be legally competent, meaning of legal age and of sound mind. Undue influence or duress upon one of the parties can also defeat a contract.

A second contract essential is the existence of an offer and the acceptance of that offer by the person receiving the offer. An offer can be made in writing or verbally, directly or implicitly. Stores implicitly "offer" to sell their wares by displaying merchandise with a stated price, and customers "accept" the offer by tendering cash, check, credit card or debit card to the store clerk. At a garage sale, the buyer may make an "offer" to the seller to buy a particular object for a stated price, which may be "accepted" or rejected by the seller. In the earlier example of a bus ride, the transit company offers to provide a transportation service and sets out the terms of its offer in writing either at the bus depot or on the vehicle itself. The passenger "accepts" the offer by purchasing a ticket or by boarding the bus and paying the fare.

A third contract essential is the concept of "consideration": an exchange of rights and obligations between the contracting parties. While the law does not attempt to regulate the value or inherent fairness of what rights go back and forth, nonetheless if all of the rights flow only in one direction, there is no contract and thus nothing to enforce at law. By way of example, an agreement to sell an entire city block for a mere ten dollars is enforceable, whereas an unsolicited promise to give a stranger a free book is not enforceable.

Finally, it is important to have "certainty" about the contract. The basic terms of the contract must be sufficiently clear to allow for a common understanding of the rights and obligations between the contracting parties. An agreement to build a cabin for a specified amount may fail as a contract if there is nothing said about when the work is to be carried out or completed. There would also likely not be an enforceable contract if the owner and builder had failed to agree on the specifications of the cabin to be built. On the other hand, failure to specify the exterior color of the structure would not be considered fatal to the contract, as color is not an essential term of the contract.

Entering into Contracts

While some of our contracts are routine and even seemingly mindless, there are many times when we enter into contract as a result of negotiations. Negotiation styles and skills are acquired at an early age and often do not change in adulthood. We learn to negotiate positionally by determining what we want and assessing what we are prepared to give up in order to obtain what we want. If what we want overlaps with what the other party is prepared to give up and vice versa, then a bargain is achieved and a contract can be entered into. The problem with this negotiation strategy from the Christian's perspective is that it is inherently selfish. Christ commands us to love our neighbor as ourselves (Luke 10:27). Is it possible to live out Christ's Great Command as we enter into contracts? The answer is a definite yes.

There is an entirely different approach to negotiations, which is "interest-based" as opposed to positional. In interest-based negotiations, both parties look at each other's interests (consisting of wants, needs and fears), and together they attempt to create an agreement that meets as many of those interests as possible. Where interests are mutually conflicting, the parties attempt to find some external objective criteria to help them in choosing between those conflicting interests. Not only does this approach lead to collaborative and relationally healthful negotiating, but also it increases the likelihood that agreement will be achieved and that the agreement will be a mutually satisfactory one. Consider the following situation: Susan very much wants to buy John's car but can afford to pay only $2,000. John has his eye on another vehicle and needs to get at least $2,500 for his old car. Positional bargaining results in no deal and leaves both of the parties irritated with each other. However, if John and Susan had entered into interest-based negotiations, they may have discovered that Susan operated a daycare service and that John had been looking for an opening in a daycare facility for his son. By exchanging $500 worth of services, Susan and John could have reached an agreement on both the car and day care, and both would have been very satisfied with the result.

Christians should carefully consider their contract-negotiating style. There are a wealth of resources on interest-based negotiations. Consider Paul's admonition to the Philippian church: "Each of you should look not only to your own interests, but also to the interests of others" (Phil. 2:4).

Conduct in Contracts

There are numerous examples in both the Old and the New Testament of God's people entering into contracts:

the owner of the vineyard contracted with workers to buy their services (Matthew 20:1-16);

Joseph was sold by his brothers to Midianite merchants for twenty shekels of silver (Genesis 37:28);

the "shrewd manager" contracted with his master's debtors to greatly reduced their debts in exchange for early payment (Luke 16:1-9);

Moses contracted with Pharaoh to pray to God for relief if Pharaoh released the Israelites (Exodus 8:8).

While there are few direct references to contracts in scriptural teaching (Leviticus 25 perhaps comes the closest to articulating rules of contracting), there are many relevant scriptural principles to guide the Christian in contractual relationships. The Christian should be fair in agreements and not take advantage of others (Leviticus 25:14). Special consideration should be given to the poor (Leviticus 25:25, 35; Proverbs 28:28). Exhortations to honesty and integrity in all business dealings appear frequently throughout the Bible. God's people are to use honest scales and measures

(Leviticus 19:36; Deut. 25:13; Proverbs 11:1). "Woe!" says the prophet Micah to those who act in a fraudulent manner (Micah 2:2). Isaiah laments the lack of integrity of his people (Isaiah 59:4). The book of Proverbs contains several principles that would be applicable as Christian behavior in a contractual setting: generosity, restraint, special care for the poor, honesty, acting without deception and keeping the law (see also Romans 13).

Another common theme, especially in the Old Testament, is justice. The Christian should not use contracts for unjust gain or to take advantage of those who are disadvantaged or disempowered. The law allows the courts to strike down contracts that are considered to be "unconscionable." How much higher, then, the standard for Christians who, in following Christ, are to act and live out of love in all dealings and relationships.

When Things Go Wrong

In our imperfect and fallen world, commitments made in contract will from time to time fail to be carried out, sometimes intentionally and sometimes for reasons beyond the control of the defaulting party. How is the Christian to respond when others fail to carry out their contractual obligations? First, we are encouraged in Scripture to be patient and long-suffering. Indeed, patience is one of the fruits of the Spirit (Galatians 5:22). Tolerance and a willingness to give others a second chance ought to characterize the Christian's response to broken contracts. We are also told not to repay evil for evil (Romans 12:17). Thus, our response to another's default ought never to be an act of vengeance or "evening the score."

But when the breach of contract is serious or repetitive, what is the Christian to do? Again, as with the process of entering into a contract, the normal choice is between a positional approach and an interest-based approach. A positional approach may be to confront in an attacking manner or perhaps to seek legal recourse in a court of law. An interest-based approach would be to deal directly with the other party in the manner described earlier, seeking to bring out the needs, wants and fears of the parties to the contract. This may be very difficult when the relationship has been strained through a breach of contract. Fortunately there are professional mediators skilled in interest-based negotiations who can assist the parties toward a collaborative resolution (*see* Conflict Resolution). The interest-based approach is appropriate for Christians both because there is a scriptural admonition against lawsuits (1 Cor. 6:1-8) and because the positional adversarial approach is usually antithetical to the response of love commanded in the Gospels.

When the Contractual Model Is Not Appropriate

While there are no general or specific biblical prohibitions on contracting, there are situations and relationships where it would be inappropriate for the Christian to act or think in contractual terms. Our relationship with God is clearly not to be thought of in contractual terms. Such a view would lead quickly to a doctrine of justification through works: if one obeys God's commands, then one can earn God's love. But, argues Paul, "all have sinned and fall short of the glory of God, and are justified freely by his grace through the redemption that came by Christ Jesus" (Romans 3:23-24). God has chosen not to contract but rather to covenant with his people. Whereas a contract involves an exchange of rights and duties, the biblical notion of covenant involves a unilateral act of love and promise on the part of God and a promise that all can appropriate. This results in a loving and grateful desire on our part to live according to God's purposes, priorities and values.

The covenantal model of relationship is the New Testament standard not only for God but for his followers. We are instructed by Jesus to love our neighbor not on a contractual basis (an equitable exchange of one's rights and duties) but on a covenantal basis, out of response to being first loved by God. That is the point of the parable of the unmerciful servant (Matthew 18:23-35). The best that the state can legislate is mutual tolerance toward each other: that is all that public law can accomplish. But God's call to love one another is a much higher standard. We understand this in our relationship with our children. Our love for them is not conditional upon their behavior. In our marriages we make vows or covenants to behave in a certain way regardless of the response of our spouse. Now the challenge is for followers of Christ to act and behave covenantally in all of their relationships and bring his covenantal grace into our contractual relationships.

See also INTEGRITY; CREDIT; CREDIT CARD; DEBT; INVESTMENT; MONEY; STEWARDSHIP; WEALTH

—Peter Mogan

CREDIT

"Having lost its value, money may no longer be the root of all evil: credit has taken its place." (Dalton Camp, *Saturday Night Magazine*).

Credit is a controversial topic and not just in Christian circles, as the quotation by Dalton Camp illustrates. Nevertheless, credit has become a way of life for most North Americans. In Canada, for instance, there are more VISA cards and MasterCards combined than there are adult Canadians. According to the office of Consumer and Corporate Affairs, credit cards in Canada in 1990 were used for more than a half billion transactions, with interest charges totaling approximately $1 billion.

Attitude Toward Credit

For most people the controversy lies in the *abuse* of credit, but there are some Christians who feel that credit is *inherently* wrong. Those who are strongly opposed to the use of personal credit might say that credit cannot be used wisely, but only with differing degrees of foolishness. A study of the typical criticisms of credit use raises many of the theological dimensions of financial life and stewardship.

Credit is inherently wrong. One cannot come to a conclusion about the acceptability of credit without first determining the biblical teaching concerning debt. A brief summary follows (*see* Debt).

Two kinds of debt are discussed in Scripture: (1) consumer debt, which was usually associated with some kind of personal misfortune such as crop failure, and (2) commercial investments, where a well-to-do Israelite might get involved with a traveling merchant.

With respect to the first kind of indebtedness, God's people were to be generous in meeting the needs of covenant brothers and sisters (see, for example, Deut. 15:7-10; Matthew 5:42). Israelites with means were to lend whatever was needed to the poor to fend off temporary misfortune and to restore the borrower and his family to financial stability. No interest (usury) was to be charged, and insignificant collateral was to be demanded. Borrowers were obliged under normal circumstances to repay their debts. However, if a debt remained unpaid by the sabbatical year, it was to be forgiven. As was typical with all aspects of the covenant relationship, no one's poverty was to be taken advantage of by better-off Israelites (Isaiah 5:8).

Commercial debt is hardly mentioned at all. Israel was an agrarian nation and little involved with commercial life. However, such transactions were permitted, and unlike the case of poor covenant brothers and sisters, interest could be charged. Israelites were warned of the dangers of being in debt to another who might well exploit them (Proverbs 22:7).

To summarize, debt was not inherently evil but could be dangerous if the moneylenders were unscrupulous, as they often were. The purpose of consumer debt was not to cater to self-indulgence but rather to ease a person through temporary misfortune and to restore the family unit to stability. Debts were forgivable at legislated intervals (that is, every sabbatical year) to achieve some higher purpose, such as the preservation of the family unit.

Credit is a temptation to materialism. A further criticism of credit is that its easy availability is a temptation to make purchases one cannot afford at this time, or do not really need at all. Businessman and author Jake Barnett puts it very well: "Credit's main function is to serve materialism" (Barnett, p. 164). Doubtless this is an astute observation. North Americans have realized an increasing standard of living over the past many decades. But with that improving standard has come a greater readiness to take on a larger debt burden. Levels of consumer credit have exploded since the early 1950s. Much of this, of course, is attributable to population growth and inflation. But with these effects removed (in other words, when indebtedness is measured in *constant* as opposed to *current* dollars), we are still vastly more prepared than our grandparents were to use, and abuse, credit in larger and larger amounts. In Canada, for instance, per capita increase in the use of credit between 1950 and 1985 was fivefold using constant dollars.

An analysis of consumer bankrupts done by Consumer and Corporate Affairs of Canada in 1982 revealed much disturbing data about the abuse of credit. First, consumer bankrupts tended to be younger than the adult population generally. About 63 percent of these bankrupt individuals were under age 35, a disproportionate number as only 43 percent of Canadians were in this age group. Only 8 percent of consumer bankrupts were age 50 or older. Second, a disproportionate number of personal bankrupts lacked employable skills. Managerial and professional people represented 9.8 percent of the Canadian labor force, but only 2.9 percent of consumer bankrupts. At the other end of the spectrum, unskilled clerical, sales and service personnel and unskilled manual labor constituted 23.4 percent of employees but a whopping 38.8 percent of those who declared personal bankruptcy. Third, and most important for our purposes, the major cause of personal bankruptcy was consumer debt. The median indebtedness of those in the study was $10,865, while median assets were about $400. A breakdown of their creditors is rather interesting. Finance and insurance companies were the major source of credit (74 percent of bankrupts owed these institutions at least one debt), followed by Canadian chartered banks (61 percent), department stores and other retailers (46 percent and 41 percent, respectively) and bank credit cards (30 percent of bankrupts reported money owing on such cards).

A senior employee of an accounting firm specializing in bankruptcies addressed this issue of why younger people who lack good occupational skills and financial prospects are so prepared to burden themselves with consumer debt.

> Bankruptcy is very much an attitudinal thing, a commitment to one's obligations. It takes very little to be technically in a situation of going bankrupt. . . . Many use bankruptcy as a tool to avoid paying debts, especially younger people who believe that they have the right to a certain standard of living without putting out for it. (Sutherland, p. 51)

In summary, we have fueled the rising standard of living with greater and greater amounts of consumer credit. Clearly we are not content to live at the level of previous generations, nor are we prepared to improve our standard strictly through earnings. While income levels have increased in recent decades, debt burden has increased even more. Being able to afford more material things has given many a hunger for an even greater accumulation of goods than can be provided through earnings. Credit as an impetus to materialism is wrong.

To be truly effective, a Christian must be debt free. While this statement sounds plausible, it does ignore the fact that for many, many North Americans the wise use of credit in its various forms has put them on the road to long-term stability and effectiveness in their families, careers, churches and communities. Had I not taken out student loans, I might have avoided a level of indebtedness for some time, but I would have never graduated from either university or seminary. Were it not for my mortgage, I would never have owned a home. Most businesses have relied at least in part on credit to get started or to meet short-term working capital and long-term expansion requirements. The careful use of credit can be a tool toward long-term effectiveness. But the many perils associated with the use of credit must be avoided.

We have established that while credit can be greatly abused, it is not inherently wrong. Used wisely, credit can be a highly effective tool in establishing long-term stability for a family or a business. The issue that remains then is how to use credit properly.

The Right Use of Credit

Incurring debt is a decision to pay for something you bought in the past, rather than saving in order to buy something in the future. Given the cost of credit charges, it usually makes better financial sense to save. However, there are important exceptions, such as purchasing a home or financing an income-producing asset. Therefore, principles concerning how and when credit should be used must be established.

Setting your own credit limits. Merchants are always happy for customers to use credit. Over half of retail sales are made this way. Credit often provides a tie between a merchant and a customer if a person is using the store's credit card, charge account or installment contract. Consequently, the last place to which you should look for advice in setting your own credit limits is the institution granting the credit. Lenders consider two things when granting any particular level of credit: your total earnings and your other debts. They never ask you what your personal financial objectives are. Unfortunately, many Christians have not taken the time to set such objectives either. This must come first! How is it done?

First, Christians must see their financial resources as gifts from God with which they have been entrusted (*see* Stewardship). Too many Christians assign this view strictly to the tithe (not that most Christians actually tithe, but that is another story). It is pointless to talk of financial objectives without first accepting that our resources are from God's hand and that we are accountable to God for their use. This attitude provides a check on materialistic impulses.

Second, calculate net family income, that is, total gross family income minus all the usual deductions plus other costs of earning that income, such as day care, necessary additional clothing, running a car and so on. Then basic necessities of life must be calculated, for example, mortgage or rent payments, utilities, groceries, clothing and so on. As Christians, we should consider a regular schedule of offerings to further the work of God's kingdom as part of these necessities. All long-term savings needs must be considered as well. These include investments and capital goods, such as a car or a down payment on a home. Noncapital purchases can be anticipated and saved for also, for example, property taxes, Christmas presents and this year's family vacation.

Finally, ask yourself how much money you can afford to take out of your net family earnings to pay back credit charges that will in no way hinder meeting your financial objectives. This constitutes your personal credit limit.

Deciding what kind of credit to use. This is a complex subject, and the reader is urged to consult the many fine books on the subject of personal finances, including those written from a biblical perspective. Such books are legion. A visit to any decent bookstore will reveal dozens of books on personal finance often tailored to specific situations. What follows are a few brief remarks about some of the most common forms of credit.

The most significant debt that most borrowers will ever experience is a mortgage. Aside from interest rates, features of mortgages vary greatly from lender to lender, for example, how much can be prepaid without an interest penalty. Do not limit your comparison shopping to the interest charged. In addition to the purchase of a home, income-producing assets may rightly be purchased on credit, especially if the interest on the loan is deductible from the taxable income generated.

Items that do not appreciate in value offer fewer advantages as credit purchases. The consumer must weigh the advantages and disadvantages of purchasing via credit, in order to have immediate use of these goods, versus postponing the purchase until sufficient savings are accumulated.

As far as credit cards are concerned, it is best to limit the number you possess because multiple cards only increase the credit limit your lenders have decided is yours and because their availability increases the likelihood of impulse purchasing. In addition, use them only when you can repay the charge within the interest-free period. If you are unable to do this, then you should resort to a cheaper consumer loan from your bank. As with mortgages, shopping around for bank loans is highly recommended. Terms differ greatly.

Conclusion

Credit is often wrong—when it is an impetus to materialism or when it undermines carefully thought through financial objectives. But like many other aspects of material life, credit is amoral. It can be used wisely, or it can be abused. The challenge to the Christian is to see credit in its proper context—as one way of utilizing the resources with which God has entrusted us.

References and Resources

J. Barnett, *Wealth and Wisdom: A Biblical Perspective on Possessions* (Colorado Springs: NavPress, 1987); J. R. Sutherland, *Going Broke: Bankruptcy, Business Ethics and the Bible* (Waterloo, Ont.: Herald, 1991).

—John R. Sutherland

CREDIT CARD

More than half of North Americans have a credit card in their wallet or purse. It is a handy way to obtain consumer credit for the purchase of goods or services without carrying cash or making payments instantly, especially while traveling. This American innovation became popular in 1938, when oil companies set up a national system to honor one another's cards for the purchase of gasoline. But it was not until the 1950s, with the development of the computer, that credit cards became almost universal, since this new technology permitted accurate and fast accounting. The *debit card,* a variation on this, instantly withdraws the money from one's bank accounts and does not extend the usual thirty-day credit. Credit cards produce profits to the institution granting them by direct user fees, by high interest rates on unpaid balances and through payments from retail establishments, or some combination of these. Many cards now offer further incentives by giving points that can be redeemed for airline travel (*see* Traveling) and penalizing, so it seems, the use of cash or checks.

As with all forms of credit, the credit card is based on the trust expressed in an individual by a bank or lender. The word *credit* comes from a Latin root meaning "faith" or "trust." An individual's credit rating is a measure of trust placed in him or her by a financial institution. Thus, the process of getting and maintaining a credit card is a form of financial testing, proving that one is a reliable person who will pay his or her bills. As with all forms of credit, this one facilitates the transfer of money in a way that increases its productivity by placing it where it will work. At the same time it economizes on the use of currency.

As with many technological advances, the use of credit cards has changed the way we live and think. We now carry "plastic money." We can make large purchases quickly without a penny in our pockets or guarantee a hotel room halfway around the world by simply using our number. Instead of providing a large cash deposit to guarantee a car rental, we simply use the line of credit provided with the card.

But there are several disadvantages. It is well known that credit cards make theft and fraud quite simple. The more serious problems are less obvious. We no longer have to wait, for we can buy it now, even if we are not carrying cash. We can "afford" it because we have thirty days to pay, even if we do not have the money in the bank ("It will come!"). It is undeniable that easy credit feeds consumerism and stimulates impulse buying. Many people are tempted to live beyond their means, accumulating debt beyond their ability to repay. Young people in particular are tempted to abuse credit and are filing for bankruptcy in distressing numbers.

So the use of a credit card is in one sense a test of our maturity. Put differently, it is an invitation to grow to an increasing maturity. We can do this by determining not to make purchases unless we actually have the money or a clear and workable plan for repayment of the debt (*see* Credit; Debt). We can reduce the number of credit cards we have to one or two to resist spreading credit—really debt—over multiple institutions.

Further, we can take our credit-card invoices as statements not only of purchases made but values held and carefully reflect on how we should exercise stewardship by preparing a budget and living by it. The last place we should look for help in setting our own credit limit is the institution granting it. Sometimes it is good to fast from credit-card buying, as my wife and I have done, and to use only cash. This gives us a more accurate experience of the flow of money through our hands.

The book of Proverbs speaks to the use of money and credit. It takes wisdom from God to possess money without being possessed by it (Proverbs 1:17-19). Without wisdom we can have wealth but no true friends, food on the table but no fellowship around it, a house but not a home, the ability to buy things but no financial freedom. Without wisdom we will use a credit card to indulge ourselves (Proverbs 21:17) and still never be satisfied (Proverbs 27:20; Proverbs 30:15-16). Credit card in hand, the unwise person "chases fantascies" (Proverbs 28:19) and so comes to ruin, but the wise, accumulating as stewards "little by little" (Proverbs 13:11), "will be richly blessed" (Proverbs 28:20). It takes wisdom to have a credit card and not be possessed by the power in our pockets.

See also CONSUMERISM; CREDIT; DEBT; MONEY; STEWARDSHIP; WEALTH

References and Resources
R. N. Baird, "Credit Card," in *The Encyclopedia Americana* (Danbury, Conn.: Grolier, 1989) 8:166-67; J. Barnett, *Wealth and Wisdom: A Biblical Perspective on Possessions* (Colorado Springs: NavPress, 1987).

—R. Paul Stevens

DEBT

Ben Franklin once said that it was better to "go to bed supperless than run in debt for breakfast." In more recent times North Americans have failed to heed his advice. The result has been an explosion in personal debt—and bankruptcies! Though I will focus on the subject of debt, one cannot really talk about this without also considering the related topic of credit.

While debt has been a subject of considerable discussion in Christian circles for a long time, it was probably the explosion of business and personal bankruptcies in the 1980s that brought unusual attention to the topic and even caused some Christians to doubt their standing before God. Over five million Americans filed for bankruptcy in the decade of the 1980s. Canada realized proportionately similar numbers. In fact, it was only in 1993 that bankruptcy statistics actually began to decline from the record total realized the previous year.

Many Christian commentators were quick to condemn Christians who took this avenue of escape from their debts. American businessperson and author Albert

J. Johnson suggested that those considering voluntary bankruptcy to resolve debt problems should read Psalm 37:21, "The wicked borrow and do not repay." He argued that a person considering bankruptcy was in financial trouble because of past violations of scriptural principles (Johnson, pp. 82, 85). Widely published financial and business adviser Larry Burkett is similarly outspoken, as is evident in one of his taped addresses:

> Now isn't that amazing to you, that somebody would actually default on a debt that they created legally, morally, ethically, and then they would default on it? See, it ought to never happen with Christianity, or it should happen so rarely that we would take that person, and we would admonish them according to Matthew 18, and bring them before the church to restore them back to the faith.

This hard-nosed attitude toward bankruptcy is sometimes held toward taking on debt generally. Some commentators have argued that debt is a substitute for trust in God and that to be truly effective a Christian must be financially free. Furthermore, debts are viewed as lifelong obligations, ruling out any possibility of their being forgiven via the bankruptcy process. Taken to its extreme, financial success is, in some circles, linked with divine favor and right standing before God, while debt problems are seen as an indication of a Satan-defeated life.

Given the fact that North Americans have taken so readily to consumer and business credit and that indebtedness has become a normal aspect of life for many Christians, it is crucial to know just what the Bible says, and does not say, about the topic of debt. This will enable us to come to sound conclusions about the use of credit.

Is Debt Evil?

If one were to adopt a proof-texting approach to this topic, confusion would assuredly be the result, for the biblical message concerning debt appears at quick glance to be a mixed one. On the one hand, many times God's people are urged to lend to the needy. Deut. 15:7-10 is particularly forceful:

> If there is a poor man among your brothers . . . do not be hardhearted or tightfisted toward your poor brother. Rather be openhanded and freely lend him whatever he needs. Be careful not to harbor this wicked thought: "The seventh year, the year for canceling debts, is near," so that you do not show ill will toward your needy brother and give him nothing. He may then appeal to the LORD against you, and you will be found guilty of sin. Give generously to him and do so without a grudging heart; then because of this the LORD your God will bless you in all your work and in everything you put your hand to.

Our Lord takes a similar view, not only with respect to one's brothers and sisters, but even with one's enemies: "Love your enemies, do good to them, and lend to them without expecting to get anything back. Then your reward will be great, and you will be sons of the Most High, because he is kind to the ungrateful and wicked" (Luke 6:35) and "Give to the one who asks you, and do not turn away from the one who wants to borrow from you" (Matthew 5:42).

On the other hand, in the Bible we see borrowers, desperate to avoid the exactions of hardhearted creditors, attempting to persuade a third party to act as a guarantor for their debts. The Old Testament frequently warns against this practice (Proverbs 6:1-5; Proverbs 11:15; Proverbs 17:18; Proverbs 22:26-27). In fact, being in debt is sometimes linked with being in a hopelessly vulnerable situation, as Proverbs 22:7 suggests: "The rich rule over the poor, and the borrower is servant to the lender" (see further Deut. 15:6; Deut. 28:12, 44). We also have the Pauline injunction "Avoid getting into debt, except the debt of mutual love" (Romans 13:8 JB).

Given the many times that God's people are urged to lend, compassionately and generously, to the needy, it would be ridiculous to assert that borrowing, and therefore debt, is evil. However, it is realistic to conclude that incurring debt can be dangerous. This two-edged characteristic is typical of most aspects of material life from the biblical point of view. For example, wealth and property can be seen as gifts from God and even as a reward for obedient living (Deut. 28:1-14). Their value is in the opportunities that they provide for increased service to humanity (2 Cor. 9:11), rather than for self-indulgent use (Luke 8:14). But material wealth at the same time is one of the chief obstacles to salvation (Luke 12:13-21; Luke 16:19-31; Luke 18:24-25).

One cannot arbitrarily conclude, then, that debt is inherently evil. God would not command his people to proffer help that was wrong to receive. But debt, like so many other aspects of economic life, can be abused by the lender and borrower alike. Thus, care must be taken to use debt wisely.

What Was the Purpose of Debt?

Virtually all of the ethical teaching about debt is found in the Old Testament. In the economy of Pentateuchal times, Israelites were involved almost exclusively in agriculture. The most common commercial participant in those days was the traveling merchant or trader, called simply a "foreigner" (Deut. 23:20) or sometimes a "Canaanite" (Zech. 14:21). While Israelites were to lend to their fellow Israelite farmers interest free, making loans with interest to foreigners (or traders) was permissible.

It was with respect to the interest-free loans to covenant brothers and sisters that the lender was urged to be compassionate, taking minimal collateral and forgiving unpaid debts by the sabbatical year (more on this below). Loans would have typically been solicited not for commercial investment purposes but as a result of economic hardship, for example, crop failure or the devastation that resulted from enemy raids (Judges 6:1-4). Borrowing was an indication of serious financial trouble, imperiling the well-being of the family unit, which was the fundamental building block of society. Thus, while the debtor was to be treated with great compassion, he or she was usually in debt not because of self-indulgent motives but because of the inability to meet the basic needs of life.

Commercial debt is mentioned but with very little comment. Clearly it was not wrong for God's people to be involved in commercial investments. They had to recognize, of course, that a loan carried with it not only responsibilities but also dangers, whether of loss or of exploitation. (This is evident in the many warnings about unwise involvement with lenders which could bring a borrower to the point of losing personal independence.)

So we see two kinds of debt in the Old Testament: interest-bearing loans to foreigners and interest-free loans to fellow Israelites. It was with respect to covenant brothers and sisters that more well-to-do Israelites were enjoined to be generous and forgiving. So important was this principle to God that it even appears in the Lord's Prayer as the perfect example of godly forgiveness (Matthew 6:12: "Forgive us our debts, as we also have forgiven our debtors"). Neither of these types of debt is condemned. But the former tends to be discussed within the context of risk and the need to avoid being exploited. The latter is found within the context of generosity and forgiveness and the requirement not to exploit.

Are Debts Forgivable?

According to biblical teaching, borrowers were obliged under normal circumstances to repay their debts. This responsibility to meet one's financial obligations is vividly illustrated by a provision recorded in Leviticus 25:39. Here a debtor in default could go so far as to sell himself into slavery. Obviously the responsibility to repay one's debts was taken extremely seriously. However, the possibility of those debts being canceled (or debt-slaves released) was not ruled out. In accordance with sabbatical-year legislation, debtors were automatically relieved of their obligations every seventh year, whether or not they deserved compassionate treatment.

Compassion of this sort—the setting aside of the legitimate rights of lenders—was typical of all economic relations envisioned in the covenant community. God's desire for his people was that they would enjoy economic stability and security as family units. Wealth was viewed as a divine blessing (Deut. 8:11-18, 28). This blessing was associated with God's people living in obedience and was based totally on God's compassion. Such financial mechanisms as the poor tithe (Deut. 14:28-29; Deut. 26:12), gleaning in the field (Deut. 24:19) and interest-free loans (Exodus 22:25-27; Leviticus 25:35-37; Deut. 23:19-20) were tangible ways by which God's people could, in turn, show compassion for each other. Beyond income-maintenance programs, God provided for permanent mechanisms—such as the sabbatical year and Jubilee—to ensure that temporary misfortune barred no family from full participation in economic life (see Exodus 21:2; Exodus 23:11; Leviticus 25:1-7; Deut. 15:1-15).

It is important to keep two points in mind. The cancellation of debts in the Old Testament was done at legislated intervals, that is, every seventh year (sabbatical year) and every seven sabbaticals (Jubilee year), regardless of the performance of the debtor, good or bad. In addition, these borrowers were not involved in commercial life. They were usually poor farmers borrowing to preserve their ability to make a living and to feed their families. But the principle that can be legitimately extracted from the biblical model and applied to our modern free-market economies in North America today is that while debt is to be taken seriously, it could be canceled to achieve some higher purpose, such as the preservation of the family unit. No desirable goal is achieved when unscrupulous debtors are allowed to escape from their financial obligations. But the Old Testament did provide for the cancellation of debts as an act of mercy, with no stigma attached.

Conclusion

Debt, like so many other topics that Christians must evaluate in contemporary society, is a morally neutral concept. Never are God's people told that debt is wrong—quite the opposite! In fact, one of the reasons that God entrusts his people with material means is because "there should be no poor among you" (Deut. 15:4). Loans were one way of restoring the poor to economic stability, especially if the lending was accompanied by a merciful and forgiving attitude. Well-off Israelites could also participate in commercial ventures provided that they made careful allowances for the risks involved. But access to loans brings with it all of the temptations associated with material life: self-indulgence, riskiness and exploitation. Debt is a two-edged sword, to be handled with care.

See also CONSUMERISM; CREDIT; CREDIT CARD; MONEY; STEWARDSHIP

References and Resources
L. Burkett, *God's Principles for Operating a Business* (Dahlonega, Ga.: Christian Financial Concepts, 1982), audiocassette; A. J. Johnson, *A Christian's Guide to Family Finances* (Wheaton, Ill.: Victor Books, 1983).

—John R. Sutherland

DISCRIMINATION, WORKPLACE

As a term, *discrimination* can be understood in different ways. Historically it has meant the process of observing differences and making distinctions in our choices. Whenever we are hiring an employee or choosing an employee for promotion, the process of selection involves a form of discrimination. In this respect all judgments are discriminatory.

In recent decades, however, *discrimination* has taken on a negative connotation. Current usage most likely refers to *unjust* discrimination that is the result of improper judgments. Here discrimination means choosing for or against a person based on their group or class, or some characteristic (attribute) related to their group, and not on individual merit. This subjective judgment is the basis for giving an individual unjustifiably positive or negative treatment.

Discrimination in the workplace is manifested in different forms. It can be seen in the selection, hiring and promotional practices of organizations. The most conspicuous forms of workplace discrimination are *sexism, racism* and *ageism*. It is naive to believe that Christians are not susceptible to workplace discrimination issues. Should a Christian manager not promote someone because of moral issues (perhaps the worker is racist, makes crude jokes, is a practicing homosexual), or should she or he consider only the employee's work performance record? Should a Christian be promoted over a non-Christian? Or should a "nice" person be promoted ahead of a profane but more competent worker? Such questions suggest the breadth and complexity of choices involving discrimination. To answer any of these situations without being aware of the myriad variables that make up each set of circumstances would be both unfair and simplistic.

One business ethicist observes that at its core, workplace discrimination involves adverse decisions against employees based on their membership in a group that is viewed as inferior or seen as deserving of unequal treatment. This discrimination can be institutional or individual, intentional or unintentional (Shaw and Barry, p. 364).

Diversity and the Changing Workplace

Diversity and *multiculturalism* are two words often applied to today's work environment. Here are some facts about the changing workplace in the United States:

• Women, people of color and immigrants account for more than 50 percent of the present work force.

• By the year 2000, 85 percent of the those entering the job market will be female, African-American, Asian-American, Latino or new immigrants.

• Two million "older" workers, between ages fifty and sixty-four, are ready, willing and able to work but are not being utilized.

• Encouraged by the Americans with Disabilities Act of 1990, many of the forty-three million Americans with disabilities will seek equal opportunity in employment (Blank and Slipp, p. 3).

There is considerable agreement that an ethical organization operates on ground rules which encourage managers to communicate and treat the diversity and differences in their work force fairly. However, dealing with diversity in the workplace without practicing some discriminatory behavior has become a more complex task today than it was a decade or two ago.

A comprehensive 1980s study done by the Hudson Institute, *Workforce 2000: Work and Workers for the 21st Century,* made significant predictions that are worth examining. It projected that of the twenty-five million people who would join the American work force between 1987 and 2000, only 15 percent would be white males;

almost 61 percent would be women; and 29 percent would be minorities (minority women were counted twice; cited by Garfield, pp. 8-9). For companies committed to a corporate culture that will include groups besides white males, this raises two dilemmas: first, how to ensure a diverse work force without antagonizing either white males, whose support is critical for change, or women and minorities, who may resent efforts to win over white males; and second, how to correct historical discrimination without creating new forms of it (Galen and Palmer, pp. 50-52).

Sexism, Racism, Ageism and Other Forms of Workplace Discrimination

Sexism occurs when people are treated in a biased or prejudiced manner based on gender rather than on personal traits or abilities. Sexism can be blatant or subtle and is often complex. There are numerous accounts of how successful professional women today had to surmount serious sexist roadblocks to advance in their careers. It has only been in the last few decades that women have been able to make substantial inroads into such fields as medicine and law, for example.

Sexism can be subtle because people may interpret a particular behavior differently depending on whether it is exhibited by a man or a woman. Some may see a man as assertive but a woman as aggressive, a man as flexible but a woman as fickle, a woman as sensitive but a man as a wimp, or a woman as polite but a man as patronizing (Range, p. 791). Women frequently encounter a "glass ceiling" as they attempt the ascent to upper-management levels. Only about 3 percent of American women have gained high-level management positions. Furthermore, in the United States a woman earns only about 70-75 cents for every dollar earned by a man having the same job (Reder, pp. 23-25).

In the work arena, *racism* or *racial prejudice* occurs when there is an unfair or unequal valuation of persons on the basis of race. Racism assumes that hereditary biology determines the differences between groups, that cultural differences are predetermined and unchangeable, and that the identifying social and cultural features of the subordinate group are inferior (Thoms, p. 342).

African-Americans in particular have experienced discrimination at work. Their representation in management positions falls dramatically short of their overall representation in the work force. As of 1991, according to U.S. Labor Department statistics, fewer than 24 percent of African-American workers held managerial, professional or administrative jobs, compared to about 60 percent of whites (Reder, p. 31).

While diversity studies tend to focus on differences in gender, culture and ethnic background, the broadest definition of diversity will also encompass differences in *age*. As the American population ages, new concerns about staffing shortages, mandatory retirement and age discrimination are arising. Ageism is a much more subtle bias than racism and sexism; therefore it often goes unrecognized.

Sexism, racism and ageism are not the only areas where discrimination occurs in the workplace. Individuals may also suffer discrimination because of religious beliefs, sexual preference, disability status, educational background and even physical appearance. For example, some qualified individuals may be passed over for extremely attractive, less qualified individuals who broadcast the "ideal" organization image.

Group Characteristics Versus Stereotypes

Managers must take time to get to know and appreciate an individual's unique qualities and not take the dangerous, ill-considered path of using stereotypes as a shortcut means for labeling people. Unfortunately, stereotyping happens too often—consciously or unconsciously—without any thought to its potentially adverse effects on others. The following are examples of common stereotypes:

- People with disabilities are unable to work regular hours.
- Women who are mothers are not committed to their jobs.
- White men are racist and sexist.
- Immigrants have no desire to learn English. (Blank and Slipp, p. 9)

Management must be aware of the difference between a group characteristic and a stereotype. For example, a legitimate characteristic of many people with disabilities—although not all—is that they need some accommodation to perform their jobs optimally. A stereotype is the belief that people with disabilities cannot work regular hours because it is too hard for them; such a stereotype may lead managers not to hire anyone with a disability.

Scripture and Discrimination

As Christians, when we make moral choices, we are involved in a type of discrimination because our intent is to select the best moral alternative over less favorable ones. However, when we use inappropriate criteria for making our moral judgments, we are practicing *unjust* discrimination. Richard Chewning astutely points out that unjust discrimination reveals an ungodly form of favoritism and rejection that violates biblical norms. Scripture reveals that God is not a respecter of persons and that unjust discrimination is an abomination to him (see Deut. 10:17; 2 Chron. 19:7; Acts 10:34; Romans 2:11; Galatians 2:6; Ephes. 6:9; Col. 3:25; James 2:1-9; 1 Peter 1:17). Christians need to be aware, Chewning says, that our "old nature" has a tendency toward becoming protective and defensive whenever our psychological comfort is threatened. Sadly, this perverted reflex is often at the root of discrimination and generally reveals personal insecurities and pride (Chewning, p. 277).

For Christians, unjust discrimination is morally objectionable not only because it is wrong and evil but also because it stands against the revelation of God, who loves all people and offers them reconciliation through Christ. Our worth is tied to the belief that men and women are created in God's image (Genesis 1:27), that all people have sinned and come short of God's glory (Romans 3:23) and that God's love for the world culminated in Christ's death on the cross, which covers the sins of those who put faith in him (John 3:16). This egalitarian ideal is also critical to Paul's conception of the church, where "there is neither Jew nor Greek, slave or free, male nor female, for you are all one in Christ Jesus" (Galatians 3:28; compare Col. 3:11). Paul's view was in juxtaposition to that of ethnic Jews who saw themselves as being a superior race because they were God's chosen people.

The Israelites were commanded to deal with people in a just and loving manner (Deut. 1:17; Deut. 24:17-18); special consideration was to be given to the poor, the widow, the orphan and the needs of the alien, who did not have equal political and economic status with adult Israelite males (Exodus 22:21-27; Leviticus 19:10; Deut. 15:7-11).

Jesus' teaching and behavior exemplified the importance of dealing with others in an impartial way (Luke 20:21) by practicing love and justice. In so doing he collided with many discriminatory practices of his day. Jesus took a strong stance in his radical inclusion and acceptance of women and children (Mark 10:13-16; John 4:1-27; John 12:1-11); he openly befriended social outcasts (Luke 5:27-31; Luke 18:9-14; John 8:1-11); and he healed the sick and unclean (Luke 5:12-26; Luke 17:11-19). Compassion, not correctness, was his guide.

One of the most important New Testament passages addressing discrimination is the parable of the good Samaritan (Luke 10:25-37). In this parable, a man who is robbed and left half dead is passed by "on the other side" of the road by both a priest and a Levite. Yet a Samaritan, despised by Jews as an unclean half-breed, takes pity on him, attends to his wounds, puts him on his own donkey, takes him to an inn, and generously gives the innkeeper enough money to provide for the man to stay for up to two months at the inn.

What makes this parable striking is that the most likely candidates for attending to the man not only ignore his plight but also deliberately pass by on the other side. The person Jesus commends in the parable was neither the religious leader nor the lay associate but a hated foreigner—the Samaritan. If anyone has a reason for passing the injured man by, it is the Samaritan, since Samaritans and Jews were openly hostile toward one another. In this parable, then, Jesus pointedly asserts that authentic love transcends national boundaries.

When Jesus asks, "Which of these three do you think was a neighbor to the man who fell into the hands of robbers?" the answer is "The one who had mercy on him." To this Jesus adds, "Go and do likewise."

The parable of the good Samaritan is given in response to the poignant question "And who is my neighbor?" Immediately preceding this question in Luke 10:27—and in other passages (Matthew 22:35-40; Mark 12:28-33; compare Leviticus 19:18)—Jesus succinctly provides guidance concerning our priorities and relationship to God and our neighbors.

Jesus replied: " 'Love the Lord your God with all your heart and with all your soul and with all your mind.' This is the first and greatest commandment. And the second is like it: 'Love your neighbor as yourself.' All the Law and the Prophets hang on these commandments." (Matthew 22:37-40)

Christians are called to accept all persons, regardless of race, creed or sex, on equal footing as children of God. In the final analysis, the problem of discrimination (in its negative sense) finds a certain resolution for Christians in the attempt to fulfill God's law as given in the "new commandment": "If you really keep the royal law found in Scripture, 'Love your neighbor as yourself,' you are doing right. But if you show favoritism, you sin and are convicted by the law as lawbreakers" (James 2:8-9).

See also BUSINESS ETHICS; FIRING; MULTICULTURALISM; OFFICE POLITICS; ORGANIZATIONAL CULTURE AND CHANGE; POWER, WORKPLACE; RACISM

References and Resources
R. Blank and S. Slipp, *Voices of Diversity* (New York: American Management Association, 1994); R. C. Chewning, *Biblical Principles and Business: The Practice* (Colorado Springs: NavPress, 1990) 272-84; M. Galen and A. T. Palmer, "White, Male and Worried," *Business Week,* January 31, 1994, 50-55; C. Garfield, "Embracing Diversity," *Executive Excellence,* October 1994, 8-9; D. J. Miller, "Discrimination," in *Evangelical Dictionary of Biblical Theology,* ed. W. Elwell (Grand Rapids: Baker, 1984) 320-21; L. M. Range, "Sexism," in *Ready Reference: Ethics* (Pasadena, Calif.: Salem, 1994) 791-92; A. Reder, *In Pursuit of Principle and Profit* (New York: G. P. Putnam's Sons, 1994); J. Richardson. ed., *Annual Editions: Business Ethics 96/97* (Sluice Dock, Guilford, Conn.: Dushkin, 1996); W. H. Shaw and V. Barry, *Moral Issues in Business* (Belmont, Calif.: Wadsworth, 1992); D. E. Thoms, "Racism," in *Encyclopedia of Biblical and Christian Ethics* (Nashville: Thomas Nelson, 1992) 342-43.

—John E. Richardson

DRESS CODE, WORKPLACE

In the book of Genesis people began to wear clothes when they first become aware of their sin: since the day Adam and Eve covered themselves with fig leaves, clothing has been a blessing and a curse—a cursed blessing to be exact (Genesis 3:7). In the New Testament we are assured that God will provide us with the necessities of life, including clothing (Matthew 6:28-30), and not just any old hand-me-downs but perhaps even designer labels, as Matthew claims the lilies of the field surpass "Solomon in all his splendor." Although we know intellectually about God's promise to care for us, many of us still fret about what to wear when we get up each morning. Moreover, while daily work can be a blessing, it is interesting that in Genesis 3 God also declares that people will be cursed by daily toil as a result of their sin (Genesis 3:17, 19).

The Corporate Image

On a basic level a dress code may be crucial to ensure an employee's safety (or at least to protect the company legally in case of worker injury). A dress code may also function to increase an employee's efficiency or to provide customers with easy identification of helpful staff. On a higher level, however, a company uses uniforms or a dress code to communicate a certain image to the public—a promise to get the job done right. While a dress code may indicate a company's lack of trust in its employees' judgment, it is useful in that it removes any ambiguity about what an employee should wear to work. To the extent that the employees themselves perform their jobs as professionally as they are dressed, the dress code serves a purpose.

Humans: Made in God's Image

We have all had experiences in which a professionally dressed salesperson does not give us the service promised. It is then that we realize how superficial worldly image can be. We are warned in the Bible that appearances may be deceiving: some people are merely wolves in sheep's clothing (Matthew 7:15). We cannot fool God simply by putting on the right clothes (1 Samuel 16:7), for God looks straight into our hearts and knows our true character. A Christian's daily struggle is to discern how God wants him or her to behave and to allow the inner character to shine through to the outside. As Christians, our true image comes from God (Genesis 1:27), who created us to have a relationship with him such as no other living creature does, one so loving that it led to his Son's paying the ultimate sacrifice for our sin (John 3:16). Therefore, it is important when we report for work that we not only dress the part but do our best work, for, as the apostle Paul exhorts the Colossians, "Whatever you do, work at it with all your heart, as working for the Lord, not for men, since you know that you will receive an inheritance from the Lord as a reward. It is the Lord Christ you are serving" (Col. 3:23).

The Christian Image Paradox: Looking Good Matters

Christian workers have a double duty as ambassadors for both their earthly employers and their heavenly Father. In movies and television, Christians are often portrayed as prim and strait-laced with no style or adornment (except a large cross pendant), wearing either paramilitary uniforms or ill-fitting, drab-colored, mismatched garments. The contrast between the joyous good news they are supposed to be spreading and their dowdy, lackluster appearance is laughably unattractive. Although this is a media caricature, it pinpoints a paradox: Christians need to have a healthy concern for what is on the surface even though God can see straight through it. This is because judging others by the way they look is a basic human characteristic. Even in biblical times dishevelment and dirtiness were considered a sign of mental derangement or demonic possession! In terms of a Christian witness, therefore, we need to work with this tendency rather than to ignore it.

Non-Christians are already convinced that to become a Christian means to adopt a life of restriction and mindless conformity. But when Christians present an attractive image, it is not to deceive but to demonstrate a healthy self-respect and to celebrate that each person is a unique creation of God. At the same time, when Christians are confronted with an office culture in which other employees spend extraordinary sums of money to compete for the best image, the Christian may consider being countercultural without being unattractive or obnoxious.

Dress Code as Authority

The dress code is a company rule that must be obeyed. Unfortunately, humans have a natural tendency to rebel against authority of any kind (Ephes. 2:2). An obvious incentive for obeying a company dress code is to avoid being fired! But an even better reason is to show proper respect for authority when that authority is acting reasonably. Paul commands the Ephesians, "Slaves, obey your earthly masters with respect and fear, and with sincerity of heart, just as you would obey Christ" (Ephes. 6:5). When our bosses are acting unreasonably, however, it might be right to rebel, such as when a dress code regulation is humiliating or discriminatory. For example, in the United States during the 1980s a female airline employee who was fired because she refused to wear makeup took her employer to court. Her grievance was that her employer valued her more for the way she looked than for the high caliber of work she performed. In the book of Acts the apostle Peter justifies disobedience to earthly authority in cases where it is clearly superseded by God's authority (Acts 4:19-20). But ultimately we cannot go wrong if we adhere to God's own dress code as itemized by the apostle Paul: "Put on the full armor of God, . . . the belt of truth, . . . the breastplate of righteousness, . . . the shield of faith, . . . the helmet of salvation and the sword of the Spirit" (Ephes. 6:13-17).

See also WORKPLACE

References and Resources

"Business Etiquette: Dress," in *Merriam-Webster's Secretarial Handbook* (Springfield, Mass.: Merriam-Webster, 1993); J. Martin, *Miss Manners' Guide to Excruciatingly Correct Behavior* (New York: Atheneum, 1982); A. Sterk and P. Scazzero, "Self-Image," in *Christian Character* (Downers Grove, Ill.: InterVarsity Press, 1985); R. P. Stevens and G. Schoberg, "Work: Curse or Blessing?" in *Satisfying Work: Christian Living from Nine to Five* (Wheaton, Ill.: Harold Shaw, 1989).

—Kathryn E. Lockhart

DRIVENNESS

Drivenness is behind one of the most respectable of all addictions—workaholism. But it is also expressed in a wide variety of addictive behaviors not covered in this article: chemical abuse, religious zeal, sexual addiction, perfectionism and fitness, which are all subject to the law of diminishing returns as people try to meet their deepest needs in these ways. The condition of drivenness usually arises from sources deep within the human personality, as well as systemic problems in our society. Drivenness reveals a spiritual dysfunctionality usually associated with a failure to accept the unconditional love of God. Driven people tend to focus all their energies on an activity that feeds their inner dysfunction, and this activity becomes an addiction.

Workaholism: The Respectable Addiction

The now commonplace term *workaholism* was coined by Wayne Oates, an American minister and psychologist, in 1968. In that year he wrote a humorous and insightful confession in an article entitled "On Being a 'Workaholic' (A Serious Jest)" in *Pastoral Psychology*. Comparing himself to an alcoholic, Oates says that he started with "social" working, boasting about how much work he could "hold" and how he could work others "under the table." But then it progressed to a true addiction. He was hooked. Drawing on his own experience, Oates describes the progression. Workaholics "pass out" (become emotionally dead) either on the job or at home, usually the latter. Whereas formerly they attained social approval for working addictively, now they are besieged by well-meaning advice to slow down, though friends and family expect them to be too busy to attend to them. If they try to slow down, they suffer "withdrawal symptoms" and fight a terrible battle when they leave the office, factory or church, resolving it by taking some work home or by doing a "weekend binge" of work. Christmas, other holidays and family vacations are terrifying experiences, and workaholics can only tolerate them by taking work with them.

Workaholics dread thinking about retirement, and when they finally retire, they may die prematurely. Work is their love, and they may even feed this love by planning another report or sermon while making love to their spouse! In this seminal article Oates recognizes that the problem is profoundly theological and spiritual: the workaholic has made an idol of work. Salvation depends on work: "Far from thinking of God as someone who loves us whether we produce or not, this is unthinkable to workaholics. Acceptance is pay for work done" (Oates 1968, p. 17).

Since Oates's initial contribution, an extensive study has been undertaken by Barbara Killinger of what she calls the "respectable addicts." A workaholic is "a person who gradually becomes emotionally crippled and addicted to control and power in a compulsive drive to gain approval and success" (Killinger, p. 6). She describes the typical workaholic family of origin: one is born in a home where love is conditional on good performance and behavior. Instead of communicating the value of a child for who he or she is, parents in such homes communicate only the value of the child's accomplishments. Thus the child does not learn to separate doing and being, performance from personhood. Instead of hearing, "The grass you cut looks terrific; you must be proud of yourself!" they hear, "You did a great job cutting the grass; you are a good boy" (Killinger, p. 21). In the words of Killinger, "conditional love teaches a child to be dependent on others for approval; unconditional love encourages independent appraisal, objectivity, and self-affirmation in deserved pride" (p. 22). Many children raised in such environments become chronically overinvolved with work, usually as a way of avoiding anxiety or emotional pain.

Workaholism is the condition of persons whose self-worth is linked to what they do rather than who they are. The result of this orientation is that work moves from being an other-centered to a self-centered activity, defining every aspect of their existence.

Workaholics do not work because they have a desire to be gainfully employed; they work to prove something to themselves. Though they keep trying by working harder, working better or trying to find the perfect job, they can never do enough to give full meaning to their lives. With some women workaholism takes a unique form in compulsive motherhood. The workaholic housewife has been well researched. Less recognized is the phenomenon of some women who become pregnant repeatedly for largely unconscious reasons: the inability to enjoy sexual relations apart from impregnation, being unhappy with any child except a new and helpless one, needing to control her husband or other children. The end result of this repeated "labor" is the martyred wife and mother, usually perfectionist and depressed (Oates 1971, p. 72).

Understanding Workaholism

The workaholic does not normally come from the ranks of the nine-to-five workers but more likely comes from a self-employed, small business, professional or homemaking background. All these people decide for themselves whether they should be working more or less (Oates 1968, p. 20). While this helpfully targets the part of our population that may be most likely to exhibit workaholism, it does not help us make an important distinction. Not all people who work hard or work long hours are workaholics. Indeed, some studies indicate that people highly involved in their work may indicate little or no sign of personal problems and may function in a healthy way on the job (Naughton, p. 181). Such persons typically find a lot of satisfaction in their work, more than they find in nonwork-related activities. Thus in developing a typology of workaholism for career counselors, Thomas Naughton distinguishes between the *job-involved workaholic,* who has high job satisfaction and performs well, and the *compulsive workaholic,* whose work reflects a ritualized pattern of thoughts and behaviors that are destructive to himself or herself and colleagues. In this latter case workaholics are not good workers, not an asset to a company or a church. They have nothing to give their families and friends. Like the idlers in 2 Thes. 3:10-12, they are sponging on the goodwill of their family and friends.

There are signs of workaholism. Workaholics typically (1) keep excessively long workdays, (2) talk a lot about their accomplishments, (3) are unable to say no and (4) cannot rest or relax (Minirth et al., pp. 29-31). Frank Minirth and his colleagues note how the deeply reflective words of Eccles. 2:17-23 are applicable to the workaholic: "All his days his work is pain and grief; even at night his mind does not rest" (Eccles. 2:23). In contrast, the godly person finds enjoyment in eating, drinking and work (Eccles. 2: 24-25).

There are substantial effects of this addictive behavior: disruption of family life, neglect of spiritual growth, diminishing returns for work, physical tension, loss of perspective on life and misdirected resentment in which others are blamed for the pain they experience (Walters, pp. 103-4). The children of workaholics are especially disadvantaged. Sons may recall very few moments when their father (or mother) attended a sporting event with them. They may be preoccupied with getting good grades. Daughters of workaholic fathers have special problems. Speaking to this, therapists note: "Their fathers are apt to totally ignore them because of a feeling that females are less productive in terms of work than are males. . . . This can be devastating for the daughter and she may go to extreme lengths to gain her father's attention . . . [including] drugs and/or sexual misconduct" (Minirth et al., p. 46). Not only do the children of workaholics suffer direct effects in the circumstances of their lives, but the workaholic pattern gets ingrained in the children, thus passing the sins of the fathers (and mothers) to the children, sometimes for three or four generations (Exodus 20:5).

Reflecting on Drivenness

Earlier I used the word *idol* in a description of a workaholic. *Idolatry* is a misplaced devotion; it is simply making something one's ultimate concern other than the One who is ultimate. The apostle Paul was a driven person until he experienced the call of God on the Damascus road. But perhaps this observation does not go deep enough. Was he obsessed and compulsive or ambitious and determined?

Prior to meeting Christ, Paul was determined to find acceptance and righteousness with God through Jewish legalism and performance and was simultaneously compelled to eliminate Christians as a threatening sect. What happened at Damascus was not the changing of Paul's personality from one type to another. Rather, Paul was released from the self-justifying paralysis of his personality by an empowering and liberating experience of grace through which he knew himself to be unconditionally accepted by God. Since the great resources of his personality were liberated by his meeting with Christ, he was able to devote himself in an entirely healthy way in a magnificently liberating passion—his passion to love God and love his neighbor as himself. Paul confessed, "To this end I labor, struggling with all his energy, which so powerfully works in me" (Col. 1:29).

It is tempting to say that the driven person and the called person may appear to be very similar to an outside observer. But this is too superficial an observation. The driven person has an obsession that destroys him and those around him. The called person is a liberated person who empowers and liberates others. Having a different source results in a different expression.

What is seldom mentioned in any discussion of addiction is that we were made for an all-consuming passion, love for God and love for our neighbor. The comparison Paul makes between being intoxicated with alcohol and being filled with the Spirit in Ephes. 5:18 is intentional. Canon Stanley Evans once described a Christian as "a controlled drunk, purposively intoxicated with the joy of the life which is perpetually created in God himself" (quoted in Leech, p. 103). "Be filled with the Spirit" (Ephes. 5:18) is in the imperative mood (it is not an option), in the present tense (it is an ongoing continuous experience) and in the plural number (it is something we experience in the community of faith). The similarity of this experience of completeness and profound pleasure in God with the sexual experience is a subject often noted.

Workaholism provides an alternative ecstasy. In an insightful section on "erotica," Killinger compares work experiences with sexual orgasms: "When there is a passionate obsession with work, erotic feelings can be expressed towards the accomplishments or products of work. The senses are aroused and alive when a coveted contract is signed, a record becomes a hit, or a sought-after degree is conferred" (p. 34). Failing to find the divine source of legitimate ecstasy, people find unsatisfactory substitutes. But how do people move from a debilitating compulsion to a magnificent obsession? In establishing a theology and practice of self-control, we must observe that self-control is not a human accomplishment, not even a religious work, but a fruit of the continuous inundation of the Holy Spirit (Galatians 5:23). How can we become accessible to such an indirect grace?

Toward Substantial Healing

Self-knowledge. The deepest sources of drivenness may be understood and resolved only through professional counseling, but a beginning can be made through reflection on why you as an individual work so hard and why praise is so important to you. Getting in touch with your own story and understanding the influence of one generation on another may be especially helpful. One aspect that is frequently neglected is simply listening to your own body-talk. Sometimes a specific illness serves as a reminder of the need for the seventh day of rest and for relief from the demands of work (Oates 1968, p. 20).

While choices can be made by a workaholic, a profoundly addicted person is not likely to gain freedom simply by making resolutions or decisions. Just as alcoholics must come to the place of recognizing that they are unable to free themselves, so workaholics must recognize their helplessness. The theologian Reinhold Niebuhr once said that to be a sinner is our distress, but to know it is our hope. To come to the end of self-deception, excuses, alibis and hiding is a profound moment of hope. God can help the helpless. Because Western society, and most of the industrialized world, sees nothing wrong with a person's wanting "to get ahead," the workaholic is tragically often permitted to remain in denial much longer than with substance abuse.

Many workaholics are helped with a personal inventory, such as that used by Alcoholics Anonymous and other self-help groups. These inventories deal with self-centeredness (my workaholism is driven by my narcissistic need to prove that I deserve to exist or to be loved or . . .), aggressiveness (my aggressiveness is really a self-centered expression of my need to be in control or to rebel against a parent or . . .), anger and resentment (I have put the following people on my grudge list, and I am affected by my anger in this way: . . .) and fear (behind my anger and resentment is my fear that I will not be loved by . . . or that I will lose control of . . .). As we take off the mask that covers our resentments, we usually discover that our adult drivenness is a desperate attempt to outrun our fear of abandonment. The deepest answer to our self-preoccupation is not through deprivation or condemnation but experiencing the unconditional love of God (Hemfelt, Minirth and Meier, pp. 263-64). But this liberating process is often complicated by the fact that those closest to us may not want us to change!

Coconspiracy for health rather than codependence in drivenness. People making a transition out of job-involved workaholism may encounter social pressures that make change very difficult. Recovering workaholics may experience shame, guilt and fear as they continue to relate to peers and employers whose work styles require long hours and who communicate social disapproval for people who fail to conform (Naughton, p. 186). Controlling workaholics need to learn to trust others and to share power.

If you are a recovering workaholic, it is most desirable that you ask colleagues and peers to hold you accountable for reasonable work hours and to ask them for feedback (and listen to it!). The same holds true for your spouse and children. Instead of playing the nurturing "fixer" who compensates for the effects of workaholism, invite your spouse to verbalize how you can take greater responsibility for your lifestyle to help diversify your interests. Those responsible for shaping the environment of a workplace have the privilege of creating organizations based on grace, celebrating who people are and not just remunerating their performance, and giving people a second chance (Oates 1971, p. 108).

Lifestyle changes. You should "give yourself the freedom to live each day well" (Killinger, p. 209). To do this, a driven person needs to stop rushing, to enjoy play, to learn to say no, to put energy into a wide variety of baskets. Killinger advises making a regular date with your spouse and a regular special outing with each of the children. Regarding your job, it is sometimes wise to ask whether you are in the right job and whether you should reduce your responsibilities rather than to seek another promotion (Killinger, pp. 208-21). Big changes in lifestyle are enormously difficult, but they can be accomplished through a succession of little changes in the right direction.

Experiencing sabbath. Some addictions, such as to pornography, require complete cessation, while others, like workaholism, require a balance of work, play, activity and rest, not unemployment. To achieve this balance, recovering a Christian experience of sabbath is essential. People who are on a treadmill of working harder and harder to support a particular lifestyle, or, in the case of the academic world, to publish more and more to justify tenure, desperately need sabbath. Our society offers work and leisure. While leisure is often a good thing, it is not contemplative; it does not direct us to reflect on the meaning of our lives and what God's view of our lives really is. Sabbath is not merely stopping work or resting. It is getting God's big view of the meaning of our lives and playing heaven.

Personal spirituality. Workaholics frequently doubt their own salvation. Not having felt unconditionally accepted as a child, they can hardly believe that the one who comes to Christ will not be cast out (John 6:37). To overcome workaholism, a person needs to deeply internalize the gospel and then to express it confidently in concrete everyday life. Experiencing gospel confidence is not like having one continuous spiritual orgasm; we were not made for continuous excitement. Practical steps for dealing with lust for more excitement all concern a deepening spiritual journey: (1) begin by reordering your spiritual values and beliefs about the root of pleasure (Proverbs 21:17); (2) accept a "deficit in excitement" as normal as being overcome by pleasure; (3) watch where and how you get your excitement; (4) come to appreciate *satisfaction* over *excitement* (Hart, pp. 60-63).

This last point hints at the seven dimensions of the fruit of the Spirit (Galatians 5:22-23), especially joy. We were made for a magnificent and liberating passion—the constant, continuous filling of the Holy Spirit. But Spirit-filling is primarily not for ecstasy but for redeemed living, for submissive and loving relationships (Ephes. 5:21) and for joy. Thus being in a community of faith, reading the Bible, practicing a life of prayer and inviting the Holy Spirit to inundate us continuously constitute the deepest answer for drivenness. This answer is not an alternative to dealing with the masks of denial, but without it we would be powerless to discover the intended content of the God-shaped vacuum in our souls.

Saint Augustine once said that God is always trying to give good things to us, but our hands are too full to receive them. Often our hands are full of the results of our drivenness. Gerald May suggests we may not be able to empty our hands by sheer willpower (p. 17). But we can relax them a little and admit that God's strength will be demonstrated in our weakness (2 Cor. 12:9), for "sooner or later addiction will prove to us that we are not gods," thus becoming to our extreme amazement a kind of good gift (May, p. 20). A German philosopher enigmatically expressed this same thought: "My burden carries me!" (A. A. Schröders, quoted in Thielicke, p. 238).

See also CALLING

References and Resources

S. Arterburn and J. Felton, *Toxic Faith* (Nashville: Nelson, 1991); A. D. Hart, *Healing Life's Hidden Addictions: Overcoming the Closet Compulsions That Waste Your Time and Control Your Life* (Ann Arbor, Mich.: Servant, 1990); R. Hemfelt, F. Minirth and P. Meier, *We Are Driven: The Compulsive Behaviors America Applauds* (Nashville: Thomas Nelson, 1991); B. Killinger, *Workaholics: The Respectable Addicts* (New York: Simon & Schuster, 1991); K. Leech, *True Prayer: An Invitation to Christian Spirituality* (San Francisco: Harper & Row, 1980); G. G. May, *Addiction and Grace: Love and Spirituality in the Healing of Addictions* (San Francisco: Harper, 1988); F. Minirth et al., *The Workaholic and His Family* (Grand Rapids: Baker, 1981); T. J. Naughton, "A Conceptual View of Workaholism and Implications for Career Consoling and Research," *The Career Development Quarterly* 135, no. 3 (1987) 180-87; W. E. Oates, *Confessions of a Workaholic: The Facts About Work Addiction* (London: Wolfe Publishing, 1971); W. E. Oates, "On Being a 'Workaholic' (A Serious Jest)," *Pastoral Psychology* 19 (October 1968) 16-20; A. W. Schaef, *When Society Becomes an Addict* (San Francisco: Harper & Row, 1986); H. Thielicke, *Und Wenn Gott Ware* (Stuttgbart: Qwee Verlag, 1970); R. P. Walters, *Escape the Trap* (Grand Rapids: Zondervan, 1989).

—R. Paul Stevens

FAILURE

No one is immune to failure. Human weakness, ignorance and the effects of sin promise that failure will be a familiar companion, even to people who walk with God. The Bible accepts the idea of failure as a part of life. Solomon observed, "Though a righteous man falls seven times, he rises again" (Proverbs 24:16). Famous Bible failures who rose again include Moses, Samson, David, Peter, John Mark and Jesus Christ.

In Western culture, success is often judged on the basis of the visible accomplishment of such things as wealth and security, public appearance and notoriety, power and influence, physical beauty and talent. Accordingly, failure is judged on the basis of the lack of these things. Even Christians, reflecting the culture, tend to evaluate persons and work on these cultural grounds. A closer look at Scripture, however, reveals that God's view of success and failure is quite different.

Neither the Old nor the New Testament uses words that coincide exactly with *success* or *failure* as we understand the terms. In the languages of the Bible the words that most nearly approximate the concept of success are ones that mean "blessed." In Hebrew the word is *barak;* in Greek the work is *makarios.* Both convey ideas of success, prosperity, happiness and enviably abundant life.

In the Old Testament the key issue in success, or blessedness, is to live in right relationship with God and to obey his instructions (Deut. 11:26-28; Psalm 1:1; Psalm 5:12). In the New Testament Jesus describes success in terms of personal transformation. The Beatitudes (Matthew 5:3-12) indicate that the changed person, not his or her measurable accomplishments, is the key to blessedness. A definition of success quickly emerges by reading the Beatitudes and substituting the word *successful* for "blessed," as in "Successful are the poor in spirit." Success as Jesus defines it has nothing to do with worldly wealth, power or honor. True success is the inner riches of personal character conformed to God's character. According to the Beatitudes, success is in the riches of inner qualities like vulnerability, brokenness, gentleness, craving for righteousness, compassion, single-mindedness, reconciliation and joy in suffering for Christ's sake.

In the Old Testament the word that stands opposite "blessed" and most closely approximates "failure" is the word *cursed* (Deut. 11:26-28). *Cursed,* as the Bible uses the term, does not represent something magical, such as casting spells or being under a hex. Lawrence Richards interprets the Old Testament word for curse as "the loss or absence of the state of blessing" (1985, p. 208). To fail is to have God's blessing withdrawn, lose the esteem of God, shrivel up spiritually, become small-souled. Obedience to the commandments of the Lord is the secret of success, and disobedience is the pathway to the withdrawal of God's blessing, reduced position, reduced power, reduced wealth, reduced honor and a broken relationship with God, which is the substance of failure (Richards, 1985, p. 207). To fail is to exist in a state of separation from God; to try to live without God is to die (Deut. 30:19). The New Testament updates this fundamental concept to include a person's response to the revelation of God in Jesus Christ. According to Jesus, the ultimate failure is to fail to be recognized as belonging to Christ (Matthew 7:21-23).

Success, Failure and Material Prosperity

The Bible encourages the expectation that if things are right between people and God, material abundance will follow. However, in Deut. 8:12-20 the promise of material blessing is immediately followed by a warning: If, after God has made them rich, his people become proud and think they have won prosperity by their own strength and hard work and if they forget the Lord and give allegiance to other gods, they will be destroyed! This same destiny awaits any nation that refuses to obey the Lord. The link between material prosperity and a relationship with God is unmistakable. But sometimes other issues are at stake.

The biblical portrait of success is often a picture of people surviving amid harassment, poverty, disaster and famine. Merely amassing material wealth and the power that goes with it is not success. Many wealthy, powerful people are in rebellion against God. God declares them of slight value (cursed). Indeed David composed a song against people who "succeed in their ways, when they carry out their wicked schemes" (Psalm 37:7).

The plutocracy of which David sings did not gain its power because of God's promises to bless the obedient. The people he describes have climbed to power and wealth on the backs of the oppressed and possess their wealth and power while the righteous have little (Psalm 37:16-17). They flourish "like a green tree in its native soil" (Psalm 37:35), but they have no future (Psalm 37:9-10, 15, 17, 38). The wealthy and powerful will be brought down in full view of the righteous poor whom they have oppressed (Psalm 37:34). The secret of the resilience of the righteous is that they trust God (Psalm 37:3). He is their delight (Psalm 37:4); their way is committed to him (Psalm 37:5); they are waiting for his justice (Psalm 37:6). The righteous are promised a home (Psalm 37:3), security (Psalm 37:3, 27), heart's desire (Psalm 37:4), justice (Psalm 37:6), peace (Psalm 37:11), protection (Psalm 37:14-15, 28), support (Psalm 37:17, 24), plenty to eat (Psalm 37:19, 25), enough to share with others (Psalm 37:21, 26), blessing-success (Psalm 37:22), confidence (Psalm 37:23), God's love (Psalm 37:28), deliverance (Psalm 37:33), a future (Psalm 37:37), salvation (Psalm 37:39), a refuge from the wicked (Psalm 37:39-40) and the Lord's help (Psalm 37:40)—an inventory of success with God in the midst of circumstances that, in the world's view, constitute failure. Psalm 37 promises spiritual abundance more than material prosperity. Believers are led to expect that basic necessities will be supplied, not that trusting and obeying will lead to a cushy life.

Worldly Success Is Failure Waiting to Be Exposed

In the last book of the Bible a great city called "Babylon the Great" is destroyed by the judgments of God. This Babylon is the symbol of worldly wealth, power and success that, according to the description given in Rev. 18, is measured in terms of profits made from commerce in everything from gold to "the bodies and souls of men" (Rev. 18:13). The destruction of this symbolic Babylon is a picture of "the inevitable judgments of God upon . . . the worship of false gods, which include riches, power and success" (Phillips, p. 516). The world's success story concludes with God's disclosure of the ultimate failure of worldly success (Rev. 18:14-24). It is not that it is intrinsically wrong to succeed in commerce or business, but it is a serious mistake to look to these things as true security and prosperity or the source and meaning of life. The real world of commerce and business is a system riddled with injustice and greed, which will finally fall to God's judgment. Those who have built their lives on it will be left impoverished and broken.

Where Is Prosperity When You've Lost Everything?

Success and blessing do not depend on material prosperity; they are found in the joy of knowing God as Savior. In the days of the prophet Habakkuk, the righteous remnant of Judah was overrun by the Babylonian war machine and carried into captivity along with those who deserved God's wrath. Everything was taken away from them. As Babylonian hordes bore down on Jerusalem, Habakkuk composed a prophetic poem (Habakkuk 3). At first he writes of God's sovereignty and mighty acts: "Suddenly Habakkuk is shown overwhelming waters of judgment, rushing like some Genesis cataclysm . . . to burst over the prophet and his people" (Richards, 1987, pp. 414-15). He trembles with fear; his knees buckle (Habakkuk 3:15-16). He knows God's faithful will not escape the bitter disaster coming on their rebellious nation. How will those who trust God find hope and see God's promise of prosperity when starvation, deprivation and defeat are the orders of the day? Habakkuk knows:

> Though the fig tree does not bud
> > and there are no grapes on the vines,
>
> though the olive crop fails
> > and the fields produce no food,
>
> though there are no sheep in the pen
> > and no cattle in the stalls,
>
> yet I will rejoice in the LORD,
> > I will be joyful in God my Savior.
>
> The Sovereign LORD is my strength;
> > he makes my feet like the feet of a deer,
> > he enables me to go on the heights. (Habakkuk 3:17-19)

Because he knew God, Habakkuk experienced spiritual success-blessing even as everything he possessed was swept away in the judgment of the condemned society in which he lived.

The Therapeutic Effects of Failure

For the person who believes God, failure is not fatal. The Bible affirms that failure will come, but when it does, it cannot destroy the believer (see Micah 7:8-9). The grace of God meets us at the point of failure.

Pressure produces sterling character (Romans 5:2-5). The Greek word for suffering means "pressure, distress of mind and circumstances, trial, affliction." The restoration in us of the likeness ("glory") of God takes place through a process involving pain and pressure, which produce perseverance, refined character, hope and the experience of God's love.

Jesus emerges through our struggles (2 Cor. 4:7-18). Normal Christian experience includes reversals, inadequacies and failure. God distills positive results from such experiences: (1) Jesus is seen living in us (2 Cor. 4:10-11); (2) spiritual blessing touches other people through us (2 Cor. 4:15); (3) even though outwardly we fail, our inner self is being thoroughly renovated (2 Cor. 4:16); (4) we learn to see from God's perspective (2 Cor. 4:17-18).

God's power is visible in weak people (2 Cor. 12:7-10). The apostle Paul could not get rid of a troublesome personal weakness he called his "thorn." It undermined his self-confidence and kept him from being the strong leader people expected. Three times he prayed about it. His prayer failed to make any difference. As he nursed his stinging disappointment, he heard God say, "My grace is enough for you. My strength is demonstrated as effective through your weakness" (see 2 Cor. 12:9). It gave him a new perspective on failure. If God could demonstrate his strength through human weakness, Paul, instead of feeling embarrassed, would make his failure a focus of rejoicing and hope.

Difficulties move us toward destiny (Romans 8:28-29). No matter what happens, what we try and fail to accomplish, what opposition we face, what mistakes we make, what weaknesses plague us, what pressure, distress or pain we suffer—all of it has a sign over it that reads "God at work!"

Through failures people move from bragging to brokenness. Peter is one of the world's most famous failures. Before Jesus was arrested, Peter bragged, "I will lay down my life for you" (John 13:37). He miserably failed. A few hours later, Peter cowardly denied three times that he knew Jesus (Luke 22:54-62). After the resurrection, Jesus met him and asked three times, "Do you love me?" (John 21:15-19). The Greek New Testament reveals that the first two times Jesus used the word for perfect love. But Peter's swagger was gone. He responded with a word meaning "friendship." "I would like to be able to boast that my love for you is perfect," he seemed to say, "but my failure has taught me the truth about myself. The best I can do is tell you that I love you as a dear friend." Peter could never have been the useful instrument he became had he not gone through his humiliating collapse at the point where he felt strong.

Based on Peter's experience we can see that failure accomplishes several things. First, failure enables us to more accurately assess ourselves and our situation. Second, failure helps us to see our weaknesses. Third, failure takes the wind out of our spiritual boasting. Fourth, failure provokes us to find answers. Fifth, failure shows us how dependent we are on God and others. Sixth, failure frees us to love genuinely and honestly.

See also AMBITION; DRIVENNESS; SUCCESS

References and Resources

R. C. Girard, *When the Vision Has Vanished* (Grand Rapids: Zondervan, 1989); J. B. Phillips, "Introduction to the Book of Revelation," in *The New Testament in Modern English* (New York: Macmillan, 1960); L. O. Richards, *Complete Bible Handbook* (Waco, Tex.: Word, 1987), L. O. Richards, *Expository Dictionary of Bible Words* (Grand Rapids: Zondervan, 1985).

—Robert C. Girard

FIRING

In a culture in which one's identity is usually defined by what one does, being fired is always a traumatic experience. If I no longer am a chemist, then who am I? If I no longer work for DuPont, then what am I? Losing one's job, for whatever reason, carries with it the stigma of failure. It is considered one of the major causes of stress that we humans can experience. Invariably the typical emotions connected with grief are experienced—shock, denial, loneliness, depression and, finally, anger.

Unjust and Just Reasons for Firing

The firings that are generally most easily understood by all parties are instances in which an employee knowingly violates the law or an organization's written policy. Immediate dismissal without due process usually follows theft of the employer's property, physical violence against another employee, arson, the willful destruction of equipment and the operation of dangerous machinery while under the influence of alcohol or other drugs. In most cases where an employee willfully violates those rules established as cause for dismissal, the employee has no one to blame but himself or herself.

Other violations of written company policy may be less obvious, and due process should be granted. Habitual tardiness may be cause for dismissal. But is some consideration given for a public-transportation system that is unreliable? The harassment of another employee, be it sexual, racial or based on age or some form of disability, is generally considered cause for dismissal. But in cases where harassment is not clearly defined, there must be due process, and the employee should be put on notice regarding any repetition of the wrongful act.

The matter of blame becomes more cloudy when one is fired for poor performance. It has been said that almost every firing due to poor performance represents a failure of management. This is certainly true for employees who truly want to do well, and most of us do. Did management fail at the point of hiring? Was the job description accurate? Were the performance standards reasonable? Was there a failure in the interviewing and selection process? Was the employee adequately trained? Were there any impediments to the employee's performance (poor equipment, distractions by others, too hot, too noisy, etc.)? Was good performance rewarded negatively? That is, is the best or fastest employee given the most assignments or asked to complete the work of a slower employee? Was there a periodic performance evaluation that was done honestly and professionally? Was the employee given realistic, measurable and attainable work goals on which to be evaluated? Was coaching provided to correct areas of substandard performance? Was there a system of warnings that alerted the next level of management of performance problems? Failures of any of the above are really failures of management.

In too many organizations supervisors and managers themselves are either poorly trained or incompetent. Time and time again managers and supervisors do not give employees honest evaluations of their completed work. Under such circumstances it should not be surprising that employees are shocked and angry when they are fired. They may not recognize the problem of poor management, but they do sense that something is unfair.

The Sacred Responsibility of Managers

Anyone who manages or supervises another has a sacred responsibility to his or her employees. When one considers the devastating effect firing has on most people, it should be apparent that the position of management carries with it a heavy responsibility. Top management should insist that all levels of supervisors be well trained and highly competent. If one is a manager who works for an organization where a high commitment to management excellence does not exist, each manager has the responsibility to educate oneself in the techniques of quality supervision. Just as we would expect a physician to have the highest professional commitment to the welfare of the patient, so also should we expect the supervisor/manager to have the highest professional commitment to the welfare of the worker.

Every employee is entitled to a periodic one-to-one sit-down evaluation of his or her performance by the immediate supervisor. Absolute honesty is crucial. Some Christians in management feel that they should be kind and forgiving in instances of unsatisfactory performance. They will, therefore, overrate the employee and avoid discussing unpleasant or difficult issues. Such a philosophy cheats an employee out of the help he or she is due and, in the long run, will hurt the employee's career. Christian managers need to be as perceptive, fair and honest as possible. If an employee is not suited for the job, the sooner he or she learns about it, the sooner a job change can be made. It is unconscionable that some employers continue with poor performers for years and then, when the employees turn fifty, tell them they were unsuited for the work in the first place and must be let go.

A caring manager will give a poor performer an honest appraisal of the future of his or her career and then help the employee to find another position where the potential for success is greater. This process may take as long as a year or so, but it is the most caring way of firing someone. But before concluding that a marginal performer cannot improve, the supervisor/manager should provide personal coaching and additional training. The human-resource professional should be called in to help, and every effort should be made to help the employee succeed. If personal problems at home are involved, there should be a search for supportive resources, and if possible flexible working hours should be arranged. For those who argue that such special attention to marginal performers will cost the company money, there are two things to be said: the cost of hiring and training a replacement (with unknown future performance) costs money also, and an employee whose career has been saved and enhanced by management concern frequently turns out to be a highly productive and loyal employee.

"Innocent" Firings

While the preceding comments relate to employees who may have been fired for willfully disobeying the law or company rules or who have failed to perform up to standards, there are hundreds of thousands of people who have been fired through absolutely no fault of their own. These are the victims of corporate takeovers or of downsizing (or its more sanitized term *rightsizing*). For instance, company A merges with or purchases company B. There is a duplication of some departments (accounting, human resources, etc.), so entire departments in one company are abolished. In another case a company or organization may be losing money. In order to save the company from bankruptcy, and the probable loss of all jobs, it downsizes in one or more ways. Management might close one part of the organization that is a financial drag on the others, thereby leaving all employees in that entire unit without work. The company might discontinue certain functions previously carried out by employees (for example, food services, payroll or advertising) and contract out for these services, thus saving the costs of health care, pensions and other benefits. The organization might consolidate functions or locations, thus reducing the number of employees needed, and retain younger employees (at lower employment costs).

While being fired for poor performance should not come as a surprise, losing one's job due to corporate takeovers or downsizing can be unexpected and quite sudden. The general practice seems to be that employees are given virtually no advance notice: "Pack up your belongings and leave—now!" The fear is that if employees are given advance notice, they may destroy company equipment, steal company secrets or take other vindictive steps. The effect of all this on the employees who are fired is devastating. *Why me?* is the first question. It matters not that an employee has been a top-rated, extremely loyal and conscientious worker with a perfect attendance record. If the unit is abolished, the employee is out on the street. And, to top it off, there was no advance notice—even though top management had to know of the action weeks in advance. The final indignity sometimes is the appearance of hired security guards to prevent vengeance. Employees feel utterly betrayed.

Some businesses feel it is more compassionate to take the route of announcing publicly that in the next twelve months or so they will reduce the work force by a specified number. The effect of this procedure is that people wait for the ax to fall. The entire organization is on edge as rumors fly. The dismissals begin. Morale is terrible. Families are consumed by fear. Substance abuse and family violence are not uncommon.

The one redeeming belief in all this is that the downsizing is being done in order to make the organization profitable again and, thus, to save jobs. But what do we say about the profitable company that downsizes with the assertion that these steps are being taken to keep the company profitable? And what do we say about the profitable company that downsizes in order to reduce costs, improve profits and, thus, give its stock a good boost in price? Can workers take some solace in the knowledge that they were fired due to no fault of their own? Not usually. Once again we are back to the identity issue—no job, no identity, regardless of the reason. And whether or not you were responsible, society stigmatizes the unemployed. The unemployed are failures.

The Effect of Firings

The effect of mass firings is not felt exclusively by those who have lost their jobs. While companies reduce the number of workers, they seldom reduce the amount of work. Those who survive the firings are frequently burdened with more work. The pressures to perform are enormous. The employer has already demonstrated a propensity to reduce the work force. Who would risk being seen as uncooperative in such an environment? The byproduct of mass firings frequently is a fifty- to sixty-hour work week for those who have escaped. The impact on family life and personal health is great.

Some companies overshoot the mark in their mass firings. It becomes apparent in time that the survivors cannot handle all the work. So are some of the recently laid-off workers called back? Seldom. Instead temporary workers are secured from an agency. The "temps" are never on the corporate payroll and, therefore, do not get a pension, health care and other benefits. There have been instances in which a temp was secured to do the exact work he or she once did as an employee. The move toward firing more employees and securing temporary workers is growing. It is estimated that by the year 2000 three out of every seven workers will be temps.

Another impact mass firings often have on the survivors is the sense of guilt. They were spared but their friends were fired. Psychologists say it is not unlike the feelings experienced by survivors of a fatal airplane crash or other catastrophe. It is called *survivor sickness*. Overwork, insecurity and sometimes guilt—these are the legacies of mass firings for those who have escaped the ax.

There is yet another group of workers hurt by downsizing: those who do the firing. As indicated earlier, some managers are reluctant to consider firing employees who are not performing well, for it is a painful task. How much more painful it is to fire good, loyal, competent workers whom top management has declared "redundant." Many might be close personal friends. How painful it must be to be told to reduce a department by an arbitrary 20 percent. Which ones go? On what basis do managers decide? How is it all explained to these fine people? For managers who have worked to develop an atmosphere of growth, expansion, hiring and training, the reduction of the work force runs counter to all their instincts. Increasingly, managers are electing to take a walk from their company rather than continue to be a part of a downsizing with which they disagree.

The Church's Response

Firing has become a commonplace event in America, but the shock, anger and pain do not lessen. As long as work and identity are so closely linked, the loss of work will continue to attack people's sense of identity and self-worth. Some Christian churches have helped their unemployed members by providing support, paying for career counseling, establishing support groups and offering job-search programs. Typically, the job-search programs involve weekly meetings in which the unemployed gather to receive help from professionals in writing résumés, developing networks and having employment interviews.

There is one vital area in which the churches could do a better job: the Christian faith proclaims that a person's work does not define his or her worth in the eyes of God. The grace of God extends to all who live in a relationship with God. If the Christian church could somehow convince all believers that the loss of a job does not diminish one's worth in the eyes of God, perhaps firing could be less traumatic to all those involved. The question is, are the churches even trying?

See also ACCOUNTABILITY, WORKPLACE; INTEGRITY; LOYALTY, WORKPLACE; MANAGEMENT; WORK

—William E. Diehl

GLOBAL VILLAGE

The generations living today are the first to experience earth as a planet. Pictures taken from a spacecraft of this immensely beautiful, but surprisingly fragile, planet have had a profound effect on our worldview. But even before these first pictures flashed back from space, in 1962 the Canadian Marshall McLuhan had already coined the phrase *global village* to express the effect of technological advances in electronics on our consciousness: "The human family now exists under conditions of a 'global village.' We live in a single constricted space resonant with tribal drums" (p. 31). We feel the world has shrunk to a single town in which everyone knows each other's business. Everyday life is now a global matter. We eat, play, think, work and pray globally, even when we are not conscious of it. Martin Luther King Jr. said, "Before you finish eating breakfast this morning, you've depended on more than half the world" (quoted in "Who Are Our Suppliers?").

Understanding Globalization

Globalize (as an active verb) is "to make worldwide in scope and application." This definition hints that human beings have a part in creating a global consciousness, that we are world makers—something which the Bible affirms. In this article *globalization* will refer to consciousness of one earth, one world and one church and our response to that in living as responsible stewards of one earth and one world and as members of one church. There are several dimensions of this global-village experience (Snyder, pp. 24-25).

First, the environment is a global issue. Toxic chemicals used on a grand scale in North America can affect the quality of the shield around the earth that protects all human beings from harmful radiation. Second, transfer of technology from country to country and global cooperation in major projects, such as space travel and medical research projects, have led to one world of scientific expertise. Third, communication is globalized. The information superhighway allows us to access information from computers worldwide. Fourth, we are moving toward a global culture. Popular music, dress styles, soft drinks, equal roles for women and more egalitarian social relationships are becoming increasingly "the same" worldwide. Fifth, the economies of all nations are linked in one giant system. A *Time* article noted, "The world's financial markets are so intertwined that when one itches, the others scratch" ("They're All Connected"). Sixth, the whole world is viewed as a single market with a global business culture. Seventh, politics is being globalized in the worldwide trend toward democracy, though this trend lacks a unified ideological or philosophical basis. We are witnessing the relativizing of everything, including values, morals and faith. Eight, travel is not merely the means of getting somewhere to do business or experience leisure. It is a way of life, a global lifestyle. Ninth, urbanization is a global phenomenon with people moving from rural areas to cities. But there is a sameness in all cities, especially their slums. These nine trends seem to be irresistible directions, but they are not welcomed by everyone and are possibly not as omnipotent as is sometimes claimed.

Paradoxically, on the edge of realizing one-earth and one-world consciousness, we are finding the village breaking down into warring neighborhoods, cliques, ghettos and clans—possibly out of the need for survival culturally and economically. When you belong to everyone, you belong to no one. And you do not know who you are.

Tribalism is on the rise, as is ethnic consciousness. There is a resurgence of religious fundamentalism, especially in Islam. Smaller political units, based on race, language or clan, are emerging in the struggle to find identity in one world culture, as evidenced in Canada and the Balkans. Poverty, far from being eradicated, is on the increase with threatening possibilities. Tad Homer-Dixon says,

> Think of a stretch limo in the potholed streets of New York City, where homeless beggars live. Inside the limo are the air-conditioned post-industrial regions of North America, Europe, the emerging Pacific Rim, and a few other isolated places, with their trade summitry and computer-information highways. Outside is the rest of mankind, going in a completely different direction. (quoted in Kaplan, p. 60)

Is it really true, as Ted Turner stated in a CNN (Cable News Network) memo to his staff, that "there are no foreigners in a global world"?

Thinking Christianly and Globally

Biblically, we have global work to do. Our basic human vocation in Genesis 1-2 is a threefold call to commune with God, to build community on earth and to be cocreators with God as we take care of God's world. This involves not only creating a global consciousness but developing the earth and the world as responsible stewards. The computer technician's work is as holy as the ministry of the pioneer cross-cultural church-planter.

We also have a global mission. Fundamental to the idea of *mission* is "to be sent" or "to be on the go." The earth cannot be "filled" (Genesis 1:28) without moving. The Great Commission (the "go" of the gospel) does not replace or even subordinate the cultural commission; it rather creates the context for its fulfillment and, by reconciling us to God, empowers people to become fully human and to humanize the world as world makers. Much of the Christian mission in the first century was undertaken in the context of movement: Lydia, a textile merchant from Thyatira whom Paul met at Philippi; the planting of churches along the trade routes in Asia, such as Colosse; through the conversion of people in the Hall of Tyrannus during Paul's two-year marketplace mission in Ephesus. Today we should expect international travelers, people on overseas assignment, people doing business with multinationals, to be frontline people in God's mission of both humanizing the world and sharing the gospel.

We are also called to develop a global unity. The command to "fill the earth," as we have already noted, required movement, the scattering of people. Genesis 11 then must be understood as both judgment and fulfillment. The people of Babel refused to scatter under God to populate and develop the world. Instead they attempted to solidify their autonomous life apart from God by building a tower that symbolized their identity, forging a "community" that was uniform and homogenous. This bland sameness is not unlike much of what is happening today in the globalization of culture and spirituality. But God judged this experiment in unity and forced the

Babelites to scatter. Not until Pentecost do we see what God is really after: a richly diverse community of people who are more one, rather than less one, because of their diversities, but united in their love of God and each other.

Global unity is not, however, a "mashed potato unity" in which peoples lose their identity, culture, spiritual gift and personality in one merged communalism. Rather it is the rich social complex for which Jesus prayed (John 17: 18, 21-22), resembling community in the triune God. In this richly diverse unity there is a need for nations (Acts 17:26) and for cultural diversity. Neither monoculturalism (the celebration of unity without diversity) nor multiculturalism as commonly promoted (the celebration of diversity without unity) fulfills God's intent.

In this matter the church of Jesus Christ is positioned to do a most exemplary thing: to demonstrate how believers in the developing world and in the developed world, believers from different races and cultures, can be truly one in a way that celebrates, rather than blurs, the differences. Paul's great missionary passion was not simply to win converts but to build a great interdependent, international and transcultural church of Jews and Gentiles, one new humanity (Ephes. 2:15), in which there would be both unity and equality (2 Cor. 8:14). It is only "together with all the saints" (Ephes. 3:18) that we can know Christ fully or even be fully human. So what can we do to realize this vision?

Acting Christianly and Globally

It has been said that we should think globally but act locally. That comment can be questioned both descriptively (our neighbors are now global neighbors) and theologically (God's mission is both local and global). Much can be done both locally and globally to be world makers in a fully Christian sense.

First, we can become consciously aware of our global interdependence every time we eat a meal or go shopping. We should find out where things came from, express our gratitude to God for the gift of international labor (perhaps during a grace) and do what we can to exercise Christian justice when we make purchases.

Second, we can learn from the global experience in microcosm in the diversity we experience in our schools, colleges, businesses, churches and neighborhoods. To do this, we must address our own ethnocentrism, confront our prejudices and learn to prize the contribution of people who are different from us. We need to go and listen before we go and tell.

Third, we can educate ourselves on the systemic nature of globalization: how political, economic and social structures and systems are so interdependent that all the elements in the world "mobile" are interconnected. This will keep us from assuming that our unemployed neighbor is simply lazy. It will also help us pray for, vote for and lobby for global justice and peace. To deal with one world today, one must understand the complexity of the principalities and powers.

Fourth, we should seek opportunities to experience other cultures, preferably in situations that take us beyond our own comfort zones. Better than roaring through

113

Cairo on an air-conditioned tour bus is returning to the same village or business enterprise annually to build relationships and learn interpersonally. Local churches in the West can be linked with local churches overseas. Both will be transformed by the connection.

Fifth, we can find ways to express stewardship on a global basis. What would it mean, for example, (heeding Paul's request in 2 Cor. 8:13) to achieve equality between the poorer churches of the developing world and the richer churches of the developed world? What spiritual growth would come to a family that engaged in practical sharing to alleviate world poverty, including alms giving, development and confronting the powers?

Sixth, some Christian people can serve globally without becoming traditional missionaries. They can gain a marketable skill and be tentmakers, supporting themselves in a short-term or long-term mission cross-culturally.

Seventh, we should regard global business (largely through multinationals), global education (with the great learning exchanges), global technology and global travel as opportunities to engage in mission that is equally important to the traditional church-planting missionary. People doing this should be prayerfully supported in their local churches and treated as tentmaking missionaries. The world will never be reached or humanized by traditional missionaries that are fully supported financially.

Eighth, we must confront our own religious imperialism and colonialism. An African once commented that most church-growth specialists come from the part of the world where the church is not growing! Western theological education, church technology and spirituality should not be marketed globally with colonizing intent but shared in a true dialogue in which all are enriched. The center of the Christian world has undoubtedly shifted from Europe to North America and now to Africa and Asia. Will Singapore, or in a few years Bejing, become the new Antioch?

However threatening or exciting we take globalization to be, the new consciousness and the practical opportunities afforded by the global village offer Christian people an unparalleled opportunity to know God better and fulfill God's mission on earth. If the church does not take up its global mission, perhaps God will raise up business to do it. Cynthia Barnum's challenge to business-people is worth repeating to Christians: "Are you ready, able and willing to do what you do anytime, anywhere, with anyone?" (p. 144).

See also STEWARDSHIP

References and Resources
C. F. Barnum, "Effective Membership in the Global Business Community," in *New Traditions in Business,* ed. J. Renesch (San Francisco: Berrett-Koehler, 1992) 141-56; R. D. Kaplan, "The Coming Anarchy," *Atlantic Monthly,* February 1994, 44-76; M. McLuhan, *The Gutenberg Galaxy* (Toronto: University of Toronto Press, 1962); B. Nicholls, *Contextualization: A Theology of Gospel and Culture* (Downers Grove, Ill.: InterVarsity Press, 1979); H. A. Snyder, *Earth Currents: The Struggle for the World's Soul* (Nashville: Abingdon, 1995); M. L. Stackhouse, *Apologia: Contextualization, Globalization and Mission in Theological Education* (Grand Rapids: Eerdmans, 1988); R. P. Stevens, "Marketing the

Faith: A Reflection on the Importing and Exporting of Western Theological Education," *Crux* 28, no. 2 (1992) 6-18; "They're All Connected," *Time* 140, no. 5 (3 August 1992) 25; "Who Are Our Suppliers?" *Marketplace,* March/April 1991, 11; L. Wilkinson, "One Earth, One World, One Church," *Crux* 28, no. 1 (1992) 28-36.

—R. Paul Stevens

GOSSIP

The word *gossip* comes from the Anglo-Saxon words for *God* and *sibling* and originally meant "akin to God," thus referring to someone who was spiritually linked with another by giving a name to the other as a sponsor at his or her baptism. Then *gossip* came to denote "talking about another who belonged to the same community." Gradually it began to have a pejorative meaning. Now it means "taking an unwarranted interest in people's affairs," often by passing on unfavorable information about them.

Good and Bad Gossip

There is a proper place for talking about other people in their absence in a constructive way, whether positively or negatively, even if the line between these two is not always easy to discern. There is also room for talking about others playfully, indeed as a form of play. This is just one form of talking about "nothing in particular," of talk for talking's sake, without any further intention.

So far as we can judge, gossip in the pejorative sense has always been a part of human life. There are many references to it in the Old Testament, especially in Proverbs. The gossip is one who betrays a secret or confidence and therefore cannot be trusted (Proverbs 11:13). The person who listens to gossip finds it hard to resist because it is so tasty (Proverbs 18:8; Proverbs 26:22). It is a destructive activity, for it inflames quarrels (Proverbs 26:20) and breaks friendships (Proverbs 16:28). Gossips are also referred to negatively in the New Testament (2 Cor. 12:20; 1 Tim. 5:13).

Later times contain many examples of the way gossip based on untruths or half-truths has ostracized or destroyed a person in a small community (such as the condemnations of witchcraft in seventeenth-century Salem, Massachusetts) or in a particular institution (as in Lillian Hellman's variously titled play and film *These Three* and *The Loudest Whisper*). Today gossip in general has become a full-time industry. The rise of the mass media, beginning with newspapers and culminating in television, has broadened the number of people who can eavesdrop helpfully or unhelpfully on the doings of others. The local gossip has given way to the gossip columnist, whose sole profession is to relay news about people that others do not strictly need to know. While all societies have taken an interest in the doings of elite or disreputable groups within them, the focus on celebrities and criminals in modern societies has exponentially increased. Much of what passes for news today is simply a form of gossip, some defensible or harmless but much of it a form of public voyeurism in which we too readily become accomplices.

At the everyday level, gossip continues to be a fact of life in all kinds of groups. With the growth of large cities and breakdown of local neighborhoods, this is now concentrated more in the workplace and in voluntary organizations like the church or school, though it can still appear anywhere. In some cases talking about others at work or at church is simply an informal way of keeping in step with what is going on and who is involved. It is a kind of human bulletin board or information exchange. In others it is simply a form of playful interaction, which is not designed to put anyone down or advance ourselves. Unless we are careful, however, this already contains some dangers and can easily spill over into something that is actually or potentially damaging.

We all have experience of the way in which one person or a small group can start unfounded or half-true rumors about others that soon become common property and are assumed to be basically true. Sometimes this is done unthinkingly, sometimes deliberately. Either way, even if the objects of gossip get a chance to privately or publicly respond, they find it difficult to clear themselves absolutely. Gossip has a way of sticking, partly because it throws its target on the defensive and into a self-justifying mode (the "Have you stopped beating your wife?" syndrome) and partly because our fallen human hearts secretly enjoy hearing about other's failings (in order to bolster ourselves). In such settings, even within the family circle, we need to remember the New Testament warnings that we will be judged for every idle word that we utter (Matthew 12:36) and that a small spark can begin a raging forest fire, one that eventually consumes ourselves as well as others (James 3:5-6).

How Can Gossip Be Sanctified?

We should recognize that some forms of talking about others, even behind their backs, is a natural human activity. We belong to a wider society, and there are certain matters affecting its well-being, or our common interest, that it is not improper to hear or tell others about. We also belong to primary or more extended communities within which there is a legitimate place for talking about each other's concerns. For example, when a member of the community in difficulty shares the trouble, others are enabled to respond helpfully. Furthermore, good gossip is a way of maintaining communal awareness and communal identity and of reminding ourselves of our bonds with and obligations to others. As the poet-essayist Kathleen Norris explains, gossip can provide comic relief for people who are living under tension and can be a way of praising or thanking others who have done individuals or the community a good turn (p. 76). Gossip is often the way small groups, institutions and places express their solidarity.

We should recognize that some forms of talking about others are illegitimate. For example, we should not generally share information about others that they would not share themselves, especially when this would injure their reputation or embarrass them in any significant way. If in doubt, we should first seek their permission to do so. We should also keep people's secrets and confidences when these have been entrusted to us. This has to do directly with faith, for by this means we "keep faith" with, or remain faithful to, those who have trusted us with some private information. To breach this faith is to act in an ungospel-like way. It is also a form of theft: people's experiences are basically their property, and they have a right to share them with others. In such cases we must allow them the privilege of telling their own story.

We should recognize the necessity of avoiding the company of those who take an unwarranted interest in others' affairs and who are overly talkative about this (Proverbs 20:19). People often engage in this as a response to some weakness, failure, need or longing within themselves. The Bible suggests that when people have too little to do, or are too much on their own, they have a tendency to gossip (2 Thes. 3:11; 1 Tim. 5:13). We should exercise care ourselves when we find ourselves personally in such a situation and should help others we encounter at such a time to avoid the temptation to "say what they ought not." We should also help those who have too little to do to find a more constructive outlet for their energies and those who are too much alone to find a community within which their need to share with others will find a more legitimate expression.

Despite these clarifications and strategies, it is still sometimes difficult to tell the difference between harmful gossip and appropriate conversation. How can we discern this? We can do so through examining our motives and asking God for wisdom before we say anything; through checking with someone we trust who is also in possession of the information; through asking whether we would, if necessary, be willing to say to others face to face what we are willing to say behind their backs; through learning from the experience of being the objects of gossip ourselves. If we are wise, we also learn from our mistakes, that is, through trial and error.

As Kathleen Norris reminds us, however, at its best gossip can be

> morally instructive, illustrating the ways ordinary people survive the worst that happens to them; or, conversely, the ways in which self-pity, anger, and despair can overwhelm or destroy them. Gossip is theology translated into experience. In it we hear great stories of conversion . . . as well as stories of failure. We can see that pride does really go before a fall, and that hope is essential. Especially as through it we keep track of those who are undergoing some major lifechange, or who are suffering some major loss, if we are really aware when we gossip we are also praying, not only for them but for ourselves. (p. 76)

References and Resources

K. Norris, *Dakota: A Spiritual Biography* (New York: Ticknor & Fields, 1993).

—Robert Banks

INSURANCE

Insurance is a means by which individuals, families, businesses and other organizations reduce or eliminate financial uncertainties in areas of life where there are predictable possibilities of financial loss. People exchange a small but predictable amount of money, their premium, for a larger, uncertain loss. Because the insurer can predict average losses over a large population, the risk is evened out and shared. The fortunate many who escape major loss help the unfortunate few who experience it. Kinds of insurance normally purchased by individuals include life, fire, theft or damage to personal property, legal liability, disability, unemployment, health and travel insurance.

The Insuring of Almost Everything and Everyone

Individuals, of course, buy some of these types of insurance for personal protection. Groups like businesses or corporations buy insurance for their employees; business partners may buy it to provide the means of buying out a partner's share in business upon his or her death. In Canada and other countries with a social welfare philosophy, the government or state agencies buy insurance by means of taxes. Insurance provided by the state in this way is compulsory rather than voluntary.

Insurance, however, protects not only individuals (and by extension their families) but also corporations, nonprofit agencies and governments. They may insure to cover the safe transfer of goods, the reliability of monies deposited in banks, the nonpayment of loans and the loss or destruction of major assets. Of course, though it may not be obvious to the person or organizations purchasing insurance, many significant risks cannot be reduced through insurance: war and insurrection, nuclear holocaust, ecological disaster (acts of humankind widely and over time) and natural disasters of colossal proportion (commonly called "acts of God").

In the Western world many individuals use a significant percentage of their income to pay for various forms of insurance, in excess of 10 percent in many cases if compulsory insurance provided by taxation is also considered. Some people complain of being "insurance poor"—spending so much to cover potential losses in the future that they have not enough to live properly today. Others are underinsured and may face a future without either personal assets or social network to cover major losses or reverses. In most developing countries individual insurance is the privilege of the rich and powerful; the poor and middle class rely on the age-old securities of family and church. Significantly, before there was a major insurance industry, the church pioneered in establishing burial societies during times of plague and mutual aid societies (especially for widows, orphans and the destitute), providing hospitality and asylum to fugitives, travelers and shipwrecked seamen; and setting up the first hospitals for the sick—a stunning and little-told story (Oliver, p. 116).

Is insurance merely a modern invention to satisfy an artificially induced need in the consumer society? Is there a biblical foundation for buying and selling insurance? When does protecting against risk become a refusal to trust God?

The History of Insurance

While widespread provision of insurance is a relatively modern affair, the idea of insurance has a long history, dating to ancient Babylon many centuries before Christ. Marine insurance was the first. It covered potential losses by traders and merchants who had to borrow funds (using their ships as collateral) to finance their trade. According to contract, if the merchant was robbed of his goods, suppliers agreed to cancel the loan in exchange for a premium paid. This was formalized in the Code of Hammurabi. The Greeks, Hindus and Romans borrowed some of these codified arrangements and adapted them.

Life and health insurance had beginnings in ancient Greece (600 B.C.) and became part of the benefits of belonging to guilds and trade associations, the precursors of modern unions. The first insurance contract was signed in Genoa in 1347, and the first life insurance with "insurable interest" (A.D. 1430) concerned the lives of pregnant wives and slaves. England developed "Friendly Societies" to insure industrial workers, and the Great Fire of London (1666) propelled the fire insurance industry forward. Lacking solid actuarial research and administrative know-how, many fledgling attempts to provide insurance folded, including some early attempts to establish insurance companies in the North American colonies. The first permanent life insurance company was formed in the U.S. in 1759; then followed health insurance (1847), automobile (1898) and group hospitalization (1936). Some of these companies were and are mutually owned by the insured; others operate as corporations with shareholders. Major factors in the evolution of multifaceted and near-universal insurance in the Western world are industrialization (with its hazards for injury and loss), urbanization (with its attendant risk of theft), mobility (with the loss of a stable family support group and land that can be worked) and privatization (with the reduction of society to the autonomous individual [see Individual]).

Thinking About Risk

At first glance the Bible seems to advise us not to think about future risks. The birds and lilies do not worry. "Yet your heavenly Father feeds them" (Matthew 6:26). It is the unbelieving Gentiles who run after all these things (food and clothing). But Jesus is not condemning us for planning for the future so much as warning us not to be anxious about it: "Do not worry about tomorrow, for tomorrow will worry about itself" (Matthew 6:34). We cannot add a day to our life by worrying; probably we will do the reverse. Indeed the way we respond to risk is a significant thermometer of our faith and spirituality.

Insurance does not deal with all risks, and perhaps not even the most important risks, such as losing friendships, personal worth, love, hope or faith. No one through buying insurance can guarantee long life, good health, satisfying work, personal contentment, a happy marriage, good neighbors, intimate friendships and children that bring joy to the heart. On a grand scale we cannot insure against the breakdown of a whole society or the ecosystem (though there is much we can do to prevent these). There is no insurance that can be purchased against marriage failure, loss of meaning, personal suffering or, most crucial of all, our eternal salvation.

We cope with risk in several ways: by ignoring it, assuming (or retaining) it, eliminating the possibility of loss, transferring the loss to someone else, or anticipating the loss and planning toward it.

On the first two options, it is folly to ignore risk, a game of let's pretend that is bound to catch up disastrously with reality someday. We must assume or retain the most important risks and the most crucial potential losses. For the Christian this means trusting in God's providential care, believing that even temporary reverses will be transformed into general good, as exemplified by the victory of the cross of Jesus. By retaining or assuming these noninsurable risks, we are called not only to trust God but to exercise faithful stewardship of our life, marriage, home, driving, possessions and ultimately the environment. God is the ultimate owner of everything; what we render is stewardship or regency. So the proper management of our lives is intended to reduce risk. Keeping an automobile in good repair, for example, is assuming the risk and managing it by good stewardship.

In most cases the third option, eliminating the possibility of loss, can be done only by refusing to accept the adventure of life. Driving a car, traveling, investing our talents in a community, getting married, having children and even joining a church are risky enterprises. Tragically, some people are like the one-talent man in Jesus' parable (Matthew 25:24-25), protecting themselves against any possible loss and so losing what they thought they had. People who refuse to invest themselves in order to eliminate all possible losses end up losing something more precious than what they protected—the joy of life.

Transferring risk to someone else, the fourth option, is not something we can normally do with risks that we must personally undertake. But this is an acceptable way of coping with some potential financial losses that could ruin one's business in a single stroke. For example, a surety bond guaranteeing the completion of a building according to written specifications transfers the risk from the person building the structure to the insurer. Such ways of managing risk are called for in a society that is composed not merely of a collection of individual farmers or tradespeople but of corporations and powerful structures.

The most common way to manage risk is to share it through buying insurance. Most insurance is simply a form of neighbor love expressed impersonally without knowing who our neighbors are. The insurance company becomes our symbolic neighbor. Through knowledge of past experience, careful prediction of future possibilities and accumulation of funds over a wide population base, insurance companies are able to cover the enormous losses of a few and the minor losses of the many, and have enough left over to cover their operating costs and make a legitimate profit for the shareholders.

Prayerful Insurance

Here are a few guidelines for Christians to consider when thinking about insurance.

Plan wisely for your family's future. In many cases it is unloving *not* to buy insurance, since it may force your family to embrace involuntary poverty to care for you in a time of extreme need. Wisely insuring is a form of neighbor love and part of our stewardship. But one must be careful that the companies trusted with funds are reliable since there are many cases of bankruptcy. Companies like Standard & Spoors and Moody's, and a new index called TRAC rate insurance companies for their strength, liquidity and solvency. Advertised reliability is not a sufficient guide.

Keep insurance in perspective; don't overvalue it. Our eyes can all too easily be diverted from the uninsurable risks that are much more deserving of our stewardship and prayerful attention: marriages, self-esteem of children, friendships and the joy of our salvation.

Never let buying insurance be an alternative to trusting God. An advertisement for an insurance company boasted, "A promise I'm forever watching out for you." Only God can do that. As Jesus said, our heavenly Father knows what we need and cares for us. Even more, we have an exuberant, risk-taking God who wants his creatures to experience life as an adventure. Significantly, the problem of the fearful investor in the parable of the talents (Matthew 25:24) was not his analysis of a potential loss but his conception of his master (representing God) as one who could not be trusted with his mistakes and reverses.

Beware of overinsuring. It is just as foolish to become "insurance poor" as to ignore insurable risks. We are meant to enjoy life and to thrive, not live cramped little lives. Often, insurance can be reduced or not even purchased (as in the case of collision insurance on a car) if one has put aside savings that can be used in the eventuality of a sustainable loss. Very valuable possessions (like inherited items) may be too expensive to insure, and wise management, combined with the attitude of "holding things lightly," is more prudent than covering every eventuality. Simpler living is a matter of perspective and not just net worth. A wise philosophy is to self-insure for small problems and use an insurance company's money for large ones. When looking at disability insurance, for example, we should choose a longer waiting period (90 to 120 days) so that in the event of disability we can use our own resources for the short term, thereby reducing the cost. Some people recommend as a rule of thumb purchasing ten times one's income in life insurance.

Help family members sustain their losses. It is lamentable that the basic unit of Western society has become the isolated individual covering all his or her potential losses rather than the family looking after one another. Insuring everything possible may inadvertently assist in the dissolution of the one organic community, besides the church, that can provide care and support during times of crisis and loss. Families can agree together what risks they will undertake mutually, including care of people when they are sick or old. Jesus roundly condemned the Pharisees for neglecting their responsibilities to their parents, a form of "honoring" them (Exodus 20:12) by dedicating their assets to the Lord's work, a system called corban (Matthew 15:3-6). Paul says that if we do not care for our own families we are worse than unbelievers (1 Tim. 5:8).

Lend aid to others in the body of Christ who need it. The church has an important role to play as the equalizer of risk. In the earliest church in Jerusalem, people sold their surplus goods to provide for anyone in need (Acts 2:44-45; Acts 4:32-37). Later came other forms of economic sharing, such as famine relief (Acts 11:27-30), occupational sharing (Aquila and Priscilla with Paul in making tents) and mutual aid gift-giving (the great love gift from the Gentile church—1 Cor. 16:2; 2 Cor. 8-9). It is all too easy to claim it would never work in our urbanized, mobile society where most people move every four or five years. But a commitment to a house church or an intentional community not to move (*see* Mobility), while countercultural, may be a concrete step toward true community (*see* Fellowship). We have something to learn from churches in the developing world on this matter. When someone dies in Kenya, the church gathers to make gifts to the family —not just the grieving spouse—to provide a living and a future for the survivors.

Remember those in society who are uninsured (the disadvantaged and destitute), and act on their behalf. In our modern times risk and loss are systemic problems, not merely matters of personal character and integrity. The Scriptures warning against idleness assume that unemployed people are lazy, whereas today the unemployed are often victimized by systemic problems, sometimes through economies halfway around the world. So in coping with risk today, we must exercise cultural and organizational as well as personal stewardship (*see* Principalities and Powers). We must fight against the abuse of unemployment and health insurance schemes if they are government-funded and abused. We need to lobby for legislative change to care for disadvantaged and marginalized people in our society.

Conclusion

Like most advances in the Western world, the growth of the insurance industry is a mixed blessing. With careful management, reaffirmation of the providence of God and wise stewardship of our lives, buying some insurance is an act of neighbor love and personal responsibility, doing what we can so we won't be a burden on others (1 Thes. 4:12; 2 Thes. 3:8). In reality, we can never eliminate that possibility fully. And where true family and church community exist, mutual caring is not a burden but part of the unlimited liability of family love. The temptation of too much insurance, or a wrong attitude, can lead to an illusory feeling that we can control our own futures and live autonomously without God. Like many facets of everyday life, this one calls us to a life of prayer, spiritual discernment and loving action.

References and Resources
J. L. Athearn, *Risk and Insurance* (St. Paul: West, 1981); K. Black Jr., "Insurance," in *The Encyclopedia Americana* (Danbury, Conn.: Grolier, 1989)15:233-39; K. Black Jr. and S. S. Huebner, *Life Insurance* (Englewood Cliffs, N.J.: Prentice-Hall, 1982); E. H. Oliver, *The Social Achievements of the Christian Church* (Toronto: United Church of Canada, 1930); N. A. Williams, *Insurance* (Cincinnati: South-Western Publications, 1984).

—R. Paul Stevens

INTEGRITY

"Teacher," they said, "we know you are a man of integrity and that you teach the way of God in accordance with the truth" (Matthew 22:16). Teaching in accordance with truth: his hearers saw in Jesus a person whose words and actions came together with the ring of credibility.

A Character Issue

Integrity is about character. Character encompasses more than beliefs and opinions. It denotes the core values and commitments that define a person and ultimately shape the person's life. We live out of our character regardless of the stated beliefs, opinions or values that we proclaim. Character flows from the soul of the person. *Integrity* refers to the consistency of character that matches words and actions, vision and choices, values and behaviors. It is life lived with consistency. *Character* refers to those internal core values that shape all that a person does.

A life lived with integrity is one in which all aspects of a person are fully integrated; it is a holistic life. In mathematics an integer is a whole number that cannot be divided into parts which are themselves whole numbers. Integrity is like that. It is that coherence of character that presents a single face to the world: "What you see is what you get."

In his marvelous book *Leadership Jazz,* Max DePree talks about voice and touch. Integrity keeps voice and touch together, being sure that what you say is matched by what you do—external consistency—living what you believe, communicating the same truth in your words and your living. DePree's comments focus on the second level of integrity—internal consistency. At its core integrity is living with words and actions that reflect the internal values of your soul.

Integrity is about truth and honesty. It means saying what you mean and meaning what you say, letting "your 'Yes' be yes, and your 'No,' no" (James 5:12). Integrity assumes a correlation between what you say is true and what is actually true. This is difficult in a world in which truth is increasingly seen to be relative, but for the Christian that means correspondence with truth as it has been revealed by God.

Being Trustworthy

Internal and external consistency produce credibility and trust, which we might call *integrity of relationship*. Personal relationships are built on trust; they require that persons be credible, believable, trustworthy. Trust is both earned and given. Relational integrity assumes that the person who presents himself or herself to you in relationship is in fact a true expression of that person—the assumed consistency of word and action, the assumed correlation between character and presentation.

Just as trustworthiness between people is based on consistency in character, so in organizations there should be coherence between the culture or values of the organization and the actual policies, processes and behaviors of the organization. In *Organizational Culture and Leadership,* Edgar Schein argues clearly that every organization has its own culture, that is, an underlying set of assumptions, beliefs and values that control the way it lives out its organizational life. The actions of an organization over time always reflect this organizational character or culture. Many organizations these days also are attempting to express their corporate values in creeds or other publicly stated value commitments. In this case integrity refers to the consistency between the stated values of the organization and the actual actions of the organization that flow from its culture. Where there is consistency, there is integrity. Where there is no consistency, there is organizational dissonance, and people get caught in the middle and trust is lost.

Integrity is about consistency of living that allows the character of one's soul to find expression in the living of one's life—in word and deed. Organizationally integrity means the culture of an organization finds congruent expression in the policies, procedures and stated values of the corporate community. Integrity is about truth, honesty, trust and consistency; it is a matter of character.

References and Resources

J. P. Hess, *Integrity: Let Your Yea Be Yea* (Scottdale, Penn.: Herald, 1978); W. L. Sullivan, *Work and Integrity: The Crisis and Promise of Professionalism in America Today* (San Francisco: Harper, 1995).

—Walter Wright

INVESTMENT

Investment is the employment of assets (money or otherwise) into a scheme that is potentially profitable in the foreseeable future. This simple definition contains four assumptions: (1) assets should be put to work; (2) they should be profitable and fruitful (that is, you should get more than you put in); (3) the future rather than the immediate present is in view; and (4) there is managed risk of loss or failure. In this article we will consider these assumptions, reflect on them theologically and offer some general guidelines, leaving specific investment advice to qualified professionals. In addition we will consider the Christian life as a form of investment in which both monetary and nonmonetary investments may accumulate what Jesus called "treasure in heaven."

The Confusing Array of Investment Opportunities

Investment takes several forms: savings accounts, ownership of one's home, pension plans, putting money into one's own business, purchasing government bonds or bank-guaranteed investment certificates, owning a fraction of a corporation (stock) and gaining a promissory certificate from a corporation with specified amount of interest (debenture). The option of hiding money in a mattress or burying it in the back yard is always present, but besides the obvious risk of theft there is inflation, which means that one hundred dollars tucked into a mattress in 1945 had only fifty dollars' purchasing power in 1970. Hence, not investing means reducing the value of your capital.

Most people recognize the importance of putting aside some of their disposable income into a *savings account* to be kept for emergencies or a rainy day. This form of investment has the advantage of permitting the money to be withdrawn anytime but the disadvantage that it earns a small rate of interest (a percentage of the total) while it is "working" for the bank or credit union. Usually the interest paid on savings accounts is less than inflation—the increasing price level of a basket of defined consumer goods, usually measured as the annualized increase in the Consumer Price Index. In some Third World countries the inflation rate is so high (upward to 100 percent a year) that investing in savings accounts appears counterproductive. One usually finds the wealthy minority investing in foreign so-called hard currency countries, draining the home country of desperately needed capital.

Another common investment worldwide is one's own *farm* or *home*. This is generally a double-duty investment: first, property like this meets a family need for housing, and, in the case of a farm, income; and second, it is a hedge against inflation since the value of a home normally increases through time. In Canada and the United States it remains one of the few legitimate investments that do not attract taxation for the profit earned. (The other tax-exempt gain is proceeds from life insurance and, for Canada only, the winnings of a lottery or other "windfall" venture.) Indebtedness associated with home ownership usually is in the long run wise (*see* Debt; Home). Real estate, however, is not a "liquid" (easily converted to money) asset, may take months to sell and is susceptible to cyclical market trends.

In urbanized, industrialized or information societies a *pension plan* is usually an important investment because it is likely that we will be forced to retire from remunerated employment before we die, and it is unlikely (though desirable) that family, community and church will be able to care for us in our extended declining years. In older societies and in some Third World countries the family farm provided free housing and food, and one's children cared for the aging until they died. But even in these countries rapid urbanization and industrialization is breaking down the family pension-plan system. In most Western countries pensions are wisely built up over one's working years through participation in a government plan, and wisely augmented through one's own workplace and/or a voluntary program such as a registered retired savings plan (RRSP or IRA). Most corporation or voluntary pension plans involve a wide selection of investment vehicles (stocks, bonds, mutual funds, mortgages and real estate) that are calculated to grow continuously with only a reasonable managed risk of loss, since the risk is diversified into many different investments. The expected return should be rationalized to the managed risk to the capital: the more risky the venture, the greater the "cost" expected for the capital loaned.

In addition to the above investments, many citizens are able to invest in private businesses (through personal loans), the government (through bonds), banks (through investment certificates) and public corporations (through purchasing stocks and convertible debentures). Principles that are important to consider in making such investments are safety and preservation of the invested capital; diversification (not having "all one's eggs in one basket"); liquidity (how easily the principal sum could be recovered); expected income and the previous performance of the investment; and tax consequences. For example, an RRSP or IRA allows investors to defer taxes on the principal amount invested until the pension is actually used. Through the magic of compound interest (interest earned on the capital increased by the interest), with time and prudent investing one could have a sizable nest egg in this tax-deferred program for retirement.

Toward a Theology of Investment

Some Christians think it is wrong to plan for the future. After all, have you ever seen a worried bird (Matthew 6:26)? What if Jesus comes tonight? Isn't it wrong to think about making money—a form of greed? The only safe investment is in the Lord's work: "Only one life, 'twill soon be past, only what's done for Jesus will last."

Return to our original assumptions about investing. First, we said that money or assets should be put to work. This is in effect what God said to Adam and Eve in the Garden of Eden: put it all to work (Genesis 1:26-29; Genesis 2:15). Second, we said that it should be profitable or fruitful. God's creation mandate to the first couple was to be fruitful, to fill the earth and to flourish. Seeds are not meant to be kept in bottles or bins forever. That way they can never bear fruit. Rather they should be sown into the soil and produce a hundredfold—a rather good return on the original investment (Matthew 13:23).

Third, the future rather than the immediate present or the past is in view. Some African and Asian cultures are oriented backward as the spirits of ancestors keep "catching up" to the present generation. We would then be like people standing on a bridge over a fast-flowing river watching the water come toward us. But the Christian perspective is to turn around and watch where the river is going. We are future-oriented. Heaven calls us. The Second Coming of Christ beckons us toward the new heaven and the new earth. We are, as Jürgen Moltmann so accurately says, living not at sunset but at the dawning of a new day. Christ might come today—we should be ready. But he may not come for a thousand years—we should be ready for even a long wait like the wise virgins in Jesus' parable (Matthew 25:1-13). It is precisely this balanced Christian view—longing for Christ to come soon but building for the long haul—that is the eschatological perspective provided by the New Testament. Martin Luther once said that if he knew Christ was coming tomorrow he would still plant a little tree today. Investment in the future is exactly what Christians should do, no matter how black the sky may seem according to a secular analysis.

Then take the fourth assumption—that risk must be assumed. Most people think that investment risk is simply the potential to lose money. But there are at least four kinds of risk to be considered: *business risk* (that the business or corporation will go out of business and not be able to meet its financial obligations); *liquidity risk* (that there may not be a buyer if you want to sell an investment quickly); *market risk* (that the fluctuating financial market may render your investment of less value); *purchasing power risk* (that the investment will not be able to exceed inflation by a satisfactory margin). All four kinds spell the potential for some kind of loss or failure. The more immediate issues are to consider whether the process is in place for continuously monitoring the risk and whether the expected return is proportional to the monitored risk. But it is impossible to invest without some risk. And failure might even become one of the most important learning moments. Wisdom comes more from failure than from success.

We explored a theology of risk briefly in the article on insurance. Risk theorists note that there are several ways of coping with risk: ignoring it, assuming (or retaining) it, eliminating the possibility of loss, transferring the loss to someone else, and anticipating the loss and planning toward it. On the first, it is folly to ignore risk, a game of let's pretend that is bound to catch up disastrously with reality someday. On the most important possibilities and uncertainties, we must assume or retain the risk. By retaining or assuming these noninsurable risks we are called not only to trust God but to exercise faithful stewardship of our lives to reduce risk. In making investments this means diversifying, seeking wise counsel and not taking unnecessary risks to make big money quickly, the latter falling into the category of speculation or gambling. The proverbs counsel rejecting get-rich-quick schemes in favor of making small regular gains over a period of time, so accumulating wealth through wisdom and patience. "Dishonest money dwindles away, but he who gathers money little by little makes it grow" (Proverbs 13:11). In all cases eliminating the possibility of loss totally is possible only by refusing to accept the adventure of life, for there is the dwindling of our purchasing power through inflation.

What would make us accept the risks attendant on making investments? One thing would be a God who takes risks! God took an enormous risk in making a creature with free will, in committing to the family of Abraham, in slipping into the human family as a vulnerable child. But the lamb was slain from the foundation of the earth. For the Christian this means trusting in God's providential care of us and of God's world, and believing that even temporary reverses will be transformed into general good, as exemplified by the victory of the cross of Jesus.

God Loves Investment

Although not addressing the issue of financial assets, the parable of the talents in Matthew (Matthew 25:14-30) and the parable of the ten minas in Luke (Luke 19:11-27) are suggestive with regard to a theology of investment. There are three things we can do with what God has entrusted to us. First we can *squander* it, wasting it as the younger prodigal did in the far county, as humankind has largely done with the created earth. Some people think they are undertaking Christian stewardship when they give away large amounts of money without any regard to the effect it has. They feel good, but the recipient feels obligated, patronized or disempowered. In reality it is squandering—disinvestment.

Second we can *hoard* it, like the one-talent man who, with his wrong view of his God (Matthew 25:24-25; compare Luke 19:21), wrapped up what he had in a handkerchief because he was afraid to lose it. He did not realize that he could keep this only by giving it away! What motivated the one-talent man was fear. Most people would commend him for his prudence and find the judgment of the master unbelievably severe. After all, did not the one-talent man return what was trusted, all in one piece with nothing lost? Did he not treasure what was entrusted to his stewardship? Yet the master condemns him. The reason for the fear of loss and failure is the one-talent man's inadequate view of his master: "I knew that you are a hard man, harvesting where you have not sown and gathering where you have not scattered seed." With that kind of God, who would want to take a risk?

In many of his parables Jesus presents an apparently ridiculous view of God—though one often held subconsciously—to shock people into converting to the real God, who is not immovable and harsh but wonderfully personal. Though Jesus does not actually say this, he expects us to think, "Believe in a God who will squeeze everything he can out of you, who will never forgive a mistake, who will swat you down to hell if you mess things up even once, and this is what you get: a pinched, unimaginative, no-risk-taking and utterly deadly life. Believe in the God and Father of the Lord Jesus, and you will be inspired to try things out, to experiment, to take risks and to flourish." So instead of squandering or hoarding with such a God, we are invited to *invest*, risky as it is. *Investment* is another word for *stewardship,* which is simply another word for Christian service. But there is more to investment than putting our money into a mutual fund.

Investing in Heaven

Giving directly to church, Christian missions and our families can be one form of investment even though the returns are not gained personally and one's personal capital is reduced (*see* Gift-Giving; Stewardship). Further, not all investments are monetary and this-worldly. Jesus' words are haunting: "Do not store up for yourselves treasures on earth, where moth and rust destroy, and where thieves break in and steal. But store up for yourselves treasures in heaven, where moth and rust do not destroy, and where thieves do not break in and steal. For where your treasure is, there your heart will be also" (Matthew 6:19-21). What does it mean to invest in heaven? How is it possible that this investment has guarantees of a "return" which can never be given for investments "on earth"?

First, we are to invest in heaven through our everyday life, work and homemaking by doing even the simplest chores with faith, hope and love. According to Paul in 1 Cor. 3:10-15, it is not the religious character of the work (Bible studies, witnessing, charitable work) that makes work last forever but Christ: this is a call to do our work with faith, hope and love. In some way beyond our imagination even simple work is actually a ministry to Jesus (Matthew 25:31-46); that is what faith points to. Love makes chores and quilt-making last forever (1 Cor. 13:8-13). And hope? There is a wonderful correspondence to work we do in this life and work in the next. Our ultimate future is not to be free-floating spirits in heaven but fully resurrected persons in a new earth and a new heaven (Rev. 21-22)—working, playing and worshiping in one glorious eternal sabbath. Just as the resurrected body of Jesus had scars, though now glorified, so this material world, scarred and worked over by humankind, will one day be transfigured into a new world in which even the glories of the nations will be brought into the New Jerusalem (Rev. 21:24; Stevens, p. 31). So our first eternal investment is simply to do everything in everyday life for God (Col. 3:22-24). It is literally true that "only what's done for Christ will last," though this does not require going into a Christian service career or spending one's time in church work, as is commonly thought.

Second, we are to invest primarily in people, especially the poor. The only treasure we can take from this life to the next is the relationships we have made through Jesus. The teaching of Jesus leaves us with the unmistakable challenge to have a hands-on relationship with the poor and to accept some form of voluntary impoverishment. We must do this for the sake of the poor and for the sake of our own souls. A newspaper article asks, "Why should we care about the Third World?" and answers, "Because our economic, environmental and political future is inextricably linked with it." But there is a deeper reason. The rich cannot be saved without the poor.

There is no doubt in my mind that in telling two parables about money and friendship (the shrewd manager and the rich man and Lazarus—Luke 16) and by placing them in juxtaposition, Jesus and Luke intend to motivate us to make friends with the poor. With outrageous freedom Jesus tells about a shrewd manager who used money to make friends by reducing the loans owed to his master so when he would lose his job these friends would look after him forever (Luke 16:1-9). The magnetic center of this parable is a shocking exhortation from the lips of Jesus: "I tell you, use worldly wealth to gain friends for yourselves, so that when it is gone, you will be welcomed into eternal dwellings" (Luke 16:9). The second parable, Lazarus and the rich man, gives an empowering negative example of a person who did not use his wealth to make friends of the poor and thus was not welcomed by them into an eternal home. Sandwiched in between these two parables is a section about the Law and the Prophets, which uniformly teach mercy to the poor (Luke 16:16-18).

The thrust of Luke 16 is the call to use our money to make friends with the poor, the sick, the powerless, the stranger and the refugee. The unconverted heart believes that there is nothing the poor can do for us. They are not worth being the object of our investment. They will not advance our cause or increase our security. But these two parables make the daring claim that what we gain through befriending the poor is love. Often the poor are richer than the rich in the treasures that really matter—in relationships. "He who is kind to the poor lends to the LORD, and he will reward him for what he has done" (Proverbs 19:17). Genuinely disempowered people cannot pay back loans, and therefore we should regard such giving as lending to the Lord. Paradoxically we gain it back with interest (Proverbs 22:9)!

Most of this article has focused on the return we are looking for in our own investments. But there is another way of considering the matter of investment. God is looking for a return on his investment in us (Matthew 25:19). What we do with assets and money entrusted to us is like a foreshadowing of the last judgment; our use declares what we really think about God. The gambler has no faith in God but hopes for good luck. The hoarder believes in a vengeful, demanding God. The investor declares that God can be trusted, that God gives what is required and that all investments made with faith, hope and love will bear a return, if not in this life then in the next.

See also LOYALTY, WORKPLACE; ORGANIZATIONAL CULTURE AND CHANGE; ORGANIZATIONAL VALUES

References and Resources

F. Amling, *Investments,* 5th ed. (Englewood Cliffs, N.J.: Prentice-Hall, 1984); J. Chrysostom, *On Wealth and Poverty,* trans. Catherine P. Roth (Crestwood, N.Y.: St. Vladimir's Seminary Press, 1984); J. Ellul, *Money and Power,* trans. L. Neff (Downers Grove, Ill.: InterVarsity Press, 1984); R. Foster, *Money, Sex and Power* (San Francisco: Harper & Row, 1985); E. B. Gup, *The Basics of Investing* (New York: Wiley, 1986); R. P. Stevens, *Disciplines of the Hungry Heart* (Wheaton, Ill: Harold Shaw, 1993).

—R. Paul Stevens

LEADERSHIP

Where have all the leaders gone? Why is it so difficult to recognize displays of leadership today? Are we in a leadership vacuum? Is failed leadership behind the failure of moral and ethical patterns of service?

The answers would seem to be yes if we consider the nature of the criticism that appears in the press and is expressed by frustrated workers and volunteers in very troubled organizations. The church, academy and marketplace declare major unresolved conflicts and challenges with their identity and viability to be a result of failed leadership.

Leadership literature has expanded significantly in the last ten years. Books are coming to the bookstores each month attempting to explain this concept and give us instruction on how to lead. Unfortunately, leadership is still not easily understood, and its practice is in short supply.

The basic question is: What is leadership? Do we have an adequate understanding? Is there a Christian view of leadership that could make a difference in these difficult times?

Most of us define leadership as decisive, appropriate and timely action on the part of a person who holds a position of authority. When we say there is no leadership, we usually mean that we feel like nothing is happening to deal with growing problems within our context. We want "strong" leadership to deal with the problems we see or dilemmas we face. Is this common understanding of a leader's role an adequate description of leadership?

The answer to this question is an emphatic no. It is not sufficient even though it holds some truth. Leaders are in short supply in the church, academy and marketplace as a result of misconceptions of leadership and its secularization. A Christian theology of leadership has the most potential to respond to this problem. With a biblical understanding of spirituality, character and community, a Christian approach provides a powerful and effective model for leadership practice and transformation.

A Secular Perspective on Leadership

The standard model for leadership evolves and takes its shape from the predominant worldview. It places a high value on independence and self-sufficiency. The leader depends on learned skills, experiences and decision-making ability. These are regarded as the key attributes of leadership. The emphasis is on doing—accomplishing tasks, achieving goals—and little attention is given to relationships. When it exists, the relationship can be termed transactional (contractual). The model is focused on the uses of power, authority and position. With this secular approach leadership skills are focused on management, "bottom-line" outcomes and quantifiable models. The model has given us the independent "tough-minded" leader and suggests that leadership is essentially a masculine enterprise.

This view of leadership has emphasized a reverse service model in that "followers" provide service to the person in authority. Service flows up rather than down. An organization exists to facilitate the leader in accomplishing his or her goals. Within this model, relationships between leaders and others are merely a means to the end. There is a low appreciation of community but a strong emphasis on the needs of the organization. Persons are valued to the extent that they add value in reaching organizational goals. An influential model for this type of leadership comes from the military and gives us lines of authority with a very heavy emphasis on competing and winning.

The model also stresses the importance of personality or "persona" over against character. Moral or ethical strategies might be employed to solve problems but are considered secondary.

Vision comes from the leader or the needs of the organization as defined by the leader. The potential of the leader and organization is virtually unlimited, given enough skill and knowledge. There is no room for God or the spiritual dimension. The model does not recognize evil or sin as a part of culture; nor does it see God's active involvement in history and our daily lives.

An Evolving Secular Model

New voices have been heard within the marketplace that are reshaping the accepted view of leadership. A movement is developing around a growing criticism of graduate education, clarifying distinctions between management and leadership, the influence of cultural modeling from Japan, the idea of servant leadership, inclusion of women and the introduction of the transformational leadership standard. Character, spirituality, community and relational leadership have found new adherents. The standard model of the marketplace is evolving into an understanding of leadership as an art with a focus on character and the quality of community.

This model has been developing over the last ten years and is expressed in many recent popular leadership books: The Web of Inclusion, Leadership Is an Art, Mind of a Manager, Soul of a Leader, Love and Profit: The Art of Caring Leadership, Leading with Soul: An Uncommon Journey of Spirit, The Female Advantage: Women's Ways of Leadership and Spirit at Work: Discovering the Spirituality in Leadership. These writings and the new movement are a response to failed leadership and an attempt to find meaning in work. While this is reforming the secular model, it still lacks a developed philosophy and a recognition of where these "new" ideas originate.

A Christian Perspective on Leadership

Christian theology contemplates the model of a triune God. From this comes the powerful image of relationships and being in community. Christian leadership is about spirituality, character and community.

The idea of the presence of God's Spirit gives us a very strong notion of our inclusion in and empowerment for the community of God. Spirituality is the center, heart and beginning point for Christian leadership. This spiritual position determines everything, from the character formation of the leader, to the interpretation of the leaders' vision, to the understanding that most issues of leadership can be resolved only at the spiritual (not merely at the moral) level. Developing a Christian theology of leadership accents the centrality of a radical discipleship to Christ.

Character is the conduit for producing Christian service and leadership. We lead out of who we are in Christ. Our relationship with Christ forms and shapes our person. This is a lifelong process and relies on the bumps and bruises of life to make markings that define who we are when no one is watching. We cannot separate our service and leadership from this composite picture of our values, beliefs and godly nature. Self-insight and a learning and growing disposition ensure a maturing character and a more responsive leadership style. Courage is the character trait that provides a catalysis for Christian leadership. This is a byproduct of our relationship with Christ and a fully explored self.

The Christian leader's obedience to Christ produces service. Both the horizontal and the vertical relationship define and provide direction for leadership through service, close partnership with God and a strong concern for community. We are drawn to God's vision of eternal life, and we know that bringing God's kingdom to life on earth is a primary goal of leadership. This is our highest calling, our driving vision. We also know that the primary focus in this process is making disciples of Christ and bringing them into fellowship with God and God's community. But also central is extending justice and compassion in and through every arena of life and every place where we work. God is a partner in this process and shares with us divine "power" to help us accomplish this goal. The presence of God is actively engaged in this kingdom-making process. Building community might be the most sacred of leadership pursuits, for leaders are attempting to bring their communities into full service to each other and God.

The Christian framework understands sin and the nature of evil. Therefore it is able to define reality and cultural context more clearly. It also takes a very different position when it comes to the notion of self-sufficiency. Dependence on and obedience to God is the highest and best use of a Christian leader's time and energy. The nature of relationships in this model is covenantal and transformational.

A Definition of Christian Leadership

Christian leadership is an art form of worshiping Christ, a teaching and serving process that envisions, influences, shapes and enhances so that both leaders and followers realize God's goals for change within their community. This definition has several important key words and concepts.

• *Art form*—not necessarily an exact science, but rather a creative process that comes from the expression of an individual. There is no formula for leadership behavior or personality, as it comes in many sizes and shapes.

- *Worship*—the process holds up something higher than itself. Christian leadership from beginning to end is done sacrificially to God.
- *Teaching*—the primary process of leadership. Christian leaders are "teachers" and influence by bringing others along in the learning/shaping development process.
- *Service*—the vehicle of the leader is the needs of others. Service flows out of obedience to a master, in this case God, who directs our leadership into service to others within our community.
- *Envisioning*—we measure our leaders by their ability to interpret God's vision. Without a vision people perish, and this vision is the discovery of God's best for us.
- *Shapes and enhances*—leadership is a sculpturing exercise that creates and builds in positive ways.
- *Leaders*—leadership is not a solo event. It involves a team, and its goal is empowerment of other leaders.
- *Followers*—they are an integral and potent force in the leadership process. We judge leaders by the quality of the community formed in the exercise of leadership.
- *God's Goals*—we are obedient to God's call, both individually and corporately. We seek divine direction and wisdom for our community.
- *Change*—the end of leadership is metamorphosis within the needs of community. This is a transformation that brings God's kingdom to light and its practice into the world.
- *Community*—everything is done within the confines of relationship. Leadership accountability, service and effectiveness are measured within the standards of the community.

The Practice of Christian Leadership

The Christian leader places himself or herself into the hands of God and becomes a living sacrifice to Christ. This is expressed as a call to service. God provides the context, and the community adds the confirmation. From this spiritual relationship, accountability to God and community is exercised. To be a Christian leader is to be countercultural, to be about the process of change. The leader is a radical follower of Christ and servant to others who is marked by several key practices.

1. *Serves God faithfully and obediently.* Our attention and focus is on God. We lead out of this spiritual relationship to God as servant and friend. This requires a very special attentiveness to hearing God through Scripture, community and prayer. Our goal is to serve God faithfully.

2. *Discerns God's vision.* Leadership is about vision. The translation of this vision into specific contexts is the role of leadership. God's vision is in tension with current "reality," and leadership is the process of dealing with this dissonance.

3. *Develops the leadership team.* Leadership is about relationships and working together for a common purpose. Solo leadership is not consistent with God, nor is it a particularly effective leadership style. We need to build a team for leadership to become

effective. Spouse, family and significant others represent the informal dimensions of this, while staff and selected position holders provide the formal component.

4. *Communicates, prays and teaches.* Leaders need skills to function effectively. The teaching dimension serves as the primary stimulus and tool of leadership. Through it communication flows and prayer becomes an intervening variable. People of prayer are given greater access to God. This produces change, which is the goal of leadership. Effective leaders are communicators that keep the vision alive.

5. *Builds God's community.* The most significant leadership task is to build community. Community is a representation of God's kingdom on earth. It is culture, purpose, identity and God's love. We judge effective leadership in terms of the "tone of the body" that they build up rooted in God.

6. *Inculcates God's values.* Values (*see* Organizational Values) are a representation of culture (*see* Organizational Culture) and set the context for leadership teaching. Storytelling, word pictures and modeling are the leader's tools in embedding values in the community.

7. *Disciples and empowers God's people.* In the Christian model, power is dispersed. It is given away to those who would lead and serve. People in community are being prepared to have their gifts used for the vision and purpose of the community.

8. *Stewards God's resources.* Management is important to effective leadership. Planning, budgeting, allocating and controlling are aspects that require attention from leaders. Stewardship builds discipline and provides a view of resources as being on loan from God.

9. *Shepherds God's people.* Caring for others is the centerpost of leadership service. Knowing those who have been entrusted to us and responding to their needs is a critical leadership issue.

10. *Renews God's organization.* The process of change is about renewal (*see* Organizational Culture and Change). Leaders guide organizations and communities to higher levels through transformation and renewal. Renewal begins with the individual and moves to the edges of the community.

11. *Develops future leaders.* The preparation of leaders for the community is a primary task of leadership. The successful accomplishment of this activity results in effective leadership. This is also leadership development and succession. Emerging leaders ensure the vitality of community and renewal of the organization.

Where have all the leaders gone? They are led to misconceptions about leadership. Most are content with management practices that focus on making things work. Many follow a secular model that does not produce and mentor leaders. While some are attracted to ethical decision-making, spirituality that comes from the power within and principle-centered leadership, unfortunately these strategies fall short. They explore only the fringe of what represents the most powerful potential to deal with failed leadership in our generation. We must rediscover the biblical model of

Christian leadership that transforms our character, community and organizations and produces love and service to others.

See also MANAGEMENT

References and Resources

J. Autry, Love and Profit: The Art of Caring Leadership (New York: Avon, 1991); W. Bennis and B. Nanus, Leaders: The Strategies for Taking Charge (New York: Harper & Row, 1985); L. Bolman and T. Deal, Leading with Soul: An Uncommon Journey of Spirit (San Francisco: Jossey-Bass, 1995); J. M. Burns, Leadership (New York: Harper & Row, 1978); J. Conger et al., Spirit at Work: Discovering the Spirituality in Leadership (San Francisco: Jossey-Bass, 1994); S. Covey, The Seven Habits of Highly Effective People (New York: Simon & Schuster, 1989); M. De Pree, Leadership Is an Art (New York: Doubleday, 1989); J. Gardner, On Leadership (New York, Free Press, 1990); R. Greenleaf, Servant Leadership (Mahweh, N.J.: Paulist, 1977); S. Helgesen, The Female Advantage: Women's Ways of Leadership (New York: Doubleday, 1990); S. Helgesen, The Web of Inclusion (New York: Currency, 1995); J. Kouzes and B. Posner, The Leadership Challenge (San Francisco: Jossey-Bass, 1987); H. Nouwen, In the Name of Jesus: Reflections on Christian Leadership (New York: Crossroad, 1991).

—Patrick Lattore

LOYALTY, WORKPLACE

A generation ago organizations expected their employees to make a commitment to the company and its mission. In return for that commitment the employee could expect the organization to provide employment and growth opportunities. It was a covenant of reciprocal expectations. Both the employee and the company expected and received a degree of loyalty. This reciprocal loyalty reached its extreme in the paternalism of the Pullman company during the development of the railroad. In today's marketplace loyalty no longer works that way.

The Erosion of Loyalty in the Workplace

Peter Block in his book *The Empowered Manager* reminds us that companies are not in business to take care of their employees. Ultimately only God will take care of you. While organizations still want their employees to make a commitment to the mission and the good of the company and while employees still want organizations who will take care of them and guarantee employment, both sides recognize that the constraints of the modern marketplace make these expectations unrealistic.

Max DePree, former chairman of the Herman Miller Company—a Fortune 500 company often listed among the best places to work in the United States—regularly notes that workers today are essentially volunteers. He is talking about volunteers not in the sense that they are unpaid but in the sense that they understand they have something to offer and expect a return on the investment of their time and energy. They choose to work where they work because of the exchange that the company offers. It is not a matter of loyalty. They are mobile and understand that they can choose to leave as easily as they choose to stay, taking their time, energy and knowledge with them to a new company where the exchange is better.

Another factor is also at work today. Global competitiveness and the changing marketplace are forcing companies to drastically reduce the work force, restructuring and reengineering themselves to be leaner and more competitive. The loyalty covenant is no longer shaping their attitudes toward employees. In his recent book *The End of Work,* Jeremy Rifkin argues that the rapid progress of technology and information systems has created a rising technological unemployment, with millions of jobs being eliminated every year. Corporations are still loyal to their mission, to their investors, to their suppliers and indeed to those employees who remain, while they remain. The fact that they may eventually be replaced, however, severely limits the scope and depth of that loyalty.

On the one hand, we have workers who understand that their jobs can be eliminated and thus are looking out for themselves. In the organizations they serve, remaining competitive and providing a satisfactory return to their investors are necessary for survival and thus take precedence over loyalty to specific individuals. On the other hand, the rapid increase in unemployment following the progress in technology will eventually make it so difficult for workers to find other positions that the "volunteer's" choice may, in fact, be removed. These two views both support the current attitudes toward loyalty and at the same time are at odds with one another. So what role does loyalty play in today's workplace?

Loyalty in the Workplace Today

Loyalty is still an appropriate concept with regard to mission, to organizational values, to personal growth and relationships, and to God.

Loyalty to the mission. Every organization is formed around a mission, a specific purpose that defines each person's contribution within the organizational community. While the unquestioning loyalty to the company of earlier decades is no longer appropriate, it is appropriate for an organization to expect its people to be committed to the mission of the community in which they choose to work. That commitment should draw employees into continually improving the contributions they make to the organization so that the mission can be achieved. It is the mission that brings them into relationship with the organization, and as long as they work in that context, the mission deserves their loyalty and the investment of their talents.

Loyalty to the values. Similarly, every organization operates with an organizational culture, a set of assumptions and beliefs that, if the organization is operating with integrity, will be expressed in the values by which it lives its corporate life. Organizations have the right to expect employees who choose to work in that community to exhibit a loyalty to the organizational values. It is these values that define the relationships of the people within the organization and the environment in which they work.

137

Loyalty to personal growth, yours and others'. As Peter Block has noted, while the organization should be expected to provide a responsible return on the investment of its employees, the company cannot be counted on to guarantee employment or future employability. It is incumbent upon employees to accept responsibility for their own growth, both in their ability to make a significant contribution to the organization and in their development for future employment in that company or another. Personal growth is the responsibility of the individual, and it may or may not be assisted by the organization. At the same time, employees in most cases work in relationships. It is appropriate that the loyalty we bring as individuals to our own growth and development be extended to those with whom we work. When the Christian concept of community is brought to the organization, it is a necessary corollary that individuals make a commitment of loyalty to one another in their relationships.

Loyalty to God. In the final analysis this is where loyalty is lodged. For example, Paul wrote to the Colossian congregation a letter that was to be read at the same time they were to accept Onesimus, the runaway slave, back into their midst as a Christian brother. He said, "Whatever you do, work at it with all your heart, as working for the Lord, not for men, since you know that you will receive an inheritance from the Lord as a reward. It is the Lord Christ you are serving" (Col. 3:23-24).

Christians in the marketplace work with full loyalty to God, a loyalty that manifests itself in commitment to the mission—the work to be done. This loyalty is also expressed in a commitment to the values of the community in which they choose to work, a commitment to grow both in their knowledge of God and in their ability to make a contribution to the organization and a commitment to the growth and well-being of those around them.

See also CALLING; CAREER; LEADERSHIP; MANAGEMENT; ORGANIZATION; ORGANIZATIONAL CULTURE AND CHANGE; ORGANIZATIONAL VALUES; WORK

References and Resources

H. Blamires, *The Christian Mind* (London: SPCK, 1963); B. A. Grosman, *Corporate Loyalty: A Trust Betrayed* (Toronto: Penguin, 1988).

—Walter Wright Jr.

MANAGEMENT

Management is a relationship between a leader and followers that focuses on a specific set of tasks within an organization, business, church or voluntary society. Both management and leadership have become hot topics, with volumes written to define them and to differentiate between them. Within the organizational context, they are closely linked. Both focus on getting something done, but there is a difference. Peter

Drucker says that *management* focuses on doing things right, while *leadership* focuses on doing the right thing.

The Interdependence of Management and Leadership

Both management and leadership are concerned with results, with getting something done by involving others. Both assume three essential components: leaders/managers, followers and mission or objective. Both refer to the relationship between the leader and the follower in which the leader seeks to influence the behavior, values or vision of the follower for the purpose of accomplishing a mission shared by both leader and follower. The mission gives purpose to the relationship. So does the follower. Without followers there is no leadership, no management.

Go back to Drucker's distinction. Management tends to focus internally within the organization on the task at hand, working for stability and efficiency; leadership tends to focus beyond the immediate task, seeking change and renewal. In every organization both are necessary and complementary. Here again, the follower has something to say. Leadership and management are always determined by the followers and the expectations they have of managers and leaders. They expect from their managers coordination, feedback, plans, order or organization, the provision of resources and information, and access to the decision-making processes of the organization. They expect from the leaders of the organization vision, renewal and motivation for change. No one can lead or manage until a follower chooses to accept that influence and follow.

Management is a relationship between a leader and followers that focuses on a specific set of tasks within the organizational mission. Leadership is a relationship that involves the followers in a process that leads to the results intended by the mission.

Management Styles

There is a wide variation in leadership styles that determines what the involvement of the follower in the management process means. The relationship between leader and follower can be dominated by the leader or by the follower. Volumes have been written arguing for a variety of leadership styles, ranging from autocratic to democratic. At one end of the scale, an autocratic manager makes all decisions and announces his or her decisions to the followers, giving specific direction to their behaviors. At the other extreme, a fully democratic manager gives the decisions to the group and participates as one of the group. In between those extremes are a variety of consultative stages, in which the manager might seek feedback from the followers but still retain the decision, or might allow the followers to decide subject to his or her approval.

The general consensus today recognizes that the appropriate mode of follower involvement varies from day to day, from person to person and from task to task. There is no one right style of participation. Sometimes it is more effective for a leader to give direction, sometimes to consult and sometimes to take direction. This is called contingency theory or situational leadership. It operates on two basic assumptions.

First, the style of leadership becomes more participative as the follower becomes more competent and confident in carrying out the assignment. Second, the goal of the leadership relationship is to develop the competence and confidence of the follower to such a level that the follower can lead on his or her own.

This approach to leadership is very follower-oriented. It seeks to develop the follower and adapts the management relationship accordingly. This flexibility, however, carries some risk. Leaders who prefer a particular style of leadership may choose to stay within their comfort zone rather than adapt for the growth of the follower. This is particularly a problem for leaders who like a more controlling autocratic approach. The contingency model allows them to declare that the follower is not competent enough, and thus they must be more directive in their leadership. As an alternative James O'Toole calls for a values-based approach to leadership that begins with a respect for persons and places follower growth ahead of leader preference. Follower participation is critical to the management process as leader and follower participate in a process that leads to the achievement of the mission objectives.

Management Process

Over the years writers have identified four to seven components of the management process. In the 1960s Alex MacKenzie published "The Management Wheel" in the *Harvard Business Review,* identifying five sequential and two continuous components that make up the management process: planning, organizing, staffing, leading, controlling, deciding and communicating. In the last decade this was revised and updated by *HBR,* but the same key elements were retained. Other writers have developed variations on these components, most often combining them into planning, organizing, leading and controlling or evaluating.

Planning refers to the management process of identifying the mission and the values of the organization and developing strategies for their implementation. It involves discovering and defining the purpose that brings the organization into being as well as the culture or character that defines how things are done (*see* Organizational Culture; Organizational Values). It asks: Do we still believe the mission and follow it? Are we controlled by the mission and values? Planning involves an audit of organizational activities. It asks: What are we doing now? Does it move us toward our mission? What else could we be doing? What can we stop doing? Planning involves the development of organizational strategies—the goals, objectives and actions of the organization. It determines the specific, attainable, measurable results that the organization wants to accomplish within a determined time frame. Planning involves the allocation of organizational resources. It determines the human, physical and financial support necessary to attain the objectives and how they must be distributed. Planning involves the delegation of organizational responsibility. It determines the actions, the individual tasks that must be performed by a given date, by a specific person, to implement the plan. The management process is responsible to see that an effective plan for implementation is in place, detailing who will do what, and when, and how it will be reported and evaluated.

Organizing refers to the management process of providing the structure and resources to implement the organization's plan. This is an important part of the coordinating and stabilizing function of management. Organizing involves identifying and grouping the tasks to be completed and the assignment of each task to a specific person or group of persons. This is the point of *delegation,* where responsibility to lead is given from the leader to the follower, at least for this specific task. Organizing also involves the acquisition, distribution and control of the human, physical and financial resources needed to assure the effective attainment of mission objectives. The management function of organizing brings the organization into existence and equips it for effective operation. It provides the structure for accountability that forms the linkage between the planning and the staffing functions.

Staffing refers to the management process of providing the human resources—the gifts and skills needed to implement the plan. Traditionally staffing involves six functions: human resource planning, the identification of the organization's needs for people to carry out its activities; personnel policy development, the setting up of procedures for the care and nurture of the organization's people; employment, the recruitment, selection and orientation of the people who will form the organization; performance review, the evaluation of the people within the organization to enable them to grow in their work performance and in their lives; career development, the support and training of persons to enhance their personal and vocational development; and compensation administration, the provision of wages and benefits to the people in the organization in return for their work and commitment.

Leading refers to the management process of providing direction and involvement in every area of the organization's development. The staffing function identifies and selects the people who will form the organization. The leading function provides them with a support system to ensure their success. Leaders are always there for the staff, not the staff for the leaders. Leading involves vision—the understanding and articulation of the mission and culture of the organization in a way that empowers the people. Leading involves delegation—the assignment of responsibility and authority to persons so that they might lead within the organization. Leading involves motivation and coaching—the inspiration and encouragement of people to accomplish their assignment. Leading involves coordination. It maintains a network of relationships among the people of the organization. Leading involves service. Leaders make a commitment to the well-being of the organization, the achievement of its mission, the development of its people and the impact it has on the community in which it serves. It is important to note that power and authority are given by the organization (by its people) to be given to the people to enable them to carry out their assignment. The leader is there to serve the follower. It is not unusual to hear the question "Who reports to you?" A much better question is "For whose success are you responsible?"

Leading is the management function of taking responsibility for the success of the people within the organization to ensure that the mission will be achieved.

Controlling refers to assessing and monitoring the progress and completion of organizational objectives. How are we doing? Are we making progress toward our mission? Controlling involves the development of standards for performance. What will a good job look like? What is quality work in this situation? What do we expect from our organization? Controlling involves measurement of performance and results. It asks how we *know* how well we are doing. Controlling also involves the appraisal of performance against standards: how well we *are* doing. Controlling involves the correction of performance deviation: if I am not doing my job well, how do I improve? Controlling involves the reinforcement of performance that is up to standard: if I am doing well, tell me!

The most common control system in most organizations is the budget. The operating budget attempts to quantify the organization's plan in measurable format that allows periodic feedback and opportunity for adjustment. The information from the controlling function of the management process provides the information that fuels the planning function, and the sequential management process continues through another cycle: planning, organizing, staffing, leading, controlling.

Along with these five sequential components of the management process, MacKenzie identified two continuous functions: deciding and communicating.

Deciding is a continuous management function that occurs in each of the sequential components of the process. It includes defining the problems that make a decision necessary—opportunity, lack, choice. It identifies the decision objectives— what we are seeking to accomplish. It develops alternatives—what the options are. It takes the risk of choosing an alternative—selecting the best option. It includes the implementation of the decision—putting the decision to work. Decision-making is one of the most critical functions of leadership within the management process. Some would argue that it is the most critical function because it involves the risk of the unknown. It does not require leadership to decide between two unequal alternatives when one is clearly the better choice. Leadership is required when both options are equal and it is not clear which is the better choice. Leadership risks when making a decision when the alternatives are equal, a decision that frees the people up to get on with their work.

Communicating is another continuous function of the management process. It is the function that links all of the areas of the organization's development. Communicating is the vital link that relates people and processes to the purpose and task of the organization. Information is friendly. A major part of the management process is ensuring that the people within the organization have the information they need to make the best decisions and carry out their assignments effectively for the achievement of the mission.

In addition to all these dimensions of management, which are shared equally by Christians and those without faith, there is another vital and powerful continuous component of the management process for the Christian manager.

Prayer is an acknowledgment of dependence on God. It is a way to seek wisdom, to see things from God's perspective, to look at one's work through the eyes of Jesus. We pray not so much with the expectation that God will make the decision for us as to express weakness and dependence. Praying brings us into the mind of God so that we may understand what is important, what is at stake and what are the values that must be preserved. Praying often draws on different thinking or brain patterns and allows insights that do not always emerge from rational thinking and discussion. One of the deepest prayers of Christian managers is that we will do no harm. We pray, however, in the final confidence that we cannot frustrate the sovereign will of God.

Management is a relationship between leader and follower that involves both in planning, organizing, staffing, leading, controlling, deciding, communicating and praying for the accomplishment of the shared mission objectives that brings them into relationship with the organization.

See also LEADERSHIP

References and Resources

P. Block, *The Empowered Manager* (San Francisco: Jossey-Bass, 1993); M. De Pree, *Leadership Is an Art* (New York: Doubleday, 1989); M. De Pree, *Leadership Jazz* (New York: Doubleday, 1992); P. Drucker, *Effective Executive* (New York: HarperCollins, 1993); J. M. Kouzes and B. Z. Posner, *Credibility* (San Francisco: Jossey-Bass, 1993); J. O'Toole, *Leading Change: Overcoming the Ideology of Comfort and Tyranny of Custom* (San Francisco: Jossey-Bass, 1995); G. Tucker, *The Faith-Work Connection* (Toronto: Anglican Books Centre, 1987).

—Walter Wright

MOBILITY

Mobility is a way of life in all modern societies, especially in newer ones like the United States, Canada and Australia. In these countries approximately one person in five moves each year. Some people, and persons in some parts of these countries, are more mobile than others. For example, young couples without children in southern California move on average every two or three years, while singles in Silicon Valley, south of San Francisco, move on average more than once a year, often around the valley itself. But overall during a five-year period between 50 percent and 60 percent of the population moves, and over a decade this rises to around 75 percent.

People move not only within countries but also between them. Indeed, in the twentieth century we have probably witnessed the largest ever movements of people from one country to another. In some cases, such as the northward drift to the United States from various parts of Latin America, this is motivated by the dream of a better life. Within a generation Hispanics will number more than 50 percent of the population of cities like Los Angeles. In other cases people are driven from their own country or feel compelled to leave it because of persecution, oppression or even genocide. On a different level altogether, travel and tourism have become big business, resulting in increasing numbers of people moving intensively and extensively around various parts of the world as well as around their own countries.

Though they reside in one location, most people frequently move around cities or regions over long distances on a daily or weekly basis. Some work is mainly mobile. This is true for drivers, salespeople, journalists, deliverers, realtors, seasonal workers, cowboys, sailors and pilots. In some cases previously fixed workplaces are becoming mobile, especially as cars develop into complete mobile office systems with cellular phone, fax machine, word processor, printer and even perhaps two-way radio. Employees are also moving more frequently from workplace to workplace or from one line of work to another. Virtually gone are the days of the lifetime company employee: the average worker now holds down five or more different types of job during the course of a lifetime.

Overall it has been estimated that people today cover around thirty to thirty-five times the distance traveled by their grandparents. These high rates and varied kinds of mobility raise a number of important questions. Why are we so mobile? What are the personal and communal effects of mobility? Where is mobility talked about in the Bible, and does this throw light on our culturally different situation? When and where should we move or not move, and what criteria should govern our decision? How can we better manage the moves we feel are right to make?

Why Are We So Mobile?

The roots of mobility in newer Western societies lie primarily in their mobile beginnings. These countries were entered by people who chose or were forced to move to them. Once there, many immigrants did not stay in one place but continued to move across the countryside. It was Frederick Jackson Turner who, toward the end of the last century, first argued that the experience of successive frontiers in the United States significantly shaped individual character and democratic institutions in America. The frontier mentality was characterized by repeated hopes for improvement, by struggles with primitive conditions, by an emphasis on expediency and acquisitiveness, by restless energy and optimism, by individualism and materialism. Though the outcome was somewhat different in Canada and Australia, where the wilderness was not won but itself won against the intruders, the expansion of people into open spaces and their movement between them still had a marked effect.

Somewhere in the midst of this ongoing mobility a subtle but decisive change took place, particularly in the United States. The immigrants' belief that their hopes would be fulfilled if they could find the right place in which to settle down turned into the belief that the very process of continually moving was itself the way to experience fulfillment. In his influential book Wendell Berry calls this the *unsettling*, rather than the *settling*, of America, for people tended to exploit, rather than care for, the land on which they settled and, when they realized this, left it behind for greener pastures. This exploiting and leaving was the beginning of the disposable society, which eventually transformed itself into the phenomenon of the disposable individual, one who successively leaves a worn-out or failed version of the self behind and by moving on again and again hopes to remake or reinvent his or her selfhood.

What Are the Effects of Mobility?

Mobility can have a number of positive effects. These include freedom from persecution or a restrictive context and the opportunity to begin again especially after making a mistake, to move to a healthier or simply more pleasant environment, to get closer to family or leave behind an abusive family situation, to increase educational or cultural possibilities, to find a better job and commute fewer hours, to develop a lifestyle more consistent with basic values or last, but not least for many Christians, to fulfill a sense of vocation or mission.

There can also be negative effects. Among these are the loss of a sense of roots and place, leaving behind extended family and friends, difficulties in readjusting and higher levels of restlessness, a diminished desire and capacity to become committed to people and contexts the more one moves, and a tendency toward greater relativism in beliefs and values. Though few people are aware of it, the increase in mobility during the last century has also increased the degree of bureaucratic control and regulation of people moving or traveling.

A significant effect of mobility that people do not take sufficiently into account is an increase in levels of personal stress. The well-known Social Readjustment Rating Scale helps people determine how much stress they are likely to encounter as they undergo various experiences. As well as a change in residence (20 points), a move generally involves a change in schools (26 points), a different line of work (36 points) or work responsibilities (29 points), a spouse's having to stop or begin work (26 points), and a change in church (19 points) and social activities (18 points). Sometimes a move involves increased marital arguments (35 points), separation from a member of the immediate family (29 points), or a change in living conditions (25 points) or in recreational habits (19 points). When we add the energy expended on adapting to a different climate and to unfamiliar locations, these points often add up to a fair degree of stress: once they reach 300, there is a 90 percent probability of people's experiencing acute insomnia and developing an illness.

Finally, mobility involves a change in churches, which not only involves an additional 20 or more points on the scale but deprives the congregation left behind of the ongoing presence and contribution of those who are moving. One of the most serious unrecognized factors militating against developing community in local churches today is that roughly 20 percent of their members are turning over each year, among them some of their most committed people. How do you build deep community in such a transient setting?

What Does the Bible Say About Mobility?

The Bible presents us with a complex picture of people moving around and staying put. God's question to the heavenly court, "Whom shall I send? And who will go for us?" (Isaiah 6:8), is probably the passage that first comes to mind in thinking about mobility. Note, however, that this sending and going dealt mostly with a vocational rather than geographical change for the prophet. But other significant figures within the nation of Israel and among the early Christians—from Abraham through Jonah to Paul—were highly mobile. This was largely true of Jesus himself. The lives of others, such as Moses and Peter, were a blend of mobility and stability. In contrast, others—like Solomon and James—had a largely settled existence. The nation of Israel itself went through long stretches of stability in Egypt and Canaan, intermixed with wanderings through the desert and a time of exile. In a deeper sense, as the writer to the Hebrews puts it, all these people were "longing for a better country—a heavenly one" (Hebrews 11:16), but this is not to say that their earthly existence was made up of continual pilgrimage.

Most of the aforementioned biblical figures, even the chosen people as a whole, were called to a rather unusual work and therefore should not be treated as exact role models for all Christians with respect to mobility. But the criteria by which they decided to stay put or move on, how short or long a time to remain or travel around, and how to cope with an unsettled life when it came their way have something to say.

Paul is an interesting example with regard to mobility, for we have more evidence concerning his movements than we have for most biblical figures. The apostle worked out the geographical boundaries within which he would move around and beyond which he would not go (Romans 15:19-20). Moreover, Paul did not equate the need or opportunity to do something with the call of God to attend to it—sometimes another factor also had to be present (2 Cor. 2:12-13). He viewed his work as completed in a particular area once he had established it in an influential center from which it would spread elsewhere of its own accord (Romans 15:21-23). Except when Paul was forced out, he did not leave a place until he had completed what he had set out to do and had done so in a quality way (1 Cor. 3:10-15). Furthermore, the apostle limited how much he attempted within these boundaries to the divine gifts and instructions he had been given, allowing others to look after the rest (Romans 12:3, 6). For all the difficulties and anxieties Paul encountered (2 Cor. 11:26-27), overall he learned to be content in whatever circumstances he found himself (Phil. 4:11-13).

What Are Our Criteria for Moving?

Building on the criteria found in Scripture, and assuming there is no overriding decisive argument for moving such as the radical state of a person's health or absolute lack of work, we ask what concrete guidance can be given to those contemplating a move.

146

First, make a list of all the stakeholders in the move, that is, all those affected by the decision. This would normally include family and relatives but should also cover friends, fellow churchgoers, colleagues and neighbors, as well as other people and institutions who have been part of your life and who will lose something by your leaving. This same list will help you assess how much you will lose through being physically separated from these people. Too often a decision to move is based purely on whether it will improve a person's job prospects or provide higher pay or whether relocation will be to a "nicer" area with a better climate. I know of more than one couple who decided that what they and their children were gaining from and giving to their church at the time was more important than a higher salary and status. In all this it is important to count the hidden costs and gains, internal as well as external, that are often overlooked in making a decision.

Second, if you do not have it already, develop a clear sense of your own values and priorities. What is most important to you in your life, and what priority would you give to those items at the top of the list? What would you most miss if all of a sudden you were deprived of it? What stage of life are you in or moving into with respect to family, work, Christian ministry and spiritual growth? If you have a spouse, what does he or she most require over the next few years, and what can you most give to or gain from the one closest to you? All too often decisions about staying or moving are made without springing from or taking into account the basic values around which our lives as Christians should revolve.

Third, work out where the authority lies for making the decision. Does it lie, as is sometimes the case, with the person who will be most advantaged by the move, often the male in the household? When a couple and/or children are involved, does the decision depend on both spouses' coming to agreement or on the whole family, at least including children of a reasonable age, reaching a decision? When people belong to a small group, how much involvement should this primary Christian community have through asking questions, contributing wisdom, engaging in prayer and seeking a word of knowledge from God? What role do nearby friends have in this process, since they will be seriously affected by the outcome? In other words, how is God's will best discerned in such a corporate situation as opposed to a matter that is purely individual or familial? Should a discernment group made of several confidants and key stakeholders be called together to help work through the issue?

Further Considerations

Two clarifications are in order. Sometimes the answer to the question about moving is neither yes nor no but *not yet*. Not all moves have to be made immediately: often a delay enables some factors that are hindering to dissolve or some of the reservations people are experiencing to dissipate. So waiting, which most people find difficult, is a genuine option. Also, deciding to stay rather than move is just as much a choice in its own right. Occasionally such a process unearths stronger grounds for staying than those considering a move had beforehand. Given the rate of mobility today, and its detrimental effects on community generally, the question that God may be asking of many people is not "Who will go for us?" but rather "Who will stay for us?" How else will community be revitalized and deepened in our churches, neighborhoods and cities today?

To whatever extent we are or are not mobile, most of us would benefit from knowing how to handle mobility better. It is helpful here to begin by identifying those aspects of the move that are most threatening or that promise the quickest rewards. Also, work out with family members concrete strategies for minimizing problems and maximizing satisfactions. Consider whatever plans you make as a commitment to those who find the move most difficult and put them into practice as soon as possible. Involve any who are willing to help in the move so that the burden is shared more widely. Try to find one person in your new location who can answer questions you might have, act as an interpreter of local customs and direct you to any services that may be helpful. Give yourselves a buffer zone of at least one or two weeks to prepare for the move and to settle in and recover from it.

See also CALLING

References and Resources
W. Berry, *The Unsettling of America: Culture and Agriculture* (New York: Avon, 1972); M. B. Emerson and C. Cameron, *Moving: The Challenge of Change* (Nashville: Abingdon, 1988); J. McInnes, *The New Pilgrims* (Sydney: Sutherland, 1980); J. Naisbitt, *Megatrends* (New York: Warner, 1982); W. Stegner, *The American West as Living Space* (Ann Arbor: University of Michigan Press, 1987); F. J. Turner, *The Frontier in American History* (New York: Henry Holt, 1920); J. A. Walter, *The Human Home: The Myth of the Sacred Environment* (Tring, Herts, U.K.: Lion, 1982).

—Robert Banks

MONEY

Money matters. It seems that money, like sex, is at the core of everything that we human beings do. The life-giving power of money in modern society is godlike. Easy it is for the moral scold to declaim that it should not be so. But the simple fact is, like it or not, that money has nearly omnipotent control over the human race. Its powers range over life and death and everything in between. In its hand is authority to bestow food, shelter and facilities that are basic to lives of human dignity. In abundance money gives us an almost royal freedom to do whatever we please—to travel, to enjoy fine things, to educate our children, to grow old in good health and security. And an excess of money quite literally gives us the power of life and death over others. Even our paltry pocket money placed monthly in the right envelope can literally save people from hunger, disease and worse. Money matters so very much because if we have it, we live and if we have a lot of it, we flourish, we ascend to Olympian heights of freedom and power, and we (and perhaps others too) live long and prosper. But without money, we perish, or if we have only a precious little of it, we (as much of the earth does) wallow in a squalor of mere subsistence. It does seem that money—mammon—rules the earth.

Money is, therefore, also a matter for the religions. It is a kind of challenger to their position in the world. Karl Marx and Thomas Jefferson, two men as different from each other in their economic beliefs as they could be, had in common a deep skepticism toward religion. They were skeptical because they observed how religions often distract people from the present material conditions of life. The spiritual strategy of religions, they believed, was to evade our ancient enemy—poverty—rather than bravely to face and slay it in honest and mortal combat.

Indeed, throughout the groaning world today no matter is more urgent to the religions than the matter of what to do about money. The great powers of poverty, sickness, illiteracy, AIDS, malnutrition and starvation rage on a global scale as never before. In the pitiful, blank faces of sallow-cheeked children (who enter our homes routinely on cable television), we truly see the dark angel of death. And his darkness soars on wings made of otherworldly spiritualism; the want of money makes him strong. Money, it seems, is our only hope, the only power on earth that can fell him. Yet according to Jesus, "You cannot serve both God and Money" (Matthew 6:24). What can this mean? In what way ought money matter to the Christian? In what way ought it not to matter?

Money Matters in Christian History

In its history Christianity, unlike a good many of the world's faiths, never was purely spiritual in its vision. That is mainly because Christianity erected its entire worldview upon a strong doctrine of creation. As the first article of the Apostles' Creed implies, to the Christian the material world is something much greater than a mere physical presence or a transitory stage on which more deeply spiritual stories will play out. The material world is God's creation, and it is thus good. The material world is not indifferent, illusory or evil, as it is in many religious visions (consider the great faiths of Hinduism and Buddhism). It is itself something real, essential, good and, we dare say, even sacred.

In the Christian tradition material wealth is directly associated with God's good creation and thus with God's will and vision for human beings on earth. Upon opening the Old and New Testaments, we see in a very short time that this is so. There is something about material wealth and poverty in almost every section of the Bible from Genesis to Revelation. In the Bible it matters that we are rich or poor. The whole story connects money with the story of God and God's people. It is not too strong to say that money (or at least material life) is at the root of all that God is said to have done in history, and it is at the root of all that counts as good or evil among the people of God. No subject was addressed by Christ more often than this one, and there really is no Christian doctrine we can think about very long before we come up against questions about economic life—especially if we are relatively rich in the context of a world that is generally poor. To the Christian, then, money not only matters in a transitory way; it is somehow connected with the redemption and eternal destinies of human beings.

Christians realized from the beginning that the matter of wealth was a matter of great theological and spiritual urgency (Gonzalez, pp. x-xvi). Early Christian thinkers all knew that spiritualism or dualism would not do. From sacred tradition, especially the prophets and Jesus, they knew that how we live as economic persons reveals, even exposes, who we are as spiritual persons. The economic life, they reasoned, is a kind of incarnation of the spiritual life. It is a sequence of actions that speak our hearts more loudly than pious words can do. To the extent that our works cannot be disjoined from faith, the ancients rightly judged that the matter of money (or wealth generally) was a matter that had the mark of eternity about it.

As there are now, there were arguments, debates, disagreements and plain old muddles over the problem. Should we have personal possessions at all? If yes (as most agreed we must), then in what quantity and form? How much was too much or too little? The answers of the early Christians tended toward the ascetic (Gonzalez, pp. 71-214). Most looked upon an excess of wealth as spiritually dangerous and morally evil. Throughout the Middle Ages to the Protestant Reformation, the most brilliant thinkers were disposed to denigrate the pursuit of material prosperity. Their model was mainly Jesus, whom they interpreted to have lived a life of poverty and to have enjoined such a life upon his followers.

There is a tendency in today's consumer society for certain Christians to lionize these historic figures as models of spirituality. But before romanticism sets in, we ought to keep in mind that the moral contest of gaining and having money in their day was very different from that of our own time. Not always but generally in ancient times, it was the rule that one person's gain was another person's loss. Only a very small and powerful elite had material wealth in excess, while the vast majority lived in conditions that we would find beneath the dignity of any human being. To such a world—the world of Augustine, Aquinas and Calvin—Jesus' words about mammon were unambiguous. It was difficult to go out and acquire great fortune without doing things that amounted morally to theft from weaker brothers and sisters. But even as great men spoke old words to an old time, a new economic world was being born. It would require new words.

Like its thinking about science, philosophy, music, art and much else, Christian thinking about economic life stood well until the modern revolutions struck. Then it seemed that nothing stood very well anymore. In the centuries before, life seemed an unbroken, nearly changeless and endless rule by monarchs and a condition of poverty for the vast majority (who as the poor, it was just presumed, would always be with us). The centuries after brought one destabilizing shock after another to the older order. The social order that had stood for more than a thousand years fell like some great old tree. A new world grew up in its place at such dazzling speed that we have not caught up with it yet. All the systems of civilization were reordered, and this was made possible in large measure by the astonishing success of the new economic system that had emerged.

For the first time in human history a people began seriously to think that poverty (just as tyranny) might be erased from the face of the earth (Lay Commission, pp. 10-17). In a new land, under a new political and intellectual order, a new people began to flourish in a new way. Ordinary men and women became wealthy as only nobility had done in ages gone. But they had not attained their good fortunes through the genetic line of heredity, nor had they gained by exploiting weaker folk. They had attained it through the honest labor of their hands, even by providing needed services to others in a cycle of prosperity. Their gain had, in effect, been gain for their fellows. In a remarkably brief span of time, this new middle class of people became the majority of the population. The poor became a minority, yet even they had hope of one day being set free from poverty. They knew that we cannot serve both God and mammon, but it seemed that God had served them with it and that he had called them to serve him in prosperity. New words were needed for this new time, and they are needed still.

Money Matters to the Christian Today

Today debates rage among Christians over money and the material goods of this world. What should be done with the great fortune we have amassed? How should we live? What would God have us think and do? The trouble is that we are at sail in a sea of delights while most of the world and some of us at home are intolerably poor. Socialism was the hue and cry of some, but its glory has faded. Defenders of the free market—capitalism—have won the war of ideas, or so it seems. But that does not solve the spiritual problem of economic identity. How ought we to live our economic lives in such a world? When does our respect for money become worship of the god mammon? How much may we freely enjoy? How much ought we in justice to give? For most, the various questions boil down to one: how are we to view the realm of the superfluous, that which exceeds the mere "necessaries of life," as Charles Wesley called them?

Some rail against the having and enjoying of superfluous wealth while others in the world hunger and thirst. In their view any countenance of the superfluous is immoral. Our lives and national systems must be rebuilt upon the principle of meeting only our real needs and then the needs of others (Sider). Their appeal is primarily to the biblical prophets and Jesus who, they say, stood against the rich and for the poor.

Others disagree. They argue that the economics of necessity spell global depression of our consumption-driven systems. The outcome would hardly be liberation of the poor from poverty, but instead poverty for almost everyone. They also point to many passages of Scripture that give God's blessing on the enjoyment of extravagant and superfluous things (Griffiths). What are we to think and do about money, about the superfluous?

151

The Two Voices of Scripture on Money

We are forced by the nature of the debate to return to our first principles. We must go to Scripture and seek to hear the Word of God in a new way. But when we turn to the Bible for help, we are soon daunted by discovering (if we do not know it already) that the text seems to speak with two voices that are, distressingly, in conflict. The one voice says that to be rich is to have received a blessing from God. It says that material riches are a means by which God expresses redemptive love for his people and makes them flourish. Material riches bring to pass the very vision of delight that our good God had for us.

The other voice is dark with warnings about money. It says that money is a curse, that the rich are accursed, that riches are the wages of sin and unrighteousness, especially toward the poor, with whom God takes his stand against the rich. Many would say that this second voice is essentially the voice of Jesus and that it does not speak good news to those who have more than enough money. Can we hear the two voices of Scripture as one harmonious word from God? Or are we doomed forever to a dialect of dissonance and paradox? The harmony is difficult to hear, but with care it can be done.

Delight and Compassion Embrace

If we listen to the deepest levels of each voice—the one that blesses and the other that curses the rich—we learn that delight and compassion are not alien to each other. Since the one entails the other, in their truest shapes they embrace. Of course, they may become alien to each other—there is a delight that turns hard, into self-indulgent and unjust hedonism, and there is a compassion that turns cold, into righteous, pitiless and joyless moralism. But they need not do so. Indeed, in Scripture, we never really have delight in its truest and fullest sense without compassion, nor do we have compassionate justice, shalom in the truest and fullest sense, without delight.

Let us briefly consider four representative biblical narratives: the creation, the exodus, the exile and the ministry of Christ. For in these narratives, God has given us the elemental structures of a worldview.

In its lyrical, almost liturgical way, Genesis 1 (and Genesis 2-3) pictures God's making a material world that is, as we said before, good and even sacred. Here the spiritual and physical worlds are as one. More so, God breathed into the lump of earth that was to become a human being. Human beings are pictured as spiritually endowed physical beings that God designed to inhabit a physical world. And it was "good," as God wished it to be. Even more so, the physical realm is characterized as a pleasure garden that humans are to till and keep as well as enjoy, except that they must not touch the wicked fruit of the knowledge of good and evil. So the most basic vision of human existence as God intended it to be is one of luxurious delight in physicality within a world of moral limits and obligations. This goes to the core of life itself as the ancient Hebrews thought of it (Schneider, pp. 43-64).

The story of the exodus carries on the same double-tinged theme. God rescues the Hebrew people from physical bondage in Egypt and consummates their liberation by giving them a land flowing with milk and honey. It is God, not themselves, who makes them rich and powerful in the land. Because they represent God, they must be especially concerned with those in their midst who have no wealth or power—with the widow, the orphan, the sojourner, the poor. As the people of this God, they must also empower the powerless, enrich those without riches. In their delight they must seek justice, wherein justice means not allowing that any fellow Israelite be poor. Theirs must be a land shining on a hill to the nations, where delight and compassion embrace in a sacred and plainly political way. The whole of the law thus weds delight with compassion, compassion with delight (Limburg, pp. 25-38).

The same double-edged theme shapes the narrative of the exile. The reason God sends his people back into captivity is that the ruling rich have gorged themselves without grieving for the poor. They are not God's people in the most profound spiritual sense of that concept. The exodus is thus reversed physically, just as it had already been turned back spiritually. The prophets thunder, not against the sacred delight that God blessed, but against the dark hedonism that God warned about in the first place. We cannot elaborate how these themes unfold throughout the so-called wisdom literature—Job, Ecclesiastes, Proverbs, even the Song of Songs—but indeed they do (Van Leeuwen, pp. 36-39).

If there is a place in biblical history where we might think delight is sacrificed on the altar of compassion, it would be in the story of Jesus—the story that ends at Golgotha. But delight in the physicality of the world does not die in the heart of Jesus; in him it is reborn and set free again on its way to true shalom for this earth. It is true that in his vision of it we hunger and thirst for the day, for it is not yet. But if we inspect things a little more closely, it is here, as it was already in him.

Moral theology has awakened us in earnest to the "radical Jesus," the Jesus who, in stark contrast to the Sunday-school cliché, stood like a stern prophet against the powers of his time. He did not fear them. Without reserve Jesus used his tongue like a whip against those who were rich, and indeed he blessed the poor, who would inherit the earth (Wolterstorff, p. 73). Many have drawn from this that Jesus was himself literally poor and that material poverty went with his life of self-denial and suffering (Sider, p. 61). But this image of Jesus simplifies things too much.

Today's moral theologians have written precious little about another Jesus whose identity emerges in the Gospels. They neglect the "Christ of delight," who bewildered his religious peers by eating and drinking, rather than fasting. He was the suffering servant, but since he came eating and drinking, pious ones who knew better labeled him a drunkard and a glutton. They, like Judas, could not fathom the freedom he had for wasteful celebration. When he, at his good pleasure, permitted the woman of ill repute to pour the jar of pure nard over his head, that was worth a year's income at a good job and could have been sold and given to the poor. Jesus broke the seal of the vessel that bottled up the forces of darkness that would betray and crucify him.

Christian economic life should flow naturally from a Christian identity that is, if possible, at one, in perfect harmony, with both delight and compassion. We should be in our bodies little Israels, miniature versions of Jesus in our circumstances, those who know the difference between the blessedness of delight and the accursedness of debauchery. Of course, it is not always possible to be so blessed and faithful at the same time. At times we may have to be poorer than we would like to be in order to keep our souls from harm. But there is no ideal to be found in this, any more than it ought to be our ideal to keep the poor around us from flourishing in true shalom. If possible, let our lives be written epistles of wonder at the blessings that God lavishes upon us so that we, as God's people, might go forth and do likewise among those who hunger and thirst in poverty for the coming kingdom of God.

There is much more to say. But these biblical narratives offer us a valuable guide for mapping out the details of economic life. How much to enjoy, to invest, to spend on family; how much to give to church, charities, individuals in need—these are matters for a lifetime. What really matters, however, is that our economic lives spring forth from souls neither too withered for delight nor too hard for compassion. In that harmony we seek the right rhythm for seeking first the kingdom of God.

See also CREDIT; CREDIT CARD; DEBT; FINANCIAL SUPPORT; INVESTMENT; POWER; PRINCIPALITIES AND POWERS; SIMPLER LIFESTYLE; STEWARDSHIP; WEALTH

References and Resources
J. Ellul, *Money and Power* (Downers Grove, Ill.: InterVarsity Press, 1984); J. L. Gonzalez, *Faith and Wealth: A History of the Origin, Significance and Use of Money* (San Francisco: Harper & Row, 1990); B. Griffiths, *The Creation of Wealth: A Christian's Case for Capitalism* (Downers Grove, Ill.: InterVarsity Press, 1984); Lay Commission on Catholic Social Teaching and the U.S. Economy, *Toward the Future: Catholic Thought and the U.S. Economy* (North Tarrytown, N.Y.: Author, 1984); J. Limburg, *The Prophets and the Powerless* (Atlanta: John Knox, 1977); J. Schneider, *Godly Materialism: Rethinking Money and Possessions* (Downers Grove, Ill.: InterVarsity Press, 1994); R. Sider, *Rich Christians in an Age of Hunger* (3rd ed.; Dallas: Word, 1990); R. Van Leeuwen, "Enjoying Creation—Within Limits," in *The Midas Trap* (Wheaton, Ill.: Scripture Press/Victor Books, 1990); N. Wolterstorff, *Until Justice and Peace Embrace* (Grand Rapids: Eerdmans, 1983).

—J. Schreider

NEGOTIATING

Negotiating is part of our daily lives as Christians. Parents are constantly negotiating with their children about when to go to bed, when they can watch television, what time they, as teenagers, need to be home and so on. We negotiate the purchase of a new home or a new automobile. When we travel, we sometimes encounter cultures in which virtually everything one buys has to be negotiated.

The Universality of Negotiating

In the world of business, negotiation is a frequent occurrence. For example, the construction industry is a fertile bed of negotiations. The developer of a proposed condominium project may negotiate with an architect to do a design not to exceed a certain budgeted figure. The developer then takes bids from general contractors and negotiates with the lowest bidders to secure the best possible deal. The successful general contractor thereupon negotiates with a multitude of material suppliers who have bid on the project. Again, the general contractor seeks to get the lowest price possible from a reliable subcontractor or material supplier. From top to bottom, there are negotiations, and more often than not they involve deception and untruths.

Negotiations also appear in the Bible. Perhaps the best-known account occurs when Abraham negotiates with God, who has determined to sweep away the evil of Sodom and Gomorrah (Genesis 18:16-33). Abraham pleaded that a just God would not destroy the entire city if there were fifty righteous people therein. God agreed. Then Abraham asked if the city could be spared if the righteous numbered forty-five. Again, God agreed. Abraham negotiated for forty, then thirty, then twenty and finally ten. God agreed not to destroy the city if within it were ten righteous people. Abraham had to be pleased with his negotiations. God, who held all the cards, must also have been content with the outcome, or else God would not have given in.

Jesus refused to negotiate with the devil during his forty-day fast in the wilderness (Matthew 4:1-11; Mark 1:12-13; Luke 4:1-13), but he did give in to his mother's plea at the wedding at Cana (John 2:1-11). The Canaanite woman successfully negotiated with Jesus to heal her daughter, who was tormented by demons. He denied her request at first, but her reply that "even the dogs eat the crumbs that fall from their masters' table" caused him to relent (Matthew 15:27). Jesus must have been content with the outcome, or else he would not have yielded.

In the case of God with Abraham and Jesus with the Canaanite woman, the power was all on the side of the ones being persuaded. We call that "holding all the cards." Neither Abraham nor the Canaanite woman had any power to compel God or Jesus to change his mind. There are times in life when we hold all the cards and can be persuaded to change a position by the appeal of another. We give in to the persistence of a child or to the plea of a beggar. As long as we are in control, negotiating is easy.

When Negotiating Is Hard

But in most of everyday life we do not hold all the cards. Then negotiating can become stressful. I want to buy a certain model car, and the salesperson wants to sell it. I want to get the lowest possible price out of the deal; the salesperson wants to get the highest possible price. I hold the money; the salesperson holds the car. Arriving at an agreeable price can be a stressful experience.

Negotiating in the workplace can also be very stressful because of the high stakes involved. Most notable is the area of labor-management negotiations. When a labor contract is due for renewal, labor representatives initially come to the table with greater demands than they can possibly attain. In turn, the management representative offers less than they know they are ultimately willing to grant. Negotiations begin. Each side usually makes token concessions as a show of good faith. They remain firm, however, on their major positions. The union's ultimate weapon is a strike, but both sides can be hurt by a long strike. And both sides know that. As negotiations continue, each side makes "final" offers to the other, yet each side suspects that it can get an even better final offer. Thus, labor and management negotiators are forced to be untruthful and deceptive by the very nature of the process. Given this reality, can one be a labor or management negotiator and still be a Christian?

When Negotiating Is Questionable
Responses to that question generally take one of three forms. The first is a simple no. Where deception and untruth are the required job skills, a Christian has no place in the work. The second answer is yes because there is no connection between what goes on in church on Sunday and what one does during the rest of the week. The third response is more interesting. Here again the position is yes; one can be a Christian labor negotiator. The reason given is that all involved know the negotiations are a "game" in which both sides realize they are the victims of deception and untruth. A Christian negotiator asks, "Am I really telling a lie when my adversary expects that I will try to deceive?" It is an appropriate question for Christian ethicists. Can a labor or management negotiator, who is absolutely truthful in all parts of his or her private life, be excused for telling lies at the negotiating table because everyone knows it is part of the negotiating game? Is this really telling lies, or should such behavior be described and viewed under some other category as it would be in a game?

In areas that directly affect the public, such as government services and transportation, third-party intervention in the negotiating process is common. Arbitration by a neutral third party offers a way out of the game of untruth and deception. Arbitrators seek to find a solution in which both sides get something of what they wanted. "Win-win" settlements are the objective, but neither party wins everything it sought. But even here a game is played. To suggest arbitration, particularly binding arbitration, implies that your adversary is in a stronger negotiating position than you are. That being the case, your adversary will be reluctant to go along with the arbitration on the assumption that you are conceding that you have a weaker position.

Negotiating is frequently the required path to obtaining many business and government contracts. The federal government, including the military, negotiates many of its contracts, even though sealed bids are initially sought for specific plans and specifications. Suppliers may differ with respect to terms and conditions, delivery times or other features of a bid. The purchaser must negotiate these aspects of a bid in order to ensure that the contract is awarded to the best supplier. But when each side struggles to better the other, lies and deceit are common. Here, again, it is seen as a game, but sometimes as a game involving victory at all costs.

Christian Negotiation

From a Christian standpoint, negotiations are best carried out when each person places himself or herself in the shoes of the other. When there is a good understanding of the needs and desires of the other person, each side should strive to meet those needs. Negotiating should not be a contest in which each party strives to get the maximum from the other. Rather, it should be a cooperative effort to meet the basic needs and some desires of each other. *Win-win* is indeed the solution sought. In doing so, the Christian who negotiates on behalf of some group will be criticized for not being more aggressive. At this point the Christian negotiator will have to explain the justice of meeting mutual needs or, having failed to do so, decide to either forget about justice or quit the job.

See also BUSINESS ETHICS; COMPETITION; COMPROMISE; CONFLICT RESOLUTION; INTEGRITY; UNIONS

—William E. Diehl

NETWORKING

The importance of networking in everyday working life is dramatized in the film *Wall Street,* Oliver Stone's showcasing of the fascinating world of financial investment. The main character is Gordon Gecko (Michael Douglas), who reigns over an empire of impressive money market monopolies. The stable of people he knows, privileged information he accesses and continuous communication he engages in add up to a networking superstar. Bud (Charlie Sheen) attempts to emulate Gecko both in his competence as a power broker and in the networking skills necessary to guarantee domination in that world.

Networking as a Feature of Contemporary Life

In its exposé of stock market realities *Wall Street* demonstrates the inescapability of networking as a fixed feature of contemporary working life. Indeed, networking is most frequently associated with job and career environments. But it has evolved as a dimension of everyday life beyond the confines of the workplace. In the busy and segmented urban life of most North Americans, networking is required to find friends and to establish a community of connections. With our nostalgic and idealized notions of relationships, we are apt to suspect networking as too formal and utilitarian for our romantic aspirations. But in the reality of city life, networking becomes the necessary bridge to identify and nurture meaningful relationships. Whether practiced consciously or accidentally, networking is a relational habit for many people.

Networks require a measure of intentionality and civility. Networkers are influential precisely because they know what they want and initiate processes to attain their desires and aspirations. People, called *players,* who vigorously pursue strategic positioning recognize that in a competitive social setting, civility and a measure of concern for others in networking are crucial for any short-term or long-term gains. Because of the pervasiveness of networking, a moral imagination should be employed to appreciate and assess its contribution to contemporary daily life.

Networking in Organizational Life

The twentieth century has seen the astronomical growth of large institutions. With this organizational trend has come a dramatic increase in professionals to manage and operate these bureaucratic enterprises. Concurrent with these developments has been the globalization of institutional relations in government, business and ecclesiastical sectors (*see* Global Village). All of these new realities mandate leadership styles that mobilize networking capacities. *Networking* is the process of creating and maintaining a pattern of informal linkages among individuals and institutions. In a swiftly changing social environment, new and flexible interconnections become necessary. Leaders must be highly skilled in constructing or re-creating the linkages necessary to function effectively (Gardner, p. 62).

The recent proliferation of publications dissecting organizational culture and submitting prescriptions for successful leadership of diverse institutions frequently includes discussions of networking. The near-totalitarian presence of organizational life is the catalyst for this saturation of printed resources to assist leaders and players to operate with confidence. In today's entrepreneurial and innovative climate, internal networking emerges as a primary ingredient in being productive. The constant moving around of people and processes means that humans rather than formal mechanisms become the principal carriers of information and integrative links between different departments within an organization. Mobility is a key factor as a network-forming vehicle and thus becomes an admission ticket to the power centers. An organization's opportunity structure—movement to privileged and prestigious positions—is directly related to the power structure (Kanter, p. 164). Networking has become one of the preferred competencies to contribute to a healthy company and to procure advancement possibilities. The wise executive or manager carefully place in strategic positions individuals who are networkers by inclination. This inclusion of networkers enables the establishment of informal cross-boundary working groups that energize the entire corporate culture (Gardner, p. 163).

External networking is also a work of innovative trends in institutional development currently in fashion. The best companies relate even to their competitors (*see* Competition). Building alliances enhances communication and mutuality. In a cutthroat approach to organizational relations there tend to be losers all the way around. Healthy alliance building produces mutual benefits for each partner and for society as a whole. Leaders must nurture outside networks of allies in the many other segments of society whose cooperation is desired for a significant result (Gardner, p. 104).

Networking and the Spirituality of Daily Life

Networking is an individual and institutional activity. The movement of structures suggests the inevitability of involvement in networks. The globalization and urbanization of contemporary life also mean that institutions are interdependent and are necessarily interfacing as their respective missions and operations pull them into a marketplace of connections. Organizational life is an extension of the created world—part of what is often called the *cultural mandate.*

God, who is a Trinity, created the world in a relational manner and wired it to be a communicative network. These relational and communicative processes have been distorted and demented as they moved east of Eden. The life, death and resurrection of Jesus Christ has brought the possibility of a more complete reconciliation into these processes. It is now possible to network in a manner that is reconciling in its intent and expression.

Networking is one essential dimension of the ministry of reconciliation the apostle Paul speaks of so intently (2 Cor. 5:19). The several implications of the ministry of reconciliation for networking are exemplified in Jesus, mandated by the Creator and empowered by the Spirit. The primary implication is the deliberate communication to the neighbor (*see* Neighborhood), including the stranger. The love of neighbor and stranger that Jesus demands becomes the starting point for the networking activity associated with our job and civic life. Networking is that public part of our daily life in which we recognize our oneness, our unity, our interdependence on one another. Indeed, we are strangers and likely will remain as such, but we inhabit common space, share resources, convene around mutual opportunities and generally must learn to live and work together. The public drama in which we all are participants reveals a life in which strangers inevitably come into daily contact with others and learn to solve problems together and enrich and enlarge each other's perspectives. We are all part of a web, linked in a network (Palmer, pp. 19-20).

The church is to be a communion of communions. Jesus has called people together from disparate multicultural environments to be witnesses of the kingdom of God. Networking is a spiritual discipline of the ecumenical church to celebrate our unity in the gospel and affirm the different ministries in the world of the public. Jesus' vision of a unified and commissioned church mandates a spirituality that includes networking as part of its habit of ecumenism and mission in the world (Marty, p. 79). A spirituality of daily life recognizes the vitality of networking in the discipleship of the Christian and in the public vocation of the church.

See also ORGANIZATION

References and Resources
W. Baker, *Networking Smart* (New York: McGraw-Hill, 1994); J. W. Gardner, *On Leadership* (New York: Free Press, 1990); R. S. Kanter, *The Change Masters* (New York: Simon & Schuster, 1983); M. Marty, *The Public Church* (New York: Crossroad, 1981); P. Palmer, *The Company of Strangers* (New York: Crossroad, 1981).

—Scott Young

OFFICE POLITICS

The term *office politics* generally is seen as derogatory. Yet within any organization where numbers of people interact daily, there are degrees of office politics ranging from the simple and accommodating to the complex and highly destructive.

Levels of Office Politics

Office politics in its simplest form is politic, that is, prudent or expedient, to "fit" in with one's organization. It makes sense for a person to follow, without any objective of advancement, the customs and mores of the organization as long as his or her personal conscience is not subverted. For example, if a person's coworkers dress modestly, maintain a neat workplace and respect the privacy of others, it is not politic to wear loud clothes, be a slob at one's desk and constantly interrupt the work of others with small talk (*see* Dress Code, Workplace). If the coworkers maintain a voluntary fund in order to buy flowers for those who are sick or have lost loved ones, it is not politic to refuse to contribute. More than likely a worker can fulfill his or her job responsibilities and receive no adverse performance reviews without fitting in with the prevailing office mores. But everyday operations seem to go better in the workplace if everyone accepts the local customs.

As a worker contemplates advancement within the organization, however, the level of office politics is raised, for he or she must go beyond just fitting in. For example, if my goal were to advance, I would consider the person responsible for recommending my raises or my promotion, for I would need to be politic with that person. Furthermore, in simple innocence, I would make certain my supervisor is aware of my work product. I would turn to that person for help when I have a problem because I need to have him or her care about the quality of my work. At this political level, I am not trying to gain any special favors at the expense of others, but I would just want to make certain my work is recognized at least as fully as my coworkers.

I move to the next level of office politics when I strive to be known and recognized beyond the level of my immediate supervisor. How does upper management dress? That's the way I would dress. What seems to be the favorite sport of higher management? If it is golf, I would learn golf. If it is tennis, that would be for me. Which of the next higher managers is the boss of my immediate supervisor? Does he or she have a favorite charity? I would work for it. Does he or she belong to a church?

I would join there and hope we could serve on the same committee. Does he or she regularly go to a certain sporting event or theater or orchestra? I would be there too. If I played my cards right, my supervisor's boss would comment on what a fine, up-and-coming employee I seem to be, and in turn my supervisor would take more interest in me, giving me special attention.

Have I reached the derogatory level of office politics yet? Perhaps, but what is wrong with what I have done? Consider an example from the Bible. A bit of office politics crops up in the New Testament when the mother of James and John asked Jesus to declare that one of her sons would sit on his right hand and one on his left in his kingdom (Matthew 20:20-21). The request had nothing to do with superior performance or ability. It was purely a request for special treatment. Jesus chided the brothers and said such a request was not his to grant. The other ten disciples became angry with James and John. So Jesus called them together and told them that "whoever wants to become great among you must be your servant" (Mark 10:43).

As a worker advances into management in an organization, he or she begins to develop networks or alliances of supportive people in other departments or locations. The network is helpful in passing along information that relates to further opportunities for career advancement. The alliances are helpful in advancing the worker's projects or assignments. At this point office politics comes into full bloom. A helpful way of approaching and assessing this level of office politics is to consider an example.

A Focal Case

Let's assume that you, as a department manager, have come up with an idea for a new product line that you are convinced will be highly profitable to the company. Or, if you are in a human-service agency, let's assume you have an idea for expansion into a new field of services that you are convinced will vastly expand the importance of your agency in the community. Or, if you are in a hospital or university or financial services organization, let's assume you have a plan for a new and highly sophisticated information system that will increase efficiency and reduce costs dramatically. You take your idea to your senior vice president, and he is immediately sold on it. He wants to back it because he is convinced it will benefit the organization just as you envision and because he sees another benefit—a personal one. If the idea succeeds, he will get the credit for sponsoring it, and that may put him in line for the president's job in two years. He is in competition with other senior vice presidents, and this project may label him as the clear choice. So he gives you his full support.

As you develop the plan, you talk to others in your network and enlist their support. You have close contacts in marketing, treasury, human resources, production, legal, public relations and other departments. Some of the department heads like your idea and can see possible benefits to them or their careers if it succeeds. There is one complication: your project will tax the full financial resources of the organization. If the project fails, the organization will be in serious trouble. Meanwhile other ideas will get little attention because of the limited resources.

Another senior vice president hears of the plan and is convinced it is a bad one. She is also aware that your boss may use the plan as a vehicle to becoming president. Through her own network and alliances, she mounts a campaign to stop your plan. She, too, has contacts in all the departments you do, and so the political battle begins. Each side moves ahead with its plan to sell the board of directors on its viewpoint. The board must decide. Your senior vice president and others he has enlisted lobby the chief executive officer (CEO). The other side does the same. Meanwhile the networks are working. Members of the board are contacted discreetly. Casual contacts at country clubs or community events provide an opportunity for more discreet campaigning. Secretaries are enlisted to learn what they can from secretaries on the opposing side. You learn of some of the arguments of the opposing side and draw up ways to refute them. Both sides seem perfectly willing to discredit individuals on the opposing side who have made mistakes in the past. All this and the CEO has not even been formally presented with the plan.

The day comes, and your side is there with all the guns it can muster. A team makes an outstanding case for your idea. The chair of the board, who appears very impressed and praises everyone highly, wants to hear from those opposing the idea and indicates the board will need a few days to decide. You are disappointed, but what can you do?

Three days later the CEO calls a meeting of the senior staff. You are also invited. You are on cloud nine as everyone gathers in the boardroom. He quickly gets to the point and gives three reasons why the board has reluctantly decided to turn down your proposal. The vote was seven to six. You are stunned. So is your boss. As you leave the meeting, everyone is convinced that the other side did a better job of political maneuvering. Only one more board member voting for your side would have made the difference.

The fallout of the battle is felt for years after. Workers are angry and from time to time try to get even. Was the decision based on the merits and appropriate pressing of the idea, or was it simply a case of vicious office politics? It depends on whom you ask. Sometimes an innocent, good-willed initiative becomes polluted by the self-interest of others. The proposal in this example got into trouble when people let the idea of how to help the company take second place to the fight for personal political power. Remember Jesus' admonition that "whoever wants to become great among you must be your servant" (Mark 10:43).

Office politics can be innocent and harmless and can even accomplish very good things for an organization as long as people put the welfare of others ahead of their own. We call such actions *statesmanship*. Statesmanship is the high road of working within an organization. Office power struggles are the low road.

See also GOSSIP; MANAGEMENT; NETWORKING; POLITICS; PROMOTION

—William E. Diehl

ORGANIZATION

Everyday life is bound up in organizational life. We work for business corporations, belong to clubs, become members of churches, sit on committees, link with political parties, experience citizenship, struggle with bureaucracy, submit to government, attend colleges and schools, participate in unions, join professional societies and get health care through complex systems. Most of our waking hours are spent in an organizational context.

God, it is often thought, is interested only in people, not in organizations. In contrast, the Bible reveals a God who deals with nations and people groups, who created and upholds a structured, ordered context in which humankind can thrive (Genesis 1-2; Col. 1:15-17). God has a purpose for the largest corporations, such as General Motors, and the smallest club. In this article we will develop a theology of institutional life, which will consider how organizations function, the problems we encounter (organizational sickness and sin) and some directions for seeking organizational holiness (for specific challenges, *see* Organizational Culture and Change; Organizational Values).

Can Anything Good Come from an Organization?

An *organization* is a collection of people or entities formed into a whole composed of interdependent parts to accomplish a purpose. Organizations are characterized by regularized ways of operating (rules), repetitiveness in procedures (traditions), permanence (institutionalization), a distinctive milieu (culture), patterns of influence (power) and a governance structure (authority). No good idea in history has made a substantial impact on society without becoming incarnated in institutions and organizations. Even Francis of Assisi would have been an isolated saint with a limited influence had he not founded the Franciscan order.

Organizations are essentially created for our good. They serve to coordinate people and resources to accomplish a mission, and they often provide a context for meaningful work that cannot be done by individuals or informed groups. Organizations can be healing, energizing and life-giving. They can also be hurtful, draining and destructive. The process of becoming organized does have risks; institutions are by nature intractable and resistant to change. In the worst of cases organizations can become demonic and idolatrous. This downside of organizational life has a theological explanation: organizations, including the organizational life of the church, participate in the fallenness of all structures in this world.

It is often said that the church is an organism and *not* an organization. In fact, it is both. As an organism the church is a living entity, pulsating with the life of God's Spirit; it is the body of Christ, the family of God, the covenant community. But the church is also an organization—ordered in a structured life with officeholders, patterns of accountability and decision-making, traditions, power structures and an implicit or explicit organizational mission. In the short run the church can be the most influential organization in society, and in some countries it has been or still is. In the long run the church will outlast all other organizations and be consummated in the heavenly Jerusalem—a city-church-state-environment—though this can only be seen with the eye of faith.

The most apparently influential organization in the modern world is the business corporation. Since it is so adaptive, many thinkers today regard business as potentially the most creative force on earth for dealing with global issues: "The churches, governments, and our learning institutions . . . have become too cumbersome for today's modern pace, where constant change is the norm" (Renesch, p 11). Edward Simon, president of Herman Miller, says that "business is the only institution that has a chance, as far as I can see, to fundamentally improve the injustice that exists in the world" (quoted in Senge, p. 5). In a prophetic book edited by John Renesch, twelve leading thinkers explain what business is becoming. (1) The company is a community, not merely a corporation; it is a system for being, not merely a system for production and profit. (2) The new image of the manager is that of a spiritual elder caring for the souls of the employees. (3) Employees are members of the body working interdependently for the common good. (4) While mission statements, vision, goals and values will continue to *push* a company, a "higher purpose" (parallel to the "Higher Power" made popular by Alcoholics Anonymous) will *pull* a company forward. (5) The corporation is an equipping (learning) organization that provides an environment for every-member service (ministry) so that each person will become more human, more creative and more integrated with the higher purpose. Many firms have already progressed in these directions.

Critical to this thinking is the increased awareness of the connectedness and wholeness of everything, in other words, a systems worldview. Instead of dog-eat-dog competition, people are cultivating interdependence and cooperation: "Although we may compete, we are nevertheless each part of a unity, so that no one 'wins' unless we all do" (Harman, quoted in Renesch, p. 15). The model system is the body of Christ, in which "the eye cannot say to the hand, 'I don't need you!'" (1 Cor. 12:21). But the theoretical development of systems thinking came first from observing other living organisms.

Understanding Organizations as Systems

As early as the mid-1920s Ludwig von Bertalanffy, a practicing biologist, began to understand living organisms in a systems way (p. 12). He recognized that biological organisms could not be adequately understood by the classical Newtonian method, which regarded each object as a collection of distinct and disconnected parts. Instead of seeing the whole as the sum of the parts, he said we should see the whole as more than its parts (Bertalanffy, p. 31). This means that unity in an organism is a complex whole, an idea promoted centuries before by Aristotle.

Other concepts implicit in systems thinking are homeostasis (the tendency of any organization to return to the tried and true, like the keel of a sailboat), isomorphism (the structural similarity of fields or systems that may be intrinsically different but behave the same way) and synergy (the mutual reinforcement that comes by the total effect of two or more elements in a system or organization). Family systems theory, developed in the 1950s, works with such concepts as fusion and differentiation (the need to be both "we" and "me") and intergenerational transmission (the way problems and blessings are handed down generation after generation in both families and churches). As I show elsewhere (Collins and Stevens, chap. 6), there is substantial biblical congruency with this way of thinking, though one needs to be critically aware of the presuppositions of some of the more radical systems thinkers (Collins and Stevens, epilogue).

As a new way of thinking about reality, systems theory has recently been applied to a host of other fields, including transportation systems, national financial planning, outer space exploration, leadership, management and large complex organizations. Ministers of finance are now painfully aware that the economic health of their country cannot be achieved by tinkering with only one factor, such as the prime lending rate for banks, but is the result of many complex factors, most of which cannot be controlled. Along with its applications to family therapy and family ministry, systems theory has recently been applied to pastoral care and leadership in the church (Friedman; Pattison). So systems thinking helps us understand how organizations work; it also helps us grasp what goes wrong with organizations.

The Sick Organization

Symptoms of disease in an organization are similar to those observed in unhealthy individuals. Organizations can be directionless, weak, manipulative and addictive. Some organizations "eat people up," consuming their vitality rather than energizing them. When leaders in an organization burn out, it is often a systemic problem: an overfunctioning leader is in a codependent relationship with underfunctioning members who are adapting to his or her "all-competence." While all might complain about the status quo, they have usually contracted (often unconsciously) to keep it that way.

Some businesses, corporations and organizations can become all-consuming alternatives to family, church and neighborhood. Taken to an extreme, an organization can become demonic, turning people away from the love of God and leading to paralyzing and deadening lifestyles. The organization has become an alternative to the kingdom of God, that yeast that leavens everything in everyday life.

The addictive organization is an extreme example of what can go wrong. While we become increasingly aware of the addictions in our society—sex, money, chemical substances, power and romance—we should also be willing to ask hard questions about the addictive functioning of organizations. The first level of addiction occurs when an addict is in a key position. If the president or pastor is addicted to work or power, the members will never be able to do enough to please him or her, but they will keep trying (*see* Drivenness). The second level of addiction occurs when the organization supports addicts—perhaps alcoholics or workaholics—in their addictive functioning as an *enabler*. Anne Wilson Schaef gives an all-too-common example of a church that had an alcoholic in a key position: the church spent an inordinate amount of energy trying not to notice that the person was doing a poor job on an important committee (Schaef, p. 118). The same thing happens among old-boy networks in clubs and businesses. The third level is organizational addiction—when the organization itself provides the fix. People who look to the organization to be the family they never had are setting themselves up for disillusionment. Some people working for high-tech, high-demand firms feel they are not working for a corporation but more for a religious order. In such cases the mission of the organization (even if it is the church) has become too important. The fourth level of organizational addiction is when the organization itself functions as an addict. "In these cases," notes Schaef, "there is an incongruity between what the organization says its mission is and what it actually does" in personnel practices, emphasis on control and how it interprets and works with power (p. 18).

The Sinful Organization

Are the organizations described above sick or sinful? Can we speak of organizational sin and repentance, organizational conversion? The analogy between individuals and organizations applies once again. Organizational illness predisposes to sin; organizational sin makes the organization and its members sick.

A theology of organizational life includes two complementary ingredients. First, God created a structured organized life as a context for human beings to thrive. Second, God gave humankind the capacity and mandate to craft organizations as part of the cultural mandate (Genesis 1:26-28). Simply put, organizations were intended to exist to serve God and God's purposes in the world in the three ways human beings were to express their calling: (1) building communion with God, (2) building community with people and (3) developing their earth's potential through cocreativity with God (*see* Laity; Ministry). The service to be rendered by the human enterprise was symbolized in the Old Testament by what is sometimes called the threefold office of prophets, priests and princes. The prophets discerned and brought justice; the priests taught and brought peace; the princes governed and brought service to the world.

Tragically all organizations have fallen, both the God-ordained institutions of state, church, family and marriage and the humanly made organizations of clubs, workplaces and all kinds of human enterprises. Individual sin in Genesis 3 leads to systemic evil, a complex of negativity that resists God's purposes in the world. Organizations have become part of the principalities and powers, which were created good but have now become tyrannical, colonized by Satan and intractable. The organization of the tower of Babel (Genesis 11) is a case in point. It is the inversion of the three God-given purposes for an organization: building a name for themselves instead of cultivating communion with God; forging a homogeneous unity of people instead of building a richly diverse community; resisting God's creative and cultural mandate by putting their energies into a single enterprise glorifying human beings and skills.

Sinful organizations are autonomous, inflexible to God's leading and self-serving. Separated from God, organizations and their memberships tend to become arrogant and take on a life of their own. This is a danger in many major corporations and governments and even in churches. Is redemption possible? Does conversion apply to organizations and not just to people? What would a redeemed organization look like? (To explore the extent to which redemption of the visible and invisible structures of life has been accomplished by Christ, *see* Principalities and Powers. To consider the ways of encountering fallen structures, *see* Structures.)

The Virtuous Organization

A virtuous organization is not merely a collection of Christians working for the same business, not-for-profit society or church. It is much more. Holiness has to do with values, the way people are treated, relationships, the way power is used organizationally and the ultimate purpose of the organization. Ironically, a group of Christians may craft an unholy organization that is self-serving and destructive to people, while a group of nonbelievers may form an organization that, unknown to them, accords with God's purposes. The following are ways in which holiness is expressed organizationally, all of them based on a biblical theology.

Trusteeship. The organization has a purpose that is larger than its own self-interest and fulfills some aspect of God's threefold call in the human vocation: communion with God, community building and cocreativity. Prophetic business thinkers today speak of this as a higher purpose that *pulls* the organization rather than as a mission statement that *pushes* or *drives* it. The virtuous organization has a sacred trust handed to it, often through the vision of its founder though ultimately from God, again usually unknown to the people working for it. Critical to this way of thinking is developing trusteeship—being stewards of a vision—rather than gaining ownership (*see* Ownership). Richard Broholm has expressed the difference this way: ownership appeals to self-interest and captures an organization for the agendas of the members ("This is *my* mission") while trusteeship appeals to a sense of calling or vocation ("This is our mission, which we have been given").

Community. The virtuous organization is concerned to build, to cultivate a rich, healthy interdependency of all the people involved: administrators and workers, employees and customers, shareholders and staff, students and faculty, caregivers and clients. All levels of personnel in the organization from the sweepers to the CEO are treated with equal dignity. People are not considered as human resources to be manipulated and used but as God-imaging creatures with inestimable value. Difference is not feared but welcomed as contributing to a rich social unity of personalities, gifts and talents. In theological terms the goal is Pentecost (the rich, interdependent unity of many peoples) rather than Babel (a bland, homogenous uniformity).

Service. The ultimate goal of the organization is to serve. Service takes us to the heart of ministry in the world, as attested by the four servant songs in Isaiah (Isaiah 42:1-9; Isaiah 49:1-6; Isaiah 50:4-9; Isaiah 52:13-53:12) and the words of Jesus (Matthew 20:26-27). If it is a business, the purpose is not primarily making a financial profit but adding value to the customers, though it is value for which customers will normally pay a fee. The organization serves, and so do its members. Since the Greek word for *service* is the same as that for *ministry,* Christians in the organization may regard themselves as those in full-time Christian ministry.

Equipping and learning. Every human interaction and every contact with the structures of the organization are regarded as an opportunity for equipping (Ephes. 4:11-12)—bringing the best out of people, drawing out gifts and talents and assisting people to become mature. The CEO and those beside her regard themselves as primarily equippers rather than do-it-yourself leaders. They equip people and the culture in their time allocation, attitudes to control and power, focus of time investment, commitment to team building and willingness to work with people developmentally. In line with this, the challenges and problems of the organization are addressed primarily in a conceptual and theological manner rather than with programmatic, expedient answers. It is, as Peter Senge expounds, a learning organization.

Values. The organizational values foundational to the company are shaped by biblical and theological realities: faith, hope and love. This frequently repeated triad of virtues (1 Cor. 13:13; 1 Thes. 1:3) can be translated into values for both persons and structures. (1) *Faith* is seeing and trusting the invisible as well as the visible potential of each and every human being and every organizational situation. (2) *Hope* is responding to the gains and losses of the present in the confidence of a future worth laboring towards—confidence and courage in relationships and organizationally. (3) *Love* is relating unconditionally to people to meet their real needs, caring unconditionally for imperfect people, communicating their worth and value independently of their performance. Love also means showing caring loyalty to the culture, structures and values of the organizational system.

Soul. The employees or members are gently nudged in the direction of living and working by ultimate sources—through inspiration that renews, rather than by principles that function as laws to direct and restrain. The organization invites and evokes faith. Those on a spiritual journey are invited to consider discipleship to Jesus not only by sensitive and appropriate verbal witness of those who are believers but by the aroma of Christ in the structures and organizational culture.

As noted before, many Christian organizations are not really Christian in terms of trusteeship, community, service, equipping, values and soul. Some secular organizations seem closer to this goal. The challenge of making organizational change in these directions is a matter for separate consideration (*see* Organizational

Culture and Change). What should be apparent is that organizational life itself is a spiritual discipline. Spirituality is not something imposed on an organization through religious practices or language; it is implicit in the challenge of working together for the commonwealth (the common good). Organizational life invites faith, appeals to the soul. It also reveals systemic sin, and it cries out for systemic redemption. The issues of competition, creativity, cooperation and cocreativity invite people in organizations to engage in a process of transformation that moves from the person to the organization and eventually from the transformation of organizations to the transformation of the world. As with all other human enterprises, organizational life will experience only partial redemption in this life and must wait for the inauguration of the new heaven and new earth.

References and Resources

R. Anderson, *Minding God's Business* (Grand Rapids: Eerdmans, 1986); L. von Bertalanffy, *Perspectives on General System Theory: Scientific-Philosophical Studies* (New York: Braziller, 1975); M. Bowen and M. Kerr, *Family Evaluation: An Approach Based on Bowen Theory* (New York: Norton, 1988); P. Collins and R. P. Stevens, *The Equipping Pastor: A Systems Approach to Empowering the People of God* (Washington, D.C.: Alban Institute, 1993); E. H. Friedman, *Generation to Generation: Family Process in Church and Synagogue* (New York: Guilford, 1985); M. E. Pattison, *Pastor and People—A Systems Approach* (Philadelphia: Fortress, 1977); J. Renesch, ed., *New Traditions in Business: Spirit and Leadership in the Twenty-first Century* (San Francisco: Berrett-Koehler, 1992); A. W. Schaef, "Is the Church an Addictive Organization?" *Christian Century* 107, no. 1 (1990) 18-21; A. W. Schaef and D. Fassel, *The Addictive Organization* (San Francisco: Harper & Row, 1988); P. M. Senge, *The Fifth Discipline: The Art and Practice of the Learning Organization* (New York: Doubleday, 1990).

—R. Paul Stevens

ORGANIZATIONAL CULTURE AND CHANGE

Culture is a dimension not only in the life of countries and ethnic groups but also in organizations. Every organization has a corporate "feeling" or environment that communicates to new and old members what is important and what is permitted. This is true of businesses, small groups, clubs, churches, nonprofit and parachurch organizations. The minute a person walks into the meeting room, the store, the office or the sanctuary, he or she picks up a nonverbal message that is more powerful than such mottoes as "The customer is number one"; "We exist to give extraordinary service"; "This is a friendly, family church." Culture turns out to be profoundly influential in determining behavior, expressing values and enabling or preventing change.

Understanding Organizational Culture

People are sometimes frustrated, without understanding why, in trying to bring about change in an organization. Try to introduce women into an all-male kayaking club, and one encounters almost irresistible forces, none of which is rationally expressed or constitutionally codified. Further, some successful changes get reversed in a few months because they were not congruent with the culture of the organization; other changes are made easily for reasons that are not apparent unless one understands the invisible but all-pervasive impact of organizational environment. To change the culture itself is possibly the most substantial change that can be made. It has a multiple impact on everything else. A man in a museum looking at the colossal skeleton of a dinosaur that once triumphantly roamed the earth turned to the woman beside him and asked, "What happened? Why did they die out?" She said, "The climate changed."

Motivation is primarily related to the culture. We draw motivation out of people in a healthy, life-giving organization. It is inspired, not compelled. Motivation is a result of a process in a group or system and is not just generated exclusively from within the individual. So motivation is only marginally increased by trying to get *people* motivated through incentives or threats. It needs to be considered culturally and systemically (*see* System).

The classic study on organizational culture is Edgar H. Schein's *Organizational Culture and Leadership*. His central thesis is that much of what is mysterious about leadership becomes clearer "if we . . . link leadership specifically to creating and changing culture" (Schein, p. xi). According to Schein, culture includes each of the following but is deeper than any one of them: (1) the observed behavioral regularities in a group (for example, really good employees show up for work fifteen minutes early); (2) the dominant values of the group (for example, church attendance is the ultimate expression of spirituality in a local church); (3) the rules or "ropes" of the group (for example, the usual way to climb the hierarchy is to engage in leisure-time diversions with your superior); and (4) the feeling or climate that is conveyed (for example, while not prohibited, it is also not acceptable to bring forward negative comments in staff meetings). Schein says that culture concerns the underlying assumptions and beliefs that are shared by members of the organization and often operate unconsciously (p. 6).

The factors at work in an organizational culture can be pictured as three concentric circles. On the outside are the symbols, artifacts and visible signs of the culture, which are often incarnated in logos, mottoes, the appearance of a building, the way people dress and the titles by which people are addressed. The middle circle represents the values that underlie the more visible processes (*see* comments on faith, hope and love in Organizational Values). Values are simply what is cherished by the organization. Often these are unexpressed and unconscious. Sometimes the stated values are incongruent with the real values that inform the culture. For example, a business may claim that it cherishes strong family life for its employees but actually requires the sacrifice of family for the corporation. The smallest circle (and the least visible) represents the beliefs that inform the values. For example, a church may believe that women should be under men in a hierarchical arrangement. That belief will fundamentally affect the values and visible "artifacts" of the congregation. Beliefs are expressed in values, and values are expressed in symbols, cues and visible patterns of behavior.

Forming the Organizational Culture

In most organizations, culture is not formed overnight but through a long process. In the church, culture often originates with the founding pastor, who projects his or her own vision of what is right and valued and how people are to be treated. In a business it is often the founding president. In a college it is the founding principal. One element of the mysterious quality of leadership called *charisma* is how it enables a leader to embed his or her fundamental assumptions into the organization or group. This is done by whom the leader pays attention to, how the leader reacts to critical situations, whether the leader intentionally coaches other leaders, what criteria the leader uses for praising and rewarding others and on what basis the leader recruits or rejects other leaders.

Years before I understood anything about culture, I observed that each organization has something like a genetic code embedded at the time of conception that determines most of what it will become. The future of a person is in large measure the unraveling of his or her genetic code. In organizations the founding moment, person and principles are likewise exceedingly important. An organization that starts with certain assumptions about the nature of the community, its style of leadership and mission in society will find it very difficult, though not impossible, to change its culture later.

As the group evolves, members take on the founder's assumptions, usually unconsciously. Some groups never allow their founder to die or leave, no matter how many successors have come and gone. Cultures tend to incarnate not only the strengths of founders but also their weaknesses. An organization would be helped if it could have a once-and-for-all funeral service for its founder! But whoever suggests this will often be resisted by the culture. In fact, the opposite approach is usually more fruitful: finding out everything we can about the contribution our predecessors have made and appreciating their gifts to the organization. One thing is certain: founders are influential. Schein's work is extremely helpful in elaborating what happens at various stages in a group's history (p. 191) and the importance of stories (about the "good old days") in transmitting the culture of a group (p. 241).

Reflecting Theologically on Culture

Whether in a church or a business, the leader of an organization is in some sense the "minister of culture." Another way of expressing this is to think of being an environmental engineer—a person who cultivates an organization's culture so that the people in the organization will thrive. This task is implicit in the broad vocation of being human beings through which we are called to be culture and world makers (Genesis 1:26-28). God created the first culture in fashioning the sanctuary-garden for Adam and Eve, a garden with boundaries, structures, limits, challenges, work to do and pleasures to enjoy. The first human culture was a sabbath culture. There was a threefold harmony of God, humankind and creation. But once human beings sinned, they created cultures that would not bring rest to people or the earth.

The men and women of Babel (Genesis 11:1-11) wanted to create a monolithic, homogenous culture, and God judged that. Imagine what would have happened if that arrogant, self-serving and total-uniformity culture had dominated the human enterprise for thousands of years! In place of Babel God crafted a colorful, pluralistic culture at Pentecost through which those from many languages and peoples heard the wonderful works of God in their own languages (Acts 2:8). What God wants on earth is a rich social unity that thrives on diversity.

In passing, we may note that the Old Testament gives us a few hints of God's grace in secular or pagan organizations. The culture of the Egyptian prison equipped Joseph to emerge as its leader (Genesis 39:20-23). As cupbearer to the pagan king Artaxerxes, Nehemiah was able to express his concern over the state of Jerusalem and be empowered to return to rebuild the walls (Neh. 2). God was at work in both. Daniel was skilled in the culture of the Persians and in that context was able to play a seminal role in the destiny of his people (Daniel 1-6).

In the New Testament Paul was continually engineering culture. His great lifelong vision was to create under God a church culture that embraced Jews and Gentiles as equal heirs, members and partners in Christ. His grasp of the gospel meant that Jews did not become Gentiles in Christ, nor did Gentiles become Jews. Rather both were incorporated into a "new humanity" (Ephes. 2:15 NRSV) that transcended these profound distinctions without obliterating the differences. The same was true of men and women, slave and free. Central to Paul's ministry was a passion inspired by the gospel: God's community on earth must be richly diverse but, at the same time, must treat all members as equal (2 Cor. 8:14). We can only speculate to what extent this carried over into his tentmaking business in which he was essentially self-employed, though often working side by side with that marvelous tentmaking couple Aquila and Priscilla.

The final cultural image in the Bible is the most empowering. In the new heaven and the new earth (Rev. 21-22) every person's contribution is evoked in the fulfillment of the priesthood of all believers (Rev. 1:6). Every nation, tongue and tribe is preserved rather than merged into one homogenous uniformity. Our future in Christ is to become not angels but full human beings in our resurrection bodies as we work and play in this fulfilled sabbath—the threefold harmony of God, humankind and creation. Even the kings of the earth bring their wealth and gifts into the holy city (Rev. 21:24). All human creativity finds perfect fulfillment, and every tear of frustration is wiped away (Rev. 7:17). What a response this should evoke! Keeping heaven in view turns out to be the most practical thing on earth.

Making Organizational Change

We are not in heaven yet. Indeed, all human organizations are approximations. Human organizations have fallen and have been captivated by the principalities and powers. These powers have been unmasked and disarmed by Christ (Col. 2:15), but the best we can hope for in this life is substantial, not complete, redemption. Gaining that—and it is as part of our public discipleship—involves organizational change. Organizational change involves culture. And changing the culture is difficult. How difficult change is!

A cultural approach to change. Changing the artifacts—to use Schein's phrase— might involve moving the Sunday service to the church hall, where the chairs can be arranged in circles to increase participation, or having a staff meeting every Monday to improve communication. But unless the fundamental assumptions of the organization are understood, cultivated and gradually changed, such equipping initiatives may be as effective as rearranging the deck chairs on the *Titanic* when the ship is going down. When the leader and the culture collide, the culture will probably win!

Schein's research shows, however, that culture-change mechanisms are at work in every stage of a group's history—birth, midlife and maturity (which he calls maturity and/or stagnation, decline and/or rebirth; p. 270). He also shows that change becomes increasingly more difficult as a group becomes more established. While all change is motivated and does not happen randomly, "many changes do not go in the direction that the motivated persons wanted them to go" (Schein, pp. 300-301) because they were unaware of other forces in the culture that were simultaneously acting. So being the leader of this process is complex indeed.

Several strategies are useful here. First, understand the culture before you try to change anything. Give the culture its due. It influences everything. Second, recognize that the culture cannot be manipulated. While you can manage and control many parts of the environment of an organization (the president keeps her office door open all the time), the culture itself with its taken-for-granted underlying assumptions cannot be manipulated. Third, good leadership articulates and reinforces the culture, especially those parts consistent with the vision of the organization. If this is not done, people are unlikely to accept any serious change. During a time of changing culture, leaders have to bear some of the pain and anxiety felt in the group at the same time that they seek to make the members feel secure. Fourth, sometimes direct change in a culture can be promoted by introducing new people in leadership, by promoting maverick individuals from within and, more especially, people from outside who hold slightly different assumptions. The appointment of a new pastor, a new assistant, a new board chairperson, a new president is an opportunity for cultural change. Finally, change takes time (Schein, pp. 297-327).

A systemic approach to change. A systems approach treats an organization as a whole that is more than the sum of the parts, in which each member and each subsystem is influenced by and influences the others. It can be easily pictured as a mobile: movement in one element requires adjustment in all the others. Edwin Friedman, a family systems therapist, has some additional insights on how a leader can bring change to a system. He uses the concept of *homeostasis,* that marvelous capacity of human bodies and social systems to regain their balance after a trauma. Every system has a natural tendency to maintain the status quo (homeostasis), just as a keel keeps the sailboat upright. The system does this when new response patterns are required through a threat, tragedy or positive change. Thus the system returns to the tried and tested rather than shifts to operate on a revised and improved basis (morphogenesis). A negative biblical example of homeostasis is the return of converted Jews in the first few years to a less-than-full expression of Christian unity with Gentile believers, a hypocrisy that Paul fervently challenged (Galatians 2:11-21). A positive example of morphogenesis is the extraordinary resolution of the council of Jerusalem (Acts 15:1-29) in which the church changed the terms upon which Jews and Gentiles could have fellowship together.

To bring about systemic change, leaders must first join the system, becoming an integral part of the whole and negotiating their place within it. The director, pastor or president must lead the way in this. In fact this involves many stages of negotiation as the leader finds his or her place in the organization (Pattison). Then the leader might take an initiative that has a ripple effect throughout the system. Usually a problem will surface without provocation. But if a problem does not surface, something as inconsequential as changing the location of the water cooler or removing it altogether will do. How he or she responds to the ripple is crucial because the response of the system will be a reflection of all the systemic factors that make it stable, including the multigenerational influences. The provoked or unprovoked crisis is an opportunity to explain what is going on and to appeal, as Barnabas, Paul and Peter did in the Jerusalem council (Acts 15:1-35), to systemic values that can be expressed in a more constructive way. The Chinese word for *crisis* is composed of two characters, one of which means "danger" and the other "opportunity." The systemic leader welcomes the opportunity of every crisis and sometimes will provoke one.

Using family systems theory, Friedman says we bring greatest change in a system by concentrating not on the dissenting or sick member but on the person or persons in the group who have the greatest capacity to bring change (p. 22). The equipping leader must always remember that the only person open to definite and immediate change is herself or himself! A systems view encourages us to see that changing ourselves can make a difference to the those with whom we are interdependent.

In the context of counseling families, Virginia Satir makes a remarkable statement about systems leadership that applies to all kinds of organizations. She says, "I consider myself the leader of the process in the interview but not the leader of the people." This, she continues, "is based on the fact that I am the one who knows what the process I am trying to produce is all about. I want to help people to become their own designers of their own choice-making" (Satir, pp. 251-52).

So organizational leadership is not simply leading individual people in an organization. Leaders must work with the whole—culture and systems included. Process leadership asks questions, clarifies goals, orients people to their mission, maintains and explains the culture and helps people and subsystems take responsibility for their own systemic life. In the end leaders are charged with the awesome task of creating an environment in which people change themselves.

See also ORGANIZATIONAL CULTURE AND CHANGE; ORGANIZATIONAL VALUES; POWER; POWER, WORKPLACE; PRINCIPALITIES AND POWERS; STRUCTURES; SYSTEM

References and Resources
P. Collins and R. P. Stevens, *The Equipping Pastor: A Systems Approach to Empowering the People of God* (Washington, D.C.: Alban Institute, 1993; portions quoted with permission); M. DePree, *Leadership Is an Art* (New York: Doubleday, 1992); E. H. Friedman, *Generation to Generation: Family Process in Church and Synagogue* (New York: Guilford, 1985); R. K. Greenleaf, *Servant Leadership: A Journey into the Nature of Legitimate Power and Greatness* (New York: Paulist, 1977); M. E. Pattison, *Pastor and People—A Systems Approach* (Philadelphia: Fortress, 1977); J. Renesch, ed., *New Traditions in Business* (San Francisco: Berrett-Koehler, 1992); V. Satir, *Conjoint Family Therapy,* rev. ed. (Palo Alto, Calif.: Science and Behavior, 1983); E. H. Schein, *Organizational Culture and Leadership: A Dynamic View* (San Francisco: Jossey-Bass, 1991).

—R. Paul Stevens

ORGANIZATIONAL VALUES

In organizational life, values determine what is cherished and important and how an organization is shaped and managed. The human body operates on blood; an organization operates on values, whether good or bad. Ideally these values are thoughtfully conceived and clearly stated in a document that can be read by members of the organization and recipients of the organization's service. Sometimes the real functioning values of an organization are in conflict with the advertised ones. So the process of getting people to clarify what values are actually operating and what values should be foundational is one of the most important exercises that can be undertaken in organizational life.

The Virtuous Organization

Values should cover the full range of organizational life: how people are treated, especially when being hired or fired, how mistakes are dealt with, how resources are used, how people relate, how decisions are made, how power is handled, how purposes are clarified and how work is performed. A virtuous organization would be shaped by three foundational organizational values from the Bible: faith, hope and love (*see* Organization). These values can be applied to both persons and structures in organizations that are not overtly Christian but where people in positions of influence can shape the values of the organization. Obviously in a church or parachurch organization faith, hope and love can be applied directly (though they often are not!). But in a secular organization these revealed values must be translated, with loss of some of the original meaning.

Faith is seeing and acting in harmony with God's will. It is seeing and trusting the invisible as well as the visible potential of every person, situation and structure (compare Hebrews 11:1). *Hope* is expressing courage and confidence in relational and organizational contexts. It is responding to the gains and losses of the present (with both people and structures) in the confidence of a future worth laboring for and embracing. *Love* is caring loyalty for people, cultures, structures and values. It is relating unconditionally to people in order to meet their real needs, communicating their worth and value independently of their performance. Love must also be directed to the structures as part of the world that God loves.

These three values are founded on *truth* about people, situations and ultimate reality. Truth is not abstract but concrete, holistically experienced (mind, body and spirit) in a way that is reliable and stable. We will now develop these values in both personal and organizational terms.

Faith in an Organizational Context

Faith is the response of the whole person to the full revelation of God's person (Romans 10:14-17) and intentions for the created order (Hebrews 11:3). Faith is a revolt against living on the basis of appearances. It is not merely a belief system but a total life orientation involving trust and action in all kinds of life situations (Hebrews 11:4-16). Faith is better considered as a verb than as a noun. Faith is based on the Word of God, the persuasion of the Spirit and the paradigm of Jesus, but it leads to concrete action. How does this apply in a secular organization?

Personal faith. Faith requires seeing people and situations the way God does and acting in relation to them in view of the potential for change, integration and wholeness that God holds before each person and every human enterprise. While full communion with God is a possibility reserved for those who become children of God through faith (John 1:12), persons of faith working in organizations of various kinds are invited to translate their own communion with God into a form of communion with their neighbors in the workplace. This is not so much possibility thinking or a search for human transcendence as for divine possibilities and capacities for transcendence that God makes available.

Organizational faith. In the same way a person of faith sees and acts upon structures and organizational culture. Normally this results in openness to the possibility of substantial, though limited, change and transformation of an organization. Faith will inspire creative action to make the structures (as well as the people in them) reflect divine values and purposes in a way that is attractive to others.

Hope in an Organizational Context

Hope is resting in the revealed and certain conclusion of the created order to shape our response to the present gains and losses. It involves understanding and living in the present in view of the future, allowing the vision of God's kingdom to inspire our confidence in the future. Hope equips us with courage to hold essential values in uncertain times and to take appropriate steps to plan for tomorrow. The person who has been "saved by hope" can incorporate hope relationally and structurally in the life of an organization. While there is some loss of meaning in this process, incorporating hope in an organization plants a pregnant hint that there is something more and invites people to move towards it. Of the three virtues, the one most urgently needed today is probably hope, for it is the one that gives people the confidence that the other two are possible.

Personal hope. Hope means never giving up on people (confidence) and helping people deal with the reality of their lives (courage), in terms of both their need for change and the positive fruits that can be appropriated through a realignment of their lives.

Organizational hope. Hope means never giving up on situations (confidence) and empowering the structures, values and culture of an organization (courage) to live in harmony with kingdom values and realities, even if in the short haul we appear to be engaging in fruitless activity or experiencing reverses. Hope inspires people in business to see their work as "playing heaven" (as children "play house" as a way of growing up) and "speeding" the day of the Lord (2 Peter 3:12) by bringing our business and organizational ventures into greater correspondence with what will be characteristic of the new heaven and the new earth. In some way beyond our imagination, hope points toward the transfiguration, not the obliteration, of our work and enterprises in this world.

Love in an Organizational Context

In the Old Testament covenant love (*hesed*) is love plus loyalty or affectionate loyalty. It also includes *ahabah,* the love that reaches out to incorporate the outsider. Covenant love is more concerned with relationships than commodities. It is not merely a sentiment but involves active caring and creative loyalty. In the New Testament *agapē* illuminates and extends this further through the sacrificial ministry of Jesus and the generous pouring out of the Spirit that encompasses not only people but the creation itself. This means that material realities and ordered structures in this world are the objects of God's love and should, therefore, be the object of ours. How does this get translated into organizational life?

Personal love. Though we love in a more limited way than God, our love should reflect that love as we show caring loyalty to employees, members, clients, peers and

THE MARKETPLACE MINISTRY HANDBOOK

customers. This involves meeting true needs, going the extra mile in relationships, understanding empathetically the other person's situation, supporting another's integrity, remaining faithful to the published values of the organization. Love makes us stay with people even when we find them unpleasant, when they "push our buttons" or when they do not meet our expectations for development. Love means we do not jump to conclusions about the motives of our customers. And even when we must deal with negative reality, we will communicate worth and create an opportunity for people to change and have a second chance.

Organizational love. Love inspires caring loyalty to the structures and values of the organizational system—loving the company systemically, structurally and culturally. As God loved the world, we are called to lay down our selves, not only for people, but for organizations and communities so that they will be humanized and transformed. In the process hopefully some people will embrace Christ as their Lord. A being-redeemed-community can express God's kindness and so lead people to repentance for sin (Romans 2:4). Gratitude is a good enough reason to return to the seeking Father, and a loving organization should evoke gratitude.

The Value of Values

Several assumptions in this reflection invite further study and discussion: (1) that Christian values are good for everybody; (2) that Christian values are relevant not only to individual persons but to the structural and cultural contexts in which those persons live and work; (3) that people on a spiritual journey may embrace and live at least partly by Christian values—to their benefit and the benefit of their neighbors; (4) that God shows grace even to people who do not ask for it; (5) that values may serve as the law did prior to the coming of Christ—a good gift that may unfortunately become a trap through pointing to impossibly high standards—but nevertheless point us to Christ (Galatians 3:24); (6) that translating Christian values in a secular context means that Christians in the marketplace have a ministry as valuable as pastoral or missionary service; (7) that rediscovering kingdom values in the marketplace may create a learning context for Christians—a theological school in the marketplace. In the end organizational life can become for believers one more context for worship, in spite of all the difficulties.

A ministry to structures desires, but is not dependent on, the hope that other people will become believers. This ministry is worthwhile in itself—a faithful, hopeful and loving ministry of lining ourselves up with the kingdom of God. Our service is goal oriented, but the goal is beyond this life. In biblical revelation the future determines the present. All our life and work in human organizations are a dress rehearsal for the final performance in the new heaven and the new earth, which will be inaugurated when Christ comes again. The end of the human story will involve renewed structures in a new heaven and earth. In the new Jerusalem faith will be realized in sight, hope in fulfillment, but love will be the continuous plot line and experience of life in the heavenly city.

See also ORGANIZATION; ORGANIZATIONAL CULTURE AND CHANGE; SERVICE, WORKPLACE; VALUES

References and Resources
R. Benne, *Ordinary Saints: An Introduction to the Christian Life* (Philadelphia: Fortress, 1988); P. Block, *The Empowered Manager* (San Francisco: Jossey-Bass, 1987); M. De Pree, *Leadership Is an Art* (New York: Doubleday, 1992); J. Renesch, ed., *New Traditions in Business* (San Francisco: New Leaders, 1991); E. H. Schein, *Organizational Culture and Leadership: A Dynamic View* (San Francisco: Jossey-Bass, 1991); G. Tucker, *The Faith-Work Connection* (Toronto: Anglican Book Centre, 1987).

—R. Paul Stevens

OWNERSHIP, PRIVATE

The issue of ownership is a large one. At the public level it raises profound questions that have preoccupied philosophers, economists, legal thinkers and political scientists, as well as creating many national and international conflicts. It has also raised complex decisions involving politicians, civil servants, lawyers and corporate managers, leading to wide-ranging antitrust laws, court battles and family quarrels. Historically, ideas of possession took root more tenaciously in North American soil than elsewhere, perhaps because so many people who came to the New World were have-nots. As the information society grows and the Information Superhighway becomes more extensive, ownership issues are becoming increasingly problematic in areas relating to copyright and privacy.

The topic raises several pertinent questions for us. What does private ownership mean? How much should we own? What is involved in saying "this is mine" or "that is yours"? When should ownership be an individual and when a joint affair? How does private ownership—of property, vehicles, possessions—appear and work within the economy of God, not just human economy?

The Nature of Private Ownership Today

In our society ownership involves primarily our right to acquire, use, enjoy and dispose of our assets—whether land, wealth, home, animal, goods or copyrights, trademarks, policies or professional rights of tenure—in whatever way we choose, subject to legal provisions. The foundation of ownership is possession, but this is not enough when someone else has a stronger claim. We can own things individually or in partnership with someone else, such as a spouse or family, or with strangers, such as a time-share arrangement in a condominium. We can own something permanently or temporarily (for example, until someone comes of age). We can own things in the absolute sense or in a derivative but de facto absolute, such as holding a ninety-nine-year housing lease from a government agency. But ownership involves not only the claim *this is mine* but in some sense *this is me*. For in some measure what we own tends to reflect who we are. It is a symbolic expression or concrete extension of ourselves. In other words, it has to do with being as well as having.

Ownership can be established in many ways, in some cases simply by holding possession or by shaking hands, in others only after finalizing protracted agreements. People may also exercise their ownership in a wide variety of ways—well or badly according to their care for what they own, selfishly or generously depending on how little or much they share with others, ostentatiously or modestly according to whether they flaunt their possessions, carefully or casually according to whether or not they give forethought to the fate of what they own when they die (*see* Will, Last).

Christian Attitudes Toward Ownership

In Christian tradition, the moral dimensions of private ownership have been often addressed. Thomas Aquinas taught that private property was not a right in natural law but only in human law, and that its use must not reflect avarice or waste but temperance, generosity, benefaction and almsgiving. The Puritans also tended to encourage modesty in the area of possessions, thrift with respect to money, and generosity with respect to giving. Apart from occasional documents, such as the *Pastoral Constitution on the Modern World* or certain World Council of Churches reports, in recent times the church has done little to question widespread possessive attitudes toward ownership or the social obligations attached to it. This is no doubt partly because church congregations themselves often own large holdings.

What happens when we view ownership from God's point of view? For many Christians this changes little. They may view what they own as coming from God's hand and as a sign of God's blessing, but that is the extent of the issue. This is the position of some conservative believers who regard the right to private ownership as an integral part of the Christian message. They may see this right as an indispensable element of being an individual. "Without property, without something that really belongs to a person and characterizes him, it is difficult to be more than a cipher or a cog" (Harold Brown in Chewning, 2:127).

In other cases, looking at ownership from God's perspective has led Christians to the view that they should own things only in common, not privately. This is the position of some branches of the Christian community movement. These people often regard the practice of common ownership as indispensable to being a disciple of Christ. As with monks and nuns in the older Catholic tradition, unless a person yields up their private property, or future right to it, they have not reached a mature level of Christian obedience.

Ownership in Biblical Perspective

The Old Testament concern to grant each Israelite a portion in the land suggests that having some property is an important part of belonging to God's people (Numbers 26:52-56; Joshua 13-19). There were laws against moving landmarks and therefore stealing another's property (Deut. 19:14; Proverbs 22:28), and injunctions against stealing others' property (Exodus 20:15; Proverbs 11:1; Proverbs 16:11). Property may be acquired on the basis of a gift (Deut. 1:8) or inheritance (Deut. 21:16; Proverbs 19:14). Its use by the owner is guaranteed even when someone else is using the goods involved (Exodus 22:7-8). It is the inalienability of land that lies behind the provision that every fiftieth year, the year of Jubilee, lands and houses that someone had been forced to sell to another for the sake of survival were to resort to the original owner (Leviticus 25:8-34; Leviticus 27:17-24). For though people might sell their land, it must always be possible for the family to get it back (Leviticus 25:25). In this respect the old covenant is unapologetically materialistic.

On the other hand, there is a continuing emphasis on God being the ultimate owner of the land: "The land must not be sold permanently, because the land is mine and you are but aliens and my tenants" (Leviticus 25:23). The highest possible use of property is also to honor God with any increase that it brings (Proverbs 3:9). Apart from land, houses and possessions, there were other objects a person could own that exceed what we are accustomed to today: in the case of a man they included his wife and daughters as well as slaves (Exodus 20:17). Though some people owned a great deal, exemplary servants of God rate other things as more important than material wealth (Genesis 13:8-12). An excessive view of owning, which tends to trust in riches, love of luxury and oppression of the poor, is consistently condemned by the prophets (Isaiah 3:16-23; Isaiah 10:1-2; Ezekiel 7:19-21; Amos 6:1, 4; Micah 2:1-2).

In light of the full teaching of the New Testament—which does not insist on common property for all Christians but on the generous, sacrificial sharing of one's resources (see 1 Cor. 16:1-4; 2 Cor. 8:1-9)—a place for what we call private property appears again, though, for reasons I shall indicate in a moment, this is not the best way of describing it. On the other hand, the practice of Jesus and his disciples suggests an abandoning of ownership for those involved in a common mission (Luke 5:11, 28; Luke 14:25-33; Luke 18:18-23, 28-30). There was financial sharing among the disciples as well as among Paul and his coworkers, though the apostle certainly earned wages for distributing to others (John 12:4-6; John 13:27-29; Acts 20:34). Though the example of the early church in Jerusalem is often cited in support of this practice, a closer reading of the text shows that it was surplus property that was sold and distributed to those who had need (Acts 2:44-45; Acts 4:32; Romans 12:13). In the early churches this practice may not have been as exceptional as many think, nor mainly a product of intense apocalyptic expectation. Certainly Paul regards one of the purposes of possessions as the possibility they provide of giving to others (Ephes. 4:28). There is evidence of Christians sharing some of their possessions throughout at least the next five centuries (Grant).

Underlying both approaches is something more fundamental that does not always come to the surface. What we call ownership, whether individual or joint, would be better termed trusteeship or stewardship. In a profound sense there is only one Owner. Everything comes from and belongs to God (Psalm 24:1-2; Psalm 95:4-5). What we have is, strictly speaking, not given to us to own in any absolute sense. It is rather entrusted to us: we are made trustees of what comes our way and are accountable for how well we use it to serve God and to serve others. We do not have a right to any of our possessions; they are given from God, who could take from us at any time. It is our responsibility to view what we "own" through the lens of our calling to reflect God's character and ways, to fulfill the ministry and vocation God has given us, and to share with others in the church or who are in genuine need.

Some Principles of Responsible Ownership

The first time I encountered an attitude toward ownership based on trusteeship rather than possessiveness was in the form of a churchgoer who offered me the use of his automobile on Sundays whenever I needed it. I thanked him profusely for his generosity, but he replied, "There is nothing generous about it. This car is not mine but God's. God has entrusted it to me for my own use and for my family, as well as any of God's people who would benefit from it. I am simply trying to put it to the use for which it was intended."

This is how we should regard all that we own. By no means does this require us to be undiscerning about who we entrust what God has entrusted to us to. Some people will demand that we share; of these we should beware. Others will accept our open-handed offers but not handle what we share with them carefully, as we would handle it ourselves or as they would want us to handle something of theirs. Some will even abuse or exploit what comes their way, or only receive but never reciprocate, even when they could do so. Precisely because we are trustees of what we have, we must learn how to balance our own and our dependents' or Christian community's needs with those of other needy people with whom we come in contact. We also need to ensure as far as we can that what we share with others is kept in the best possible condition so that it can continue to be of benefit to people. Sometimes this will mean saying no to otherwise appropriate people.

We should also consider carefully how much we need to own as individuals or as a family, or how much we could own certain things in common with others. The danger of wanting to possess too much was strongly criticized by Jesus (Luke 12:15). Our households—inside and out—are full of possessions which we use only once a week or less. When we live close to others whom we know, we could share or jointly own many tools and implements and even appliances. Under some circumstances, within the family, this can even be arranged with cars or homes. This raises larger questions about owning property and how much we should own. This need will vary from person to person, and will depend on a whole variety of factors, such as our income level, dependents, vocation and setting. There is no uniform answer, except perhaps to say that among middle- or upper-class believers, generally much less could be owned than is generally the case. But this raises the issue of a home ownership (*see* Home) and simpler lifestyle, on which more is written elsewhere in this book.

Beyond such questions is the deeper issue of sorting out how much we own what we have or how much it owns us! It is one thing for what we own to be an expression or extension of ourselves. It is altogether another if it defines us and our life revolves too much around it. This basic issue is a matter for serious reflection, for at stake is nothing less than idolatry (Ephes. 5:5; Col. 3:5). But then the sharing of what we own also calls for much prayer, advice, discernment and learning from experience. It is a risky adventure of faith in which we will sometimes make poor judgment calls and at other times entertain angels unawares. Though they sound as if they are polar opposites, we should always remember that owning and giving are actually closely related, just as are individual and community. This is certainly the case with God, and increasingly we see the connection between the two. We live constantly within and through that tension as we gradually reflect more of God's own nonpossessive nature and large-hearted view of ownership.

See also INVESTMENT; MONEY; STEWARDSHIP

References and Resources

W. Brueggemann, *The Land* (Philadelphia: Fortress, 1977); R. C. Chewning, *Biblical Principles and Economics: The Foundations* (Colorado Springs: NavPress, 1989); E. Fromm, *To Have or to Be?* (New York: Harper & Row, 1976); R. M. Grant, *Early Christianity and Society* (San Francisco: Harper & Row, 1977); D. J. Hall, *The Steward: A Biblical Symbol Come of Age* (Grand Rapids: Eerdmans, 1990); M. Hengel, *Property and Riches in the Early Church* (Philadelphia: Fortress, 1974); L. T. Johnson, *Sharing Possessions: Mandate and Symbol of Faith* (Philadelphia: Fortress, 1981); C. B. MacPherson, *The Political Theory of Possessive Individualism* (New York: Oxford University Press, 1964); G. Marcel, *Creative Fidelity* (New York: Farrar, Straus, 1964).

—Robert Banks

PART-TIME EMPLOYMENT

We tend to regard part-time employment as the exception rather than the rule. Historically this was not the case. While some people have always performed the equivalent of what we call "a full-day's work" for pay, in many respects the Industrial Revolution was the creator of the full-time salaried job. It also increased working hours by a half or more over what people had traditionally known. For most of human history the majority of people have engaged in several activities in several locations in the course of a week, often without monetary payment, rather than a single task in one setting (*see* Volunteer Work). In the winter months most people worked less than a full day's labor, adjusting their hours according to the number of daylight hours and the dictates of the weather. Work responsibilities were also spread more evenly through the extended family rather than concentrated on one, now often two, members of a nuclear family.

The Growing Incidence of Part-Time Employment

Even in recent times, part-time employment has been the norm rather than the exception for certain kinds of people. Women have frequently held part-time or less-than-average full-time positions, and after a period of decline this older pattern is now returning. Large numbers of immigrants, even those who have been in a country for some time, also have part-time or occasional work. Many rural workers are involved in seasonal work. So too are many students in schools, colleges and universities, though increasingly these continue to hold down part-time positions alongside their studies. Overall, part-time employment has been steadily growing during the last decade and looks set to continue doing so well into the future.

There are various reasons for the trend: (1) the downsizing of many workplaces and contracting out of responsibilities to other people, (2) a lower outlay on salaries, insurance and health schemes, (3) the greater flexibility required by many new kinds of work, (4) the growing desire for self-employed or multisided work, (5) the search on the part of some baby boomers and many baby busters for a more balanced life and (6) the call of God upon some to launch out into freelance or tentmaking Christian service.

Some social commentators believe that we are in the midst of a paradigm shift with respect to work. The traditional job is dying. For example, the number of people who are part- or full-time telecommuters doubled in a two-year period, and the number of traditional or traditional-looking jobs even in a country like Great Britain is about 25 percent of the total work force. In years to come, increasing numbers of people will find themselves "dejobbed." We are moving toward a workplace without jobs as we have known them. The bulk of jobs are on the way to becoming temporary rather than permanent. Guaranteed employment and tenured positions will be a thing of the past. The existence of the much-written-about organization man or woman, who is wedded to a firm or company for much of his or her life, or the career path of rising through a sequence of jobs that increased in salary, responsibility and complexity will be rare (*see* Career).

In the entertainment and communications industries, traditional job structures ultimately became too inflexible to cope with the constantly changing nature of the work. This will prove to be the case in other kinds of workplaces. Individuals called in to perform a particular function, telecommuters working for several firms at the same time, teams or even whole firms hired for a particular project, these are the wave of the future. The result will be an ever larger number of what the freelance consultant William Bridges calls *vendor workers*, who sell their services to a variety of clients and tend to work on projects on a short-term basis. While such a development opens up the possibility of further exploitation by employers, as has often been the case with part-time employment, this will be offset by the competitiveness of certain work situations, the high quality of the people being employed and the beginning of protective structures or regulations for part-time workers.

A Survival Guide to Part-Time Employment

A greater challenge may well be the psychological, social and economic adjustments workers will have to make to manage and benefit from these changes. Those already in part-time work have always had to cope with the sense of inferiority associated with not having a full-time job. Workers who in some industries have already shifted from a five- to a four-day working week have had difficulty adjusting to not being able to socialize during their time off with their friends in traditional jobs. If, as is likely, some part-time work takes on the pattern of shiftwork or working at different hours, the long-observed problems of physical, psychological and marital problems experienced by such people will spread. Since economies—from benefit provisions to tax collection—are still largely built around traditional employment arrangements, there is still little recognition or support from the government for the emerging part-time employment economy. On the other hand, some businesses are taking responsibility to develop new financial practices and packages for the new kind of worker.

What can part-time workers themselves do to make a satisfactory transition from traditional employment into this new situation? First, it requires a more inner-directed and self-motivated attitude than a traditional job. This is not always easy in an increasingly outer-directed and peer-motivated culture. Giving additional time to prayer and meditation, especially to journaling one's daily life, strengthens one's inner life with God and develops a greater capacity for one to stand on one's own. If selling oneself is also awkward, focusing on what could be contributed to specific projects, rather than what one has to offer generally, may help overcome the difficulty.

It is also important to establish contact with others who are working part time. People can then meet regularly to talk about common concerns arising from their nonstandard working practice. Congregations and some parachurch organizations could help develop such groups. In addition, belonging to a support group or home church within a congregation creates a place where people can talk and pray about their work and provides a weekly anchor and reference point.

Since part-time work does not always have the regular rhythms of a traditional job (for example, working intensively one day or one week with little to do the next), it is important to learn and live with flexibility. This is not necessarily easy, and individuals will differ in their attempts and ability to deal with it. For most it is important to establish "islands of order" (Bridges), routines that hold fast even in the most demanding work schedules but especially during spells when there is less to do. These may include reflection and prayer times (*see* Spiritual Disciplines), hobbies, exercise or sports, ongoing commitments to others, a project or a cause. While these may expand or contract according to circumstances, they will be a consistent feature of one's day or week.

Since part-time workers, especially those who are self-employed, are often among the lowest paid, and even if well paid sometimes have highly fluctuating incomes, it is imperative for them to have a broader financial support system. This could take different forms, and I offer two from my own experience. Those in the same work position could agree to help each other out or have a common fund from which any can draw when necessary but must repay as soon as his or her position stabilizes. A church-based support or communal group could also commit itself to helping one or more of its members during the transition into part-time employment or during other difficult times.

The wider challenge of part-time work, especially if it becomes more entrenched in our society, presents considerable challenges to Christians, though no more so than those already faced by members of some industries and those involved in freelance work. It is helpful to remember that the tradition of part-time work has some significant Christian precedents. We often forget that the apostle Paul was mostly a part-time, not full-time, missionary, who made tents to support himself and his associates (Acts 18:3; Acts 20:33-34; 2 Thes. 3:6-10). The secret to living this way, he said, lies in learning "to be content whatever the circumstances," knowing "what it is to be in need" and "what it is to have plenty," doing "everything through him who gives strength" (Phil. 4:11-13).

See also CALLING; SHIFTWORK; WORK

References and Resources

W. Bridges, Jobshift: *How to Prosper in a Workplace Without Jobs* (London: Nicholas Brealey, 1995); C. Handy, *The Age of Unreason* (Boston: Harvard Business School, 1989); J. B. Schor, *The Overworked American: The Unexpected Decline of Leisure* (New York: Basic Books, 1991).

—Robert Banks

PLANNING

Thomas Carlyle said, "Nothing is more terrible than activity without insight." With even greater wisdom Proverbs notes, "Many are the plans in a man's heart, but it is the LORD's purpose that prevails" (Proverbs 19:21).

Planning is something everyone does, says they do or would like to do. It is remarkable how much personal planning happens in the course of one day: choosing clothes to wear, getting the trash and recycling out on time, planning the fastest route to the job according to morning traffic flows, scheduling errands and taxiing children to their activities, deciding how much money to withdraw from the ATM (automated teller machine), filling out the form to join the CD (compact disk) club, ensuring meal ingredients are available and cooked at approximately the same time, programming the VCR (videocassette recorder), choosing a clock alarm setting in order to maximize sleep and minimize panic the next morning. Given all of this, we have not begun to touch the planning required at work, through school and in community involvements.

Much of this planning is conscious, deliberate and efficient. When things go wrong, we resolve to plan better. Perhaps we think about buying a book or attending a workshop on the topic of planning. But the basic questions are, How do we know (before the results) what a good approach to planning might be? How do we evaluate the approaches to planning that are constantly being suggested in this accelerated, acronymic age in which we live? What is the difference between personal planning and planning as a group? Finally, if we can figure out what planning is, does a distinctively Christian view of it exist?

The Nature and Variety of Planning

There are as many definitions of planning as there are definitions of leadership. Standard dictionaries suggest two basic approaches: *planning* as arranging the parts of or designing something and *planning* as devising or projecting the achievement of something. Unless we are in a design profession such as architecture, the latter is more what we have in mind when we think of planning. That is not to say that planning to fulfill an aim is an uncreative process: once a purpose has been identified, assessing and marshaling resources, selecting structures and activities, and evaluating results related to the purpose all involve a lot of creativity. Sometimes the planning process seems unconscious or instantaneous, but by definition some kind of intentionality and mental work must be involved with planning. Very brief analyses of options for their efficiency (minimum resources), elegance (simple structures) and effectiveness (maximum results) are going on all the time in our daily lives, even if we are not very aware of the process.

For example, you want to go out for an evening and therefore begin to contact baby sitters on your list (assuming you are fortunate enough to have a list). Your first choice to phone may seem random or instinctual, but it is really the product of a rapid planning process. You have made assessments of the choices and decided on the option that is most (1) efficient (who is most likely ready and willing), (2) elegant (who comes with no strings attached, for example, with no need to negotiate with a teen's parents or to return the favor, in the case of baby-sitting exchanges) and (3) effective (who is most reliable based on reputation and experience). Or perhaps you just maximized the particular value that is most important to you at this time. No wonder these simple tasks tire us out.

In more formal group processes, such as we encounter in work settings and organizations, there are layers of planning to consider. First is identifying the purpose driving the plan (some people call this the *mission* or *vision*). Next is assessing or assembling resources (for example, money) and structures (that is, the right groupings of people, lines of communication and policies). Then there are the selection and sequencing of activities that will contribute to the purpose. I have just described various nuances of planning: planning as intention (we plan to . . .), planning as preparation (planning for a trip), planning as a program of choices (the first step in the plan is . . .) and planning as implementation (who will do what by when). Finally, there is evaluating how it all worked out. This last stage, often neglected and sometimes painful, is actually vital. A group of successful executives was once asked how they had come to make such good decisions. Their answer was "Experience." They were then asked how they got experience. The answer they immediately gave was "Bad decisions." Evaluated experience is a key raw ingredient of good planning.

There is an additional layer of the formal planning process we must note, that is, how exactly people are supposed to approach the various decisions just described. This is sometimes called *planning the planning*. This preliminary planning requires a process of its own; it too is a stage that is often neglected, for people launch into formulating a plan without thinking about how to do the planning and what kind of plan is desired. The fact is that there are many different ways to do planning or make decisions, especially in a group. Will voting or a consensus approach be used? Can closure on the discussion be invoked? Who will chair, and what will be the chair's duties and powers? What planning model will be followed? (See "How to Plan Anything," below, for one approach.)

There are also many different types of plans: long- or short-range, strategic (focused on key purposes) or action, comprehensive or single-issue. Finally, there are different approaches to the components of planning, for example, cost-benefit analysis, pros and cons, computer simulation and brainstorming. In modern technological society, planning has been reduced to a technique, thus presenting further ambiguities for followers of One who appeared not to plan, at least not in the modern technological manner (see Cadbury, *The Peril of Modernizing Jesus*). Are all these approaches equally valid for the Christian? Even more profoundly, is planning itself valid for the believer? The negative warning of James 4:13-17 is at least a prohibition against boasting in our plans as though we were gods, which is a form of practical atheism.

Divine Planning and Ours

Few would disagree that we are to be guided by plans. The main debate in Christian circles concerns how the plans originate: through a human process or as a revelation from God. There are instances when God's instructions to individuals are very specific (for example, Abram's being directed to leave his homeland for Canaan in Genesis 12:1) and detailed (for example, the plans given to Moses for the tabernacle in Exodus 26:30; compare Ezekiel 43:10). We see Jesus following a plan, for example, as he generally restricts himself to a Jewish rather than Gentile ministry, as he tries to manage the public relations around his miracles and as he sets his face toward Jerusalem. However, it is difficult in the case of Jesus to distinguish between revelation and methodical planning—in fact, we are not given much insight into the latter at all. When he selected the twelve apostles, it was after an all-night prayer session. Was there any "human" planning going on in that case, or is the planning of the faithful supposed to be merely a matter of getting in touch with God's intentions?

One textbook on social planning offered this definition of its topic: "Planning is the guidance of future actions" (Forester, p. 3). But surely guidance is to be left to God.

It is true that God is Planner. The Scriptures are full of testimony to this notion. The Lord declares through the prophecy in Isaiah 14:24, "Surely, as I have planned, so it will be, and as I have purposed, so it will stand." Paul echoes the sentiment in Ephes. 1:11: "In him we were also chosen, having been predestined according to the plan of him who works out everything in conformity with the purpose of his will" (see also 2 Kings 19:25; Psalm 33:11; Psalm 40:5; Isaiah 23:8-9; Isaiah 25:1; Isaiah 37:26; Jeremiah 29:11; Hebrews 11:40). It is clear that whereas God's plans cannot be thwarted (Job 42:2; Proverbs 21:30), God is quite capable of thwarting the plans of his creatures and is especially willing to do so when those plans are evil (Job 5:12; Psalm 64:5-8; Isaiah 8:10). One of the most famous case studies of such thwarting is the attempted construction of the tower of Babel in Genesis 11. Sometimes less-than-perfect human plans are woven into God's overall plan, as Joseph testified to his brothers in Genesis 50:20: "You intended to harm me, but God intended it for good to accomplish what is now being done, the saving of many lives." The same idea emerges in David's plan to build a temple: he is prevented, but the task is transferred by God to Solomon (1 Chron. 28). The concept of God's redeeming our plans is most powerfully seen in God's superintending the conspiracy surrounding the execution of his own Son (Acts 2:23).

The question that remains after observing this strong theology of divine planning is whether or not any room exists for appropriate human planning. Concerns about the dangers inherent in human planning have also been raised in other spheres (for example, Jacques Ellul's critique of technicized economic planning). God's word in the middle of the Babel story seems to echo these concerns: "If as one people speaking the same language they have begun to do this, then nothing they plan to do will be impossible for them" (Genesis 11:6). However, other biblical evidence seems to allow a role for human planning processes. The aforementioned story of Joseph is one case: though one knows he is in Egypt by God's design and God does reveal details about the upcoming famine in that land, Joseph also seems to play a role, based on gifting and wisdom, in coming up with the plan to save the nation (Genesis 41:33-40). Such a picture fits well with the strand in the New Testament that describes believers as God's fellow workers (1 Cor. 3:5-9; 2 Cor. 6:1; 1 Thes. 3:2). This is both a humbling and an exciting concept. A last bit of evidence is the tacit support given to planning in Proverbs. It is true that many cautions and limitations are put on planning in this book (Proverbs 19:21), but all of this assumes first that planning is a human activity that God expects and endorses (for example, Proverbs 14:22; compare Isaiah 32:8).

Personality and a Theology of Planning

Some, because of how they are shaped as people, would like to believe that planning as a human process can or should be avoided or at least severely curtailed. Resistance to planning within Christian organizations may be especially exhibited by members who are weary of planning in the rest of their lives and who, for example, come to church services for a break. But the resistance may run even deeper. Antiplanners may claim that their personality does not suit planning. They are free spirits, letting each minute, hour and day unfold as a series of spontaneous events and choices. However, as soon as they admit the notion of choice, they have admitted the reality of planning as well. To select one thing over another requires a plan, even if it is established and implemented in an instant. Moreover, even if the semblance of a Thoreau-like spontaneous life were sustainable, the decision to operate in this fashion itself represents a plan!

Further, those weak on planning may buttress personality with spirituality: they say they are guided by the Holy Spirit, making plans unnecessary. There are two problems with this approach. It confuses process and product, and it is bad theology. Whether or not the Spirit is involved with the choices that make up a plan does nothing to invalidate planning; the Spirit may very well guide you in the details of a plan, but a plan nevertheless results. Why would the Spirit be unable to influence a human planning process that is submitted to him? To believe otherwise is to be overprotective of the Spirit. Furthermore, the decision to be prayerful, or to adopt a waiting, listening attitude, involves planning, specifically planning how to plan. The bad theology of what might be called overdependence on the Spirit's leading is that it ignores God's awesome creativity in actually giving his creatures free will. Whatever the input of the Spirit, in God's economy there still are real human choices with real consequences. Without trying to solve all of the philosophical issues of determinism and free will, let it suffice to say that the notion of human freedom prevents planning from being cast aside out of some kind of respect for God's sovereignty.

Finally, action-oriented persons, though accepting the general defense of planning, may want to short-circuit the process, moving quickly to tasks rather than getting bogged down in interminable planning processes. Again, though there is wisdom in being reminded about efficient processes and the importance of implementation, the solution for frustrated activists is to leave the earlier parts of the planning process to others and come in only at the end. As Jesus himself suggested in a couple of brief parables on counting the cost, there is reason for taking time and care in planning (Luke 14:28-32).

The above discussion does suggest that a distinction can be drawn between personal planning and that done within organizations. When it comes to planning in your individual life, perhaps cautions against being overly technical are in order. We must be honest enough to admit that the idea of consciously selecting a purpose and being rigorously guided by it may be more of a modern concept than a reflection of the life of Jesus. Consider how one writer has described the Lord's approach:

> Whatever he said and did was not brought by him into accord with some external criterion; it sprang from an inner coordination of life. In such cases logical consistency is not always present and is not intended; but a moral

consistency may be there, an habitual reaction. . . . Perhaps some day in the future historical students of the gospels will realize that there is more profit in inquiring into these hidden habits of his soul than in attempting to fit the anecdotes and sayings of Jesus into a program of his life. (Cadbury, pp. 148-49)

To apply these sentiments too quickly to organizational planning, however, may be misguided.

The fact must be faced that some of the reasons for avoiding planning in groups involve the flesh more than the soul. Planning is hard work, not meant for the lazy or undisciplined; planning permits evaluation, not meant for the insecure; planning builds teamwork, not meant for the antisocial. With this having been said, it is important to recognize legitimate differences in the way believers approach planning. The key is to see that all planning is not automatically labeled as being unspiritual and all spirituality as being unplanned: "Such attitudes prejudge all planning as being carnal and ignore the validity of a third option: Spirit-guided planning. Let each be fully persuaded in his own mind, but let the spiritual nonplanner be careful lest he judge the planner as being necessarily carnal" (Alexander, p. 19).

How to Plan Anything

So what might Spirit-guided planning look like? There are many patterns that may be followed in planning for organizations. Here is one that seeks to honor God and, when used in a group, to honor God's people as your colleagues.

Commit your planning to God. Always begin with a commitment to God, not to have him bless your plans, but to have your plans caught up in his (Proverbs 16:3). This requires an understanding of God's purposes as revealed in his Word and a sober interpretation of current reality (read Isaiah 22). You cannot stop too often in a planning process to ask for God's direction and correction.

Define the planning task or the purpose. What exactly are you trying to achieve? Many wasted hours will be avoided if you can answer this question as clearly as possible (Acts 15:6).

Identify personal goals and motives that you bring to the planning process. This is especially important in planning with a group. For example, some may be interested in building teamwork through consensus approaches to planning and combined efforts in implementation; others may want to get the meetings over as quickly as possible so that they can get into action by themselves. One can imagine the different agendas that Paul and Barnabas brought to planning the second missionary journey (Acts 15:36-41). Sometimes motives need to be submitted to God and reconciled before planning can proceed (Proverbs 16:2).

Establish the facts or context. This can include a list of external constraints, an inventory of resources and an analysis of current structures (groups and policies). It also includes understanding the history of a project (Acts 15:7-18).

Generate action ideas. What could be done to fulfill the task? The more ideas, the better. If you are engaged in a personal planning process, this is the step (along with the next two) in which the biblical value of multiple advisers comes into play (Proverbs 11:14; Proverbs 15:22; Proverbs 20:18; Proverbs 24:6). The value of group planning processes is, of course, that "many heads" are built right in. The Spirit works through the plurality and gifting in a group context, and the implementation is partially done if the group is involved in the process (*see* Leadership, Church; Management).

Package the ideas into major options. Such packaging makes evaluating the options easier, for there are only so many things that can be considered at once. Do not give in to a sense of urgency and take shortcuts through the process. This logical linking of options is a distinct step in planning. As with the whole process, take time on it (Proverbs 21:5); it will make the next step easier.

Assess the option packages. Which one best serves the task or purpose? Use any tools that make sense, for example, a list of pros and cons for each option. Get input from everyone in the group (or from everyone in your group of advisers). Pray for wisdom and insight (1 Kings 3:9-10; James 1:5).

Draw a conclusion. In some ways this is easier when the final authority falls on the chair (Acts 15:19) or when you are dealing with a personal decision (though going against advice can be painful; for example, see Acts 20:12-14). However, there is power in a consensus decision, as many people will be behind it emotionally and practically.

Implement your plan with holy boldness. (Note that implementation may require another planning process.) We are saved by grace, not by works, including the works of planning. We step out knowing that God goes before us, will forgive us and will work all things together for good (Romans 8:28). He has already paid the price for our imperfection; he requires only faithfulness from us as planners.

Be prepared for course corrections. Paul did plan the itineraries for his missionary journeys (2 Cor. 1:15-17), but he also knew that plans had to be changed sometimes (Romans 1:13) and himself encountered course corrections (for example, Acts 16:6-10). We must hold all plans lightly before the Lord (Proverbs 16:1, 9; Proverbs 19:21) and before changing circumstances.

Although not a guarantee of good results, this sort of careful process can lead to an agreement between God's Spirit and God's people that brings him glory (Acts 15:28).

The Benefits of Planning

Christians can benefit from good planning in many spheres. For Christians as individuals, these spheres are career choice and attainment, marriage, budgeting, personal mission statements and family goals. For Christians as church members, these spheres are small group contracting, management and eldership decisions. For Christians as neighbors, there are increasing opportunities and needs for public participation in urban planning. Finally, for Christians as global citizens, there is a place for involvement in national and international planning issues.

There are several ways that planning can help in any of these spheres. First, there is a basis for evaluation and redirection based on a clear purpose and activities meant to serve that purpose. Second, there is a basis for saying no, for avoiding lower priorities and weaker ideas that distract from the main purpose. Time is the ultimate limited resource that must be protected in good planning: "I can do only one thing at a time, but I can avoid doing many things simultaneously" (Ashleigh Brilliant). Third, good planning means that personal and group resources can be released most powerfully: "Within most Christian groups is an enormous amount of creativity. Let us encourage and stimulate this potential in every possible way. Let us urge people to think creatively on every aspect of our purposes, to be bold to experiment with new objectives, fresh strategies . . . and tactics . . . and to innovate wherever desirable so that we can more effectively fulfill our purposes" (Alexander, p. 21).

See also VOCATIONAL GUIDANCE

References and Resources

J. W. Alexander, *Managing Our Work* (Downers Grove, Ill.: InterVarsity Press, 1975); R. S. Anderson, *Minding God's Business* (Grand Rapids: Eerdmans, 1986); H. J. Cadbury, *The Peril of Modernizing Jesus* (London: SPCK, 1962); K. L. Callahan, *Twelve Keys to an Effective Church* (San Francisco: Harper & Row, 1983); J. Ellul, *The Technological Society* (New York: Vintage Books, 1964); J. Forester, *Planning in the Face of Power* (Berkeley: University of California Press, 1989).

—Dan Williams

POWER

Power is troubling for many Christians. We are suspicious that its exercise violates the ethos of the Sermon on the Mount with its call for meekness and willingness to be last. Power is also easily corrupted. In Lord Acton's well-known words, "Power tends to corrupt; absolute power corrupts absolutely." The more power we have, the more evil we can do, and the more likely is the devil to seek to waylay us.

The Ambiguities of Power

Power is frequently used to oppress and exploit others (Micah 2:1-2; James 5:1-6). Many contemporary feminists call for the abolition of the power model of society and organizations and brand its attendant hierarchical structure as a remnant of discredited patriarchal and unchristian ways. In its place they call for an ethic of sharing and collegiality. Anabaptist and other circles that stress nonviolence warn of the seductions of power politics and instead urge us to take up the role of servants who simply and humbly follow Jesus' commands.

At the same time many Christians see no particular virtue in refusing to exercise power while the world and the church engage in oppression and injustice. We also tend to appreciate good leaders. Anyone who has sat through an unstructured meeting or a small group with ostensibly no one in charge or when no one will make a suggestion for fear of upsetting someone else knows the yearning for proper structure and authority. Christians are especially divided about whether we should ever exercise the forms of power we usually call *coercion* and *violence*. Those who do accept them insist that they can only be used as a last resort. The division roughly parallels the distinction between those who are committed exclusively to nonviolence and those who accept just war views.

Usually we end up exercising power. Some do so with sneaking guilt. Others just accept power and its consequence uncritically, whether it is the coercion that lies behind most political power, the marginalizing of others produced by intellectual power or the dehumanizing that may come from applying business models to church or vice versa. This ambiguity is reflected in the "theology of the powers," which is associated especially with Walter Wink. This view says that power formations were originally a good gift of God, but now that they have fallen, we must work with them but maintain a continuing aloofness to their seductions.

Types of Power

There are many forms of power, including wealth, appointed office, intelligence, access to information, charisma, skill, physical strength and military means. Power can include control of things, like cars or word processors, as well as control of people. It exists not only in large-scale settings, for we can speak of a powerful argument, a powerful computer or a powerful sermon. Anything that can accomplish an end is a form of power.

Biblically, all power comes from God and belongs to God (Matthew 26:64; John 19:11). The New Testament draws explicit attention to Jesus' power: his power over all things is a manifestation of his kingdom (Mark 4:14; Mark 5:17; Mark 11:20-22). God's power is delegated to human agents in the form of authority or office (Genesis 1:26-28; Psalm 8:5-8). This includes those within the church structures, such as elders or apostles, and also those in other positions, such as kings or teachers.

The Right Use of Power

We cannot reject power as such. It is a pervasive and inescapable fact of our lives as God's creatures. While it may be true that power corrupts, it is also true that an unwillingness to use legitimate power can also corrupt. We must be cautious with power, even suspicious of it, and we must carefully judge the forms of power and the ends of power, but we can never escape the God-given responsibility to exercise power. Jesus continually stressed the right use of power and the right types of power. He emphasized that the key to power is that it is a means of servanthood, thus reversing the common understanding (Mark 10:42-45; John 10:17-18). Paul also emphasized that "the governing authorities" are "God's servant for your good" (Romans 13:1-4 NRSV). This might sound trite to us, accustomed as we are to the language of public servants, but these were radical words when applied to Roman emperors and their subjects. To put it mildly, in the ancient world servanthood was not usually taken to be an attribute of imperial power.

It may also help us to use the common distinction between *power* (generally understood as the mere ability to achieve something) and *authority* (understood as legitimate power), which is close to the New Testament's distinction between *dynamis* (2 Cor. 8:3; Ephes. 3:16) and *exousia* (Matthew 21:23-27). The late Jewish philosopher Hannah Arendt even went so far as to treat these two as opposites: that is, people are reduced to exercising power when authority is not possible. We do not need to polarize these so sharply in order to benefit from the distinction. The existence of legitimate authority highlights the fact that even authority over people need not be exercised contrary to the will of those subject to it. Many forms of authority stem from leadership that wins people over gladly, something that Jesus, along with any good preacher or political leader, exemplifies. Even a great general commands not merely by military discipline and threat but by inspiring those who are commanded. A willingness to risk death comes from inspiration as well as fear.

Authority and Gift

The form of power called *authority* is clearly something we should exercise. The exercise of such authority is in turn tied to the gifts we have been given by God. When we have a particular gift—whether healing, administration, preaching or auto maintenance—we already have a factual authority in that area because we have an insight, and therefore an ability. We should follow good administrators in organizations, follow good medical advice in areas of health and learn wise ways from wise elders. In each case we are thereby recognizing an authority, a power, and at the same time we are conferring an authority and submitting to legitimate power. The key to using power well is not trying to avoid it in a desperate search for a world in which no one is ever subject to another but rather knowing its strengths and temptations. It means recognizing and submitting to giftedness as a blessing from God.

See also ORGANIZATION; POLITICS; POWER, WORKPLACE; PRINCIPALITIES AND POWERS; STRUCTURES; SYSTEM

References and Resources

K. Rahner, "The Theology of Power," in *Theological Investigations* (Baltimore: Helicon, 1966) 4:391-409; P. Schouls, *Insight, Authority and Power* (Toronto: Wedge, 1972); W. Wink, *Engaging the Powers* (Philadelphia: Fortress, 1992); W. Wink, *Naming the Powers* (Philadelphia: Fortress, 1984); W. Wink, *Unmasking the Powers* (Philadelphia: Fortress, 1986).

—Paul Marshall

POWER, WORKPLACE

Power is the ability or capacity to act. It refers to strength, influence and control. In the workplace power of different sorts is required to perform the services or create the products intended by the business or institution. Industrial power, for example, is a composite of natural resources, energy supplies, good ideas and design, capable management and productive workers. The power of a community or political organization depends on its financial and human resources, ideas, programs, leadership and constituency of workers and supporters.

Our interest in power in the workplace is focused primarily on how policy and direction are set, how plans are made and carried out, how influence is distributed among the people. Employees, including middle managers, are often frustrated by what seems to be their lack of real power. It often seems that responsibilities are not commensurate with authority or power; there is not enough of the latter to fulfill the former.

In this article we are considering *power* not in general but in the workplace. How can we better understand power and then respond as thoughtful Christians? What are the purposes of this work for which power is sought? What kind of power is to be sought by the people of God? How can Christians relate to power in the workplace as it is configured in our world?

Personal Power

First, our personal power in the workplace is dependent primarily on our competence, skill and fitness for the tasks we are assigned. Our motivation as Christians to competence and excellence is based not on the potential for rewards from our employers but on our desire to please and honor God: "Whatever you do, in word or deed, do everything in the name of the Lord Jesus, giving thanks to God the Father through him" (Col. 3:17 NRSV). This applies even to the work of a slave: "Whatever your task, put yourselves into it, as done for the Lord and not for your masters, since you know that from the Lord you will receive the inheritance as your reward; you serve the Lord Christ" (Col. 3:23-24). To be persecuted, or disempowered, in the workplace because of our failure to perform well is not praiseworthy. On occasion, despite our good performance, we may suffer unfairly. Ordinarily, however, we will be rewarded not only by God but by our employers if we carry out our tasks with godly excellence.

Second, power in the workplace is often dependent on our relational skills. It is a matter of whom you know and how you treat others. The tempting and cynical approach is to use and manipulate others for selfish purposes, but Christians reject this as the power of darkness. As the children of light, Christians model their relationships on those of their Lord. Thus we reach out in concern to the low as well as the great, to those who need us as well as those we need. Christ teaches

196

us to relate to others always as unique persons made in God's image and likeness. We care for others as God cares for us. Our basic stance is that of servants of God, freely and graciously giving knowledge, assistance and care. Our competitiveness is directed against the true enemies of human well-being—poverty, loneliness, pain and meaninglessness—not against our fellow beings. Such relational servanthood will on occasion be misunderstood, demeaned or exploited by others. In the worst case we may need to seek other employment or simply commit our cause to God. However, such servanthood will more often result in the appreciation and approval of our colleagues. The servant of all may become the leader with moral and personal power if not with institutionally recognized position (Luke 22:24-27).

Third, power in the workplace depends on our communication. The cynical approach might include a quest for power through deception and falsehood. Résumés and reports might be falsified; flattery or intimidation might be communicated in a quest for advantage. But for Christians power through communication is based on "speaking the truth in love" (Ephes. 4:15; compare Ephes. 4:25, 29). God's truthful word created the world; the Word of God became flesh and lived among us (John 1). The truth of Jesus Christ sets us free. These themes govern our workplace communications, be they internal to the company or external representations of our products and services. Though there may be short-term power payoffs through deception or gossip, over the longer haul the truth will win out. One who habitually communicates the truth in love acquires long-term personal power in the workplace.

Finally, power in the workplace, as elsewhere, is partly a function of our character. Our specific actions are always important, but our character is our ongoing constellation of traits, attributes, dispositions, habits and capacities. Our character is "who we are," not just "what we do" in this or that circumstance. Our reputation may not do justice to our real character at times, but over the long haul a Christian character that is shaped by faith, hope and love, by the Beatitudes, will experience and display the power of God as we are progressively being reformed toward the image of Jesus Christ.

Structural Power

Power is never merely a personal issue. It is also a function of corporate structures and processes and of role definition and distribution (see System). People of great skill, relational and communicational excellence, and admirable character are sometimes disempowered by forces and structures larger than themselves. To the extent we are able, we need to understand and improve this corporate and structural context. Our reform efforts may be motivated by a desire to be better able to flourish in our own work. But we also must be mindful of others in our workplace who suffer from such injustice. Christians with managerial and administrative roles will be motivated to justice and fairness knowing that they, in turn, are accountable to a Master in heaven, who is invariably just, fair, liberating and loving (Ephes. 5:1).

In order to have empowered people in the workplace, employees must be given authority commensurate with their responsibility. Employees need to be assisted in the acquisition and improvement of their personal skills and placed in work roles that allow their expression. The opportunity for helpful, meaningful relationships among employees must be maintained. Communication, both speaking and listening, needs to be free and should be encouraged. The development of the whole person, that is, character and relationships, needs to be valued.

Christians, following their Lord, will exhibit special care for those with little power and weak voice, personally or culturally. Cultural habits and prejudices based on race, gender, age and other such nonwork distinctions have too often meant that some voices were unheard, some abilities untapped, some deserving promotions overlooked. Christians must not allow their practices and attitudes to be shaped by such worldly patterns (Romans 12:1-2). Our goal is to see and recognize all our colleagues with the eyes of Christ, honor each of them in the dignity bestowed by their Creator and empower them with the strength of God.

In addition to those cultural habits and prejudices that make up a large part of the organizational culture of the workplace, the official structures defining the workplace, that is, the systems and policies, should be the focus of Christian scrutiny. An empowering corporate culture will demonstrate fairness in hiring, promotion, compensation, discipline and dismissal processes (*see* Firing). If hiring, compensation, communication, decision-making and other policies are preserving a disempowering organizational structure, then these policies may need to be examined and reformed.

The Power of God and the Powers of the World

In the workplace, where many of us spend most of our lives, we desire that we and others be set free and empowered to flourish to the best of our God-given abilities. We find, however, that the powerful weight of tradition and habit, of money and production demands, of policies, laws and regulations often severely constrain our possibilities. Struggling against more than a particular organization or oppressive boss, we often experience the spiritual dominance of what the Bible calls "principalities and powers." We find ourselves in a spiritual battle, not just a personal or organizational conflict. Many of us have come home from work, even from presumably Christian workplaces, bowed down, discouraged, powerless and feeling defeated.

While the "microresponses" suggested above are important, it is essential to recall and accept the "macroperspective" on our situation. If our struggle is ultimately a spiritual battle, albeit with identifiable human elements, then our point of departure must be spiritual. Here we reconnect with the gospel of Jesus, which, while appearing weak, is truly the "power of God" (Romans 1:16; 1 Cor. 2:5). As individuals we believe that despite our weakness, we "can do all things through him [Christ] who strengthens" us (Phil. 4:13 NRSV). Moreover, we are not alone but are part of the church, which received the promise "You will receive power when the Holy Spirit has come upon you" (Acts 1:8 NRSV).

For Christians, then, power in the workplace is not just a function of personal excellence, relational skill, communication ability and solid character. Nor is gaining power simply the result of structural reforms and improved corporate character. It is fundamentally dependent on our drawing on the powerful strength of God, his Spirit and his people. We draw on these sources as we worship, as we pray, as we share our common life and struggle together on behalf of the kingdom of God.

See also ORGANIZATION; ORGANIZATIONAL CULTURE AND CHANGE; POWER; PRINCIPALITIES AND POWERS; STRUCTURES; SYSTEM

References and Resources

H. Berkhof, *Christ and the Powers,* trans. J. H. Yoder (Scottdale, Penn.: Herald, 1962); W. Diehl, *Thank God It's Monday* (Philadelphia: Fortress, 1976); H. Schleir, *Principalities and Powers in the New Testament* (New York: Herder & Herder, 1964); W. Wink, *Naming the Powers: The Language of Power in the New Testament* (Philadelphia: Fortress, 1984); W. Wink, *Unmasking the Powers: The Invisible Forces That Determine Human Existence* (Philadelphia: Fortress, 1986).

—David W. Gill

PRINCIPALITIES AND POWERS

Life in this world is not easy. Your child watches television in a neighbor's home, and you discover later that some of the material was pornographic. Your church is denied the right to expand its building because of a residents' lobby in the neighborhood. Your boss requires you to do graphic art for a business with dubious connections. The school system teaches a godless approach to all subjects including the creation of the world. Your money seems to purchase less and less because of global economic factors over which you have no power.

The reason for the complexity of life is not simply the perversity and sin of individual human beings or even the cumulative effect of all the sinners in the world, but something more systemic, something all-embracing. For every visible foreground to a person's life—embracing family, work, community service, leisure, citizenship and church—there is an invisible background that is profoundly influential. We want to do good, to serve God and our neighbor, to do an honest day's work, but we find ourselves confronted with "the system"—with frozen tradition, with intractable institutions, with deeply engrained social patterns that resist us, and, finally, with the world of spiritual beings and forces. What makes life difficult is systemic evil. In this article we will look at the biblical evidence for an invisible world that affects us both positively and negatively, consider how people interpret and experience this world and suggest some approaches to living victoriously in the battle of life.

Identifying the Powers

The trouble we experience in the world is multifaceted and comes to us through unjust or unloving structures, systems of business and finance, principles of conformity, language and social patterns, customs and traditions that marginalize the life of faith or positively oppose it, and the ever-present influence of the mass media. In addition there is the world of the spirits. All these are interdependently, systemically resistant to God's purposes in the world and dog the steps of believers. The Bible says relatively little about the ultimate source of evil. Rather it concentrates on describing the complexity of our life in this world and, most important of all, God's ultimate supremacy over all the powers. Scripture describes the realities encountered by people in their life in this world by means of various names, among them *the world, the flesh, demons, Satan, angels* and *the divine council*. This includes a variety of evil personages and forces unified under a single head, Satan, who is totally opposed to God and God's purposes in this world. The Bible also talks about *principalities and powers*.

Naming the Powers

Paul deals with the trouble of living in this world through a cluster of terms that include *power(s), thrones, authorities, virtues, dominions, names* and *thrones* (Romans 8:38; 1 Cor. 15:24; Ephes. 1:21; Ephes. 3:10; Ephes. 6:12; Col. 1:16; Col. 2:10, 15). We will explore them under the general title *principalities and powers*. Each term must be understood in the immediate context of its use and in the larger context of the Bible as a whole. *Rulers* (*archai;* Romans 8:38; 1 Cor. 15:24; Ephes. 1:21; Ephes. 6:12; Col. 1:16) refers to those in charge. The whole of this present world is under rulers who crucified Christ (1 Cor. 2:8) and who are on their way to destruction. Satan is the ruler of the kingdom of the air (Ephes. 2:2). The *authorities* (*exousiai;* Romans 13:1; 1 Cor. 15:24; Ephes. 1:21; Ephes. 6:12; Col. 1:16; Col. 2:15) are those who have the right to decide on behalf of others, generally through the entitlements of an office, administrative as well as political, local as well as imperial, as in the case of the Roman governor (Romans 13:1).

In contrast, Paul uses some phrases that appear to deal not with earthly rulers but with heavenly realms: "the powers of this dark world" (Ephes. 6:12), "the spiritual forces of evil in the heavenly realms" (Ephes. 6:12) and "the basic principles of the world" (*stoicheia;* Galatians 4:3, 8-10). *Thrones* (*thronoi;* Col. 1:16) may allude, according to intertestamental literature, to thrones occupied by angels who were created and redeemed by Christ (see Col. 1:15-20). *Powers* (*dynameis;* Romans 8:38; 1 Cor. 15:24; Ephes. 1:21) may refer to spiritual beings and the angelic armies of God, since the term is used in the Greek version of Daniel and in *1 Enoch*. *Dominions* and *lordships* (*kyriotētes;* Ephes. 1:21; Col. 1:16) may suggest "spheres of influence formerly understood to be ruled by the gods of the nations" (Reid, pp. 746-52) or the influence of idols (1 Cor. 8:5).

The interpretation of these terms has generally followed one of three lines. First, these powers are a mythic projection of the human disease onto the cosmos. Second, these powers describe structures of earthly existence: tradition, morality, justice and order. Third, these powers are sociopolitical and spiritual forces, both the outer and the inner structures of life, both the earthly and the heavenly. It is this last view that seems most persuasive.

A stunning example of how the inner and outer realities of a power are intertwined and inseparable is the case of money. Mammon is an alternative god; the name *Mammon* in Aramaic comes from the word *Amen,* which means firmness or stability. It is not surprising that a common English phrase is "the almighty dollar." As Jacques Ellul (pp. 76-77, 81, 93) shows, wealth has some of the pretended claims of deity: (1) it is capable of moving other things and claims a certain autonomy; (2) it is invested with spiritual power that can enslave us, replacing single-minded love for God and neighbor with commercial relationships in which even the soul is bought (Rev. 18:11-13); (3) it is more or less personal. So money, "unrighteous mammon" (Luke 16:9 RSV), is a form or appearance of another power (Ephes. 1:21).

So we encounter both supernatural and earthly forces in the world. These make their appeal and persuade us to give them their loyalty, sometimes appropriately as good servants of God (such as government and social structures like marriage) but usually as intransigent and unruly alternatives to the kingdom of God. It is critical to understand these powers in the light of our current social situation.

Experiencing the Powers

Fallen social structures. Many authors, some of whom are cited, understand our experience of resistance as primarily the structures of earthly life, structures that hold society together but have gone wild. These powers can best be described by anthropology, psychology and sociology. We experience these as political, financial and juridical forces (Barth); traditions, doctrines and practices that regulate religion and life (Barth); dominant images and cultural icons like Marilyn Monroe (Stringfellow); corporate institutions like GM or IBM (Stringfellow); ideologies like communism, capitalism and democracy (Stringfellow); the power of money or mammon (Ellul); and the inner aspect of all the outer manifestations of power in society (Wink). Most people writing about these are concerned with the hermeneutical question of how to identify powers in society today rather than the metaphysical question of the nature of their existence. We do not have an adequate explanation of why structures so frequently become tyrannical. But if there are inadequacies in locating the powers exclusively in the human realm of structure and tradition, there are dangers as well in locating them exclusively in the angelic and demonic.

Personal spiritual beings. This approach assumes that the heart of our experience of multilevel resistance is the presence of personal spiritual beings that are capable of purposeful activity. Representative of this approach is the following quotation of Heinrich Schleir:

> Satan and his hordes, those manifold developments and effusions of the
> spirit of wickedness with their combination of intelligence and lust for

power, exist by influencing the world and mankind in every sector and at all levels, and by making them instruments and bearers of their powers. There is nothing on earth which is absolutely immune from their power. They can occupy the human body, the human spirit, what we call "nature," and even the forms, bearers and situations of history. Even religions, including the Christian teaching, can become tools of their activity. Their spirit penetrates and overwhelms everything. (pp. 28-29)

A number of popular novels and treatments of spiritual warfare, notably the works of Frank Peretti and David Watson, take this approach. Its strength is that without these powers we lack an adequate explanation of why structures so regularly become tyrannical. Its weakness is that too often it focuses energy only on prayer and spiritual warfare instead of also working to change structures, traditions and images in a concrete way.

Western society has largely rejected the spiritual interpretation of life. Even the church has frequently turned to social analysis to find out what is going on and left out the spiritual realities behind and within the visible and present. The influence of such people as Charles Darwin in science, Sigmund Freud in psychology and Karl Marx in politics has certainly contributed to this one-dimensional view of reality. But the Christian in the world must deal with both the seen and the unseen. And Scripture witnesses to the complexity of systemic evil: structures, spiritual hosts, angels and demons, the devil and the last enemy, death (1 Cor. 15:24-27)—all arenas for Christian resistance.

Systemic evil. The approach taken here is sometimes called "the double reference" interpretation because it regards the visible human rulers and authorities as political vehicles for cosmic, invisible powers. A truly biblical theology of the powers must include the Gospels, wherein Jesus is clearly depicted as encountering evil spiritual beings (Luke 9:1) as well as structures. So in reality many of the seemingly autonomous powers are being influenced by Satan himself. And in some cases the alien power (Satan) has home rule.

The complex vision of the last book of the Bible reveals multiple (and systemically interdependent) levels of difficulty, which can be pictured as concentric circles of influence: the red dragon (Satan; Rev. 12) at the center of it all, the two beasts (Rev. 13) representing diabolical authority and supernaturalism, the harlot (Rev. 17) representing the sum total of pagan culture and Babylon (Rev. 18) as the world system. This elaborate picture shows that the Christian in the world encounters not only a multifaceted opposition but one in which there are interdependently connected dimensions. This elaborate vision in Revelation shows us that the political power of Romans 13 (then the good servant of God) has become in Rev. 13 the instrument of Satan (in this case the same government but more colonized and corrupted)—thus showing the way in which supernatural forces and personages may influence and corrupt human institutions, structures, and patterns of cultural and social life. What we encounter in public discipleship is systemic evil, interconnected realms of dissent that do not operate in isolation from one another.

Understanding the Powers

Good theology can help us make sense of our life in this world and equip us to live victoriously. Scripture shows that God has both visible and invisible servants. All were created good. All have been corrupted. All have been substantially redeemed by Christ's saving work. All are personally ambiguous in the work they do. All will be finally and fully redeemed in the last day when Christ comes again and transfers the kingdoms of this world to the Father.

The good powers. Far from being the result of the Fall and a necessary evil to protect us from ourselves, these powers are part of God's *good* creation. They are not innately evil. They are made by Christ and for Christ! Paul claims that through Christ "all things were created: things in heaven and on earth, visible and invisible, whether thrones or powers or rulers or authorities; all things were created by him and for him" (Col. 1:16). This, as Hendrik Berkhof brilliantly describes it, is the invisible background of creation, "the dikes with which God encircles His good creation, to keep it in His fellowship and protect it from chaos" (p. 28). They were intended to form a framework in which we live out our lives for God's glory. Four such frameworks are marriage, family, nation and law, each ordained by God for our good. For example, without marriage and family, relationships would become meaningless; children would grow without the shelter of marriage.

The fallen and colonized powers. Along with some supernatural beings (2 Peter 2:4; Jude 6:2), these same structures have become broken, hostile and resistant to God's rule. Ephes. 6 claims we should resist these fallen powers as part of our daily existence. There will be no cessation of this spiritual conflict until Christ comes again or until we depart to be with Christ, whichever comes first. Some of these powers have taken on a life of their own, making idolatrous claims on human beings: government, religion, culture, various "isms" symbolized in the names and titles that dominate the news (Galatians 4:8-9; Ephes. 1:21). In Ephes. 6 Paul suggests these powers have been "colonized" (though the term is not used) by Satan himself.

The overpowered powers. No Old Testament passage is quoted as frequently in the New Testament as Psalm 110:1, which declares that all the powers have been subjugated by the Messiah-Christ. Throughout the Gospels Jesus is seen as supreme over the evil spirits. He casts out demons by the finger of God (Luke 11:20); he destroys the power of Satan (Matthew 12:26; Mark 3:23-26; Luke 11:18); he enters the strong man's house and plunders his goods (Mark 3:27). This extraordinary power of Jesus to overpower the powers is delegated to his followers (Matthew 10:1; Mark 3:14-15; Mark 6:7; Luke 9:1-2; Luke 10:1). Paul's further development of this elaborates the extensiveness of Christ's work now that he has died and been resurrected.

Paul variously describes how the hostile powers have been subjugated: they have been abrogated, stripped, led in triumphal procession or into captivity, made to genuflect, pacified or reconciled (1 Cor. 15:24-26; Ephes. 1:22; Ephes. 4:8-10; Phil. 2:10; Col. 1:20; Col. 2:15). Drawing on the three phrases of Col. 2:15, Berkhof points out three things Christ did to the powers. First, Christ made a public example of them. What once were considered to be fundamental realities are not seen as rivals and adversaries of God (Berkhof, p. 38). As divine irony, the title "King of the Jews" was placed over the cross in the three languages representing the powers that crucified Jesus: Hebrew (the language of religion), Latin (the language of government) and Greek (the language of culture). By volunteering to be victimized by the powers through his death and thus using the powers to accomplish a mighty saving act, Jesus put them in their place as instruments of God rather than autonomous regents, showing how illusionary are their pretended claims. Second, Christ triumphed over them, the resurrection being proof that Jesus is stronger than the powers, including the power of death (1 Cor. 15:26; Hebrews 2:15). Third, Christ disarmed the powers, stripping them of the power and authority by which they deceived the world, namely, the illusion that they are godlike and all-powerful and that devotion to them is the ultimate goal of life.

Oscar Cullman compares the powers to chained beasts kicking themselves to death. Between the resurrection of Jesus and the Second Coming they are tied to a rope, still free to evince their demonic character but nevertheless bound. Cullman used a helpful analogy to explain the tension. D-Day was the day during World War II when the beaches of Normandy were invaded and the battle was turned. One could say the war was "won" that day even though there were months of battling ahead and many lives still to be lost. V-Day was the day of final victory. Christ's coming and death represent D-Day, but we must still live in the overlap of the ages as we wait for the final consummation of the kingdom at the Second Coming of Christ (Cullman, p. 84).

Grappling with the Powers

There are four historic approaches to the powers, all of which have their place in Christian mission: (1) exorcism and intercession, (2) suffering powerlessness, (3) creative participation and (4) just revolution (*see* Structures). The church, however, must engage in a full-orbed approach, which includes discernment among other approaches.

Discernment. The Prayer Book of the Anglican and the Episcopal Church provides a handy summary of our multifaceted problem: "the world, the flesh and the devil." Each must be fought differently. We deal with the spirit of the world through nonconformity with it and conformity with the will of God (Romans 12:2). We deal with our lower nature by mortification (identifying with Christ's crucifixion) and aspiration (breathing in the Spirit). We deal with the devil by resisting and fleeing (James 4:7; Rev. 12:11). It is a multifronted battle. And our Lord meets us at each of these fronts: *transfiguring us* from within (Romans 12:2) so we can transform, rather than be conformed by, the world as we penetrate it in our work and mission; *bearing Spirit fruit* through us (Galatians 5:22, 25) as we determine to walk in the Spirit and regard the flesh as crucified; and *overcoming the evil one,* the devil (Rev. 12:10), as we put on Christ's armor through all kinds of prayer (Ephes. 6:13-18).

Prayer. Karl Barth once said that "to clasp the hands in prayer is the beginning of an uprising against the disorder of the world" (quoted in Leech, p. 68; see James 4:7; Rev. 12:10-11). Paul uses an elaborate metaphor for arming ourselves in Ephes. 6:10-18 by referring to the armor worn by a Roman soldier. The belt of truth means living with integrity. The breastplate of righteousness involves having right relations with God and living righteously. The "go" of the gospel implies that we are ready and "on the way" to share the gospel—there is more than defense here! The shield of faith deflects the enemy's attacks, and the helmet of salvation brings assurance to our minds that we belong to a God who will never divorce us. The sword of the Spirit is the Word of God, read, obeyed and spoken. All these are ways of "putting on Christ": Christ's righteousness, Christ's message, Christ's faith, Christ's finished work on the cross and Christ's Word. All of these are put on by prayer: prayer on all occasions and all kinds of prayer (Ephes. 6:18).

Preaching the gospel. The first and most effective strategy against the false claims of the powers is preaching the gospel. Our duty is not to bring the powers to *our* knees: this is Christ's task. Our duty is to arm ourselves with Christ (Ephes. 6:10-18) and to preach his cross. However much we attempt to "Christianize" the powers, we must not bypass preaching the gospel and calling people to embrace the reign of Christ through repentance and faith. Some of these powers deserve the loyal submission of Christians (Romans 13:1). Some of them should be Christianized by the involvement of Christians and the church in creational and re-creational tasks: directing the resources of the world in education, politics and culture to serve human beings as defined by God's intention. Some powers will be unmasked by the martyrdom of faithful believers (Rev. 12:11).

Public discipleship. Christ's complete victory over the principalities and powers, over Satan, sin and death, assures us that there is nowhere in the universe so demonic that a Christian might not be called to serve there. We fight a war that is already won. Therefore as far as is now possible, Christians should Christianize the powers, pacify the powers through involvement in education, government and social action, all the while knowing that the task of subjugating them is reserved for Christ alone (Ephes. 1:10; Phil. 2:10-11). We work on the problems of pollution, food distribution, injustice, genetic engineering and the proliferation of violence and weaponry, knowing that this work is ministry and holy. In the short run our contribution may seem unsuccessful, but in the long run it will be gloriously successful because we are cooperating with what Christ wants to do in renewing all creation.

Living with practical heavenly-mindedness. Jürgen Moltmann spoke of eschatology, or the "end times," as the most pastoral of all theological disciplines because it shows us that we are living at the dawning of a new day rather than at the sunset of human history (p. 31). Keeping the end times in view is critical to grappling victoriously with the powers: it shows us that work done in this world is not resultless but, in some way beyond our imagination, contributes to a world without end. Eschatology also liberates us from a messianic complex (or inappropriate egoism), since the future is ultimately in God's hands. The kingdom will come to consummation in God's own way and time. Lesslie Newbigin comments on this with great depth:

We can commit ourselves without reserve to all the secular work our shared humanity requires of us, knowing that nothing we do in itself is good enough to form part of that city's building, knowing that everything—from our most secret prayers to our most public political acts—is part of that sin-stained human nature that must go down into the valley of death and judgment, and yet knowing that as we offer it up to the Father in the name of Christ and in the power of the Spirit, it is safe with him and—purged in fire—it will find its place in the holy city at the end. (p. 136)

See also ORGANIZATION; ORGANIZATIONAL CULTURE AND CHANGE; ORGANIZATIONAL VALUES; POWER; POWER, WORKPLACE; STRUCTURES; SYSTEM

References and Resources

M. Barth, *Ephesians,* 2 vols., Anchor Bible (Garden City, N.Y.: Doubleday, 1974); P. L. Berger, *The Sacred Canopy: Elements of a Sociological Theory of Religion* (Garden City, N.Y.: Doubleday, 1967); H. Berkhof, *Christ and the Powers,* trans. J. H. Yoder (Scottdale, Penn.: Herald, 1962); G. B. Caird, *Principalities and Powers: A Study in Pauline Theology* (Oxford: Clarendon, 1956); O. Cullman, *Christ and Time: The Primitive Christian Conception of Time and History,* trans. F. V. Filson (London: SCM, 1951); J. Ellul, *Money and Power,* trans. L. Neff (Downers Grove, Ill.: InterVarsity Press, 1984); J. Moltmann, *Theology of Hope,* trans. J. W. Leitch (New York: Harper & Row, 1967); K. Leech, *True Prayer: An Invitation to Christian Spirituality* (San Francisco: Harper & Row, 1980); R. Mouw, *Politics and Biblical Drama* (Grand Rapids: Eerdmans, 1976); L. Newbigin, *Honest Religion for Secular Man* (Philadelphia: Fortress, 1966); D. G. Reid, "Principalities and Powers," in *Dictionary of Paul and His Letters,* ed. G. F. Hawthorne, R. Martin and D. G. Reid (Downers Grove, Ill.: InterVarsity Press, 1993) 746-52; H. Schleir, *Principalities and Powers in the New Testament* (New York: Herder & Herder, 1964); J. S. Stewart, *A Faith to Proclaim* (London: Hodder & Stoughton, 1953); W. Stringfellow, *An Ethic for Christians and Other Aliens in a Strange Land* (Waco, Tex.: Word, 1973); W. Stringfellow, *Free in Obedience* (New York: Seabury, 1964); W. Wink, *Engaging the Powers: Discernment and Resistance in a World of Domination* (Minneapolis: Fortress, 1992); W. Wink, *Naming the Powers: The Language of Power in the New Testament* (Philadelphia: Fortress, 1984); W. Wink, *Unmasking the Powers: The Invisible Forces That Determine Human Existence* (Philadelphia: Fortress, 1986); J. H. Yoder, *The Politics of Jesus* (Grand Rapids: Eerdmans, 1972).

—R. Paul Stevens

PROFESSIONS/PROFESSIONALISM

The professionalization of work, one of the characteristics of modern society, is a matter about which Christians can profitably reflect. Sociologists speak of the professionalization of everyone (Wilensky, pp. 137-58) and everything from housecleaning to car repairs. But can everyone and everything be professionalized? The word *professional* is difficult to define. The idea has Christian roots, and Christians, both professional and nonprofessional, have reason not only to reflect on this occupational trend but to respond with appropriate Christian action. This article will explore the Christian roots of professions, the difficulty of defining professionalism in modern life, the dangers of professionalism and a Christian response.

Christian Roots

Prior to A.D. 500 the generic term *profession* (*pro-fateri;* to confess, own, acknowledge) was understood only in a religious sense. Both office bearers in the church and ordinary members profess their allegiance to Christ, to the gospel and to service in God's kingdom. Though such "professions" were predated by the oath of Hippocrates and the claims of shamans to understand the mysteries of life and death, it is substantially true that "the mother of all the learned professions is the church" (Reader, p. 11). In the New Testament we read about professing godliness (1 Tim. 2:10) and professing the gospel (1 Tim. 6:12). A professional is therefore someone who makes a public declaration of service to God. In a special sense the medieval church used *profession* for the vow of poverty, chastity and obedience made by those entering the religious life, thus creating a religious professional elite. Reacting to this, Luther recovered the biblical universality of calling, insisting that all, and not just priests, nuns and monks, were called of God.

The modern world has secularized this idea of a holy calling from something with a divine source outside oneself to an occupation with a special status and special responsibilities. To be a professional is the opposite of an amateur. Instead of professing to serve God, the modern professional claims a unique role that brings him or her deep fulfillment. In answer to the question of what is professed, E. C. Hughes says, "They profess to know better than others the nature of certain matters, to know better than their clients what ails them or their affairs" (p. 1). George Bernard Shaw made one of his characters say that every profession is a conspiracy against the laity. It is vitally important to consider whether this is true.

Defining Professions and Professionalism

A broad outline of the traits of a profession include the following: (1) it is a full-time occupation (amateurs might do the same thing as an avocation); (2) it is viewed loosely as a *calling,* that is, an occupation that places behavioral and ethical demands on the person who engages in it; (3) it is based on special, often esoteric, knowledge that usually involves training of exceptional duration; (4) it is regulated by a credentialing process usually administered by a peer organization and thus excludes those not so trained; (5) it is dedicated to the service of the community and is not intrinsically self-serving; (6) it allows professionals considerable autonomy as they exercise their own judgment and authority. In practice this leads to an elitist occupation.

Wilbert E. Moore says, "The bond established by shared mysteries, exemplified in technical language and common styles of work and even common attire, bespeaks a consciousness of being set apart" (p. 9). Thus, in the modern world, not only doctors (who in England were long denied professional status because of the manual skills involved in surgery) and lawyers but engineers, accountants, the clergy and (increasingly) managers are accorded a professional status. Further, in a technological society tradespeople with esoteric skills in repairing computers, for example, have become professionalized.

The sixfold "trait" definition of a profession has been attacked by those who question the service role of professions and single out other distinguishing marks. One is wealth. While the original idea is that a professional does not work for pay but rather is paid to work, the high level of remuneration is now viewed commonly as a distinguishing mark and a motivating reason for entrance into a profession. Another mark is education; the professional is first and foremost an educated human being. To this Alfred North Whitehead said that "the term profession means an avocation whose activities are subjected to theoretical analysis, and are modified by theoretical conclusions derived from that analysis" (quoted in Hoitenga, p. 302). Since the 1960s, however, a third mark has been highlighted—power.

Professional help, it is claimed, leads to dependence on the part of clients and therefore disables rather than enables them (De Vries, p. 153). The emotional neutrality so widely promoted by professionals leads to less care than that given by those who simply love, that is, amateurs (those who work for love, as the original meaning implies). Ivan Illich calls for the abolition of occupational expertise not, as Adam Smith and Karl Marx do, because of its effect on the workers but because of what it does to the consumers (Freidson, p. 13). So added to the difficulty of defining what occupations may be called professions is this further confusion of whether professions and professionalization are good things.

Advantages

After considering the question of whether professions are necessary, Eliot Freidson makes a case for expertise, credentials and the institutionalizing of professional standards. There is simply not enough time in life to learn every form of expertise. Professions are based on a division of labor, so fundamental to a developed society. Such a division expresses a functional difference and not necessarily a difference in value and worth. Further, since ideas and skills cannot be advanced without becoming institutionalized, some form of credentialing is needed to protect society's members from the disaster of ill-informed choices (Freidson, pp. 22-23).

208

Still, the dangers of professionalization are all too apparent. Professional life can corrupt the soul of the very Christians who take up the challenge of serving God's redeeming purpose in the world, not just in the church.

Dangers

The autonomy of professional life, based as it is on advanced knowledge, all too easily leads to smug self-reliance, pride of place and position. Among God's covenant people even a king must "not consider himself better than his brothers" (Deut. 17:20) nor "accumulate large amounts of silver and gold" (Deut. 17:17).

The structure of professional life rewards success and all too easily leads to a meritocracy in which service gives way to a psychology of entitlement. Success blinds professionals to the reality that grace is Christ's gift to the broken, the needy, the blind and the wretched. Human achievement gets scant mention in the Bible. Scripture offers a theology of response to God's achievements rather than to human expertise, of wisdom rather than success, of service rather than power. Without love, excellence all too easily becomes an idol. Technique may be safely learned only when one has determined in the heart that love is the most essential thing.

Because of the sacrifices they have undertaken in their long educational preparation, professionals all too often come to believe they deserve a special status and higher income (Hatch, p. 97). Frequently professionals find their identity in their work and measure their worth by what they do, rather than by who (or more important, whose) they are.

We require a deeper analysis of what is wrong with the professions. Christians diagnosing the problems of the world usually concentrate on hunger, poverty and war. But systemic evil is more complex and comprehensive. The principalities and powers (Ephes. 6:12-13) that Christians daily battle range from fallen social structures to the demonic. The very structure of professionalism in our society reflects not only the fallen human nature of those who have polluted the original vision of people professing Christ in their work, but systemic disorder. The result is that the very institutions established to serve others now serve themselves. Christians take their places in the world with hope but not easily. The hope involves living as a Christian amateur even while serving within a profession. This is especially difficult for those who are called to the professional ministry.

Christian Amateurs

The term *professional Christian* makes no theological sense at all. At heart Christians are amateurs who serve for the love of God, the love of serving and the love of those they serve. Three things militate against the professionalization of Christian service: one cannot be a Christian for a living; one cannot be a part-time follower of Christ; one cannot base one's discipleship on peer review. *Professional ministry* itself is an oxymoron. *Ministry* is service to God and others marked by faith, hope and love. No one can be a specialist with God, though four basic models of ministry in history offer patterns of presumed specialization: (1) the sacramental model based on credentialing through ordination, (2) the cloistered religious model of monasticism, (3) the learned pastor model that has arisen since the Renaissance and (4) the organizational model of contemporary management culture. Each model offers a criterion for excellence and elitism. But it is questionable whether pastoral, missionary or parachurch service should be regarded as a professional career to be pursued for life (*see* Financial Support).

The professionalization of ministry may have some benefits (Noyce, pp. 975-76), but it normally contributes to the tragic and unscriptural dualism of laity and clergy, unless of course we return to the original meaning of professional as one who professes faith, hope, love and justice. At the heart of Christian leadership is the idea of giving away everything one has in order to equip all the saints for the work of ministry (Ephes. 4:11-12; *see* Equipping). Further, Christian ministry is never a one-way delivery system undertaken by highly trained experts but a mutual enrichment and empowerment (Romans 1:12). The recovery of a true amateur motivation is essential to the recovery of integrity in Christian ministry. But this is not the only way Christians may respond to the crisis of professionalism.

Recovering True Professionalism

One contribution the church can make is the humanization of professional education. John Stuart Mill once said,

> Men are men before they are lawyers, or physicians, or merchants, or manufacturers. . . . What professional men should carry away with them from the University, is not professional knowledge, but that which should direct the use of other professional knowledge, and bring the light of general culture to illuminate the technicalities of a special pursuit. (quoted in Hoitenga, p. 303)

Having lost the Christian (and therefore humanizing, though not humanist) foundation, the modern university has become a multiversity. Christians have the prophetic task of proclaiming a worldview for professional life that is fully integrated and includes moral education, the development of character and personal mentoring, all facets of professional education that preceded the present technical career preparation. The professional must be a person, a whole person.

Traditional professions were rooted in a special brotherhood of people who regarded their service as a special calling and *therefore* were worthy of trust by clients, patients and parishioners. The order of priority has been reversed in modern life. Professionals are expected to provide excellence in service as measured by standards, thus resulting in trust. The shift from interpersonal trust based on personal integrity to technical competence guaranteed by credentials is signaled by the widespread use of advertising to identify professional services and assure confidence in their use. Even if it were desirable, it is unrealistic to attempt to turn the clock back and eliminate the need for professional standards. Nevertheless, developing persons of integrity remains the greatest challenge in professional education and life. The Christian faith, with its emphasis on maturity as the master educational concept (Ephes. 4:13), is eminently relevant.

One of the hallmarks of professional life is excellence. The Christian serving in professional life in a so-called secular career will strive for the best. But excellence is not the goal or even the measure of Christian service, whether in church leadership or business management. Love is that goal: "If I . . . surrender my body to the flames, but have not love, I gain nothing" (1 Cor. 13:3). Emotional neutrality and professional impassivity will lead to a lower quality of care than that given in love. Love empowers and serves even when there is no immediate financial reward or even the reward of visible results. Indeed, the results of our lives are not seen in this life. So the Christian professional, who is simultaneously an amateur, lives by faith, hope and love. In doing so, Christians can recover the original meaning of *professionals* as people who profess a holy calling.

See also CALLING; CAREER; INTEGRITY; ORGANIZATION; POWER; SERVICE; TRADES; WORK

References and Resources

J. W. Carroll, "The Professional Model of Ministry—Is It Worth Saving?" *Theological Education* (Spring 1985) 7-48; A. M. Carr-Saunders and P. M. Wilson, *The Professions* (New York: Oxford University Press, 1933); R. G. De Vries, "Christian Responsibility in Professional Society: A Reply to Hoitenga," *Christian Scholar's Review* 13, no. 2 (1984) 151-57; E. Freidson, "Are Professions Necessary?" in *The Authority of Experts,* ed. T. L. Haskell (Bloomington: Indiana University Press, 1984) 1-14; N. O. Hatch, "The Perils of Being a Professional," *Christianity Today* 35, no. 13 (1991) 96-97; D. J. Hoitenga, "Christianity and the Professions," *Christian Scholars Review* 10, no. 4 (1981) 296-309; E. C. Hughes, "Professions," in *The Professions in America,* ed. K. S. Lynn (Boston: Beacon Press, 1965); I. Illich, "Useful Unemployment and Its Professional Enemies," in *Toward a Theology of Needs* (New York: Bantam New Age Books, 1980); D. B. Kraybill and P. P. Good, eds., *Perils of Professionalism* (Scottdale, Penn.: Herald, 1982); W. E. Moore, *The Professions: Roles and Rules* (New York: Russell Sage, 1970); G. Noyce, "The Pastor Is (Also) a Professional," *Christian Century* 105, no. 21 (1988) 975-76; W. J. Reader, *Professional Men: The Rise of the Professional Classes in Nineteenth Century England* (New York: Basic Books, 1966); H. L. Wilensky, "The Professionalization of Everyone?" *American Journal of Sociology* 70, no. 2 (1964/1965) 137-58.

—R. Paul Stevens

PROFIT

Profit, as defined by the accounting profession, is the excess of a business's total revenues over total costs. Economists define *pure profit* as the amount of money remaining after making all payments for productive services and raw materials after the going rate of payments for the capital invested has been deducted. Profit is the estimated claim on wealth that can be used as capital for new efforts to create wealth.

THE MARKETPLACE MINISTRY HANDBOOK

A Christian perspective on profit requires a correct understanding of what profit actually is, how it is created, who has a just claim on it and what role it plays in a business, all in the context of a biblical understanding of human nature, stewardship, justice and community.

Understanding Profit

Profit in an organization must be understood in the context of the productivity of capital. In the long term, the return on invested capital must exceed the cost of capital to the organization. If the firm fails to do this, it is technically a destroyer of all kinds of wealth in society—finances, intellect and humanity.

The corporation does not exist for its own survival. Business organizations are organized as stewards of resources to meet needs and aspirations in society. Every organization has a vocation, a specific reason for existence (*see* Calling). The primary vocation of business is the production of goods and services to sustain and enhance the human experience, thus contributing to the fulfillment of the cultural mandate given to us in creation (Genesis 1:28-30). The measure of the organization's fidelity to that vocation is the value it creates in society. As a member of an interlocking system of associations, business organizations exist for the common good and ultimately will be judged by the degree to which they cooperate with God in implementing his purposes for creation.

If an organization produces a product or service that does not fulfill a need or aspiration, it loses its legitimate reason for existence. Companies exist only as they continue to benefit customers. When they no longer create goods or services that are valued, they will be unable to create profit and will cease to exist. For example, the makers of buggies ceased to exist when customers no longer chose the horse as the primary means of transportation.

Profit and the Purpose of Business

Fundamentally, the purpose of business is to create a customer, not to make a profit. But when they are properly functioning, organizations will make a profit. This differentiation between purpose and function is critical for Christians who are trying to reflect on how they are called to express their faith in the workplace. Function focuses on economic criteria while purpose asks, Profit for what reason?

Profit is perhaps best understood analogously: profit to a business is like blood to a person. Just as persons cannot live without blood, organizations cannot live without profit. Just as healthy persons do not live *for* their blood, organizations do not live *for* profit. They cannot live without it, but do not live for it. In the same way, we eat to live rather than live to eat. Organizations must have profit to guarantee their survival. Nevertheless, any discussion of profit must first be placed in the philosophical framework of the mission or purpose of the organization. We need additional criteria besides profit for measuring a company's performance.

How Profit Is Created

The creation of profit begins with the production of goods and services that fulfil human needs. Taken from the user's perspective, the customer is the ultimate definer of value. In a market economy, customers exchange money for the value created by the goods or services.

Creating value for the customer, however, is not the same thing as creating profit for the organization. Profit from the firm's perspective is the incremental value that exceeds the cost of creating that value. So how do companies create a profit? The first determinant of this is how they create revenue. In a market economy, customers are free to purchase what they value. In the short run, the greatest influence on what price they pay is demand. The availability of the particular good in the context of its demand will determine the transaction price. But over the long term in a competitive market economy with access to information, the cost of production is the major driver of the transaction price. Taken together, demand and cost of production seem to establish the transaction price as simply "what the market will bear."

Although economists generally affirm that a just price is what the market will bear, Christians are required to reflect on this in light of the biblical message. Is there such a thing as an unethical amount of profit on a transaction?

Profit and Justice

Underlying the transaction by which the customer exchanges money for goods or services is the issue of justice, specifically commutative justice, which prohibits doing harm. Justice is a primary expression of vocation for all Christians in the marketplace. For an exchange to be just, both the seller and the buyer must receive an equivalence of exchange. To accomplish this, both must be empowered with equal competence. The price must not be established because the buyer is ignorant and uninformed about the product or service. This is the purpose of advertising. Assuming a noncoercive environment, a free exchange should take place. The seller offers a value that fulfills a need in the customer for which the customer willingly pays. In the coercive world of advertising this free exchange is usually compromised.

The biblical framework for this evaluation is covenant and justice in the context of community. Covenant implies a relationship that exists to serve the well-being of all parties to it, including the communities in which the organizations serve. They serve their neighbor with the exchange of goods and the promise that the customer will receive the goods they were promised. As Karl Marx insisted, justice in the business covenant concerns fair play not only with the customer but also with the producer. He argued that companies do so by purchasing the one commodity that can create a value greater than its own—labor power. Marx tried to dispel the illusion that laborers were well paid for their work. Labor creates value, and when it is not remunerated it is being exploited. What Marx failed to discern is that capital is never produced by labor alone, but rather reproduces itself. The amount of profit is determined not only by the price the customer pays but also by the value of the labor and the productivity of capital. So we must think deeply about not only just compensation for labor but also the stewardship of resources, especially the capital entrusted to the corporation.

Business as Stewardship

In economics, the ultimate cost of any product is the nonuse of resources for some other end. This principle is known as "alternative cost" analysis. If a firm fails to create a return in excess of its cost of capital, in the long run it is destroying the wealth that was entrusted to it. Consequently, it is the responsibility of the board of directors and stockholders of the organization—as stewards of the previously existing capital—to ensure that the resources are being deployed so that the capital reproduces itself for future sustenance. This responsibility is not just for the stockholders but also for employees, customers, suppliers and the communities in which they live and work. In the long run, all of these "stakeholders" are harmed if the organization fails to deploy its capital effectively.

The other justice and stewardship issue is the cost of labor. In the short run, as in the case of prices, the relationship of supply and demand determines the cost of labor to the firm. The *minimum subsistence level theory* (what was later referred to as the "iron law of wages") was developed by Anne Robert Jacques Turgot in 1766. This theory held that competition among workers lowers the wage to the minimum subsistence level. Wages are determined by what is required for the support of the laborer in the short run. Over the longer term, it has been argued that wages are determined by a "standard of living" which reflects the laborers' psychological requirement for sustaining family life. If wages fall below that level, the rate of growth of the working population would be negative, and decline in the labor supply would over time raise wages.

While this helps clarify how wages move over time, economic justice requires that we consider our responsibility to the whole person. Work that engages the whole person should enable the worker to provide for his or her family. Additionally, work has value beyond financial remuneration. Our calling to be coworkers with God in the world means that we have been imbued with authority and decision-making capacity. Therefore, we will consider not only the instrumental value of work to the worker and the company—wages and productive service—but also the intrinsic value of the work in the development of the whole person.

A further theological issue is what to do with profit. When the firm creates profit in excess of its cost-of-capital, to whom should the surplus go and what criteria should be used to distribute it?

Distributing Profit

The potential recipients of this "pure profit" are the stakeholders referred to above: stockholders, employees, customers, suppliers and communities. We must distribute "surplus profit" in a way congruent with the biblical witness that balances responsibilities, risk and return.

214

Stockholders entrust their capital to an organization. By doing so, they should be compensated for the opportunities foreclosed by trusting their savings to one organization over another (*see* Investment). Any profit less than "pure profit" belongs to the stockholders, who are not being justly compensated for their investment until the "profit" level equals the rate of return captured in the cost of capital.

To determine what responsibilities the company has to distribute surplus profit to the stockholders, the following issues must be considered: First, what is the level of risk in the industry? Second, did the stockholders forgo any return during a start-up period? Have all the aggregate requirements for return on capital been realized? (Capital is continuous as opposed to a sunk cost, so no static period for defining value can ever be absolute.) Third, what is the relationship among the stakeholders for creating value? Is an ongoing access to capital the primary sustainer of competitive advantage? Is the business a capital-intensive business as opposed to a labor-intensive business? (If so, it is equitable for those who are the providers of capital to be rewarded and to receive the highest return, as they are the most responsible for its success and have taken the greatest risk.)

Now we must consider whether employees should share in the profit. Profit sharing for employees is growing in popularity for utilitarian purposes; that is, it seems to work. But there is a more important reason. From the perspective of justice and community, profit sharing links performance to the community. Each member is independent and contributes to the communal well-being. Consequently, each person feels some measure of accountability for results. Because we were created as relational people, being accountable and responsible for the effort of the community as a whole correctly aligns the individual and the community in a consistent way. We were created to live and work in this way—for the common good.

How much profit relative to other stakeholders should go to employees is dependent on the following issues: First, is the business a labor-intensive business? Is the primary value related to the efforts of the employees, or is the business an extremely capital-intensive business? And second, what is the level of risk associated for the employee—physical, psychological and in terms of time or lost opportunities for the future? (Employees also have a "cost-of-capital" in that their labor value is at risk when they join a firm. They forgo future opportunities for developing their skills and knowledge when they commit themselves to an organization. Employees should be justly rewarded for that commitment when it creates exceptional profit.)

Suppliers are part of the independent community of the organization and therefore have a stake in the performance of a firm. Relationships with suppliers should be structured to reward them for the value they bring to the company. If the work of a particular supplier is a major strategic advantage, then their compensation should include access in some way to the profit they help create. This clearly enhances the relationship between the two organizations and creates the sense of common unity.

The communities where an organization conducts business are also responsible for the success of the organization. School systems, social services and arts programs all play a role in shaping the capacities and character of the employees. Additionally, they all have a stake in the ongoing success of the firm.

Customers also have a stake in the firm because they depend on it to meet their needs. Therefore, the firm has a responsibility to reinvest future funds to ensure its ability to continue to service the needs of customers. In these ways all stakeholders should share in the profits of a business.

Conclusion

Some have argued that business has no social responsibility other than making a profit ethically. This fails to understand the systemic nature of the economy and human community. A business does not operate in a vacuum but is the recipient of shared cultural and intellectual wealth and is accountable to the community. As a major influence on life in today's society, business has a responsibility to reflect on what that means. It is strategically positioned in society to express justice, covenant community and stewardship. In so doing, business can fulfill its calling and serve God's purposes on earth for the good of humankind and creation.

—Donald E. Flow

PROMOTION

Many employees have the ambition to advance into positions of greater responsibility within their organization. As organizations grow and senior employees retire, positions open up in the organization into which employees can be promoted. If the number of openings match the aspirations of eager employees, everyone is happy. The problem is that this seldom happens. Advancement in an organization seldom comes as soon or as rapidly as aspiring employees wish. Nor do the needs of the organization always fit the skills and experience of these eager employees. In both cases frustration may result.

Advantages and Disadvantages of Promotion

Promotion has some positive dimensions and advantages. First, the opportunity to advance is a high motivator; as a consequence, the organization benefits by the work of zealous workers. Second, the organization benefits by the infusion of new ideas and enthusiasm as younger employees work their way up the organizational chart. Third, a promotion is a clear indication of the worth of an employee and an affirmation of his or her good performance. It gives an employee the opportunity to grow and use his or her talents to the greater benefit of all. Fourth, promotions bring with them increased earnings at a time when younger families have growing financial needs.

Promotion also has negative dimensions and disadvantages. First, as some employees are passed over in promotions, motivation fades and negativism or indifference may develop to the detriment of the organization. Second, while promotions bring youthful thinking and enthusiasm into the organization, there may be a loss of experience as senior employees leave. Third, the self-esteem of those who are not promoted may fall, and this may spill over into other parts of their lives. Failure to win a promotion may be seen by the employee, the family and others as failure in life. Fourth, some promotions require transfer to another location. If the employee has a working spouse, the decision to accept the promotion will certainly be influenced by the spouse's ability to move also. If children are involved, the move can be traumatic for them. In some organizations, to turn down a promotion for family reasons eliminates the employee from ever again being offered a promotion. Finally, the principle of earning a promotion as a result of hard work is contrary to the theological principle of God's assurance that we are accepted (saved) by our Creator without any merit of our own. The assurance of the grace of God is difficult to accept in a workplace where good performance is the key to promotions.

Unwise or Unfair Promotions

Up to this point, the premise has been that promotions come as the result of good performance. But what if that's not the case? What if I am a member of a union where the contract with management clearly states that promotions will be based on seniority? A poor performer in my work group will be promoted ahead of me, even though she knows nothing about the job, simply because of seniority. To add insult to injury, I may be assigned to train this person. Is this fair?

Apart from union situations, my superior performance may be overlooked in favor of a less qualified worker whom my supervisor happens to like. Sometimes outside pressure is put on my supervisor to promote a poorer performer (see Office Politics). Or perhaps I am passed over in favor of a female, minority or handicapped person in order to correct the organization's past discriminatory practices against such persons. In order to reduce costs, some companies promote junior, lower-paid employees at the expense of more senior, higher-paid workers. This practice can result in age discrimination suits brought by disgruntled employees who have been passed over. Not to receive a promotion for any of the reasons above, when one knows that one's performance has been outstanding, can be dispiriting.

There are other realities at work that can be even more dispiriting. As organizations "downsize" (see Firing) or "right size" in order to reduce costs, entire departments may be abolished. Not only is the job into which I had hoped to be promoted gone, but my *present* job is gone. I am given the opportunity to accept a demotion into another part of the company or accept a special separation package and leave. A similar situation can result from mergers or acquisitions. The reality of life is that for many workers high performance and good experience do *not* result in a promotion.

Managing Promotions

Some managers, in an effort to get greater productivity, intentionally set up competition between two contenders for a promotion. It is quite commonly done at the top levels of business corporations. But regardless of the level in the organization, such competition can become destructive. The competitors can put all their time and energy into their work at the expense of family life and their own health. Such competition can even spill over into the defamation of the other's character and competence. It can become so vicious that when the winner receives his/her sought-for promotion, the loser feels obliged to leave the company.

The Peter Principle says that people are promoted to their level of incompetency. There is a great deal of truth to this statement, but the fault lies much more with those who did the promoting than those who were promoted. Management can make a number of errors in the process of deciding upon a promotion.

First, it is difficult *not* to reward a star employee with a promotion into the first level of management. But it may be a mistake. The example most frequently cited is the promotion of a star salesperson into a terrible sales manager. While selling and managing both require people skills, managers help others to work effectively while salespersons do the work themselves. The same problem can arise in promoting research scientists, computer analysts, teachers, doctors, social service providers and many others into management positions. Management should not assume that the star performers will become star managers. Perhaps a mediocre salesperson can become a top-notch sales manager.

A second fault of top management is in not providing enough training for the job into which someone is promoted. Doing computer analysis is much different from managing computer analysts. In making such a transition, it is not only wise but a matter of justice to give the employee professional help in how to be a manager. It is interesting to note that the higher one goes in an organization, the less training one gets in a promotion. It is assumed that the senior vice president in the law department will know how to be an effective president. Sometimes this is true, sometimes not.

Persons moving into their first management position encounter the problem of how to deal with their former peers. As one among equals in their work group, these new managers used to socialize freely with certain members of the group. Some were very good friends; perhaps one was the new manager's very best friend. In the new role the manager cannot have personal favorites. Will the group accept and respect the new role their former coworker has been given? And what about the best friend? Can the new manager frankly and openly address the best friend's performance weaknesses? Will the new manager try to maintain the best-friend relationship off the job but lay it aside on the job? Will it work?

Refusing Promotions

Up to this point we have assumed that all workers want and will accept a promotion. Such is not always the case. As indicated earlier, if a promotion involves a move to a new location and the interests of a spouse and/or children must be considered, an employee may elect not to accept the promotion. At times this may happen in favor of retaining links with the local church to which one is strongly committed or from which one is presently gaining some greater benefit. More and more organizations are trying to reduce the problem by helping locate a job for the spouse at the new location. But depending on where children are in school, the decision may still be negative. While some companies blacklist an employee for refusing to move, wiser organizations recognize that talent is talent and what is "no" to a move today may be "yes" to a move in five years.

Some employees may reject a promotion because they are perfectly happy ding what they are doing. They like the 9-to-5 ritual where everything is fairly predictable and change comes slowly. They do their jobs very well and will continue to do so. Why spoil a good situation? is their reasoning. Some employees turn down a promotion because the new job would subject them to stressful situations. They do not want to be held responsible for the work of a group of people. They rebel at the thought of having to evaluate another person's performance, of recommending pay raises and, perhaps, of firing someone.

Reflecting on Promotions

The Bible contains numerous accounts of good performance resulting in promotions. Genesis records the remarkable story of Joseph, who advanced from being a prisoner in Egypt to the second-in-command under Pharaoh as a result of his good work. Jesus' well-known parable of the talents (Matthew 25:14-30; Luke 19:12-27) has the master promoting the slaves who performed the best in increasing the talents with which they were entrusted. The slave who did not perform well was cast out. At the same time, the Bible also clearly reminds us of the grace of God, a grace that is freely given, without any merit of our own.

For the Christian who is dedicated to a life of service, promotions provide the opportunity to use one's God-given talents to greater good in the workplace. At the same time, the heavy influence of performance in the awarding of promotions can easily change one's focus from what God has done for us to what we have done for ourselves.

See also AMBITION; COMPETITION; DRIVENNESS; OFFICE POLITICS

References and Resources

J. A. Berbaum and S. M. Steer, *Why Work? Careers and Employment in Biblical Perspective* (Grand Rapids: Baker, 1986); D. Braybrooke, "The Right to Be Hired, Promoted, Retained," in *Ethics in the World of Business* (Totowa, N.J.: Rowman & Allanheld, 1983) 145-76; W. Diehl, *Thank God It's Monday* (Philadelphia: Fortress, 1982); R. Mattson and A. Miller, *Finding a Job You Can Love* (Nashville: Thomas Nelson, 1982); L. T. Peter and R. Hull, *The Peter Principle* (New York: William Morrow, 1969); R. E. Slocum, *Ordinary Christians in a High-Tech World* (Waco, Tex.: Word, 1986); G. Tucker, *The Faith-Work Connection: A Practical Application of Christian Values in the Marketplace* (Toronto: Anglican Book Centre, 1987).

—William E. Diehl

RETIREMENT

It is helpful to think of retirement as a time of transition when the grind of the workplace is finally exchanged for a less-stressful and more-leisured lifestyle. Retirement is, therefore, to be welcomed rather than dreaded. Nevertheless, retirement may involve some pain: reduced income (although occupational pensions are becoming more common), loss of status (particularly if there have been prestigious trappings associated with one's job) and being cut off from the camaraderie of the workplace. But if retirement involves loss, it also has its rewards. In earlier times, comfortable retirement was only possible for a select few: today, thanks to social security and retirement benefits, it is within the reach of all. Society has come to recognize that men and women who have reached a certain age are entitled to the privileges of retirement. Life has its rhythms: "For everything there is a season, and a time for every matter under heaven: a time to be born, and a time to die" (Eccles. 3:1-2 NRSV). It was a beneficent and merciful Creator who ordained that we should work only six days in the week and rest on the seventh. Retirement is to be welcomed as an opportunity for the enjoyment of life.

Traumatic Retirement

Unhappily, there are some who unexpectedly find themselves retrenched and faced with involuntary and premature retirement. It is not surprising that for them the term *retirement* has sinister overtones, for it is associated with "getting the sack." In the bad old days, that was an ever-present reality. In military parlance the word *retirement* still has negative associations. In warfare it is a synonym for "withdrawal" and was often a prelude to defeat. The editors of the fifth and final volume of *A History of Private Life* argue that retirement, however camouflaged, is a tragic misfortune: "To expel a man from social life at age sixty, when he is still able and eager to work, is an act that must be shrouded in honorable rhetoric so as to hide its ignominious character." But that is an extreme view. Involuntary retirement consequent upon retrenchment or ill health is however a special problem. Of course, the pace of retired life is so different from that of working life that the abrupt change can be wrenching and, for those not ready to retire, disastrous.

Planning for Positive Retirement

Retirement, if associated with reasonable financial security, is a richly rewarding experience, opening the door to a wealth of creative and fulfilling activities. Retirement should be approached positively. It is emphatically not a sentence of death. In our modern world most people are able to look forward to twenty or thirty or more years of retirement during which they can pursue other purposes and other goals. Nicolas Coni, William Davison and Stephen Webster, in their authoritative book *Ageing,* argue that planning for retirement cannot start too soon. Even children, they suggest, should receive instruction about retirement. Interests explored in youth can in retirement be developed and enjoyed to the full. Therefore, they argue, as retirement approaches, it is important to consider what interests you have previously enjoyed and can now revert to.

The goal must be self-fulfillment, not self-indulgence. Jesus spelled out some of the dangers. He told a parable about a man who, having accumulated ample goods, decides that this is the time to take his ease and to eat, drink and be merry. He glibly assumes that he has many years ahead of him as well as ample goods. But death taps him on the shoulder and says, "You have forgotten me, my friend." Jesus comments, "This is how it will be with anyone who stores up things for himself but is not rich toward God" (Luke 12:21). Dean Inge, the acerbic dean of Saint Paul's Cathedral in London, warns that men of fifty need to beware of a sort of fatty degeneration of the conscience when they are not much inclined to fight against anything, least of all against their sins. Retirees need to take note.

When to Retire

People are living longer and retiring earlier. At least a quarter and possibly a third of all the human beings who have ever lived beyond the age of sixty are alive today. Fortunately most people can now look forward to decades of active social life before the onset of the physical and mental handicaps that reduce individual autonomy and define old age. Those who are able to do so are, therefore, likely to retire before "the doors on the street are shut, and the sound of the grinding is low . . . when one is afraid of heights, and terrors are in the road . . . and desire fails" (Eccles. 12:4-5 NRSV). The time of retirement will depend on a variety of personal and financial considerations.

The advantages of early retirement are many: the opportunity to take up other interests, to adopt a different style and pace of living, to engage in part-time employment, to undertake charitable and volunteer work, to participate more fully and practically in the work of the church and, perhaps belatedly, to spend more time with one's spouse and family.

The disadvantages of early retirement are living on a reduced income, the difficulty of finding activities and interests that are worthwhile and fulfilling, and the tendency of allowing oneself to vegetate and go to seed. The worst scenario is being reduced to the desperate expedient of killing time. Financial considerations weigh heavily with most people. Median incomes for retirees are markedly lower than those for people in their middle years, even when adjustments are made for family size. Most retired people are dependent on social security and retirement benefits apart from savings and investments. Early retirement may mean these are diminished or postponed. Nevertheless, demographers point out that on the average older people, with their years of asset accumulation behind them, own more and owe less than younger people. Further, the majority of older married people own their own homes. Allowance needs to be made for the certainty of increasing medical expenses in future years. Whereas older people spend less than younger people on budgetary items (including leisure items), they spend more on items relating to health, particularly when there is no comprehensive program for medical insurance available.

The mandatory age for retirement is becoming progressively lower. This makes the transition difficult for those who believe they are still in full possession of all their powers and who enjoy their work. Politicians are exceedingly reluctant to admit that they ought to retire at the age of sixty-five. Ronald Reagan in the United States, Winston Churchill in England and Konrad Adenauer in Germany were all in office in their seventies; Churchill and Adenauer remained into their eighties. Pope John XXIII, who inaugurated far-reaching changes within the Roman Catholic Church, was not elected pope until he was seventy-eight. In other walks of life there is, however, widespread support for a mandatory age of retirement.

Retirement should be embraced positively as a well-earned reward. If it can be seized early, so much the better. Those who retire early by choice have happier and longer retirements than those who resent retirement and are bitter about it. Those who have enjoyed variety in life are more likely to do so in retirement than those who have not. Once the decision to retire has been made (or made for one), there are some urgent practical problems to be faced.

Where to Live?

The obvious options are to continue to live in one's own home, to purchase a condo, to lease an apartment, to move into a retirement village. The decision is a highly personal one. Some are jealous of their independence and prefer to be alone; others enjoy community living. Some prefer the country; others prefer the city. These personal factors will dictate one's choice. There are also the factors such as access to transportation and health services.

There are public as well as private factors involved in the choice of location. A characteristic of contemporary life is community planning, with its impact on the physical and social environment and its influence on day-to-day activities and human contacts. This includes proximity to one's church. Retirees do not as a rule avail themselves of freedom from occupational commitments to move away from their former homes. Rates of moving are higher among younger age groups. When older people move, they are more likely to move within the confines of their immediate locale than to change their community setting. Ties to one's place of residence become stronger as one grows older. Those who own their own home, or have strong social connections with their neighborhood, are least willing to move.

In Western society the ideal today is the nuclear family. Once the ideal was several generations together in one home—grandparents, unmarried uncles and aunts, parents and their children, all as one extended family—but that ideal does not hold today. Joy Davidman, in her little classic on the Ten Commandments entitled *Smoke on the Mountain*, cleverly adapts one of Grimms' fairy tales and satirizes the way in which the old are, in modern households, made to feel an embarrassing encumbrance.

222

Once they were lovingly cared for; the modern "serpent's-tooth" method, she accuses, is to lead Grandpa gently but firmly to the local asylum, there to tuck him out of sight and out of mind as a case of senile dementia (p. 58).

Patterns of living in today's society have changed dramatically, so much so that instead of the extended family, what we have is subdivision into two or even three generations of distinct nuclear families: the young people with their dependent children, the middle-aged parents and the aged generation of grandparents. Many family units today are single-parent families, thus complicating the picture further. As life expectancy has increased, husbands and wives are more likely to survive together, living independently. The ability to do so presupposes continued health, when in fact aging is accompanied by ills such as rheumatism, arthritis, heart disease and high blood pressure. Further, there will be increasing visits to the doctor, periodic hospitalizations, restricted activity and days spent in bed. In the United States four out of five persons over the age of sixty-five have at least one chronic condition.

If, on balance, the decision is made to relocate, one must consider a variety of practical matters: the advantage of single rather than multiple levels, sufficient space for one's possessions and visitors, ease of maintenance, heating and air conditioning, convenient access and security. Retirement villages have become increasingly popular, particularly complexes that cater to a variety of needs. The usual pattern is separate houses or self-servicing individual units within a larger complex, residential accommodation with servicing as well as meals provided, and nursing homes together with a hospital annex. The whole complex is under the supervision of an administrator. Specialized staff are employed as well as that typical twentieth-century innovation— diversionary therapists who are responsible for community activities.

Complexes that provide a full range of accommodation, from totally independent units for those who require no assistance through sheltered accommodation to full nursing care, have a very great appeal. It is necessary to buy into these schemes, and the price is high. But once in, there is the guarantee of being provided for at whatever the level of need. Churches have moved extensively into this field and provide highly professional services in a Christian context. Through the death of a spouse, many elderly people find themselves left living alone. Many married women end their lives as widows. For such people, some form of communal living is often the answer.

What to Do?

Those who have enjoyed variety in life are more likely to do so in retirement than those who have not. A full, broad education is also likely to stand one in good stead. Those who have found happiness and job fulfillment are the ones who are most likely to find satisfaction and fulfillment in active retirement. Those who approach retirement happily and expectantly are those likely to use retirement well. Of course, retirement is less likely to be happy when it occurs without warning, due to either sudden retrenchment or ill health, but even then retirement opens up new possibilities.

It is foolish to adopt the view that you can't teach old dogs new tricks. This has been clearly demonstrated when younger students and more mature students are enrolled in the same courses. The older students usually do better because of their higher motivation and their increased self-knowledge. Retirement opens the door to the pursuit of new intellectual and cultural interests. This can be immensely rewarding. The nature of the subject does not matter, provided it gives pleasure. One can learn, or relearn, a foreign language to assist with travel plans or reading. There are also adult-education courses available in most cities. For those remote from the cities there are long-distance teaching techniques (*see* Information Superhighway). Using one's mind and keeping it agile and nimble are believed to offer some protection from dementia.

Physical activity as well as cultural is important. Retirement is an opportunity to take up new sports and to improve one's skills in the sports one already enjoys. It has been said that fitness is a luxury for the young but is essential for the old! The fitter you are, the less likely you are to become ill, and the more quickly you are likely to make a full recovery should your health break down. It is the elderly who are most likely to suffer from illness in Western society, and their illnesses are probably due to degenerative changes in their bodies. It pays to invest time and energy in staying fit. Physical fitness can be regained during retirement, and muscles that have wasted due to lack of use during a sedentary life can be redeveloped. It is not necessary to indulge in dangerous or macho sports to ensure fitness; activities such as walking or swimming or cultivating a garden help.

Taking up sports and vigorous exercise in later life need not be dangerous. The secret to any new activity is starting gently and gradually working up to a peak. Whether it takes weeks or years does not matter, so long as one finds pleasure in it and practices regularly. Exertion can cause even the young to sweat, get breathless and have palpitations! The goal of *mens sana in corpore sana* (a sound mind in a sound body) is to be sought, not only for one's own sake, but for the sake of others.

Retirement can degenerate into a life of appalling selfishness, narcissism and self-indulgence, but retirement can also make possible a life of loving thoughtfulness and service. Humanitarian and charitable organizations need help; such regular volunteer work also helps the retiree. Authorities note that a common reason for seeking early retirement is the craving to be freed from the rigid routine and the exacting demands of a full-time job, but for most people, structure in one's life pattern is important and continues to be important after retirement. Retirement is an opportunity to restructure one's routine and to adopt a pattern that is less rigid and tightly packed. Demands on one's time will multiply. The ideal is balance—balance between one's physical and mental activities, one's volunteer work and one's family. Structure and routine should therefore be used to maximize the pleasure and the joy of retirement.

References and Resources
P. Ariès and G. Duby, eds., *A History of Private Life* (Cambridge, Mass.: Belknap/Harvard University Press, 1987-1991); J. E. Birren, ed., *Handbook of the Aging and the Individual: Psychological and Biological Aspects* (Chicago: University of Chicago Press, 1959); N. Coni, W. Davison and S. Webster, *Ageing: The Facts* (Oxford: Oxford University Press, 1992); J. Davidman, *Smoke on the Mountain* (London: Hodder & Stoughton); H. Humisett, *Retirement Guide: An Overall Plan for a Comfortable Future* (Vancouver, B.C.: Self Council Press, 1990); H. D. Shelton, *Older Population in the United States* (New York: Wiley, 1958); C. Tibbetts, ed., *Handbook of Social Gerontology* (Chicago: University of Chicago Press, 1960).

—Stuart Barton Babbage

SERVICE, WORKPLACE

In recent years there have been growing complaints about the weakening emphasis on service among workers. Jokes have long existed about what happened to the service promised by the description "civil servants." Tradespeople offering service seem to be less and less reliable in keeping appointments. In shops and department stores, banks and post offices, garages and government departments, customer service no longer seems to be as available as it used to be. Ironically enough, the type of work which most often heads the list in complaints about service is the so-called service sector. Typical examples are restaurants whose waiters are untrained, airlines that overbook and auto-repair shops that do not undertake quality work and often overcharge in the bargain. Many now fear that the same kind of decline in quality that took place earlier in the industry field, and led to many of the present problems, is beginning to strike the service sector.

Understanding the Loss of Service
The reasons given for this are many. Some argue that younger people are no longer committed to the work ethic of the previous generation (*see* Work Ethic). Others point to an overemphasis on scale economies involving downsizing and cost-cutting that has affected both the private and the public domain. Some suggest that schools and colleges are no longer doing their job of training people satisfactorily for the work force. Others regard the deterioration of service as part of the broader weakening of morality and concern for others in society. There is some truth in all of these, but the reasons for the lack of service today go deeper.

It helps to approach the issue from another angle. In all our complaints we tend to lose sight of the fact that this is an issue concerning people. People care deeply about this, even if this is often for purely personal reasons, because we take for granted the association between work and service. This has not always been the case in the West and is still not the case in some cultures. In such settings when little service is forthcoming, people do not complain with the same degree of disappointment or indignation. For this is the way things are, always have been, and ever will be—just a fact of life. Our complaints are more intense precisely because we had hoped for more and want to see the situation changed. In this there is some promise.

Linking Work and Service

In large measure, the link between work and service is a consequence of the impact of the gospel on Western society. The key word used to describe the activities of early Christians was *service,* generally translated as "ministry." This is occasionally used of activities in which people were engaged outside the church, and in one place even non-Christians are described as God's servants when they do their work in ways congruent with the divine purposes (Romans 13:4). This attitude and language gradually permeated other kinds of work and at times even gave rise to new titles for the work people were doing. "Civil service" or "public service" is one such example. Another is the description given to the whole "service sector" which now accounts for some 75 percent of the economy in advanced industrial societies. In places influenced by British political practice even the word *ministry* is still used of the inner circle of parliamentarians around the prime "minister." The very frequency of the word *service* in the wider marketplace of ideas today is testimony to its continuing vitality. Almost five thousand books a year contain the word in their titles.

So we already have in the way we talk an unconsciously acknowledged theological connection between work and service. Improved service in the workplace begins with realizing more fully the link between the two. It will not be enough to try to push people into giving greater service, for unless they view work itself as a form of service and find the language to convey that, all the pep talks, prep courses and pop techniques to improve this will not take us very far. Service has more to do with how we view what we do and who we are ourselves than what we actually do and how we do it. The latter are certainly important but not in themselves sufficient, for without the former any improvements in service are built on rather shaky foundations. So a major part of the task is helping the whole culture of business and the workplace to embrace again a vision of service.

Recovering the Dignity of Service

One of the ways we can do this is to help bring the idea of vocation back into the workplace (*see* Calling). Although our vocation touches all areas of life, not only our work, there is no doubt that those who see their work in some sense a calling or vocation are more likely to do it more in the spirit of service. This was one of the findings in the survey of senior managers conducted by William Diehl, as recorded in his book *In Search of Faithfulness.* It is partly because a sense of vocation has been largely replaced by notions of a career, or just the job, that the quality of much of the work people do has also suffered (*see* Protestant Work Ethic).

But we must also find fresh, practical ways of bringing service and work back into closer connection with one another. This is already taking place in significant contemporary business literature. Much is said these days about the need for firms to place service at the center of what they do. In these highly competitive times, success will go to those who are perceived by the public as really delivering on their offers of service. Some companies make this point by offering to refund some or all of the cost of their product or service if it does not live up to expectations or if it is not supplied in the time promised. This means a lot to customers, who are mostly busy people who do not have time to wait around for deliveries or to keep chasing firms that have not done what they promised.

Another suggested way forward for businesses is to add some extra benefit to the customer on top of what is usually supplied. This is the so-called value-added factor, and customers, especially those who belong to the baby-boom generation, are increasingly looking for this. They realize that these days it is mostly a buyer's, not seller's, market and that since buyers are increasingly quality-conscious, they are primarily looking for the best deal they can get. Workplaces that are taking seriously "the search for excellence" (Peters and Waterman), "total quality management" (Deming), "total product concept" (Levitt) or the "principles of completeness" (Crosby) are seeking to equip themselves to do this. Going beyond this is the idea of offering "extraordinary" or "superlative" service (as exhibited in firms like Nordstrom or Federal Express). This means treating the client or customer as a partner in a lifelong relationship of giving and receiving which changes according to the needs and requirements of the person served as much as the challenges and developments in the serving organization.

Increasingly in this literature there is an emphasis on what the person of the worker, as well as the quality of the work, brings to the nature of the service offered. It is not just about the quality of products and services, it is about the quality of those producing them and serving customers. This is especially the case in those occupations that provide services rather than goods but all too easily focus on numbers, revenue or other measurable performance indicators rather than meeting both server and customer expectations. Unless there are internal changes taking place in the lives of the workers themselves, it is only a matter of time before the quality of what they do is affected; in some cases it is affected from the outset as their approach to customers or clients gets in the way of others wanting what they are making or offering.

Servant Leader and Serving Organization

This where the idea of the "servant leader" in the workplace comes in, for such a person can model to others the importance, meaning and practice of service connected with one's work. This idea was given particular currency in the 1970s by Simon K. Greenleaf (*see* Leadership; Leadership, Church). This has now undergone significant refinement at the hands of writers like Michael Maccoby, who distinguishes the different ways in which people serve depending on the type of contribution they offer. For *helpers* service means assisting people, valuing relationships above all and responding to specific needs. For *defenders* it means monitoring and protecting those

227

who are disadvantaged. For *innovators* it means creating and implementing a more effective strategy. For newer-style *self-developers* it means facilitating a problem-solving process with customers and clients that includes an opportunity to learn and grow. These categories helpfully broaden the ways in which we should think of direct service to people. Too often we identify this mainly with the work of the first group. But even with these refinements, we need greater emphasis on such a person being a "leading servant" rather than just a leader—of whatever kind—with a service orientation.

In any case, the whole notion of leadership needs to be broadened to include a more collaborative approach and a recognition of the point at which everyone in the work force can take the lead in some respect or other. This means that we do not necessarily have to wait for designated leaders to take the lead in this or any other area. If they do, fine; if not, someone else can take the lead. But all of us—no matter how ordinary a position we might have or how ordinary our work might appear—can seek to fulfill our responsibility in a genuinely servant-like and service-oriented way. We can do this without seeking permission or affirmation.

We can exemplify service before those around us. We can make informal or formal suggestions about how our own work and the work around us can be improved. We can look for ways of generating discussion on how certain things might be done. We can both stand up for and stand up to our immediate over-seers, for example, helping to conserve their energy, being responsible gatekeepers, defining them publicly, acting in their name, defending them, helping them focus. And we can buffer others from a leader, facing them with hard facts, presenting options and playing advocate when they are in danger of deciding unwisely. Though sometimes this will encounter opposition, forcing us to make some hard choices about how far we can go or whether we might have to change our work, at other times we will find a warm reception for our efforts.

Apart from what they can bring personally to the task, those in positions of leadership can go further and develop an organizational culture, processes and training that will help others see their work as a service. The key here is for them to see themselves as stewards rather than controllers of the organization and everyone in it, exercising rank without privilege, developing partners rather than dependents and granting empowerment rather then entitlement. Practices that enhance service in their organizations include maximizing core workers' opportunity of designing and customizing policy; reintegrating the managing and doing of work; allowing measurements and controls to serve, not master, core workers; and supporting local solutions rather than consistency across all groups (Block, pp. 64-66). They should encourage people to put service before everything, and find appropriate ways of monitoring, rewarding and improving its quality, consistency and novelty, giving special attention and training to support and front-line service people on whom so much depends. Throughout the process, these leaders should be fully aware that service is not merely about giving someone a useful product or a service, but establishing a relationship with them that will encourage their looking to satisfy similar future needs from the same place.

See also INTEGRITY; LEADERSHIP; MINISTRY; ORGANIZATIONAL CULTURE; WORK; WORK ETHIC, PROTESTANT; WORKPLACE

References and Resources

P. Block, *Stewardship: Choosing Service over Self-Esteem* (San Francisco: Barrett-Koehler, 1993); I. Chaleff, *The Courageous Follower: Standing Up to and for Our Leaders* (San Francisco: Barrett-Koehler, 1955); P. B. Crosby, *Completeness: Quality for the Twenty-first Century* (New York: Penguin, 1994); W. Diehl, *In Search of Faithfulness: Lessons from the Christian Community* (San Francisco: Harper & Row, 1989); R. K. Greenleaf, *Servant Leadership: A Journey into the Nature of Legitimate Power and Greatness* (New York: Paulist, 1977); R. E. Kelley, *Power of Followership: How to Create Leaders People Want to Follow and Followers Who Lead Themselves* (New York: Double Currency, 1991); M. Maccoby, *Why Work: Motivating and Leading the New Generation* (New York: Simon & Schuster, 1988); B. Patterson, *Serving God: The Grand Essentials of Work and Worship* (Downers Grove, Ill.: InterVarsity Press, 1994).

—Robert Banks

SHIFTWORK

In earlier times almost everyone worked during the day and rested at night. This practice is alluded to in Jesus' injunction regarding mission: "As long as it is day, we must do the work. . . . Night is coming, when no one can work" (John 9:4 NRSV). On occasions people did work at night: in two places we find reference to Paul's doing this (Acts 20:31; 1 Thes. 2:9). The main exceptions to working during the day were those who were on watch or guard duty, servants at dinner parties or in taverns, traders bringing goods to market where there was a daytime curfew, or people dealing with an emergency situation. Even in these cases, working at odd hours or at night tended to be intermittent.

How Did Shiftwork Come into Being?

It was not until the Industrial Revolution that this pattern underwent serious change. What made the difference was the introduction of machines. Unlike humans, machines can run all night as well as all day, having to stop only when a problem develops or they break down. From an economic point of view, machines are more profitable if they are kept running. This development led to the formation of two, then three, shifts throughout a twenty-four-hour period. Generally workers rotated around these shifts, though in time some were compelled or chose to work a regular shift.

Minor variations of this occurred with the introduction of Morse code and then the wireless and with the creation of varying time zones within large countries like the United States, Canada and Australia. This resulted in some people operating in the time zones of places other than where they lived and worked. As a result of the introduction of the telephone and now the broader telecommunications revolution, people are able and at times required to operate according to the time zones of other countries. As larger numbers of people have become involved in shiftwork, there has been a corresponding increase in shiftwork among people in the service sector to cater to the workers' needs at the times they are available.

How Widespread Is Shiftwork, and What Are Its Effects?

Over the last few decades shiftwork has been increasing in most industrializing or industrialized economies. Overall in Western countries approximately one-third of all workers are employed at times other than standard working hours. Many of these are involved in rotating schedules, others in permanent shiftwork, including those who are operating according to the time zone of another region or country. Indeed the whole idea of normal working hours is becoming increasingly questionable. Many who work standard hours are now finding that sometimes they also have to work regularly at night or on a weekend.

There are some advantages in doing shiftwork. The pay is generally better. Time spent commuting is often shorter. The sense of camaraderie can be greater. But the disadvantages are serious, and awareness of them has grown over the years. Problems include (1) disrupted sleeping patterns, (2) greater vulnerability to fatigue and depression, (3) increased likelihood of physical illness, (4) more tensions with spouses and children, (5) less socializing and contact with friends, (6) higher incidence of divorce and (7) a tendency to die earlier. It is obvious that these are not minor difficulties.

How Can Shiftwork Be Handled More Responsibly?

For a long time the physical, psychological and social consequences of shiftwork were overlooked or viewed only as isolated cases. Now that they are well known, many employers and unions have begun to take steps to reduce them. Individual workers also need to know whether they should take on regular shiftwork at all or, if already doing so, how best to minimize its unfortunate consequences. Here are some major steps that can be taken:

1. Vary shiftwork with more normal work patterns. Though this involves adjustments to changing schedules, these are no greater than those experienced by someone traveling by air overseas.

2. With long-term shiftwork, avoid rotating shifts. Instead, have people work mostly the same hours.

3. As much as possible, it is best for people to work regular week-length rhythms, even if these do not always coincide with standard weekdays and weekends.

4. Shiftworkers need normal, generally long, weekends throughout the year so that their socializing patterns can coincide with those with whom they want to socialize.

5. Shiftworkers also need longer or more frequent holidays so that they can make up time lost through shiftwork with their families.

There are other steps that can be taken, not only by individual shiftworkers but by those associated with them. First, spouses of shiftworkers can adjust as much as realistically possible to the latter's daily rhythm so that they can have more time together. Second, friends should be prepared to do the same from time to time so that they can maintain their relationship with shiftworkers and engage in common activities. It is lamentable that shiftworkers often lose long-standing friends and only develop relationships with others also working shifts; apart from the obvious relational loss, this tends to result in having too restricted a view of life and the world. Third, shiftworkers and their spouses, preferably children as well, need to be in a communal Christian group where they can gain support, find practical help for their special circumstances and forge long-term links with people living according to more normal time patterns. Fourth, congregations—whether acting in concert or on their own—should hold some groups, corporate worship services and occasionally other activities at times shiftworkers can attend, sometimes late in the evening or early in the morning. Fifth, every so often permanent shiftworkers should try to rotate their jobs so as to have more normal employment or together with their families spend time with a counselor ensuring that habits, tensions and ailments are not building up so as to create severe problems in the future.

Since surveys suggest that the trend toward shiftwork or other unusual work patterns is likely to continue, it is important that as Christians and as churches, as employers and as unions, further serious attention be given to this phenomenon. Since the debate has now moved beyond issues of salary and time off to issues of health and lifestyle, perhaps the time is now ripe to tackle issues of spirit and community.

See also TIME; WORK; WORKPLACE; SERVICE

References and Resources

W. P. Colquhoun and J. Rutenranz, *Studies of Shiftwork* (London: Taylor & Francis, 1980); T. H. Monk, *Making Shift Work Tolerale* (1992); A. J. Scott, ed., *Shiftwork* (Philadelphia: Hanley & Belfur, 1990).

—Robert Banks

STEWARDSHIP

While *stewardship* is commonly used as a camouflaged appeal for funds for church and religious purposes, the term denotes a more comprehensive view of the Christian life affecting time, work, leisure, talents, money, the state of one's soul and care for the environment. The Greek word for *steward* (*oikonomos,* from which we get our word *economy*) means "one who manages a household." Years ago persons called stewards, rather than huge financial institutions, were employed to manage the financial affairs and households of wealthy people. Their management included not only money but everything that makes a household thrive, not unlike the vocation of homemaking but on a large scale. A biblical example is Joseph's work as steward of Potiphar's house; his master did not "concern himself with anything in the house" (Genesis 39:8).

Stewardship is a term theologically related to service or ministry (*diakonia*). If *service* denotes the motivation for ministry—undertaking God's interests for the pleasure of God—*stewardship* suggests the purpose of ministry: to manage God's world in harmony with the owner's mind. These two words, *service* and *stewardship*, taken together constitute the ministry of the laity and are roughly equivalent to the much popularized term *servant leadership.* Because stewardship integrates many facets of everyday life, we begin with a summary indicating other articles that can be consulted. Then we will consider personal and church stewardship.

Managing God's Household

God is the ultimate owner of everything (Psalm 24:1; Psalm 50:10) and has entrusted the nonhuman creation to the care of humankind. A good word to describe our double relationship with God and the world is *trusteeship:* we are entrusted with the care of the world and are accountable to God, who owns it and has declared his intended purpose. This trusteeship stems from the so-called creation mandate in Genesis 1:26-29. Humankind has "an accredited discretionary power" (Wright, p. 117) over everything except itself. The stewards are to take care of the earth (Genesis 2:15) and develop it in response to the summons of God.

This far-reaching stewardship embraces (1) care of creation, so managing the resources of earth and sea (*see* Creation; Ecology); (2) expressing creativity in all of its forms, so developing God's aesthetic creation and bringing further beauty into the world (*see* Art; Beauty; Craftsmanship); (3) maintaining the fabric of God's creation, so making God's world work (*see* Chores; Ministry; Service; Work); (4) enculturating the world and developing varieties of human expressions of values, structures and lifestyles, so bringing distinctive meanings to the peoples of the world (*see* Culture); (5) harnessing the earth's potential by inventing tools and systems for making things, so bringing benefit to humankind (*see* Technology); (6) expressing dominion over time by ordering human life around patterns of time and by keeping one day a week for rest and reflection, so expressing dominion over time (*see* Sabbath; Time); (7)

developing human society, organizations and peoples/nations, filling the earth with peoples living in distinctive but harmonious communities and states, so creating structures as contexts for human life (*see* Organization; Politics; States/Provinces; Structures). Considered together, these are the ways we take care of God's household. This all-encompassing stewardship is the stewardship of every human being; every living thing and the whole material creation are not exempted from this stewardship in favor of something more "spiritual"; this is part of their spiritual ministry.

Caring for Creation

Some significant implications stem from this stewardship. First, God's calling to humankind is not merely directed toward individuals but organizations and communities. Even corporations and nations have a call from God and should undertake stewardship.

Second, in defining humankind's relationship with the physical creation, stewardship keeps us from two extreme relationships with the earth: (1) reverencing and worshiping the earth (a trend toward which the ecology movement is moving) and (2) manipulating and ruthlessly exploiting the earth, which is still so common in industrialized countries. Unfortunately the Christian faith is accused of promoting the latter view, when it is precisely the loss of Christian stewardship that has caused the rape and pillage of the earth.

Third, in the Old Testament, God (the divine owner) gives "accredited discretionary power" to all humankind (Genesis 1:26-29; Wright, p. 117) for the benefit of everyone. The first human ownership/stewardship implies the common ownership and shared use of the material resources of the world. The right of all is prior to the right of individuals or individual nations to accumulate personal wealth (*see* Justice; Money; Ownership; Poverty; Wealth). So there are severe limitations on personal or national ownership of the earth's resources; they are a divine gift entrusted to the race for the benefit of all. As John Chrysostom said in the fourth century, the rich are entrusted with wealth as stewards for the benefit of the poor (p. 50). What a gracious revolution would be incited by the application of this principle in the global village today!

Israel as Exemplary Steward

Under the old covenant God's gift of trusteeship was especially directed to the nation Israel (Deut. 10:14-15). There are three parts to the promise God gave to Israel: the presence (God will be with them), a people (he will be their God; they, his people) and a place (the land will be theirs, that is, entrusted to the people, not individuals).

The families (more like clans or extended families today) were the basic social, kinship, legal and religious structure under the old covenant. They were family-plus-land units, as is graphically illustrated by the redemption of Naomi's land-plus-family in Bethlehem (Ruth 4:9-12). Thus in the Jubilee year (every fifty years) both

God's ultimate ownership and the family's trusteeship were expressed by the return of the land to the original family, even if the land had been mortgaged or sold in the meantime to pay debts (Leviticus 25:4-18). The reason given is this: "The land is mine and you are but aliens and my tenants" (Leviticus 25:23). This has implications for the question of providing an inheritance for one's family (*see* Will, Last).

New Testament "Household" Responsibilities

Applying Old Testament legislation to people under the New Testament must be undertaken in a paradigmatic way—with the Old providing a structure for thinking of something greater that is fulfilled in the New. All the promises of God concerning God's presence, people and place find their "yes" in Christ (2 Cor. 1:20). The Gentiles along with Jews in Christ become joint heirs (Ephes. 3:6) in a joint body so that "in Christ" answers to all that "in the land" meant to Israel—and even more! Fellowship in Christ for the Gentiles as well as the Jews fulfills the analogous function for the Christian as the possession of the land did for the Israelite. But that does not eliminate the socioeconomic dimension of stewardship. Christian fellowship (*koinōnia*' is not merely "spiritual" communion. It is total sharing of life, not regarding possessions as absolutely one's own, bringing economic and social justice and peacemaking.

Christians share stewardship of the world with the rest of humankind, but they have three additional concerns: (1) the investment and proper use of our personal time, abilities and finances for the benefit of others, something for which we are held responsible by God (Matthew 25:14-30; *see* Money; Spiritual Gifts; Talents); (2) the treasuring and distribution of the grace of God as proclaimed in the gospel (1 Peter 4:10), not only by apostles and church leaders (1 Cor. 4:1; Titus 1:7) but by all believers' being stewards and witnesses of the gospel (*see* Evangelism; Laity; Ministry; Witness); (3) the full-fledged sharing of life (including material possessions) as a sign of being "in Christ." In the early church this meant sharing available assets over and above the normal (Acts 2:44-45; Acts 4:32-35), engaging in relief missions to poor believers (Acts 11:27-30) and crosscultural giving to symbolize the mutual interdependence, equality and unity in Christ (1 Cor. 16:1; 2 Cor. 8:13).

Time, Abilities and Finances

It is unbiblical to relegate personal stewardship to merely the religious portion of our lives: to tithing, using our talents for the church or giving a percentage of our income to the Lord's work. All of us belong to God, and stewardship concerns the whole of everyday life.

The time of our lives. Instead of our squeezing yet one more Christian activity into our already overloaded schedule, stewardship of time might involve the opposite. We exercise stewardship of time in our daily occupations, fulfilling God's creational and providential calling to make the world work. We also invest time when we play with our families or enjoy conversation with friends. This everyday redemption of time springs from the sabbath, which is one of the crucial signs that we take the stewardship of time seriously. We cannot lay aside our compulsion to work unless we believe that God is running the world and can be trusted with it while we rest.

Abilities for church and world. It is a sin not to use talents and gifts that God has given. Our gifts are on loan from God. They are to be used for the upbuilding of family, church, neighborhood and society. In the end we are accountable for our use or disuse of them. Not all of this has to be organized through the local church; indeed, most of it will not be. Luther was eloquent on this subject. "How can you think you are not called?" he asked. He then reminded his hearers that they had more than enough to do in their homes, kitchens, workshops and fields:

> The idea that the service to God should have only to do with a church altar, singing, reading, sacrifice, and the like is without doubt but the worst trick of the devil. How could the devil have led us more effectively astray than by the narrow conception that service to God takes place only in church and by works done therein. . . . The whole world could abound with services to the Lord (quoted in Feucht, p. 80).

Finances, where your heart is. Contrary to the secular viewpoint—"If you don't own it, you won't take care of it"—being a steward should increase our care and diligence in the use of property and wealth. It is not ours; it will be taken back by God one day; God will hold us responsible for what we do with it. Our everyday stewardship—even maintaining a vehicle and doing chores—links us with God, who maintains the world. God wants not just an intact creation but a "return" on his investment (*see* Ownership).

It is tragic that Christian stewardship has been so often reduced to "tithing"—giving to the Lord's work one-tenth of one's income ("Is that gross or net after taxes?"). In the Old Testament tithes were like taxes paid to the temple; they were not discretionary gifts (for an exception, see Genesis 14:20). This accomplished four things. It (1) celebrated the goodness of God (Deut. 14:26), (2) acknowledged God's ownership of everything, (3) maintained places of worship (Numbers 18:21; Deut. 14:27) and (4) cared for the poor (Deut. 14:28-29). Even in the Old Testament tithing was only part of Israel's stewardship. The New Testament only once mentions tithing (Matthew 23:23)—in the context of Jesus' calling the Pharisees to something more important. The New Testament principle is not one-tenth but "hilarious giving" (2 Cor. 9:7), that is, cheerful and uncalculating. Since everything belongs to God, we should generously disperse what we can to help others. But the use of "should" destroys the very idea of Christian giving; it comes not from law, principle or obligation but from the spontaneous overflow of gratitude for Christ's blessing on our lives (2 Cor. 8:9).

The Grace of Giving

Many people give donations. The Bible calls us to stewardship. Donations imply that we are the owners and out of the generosity of our hearts we are giving some to others. Stewardship implies that it all belongs to God and is used for God's purposes.

Donation spirituality is self-affirming and calculated for effect; stewardship spirituality is other-directed and wholehearted. Donation spirituality looks for a thank-you from the recipient; stewardship spirituality aims at "Well done" when the Lord returns.

Some questions to ponder are these: How much do we give that does not come from a sense of obligation or social expectation? Do we act as if the part we retain is actually ours? Do we regard whatever wealth we have as a stewardship on behalf of the poor? Does the disbursement of monies represented by our checkbook or credit-card invoice reflect God's priorities for everyday life?

How does the grace of giving work out in practice? Of course, we should give to support Christian workers and causes as instructed in Scripture. But, in accordance with the Old Testament outlook, we should also see that we are stewards of money and assets in ways that benefit our families. To neglect family through sacrificing for the church is wrong. This is clearly something both Jesus (Mark 7:11) and Paul affirmed. Indeed not taking care of our families makes us worse than unbelievers (1 Tim. 5:8). We should also heed Jesus' injunction to "use worldly wealth to gain friends for yourselves, so that when it is gone, you will be welcomed into eternal dwellings" (Luke 16:9). This means investing in people, giving money (anonymously, if possible) to the poor, showing hospitality. As Thomas Aquinas so beautifully explained, this holistic stewardship is much more than handouts. He listed the seven corporal alms deeds—visit, quench, feed, ransom, clothe, harbor and bury (the dead)—and linked them with seven spiritual alms—instruct, counsel, reprove, console, pardon, forbear and pray (*Summa* 32.2.1).

In these matters mutual encouragement and accountability are needed. In the Western world we are modest about nothing except money. The fig leaf has slipped from the genitals to the wallet. Yet it is precisely in the way we spend time, abilities and especially finances that we reveal our true relationship to God and work out our salvation. Part of our problem is that we mostly think about and decide such matters on an individual basis or simply as families. Small groups and spiritual friendships can provide the fundamental contexts for sharing priorities, budgets and prayerfully supporting one another in becoming better stewards. In this matter the church as a whole needs to take the lead.

The Church's Stewardship

There is nothing in the Old or New Testaments to match or justify the present preoccupation of "stewardship" drives to raise money for Christian workers and church buildings. Though some workers should be freed from common toil for a specific ministry, this is entirely exceptional and is a secondary form of Christian stewardship (*see* Financial Support). Most Christian workers throughout history have been self-supported tentmakers. The primary understanding of Christian stewardship has to do with investing what God has entrusted to us, sharing the treasure of the gospel, demonstrating love, striving for economic justice and peace on earth, all of this starting with the Christian community itself (Galatians 6:10).

The church's time allocation, use of the gifts and talents of its members and allocation of financial resources are a graphic statement of its spirituality. If the local church consumes all the discretionary time of its members, not freeing them for family and neighbors, it is hoarding. If a church fails to release spiritual and natural gifts and allows people to "waste" themselves, it is squandering. If a church uses all its money on itself (staff and building), it is caring for itself rather than undertaking stewardship.

Some specific suggestions to be considered in light of this are the following: Spend half of the church budget beyond the local church. Apply simple-living guidelines to the church and not just to individuals. Invest time, abilities and finances in serving God's unity mission by linking poor and rich churches, Third World and Western churches, fighting injustice and bringing peace, unity and equality as Paul did in the great collection (2 Cor. 8-9). Devote leadership and resources to supporting people where God has placed them in the world, rather than enlisting them for the programs of the church. Send groups of people (and not just checks) to care for the poor at home and abroad (remember Aquinas's blend of corporal and spiritual alms).

Stewardship gives meaning to our lives and helps us make sense out of everyday life. It captures all our energies, assets and creativity for God's grand plan of humanizing the earth and developing it as a glorified creation. It saves us from the twin dangers of despair (What will come of the earth?) and false messianism (If we do not save the planet, who will?) because we are cooperating with a God who is determined to bring the creation to a worthy end through its complete renewal (Rev. 21:5). Stewardship is a thermometer of our spirituality and discipleship. Where our treasure is, there will be our hearts (Luke 12:34). Our response to a brother in need is a measure of our love for God (James 2:15-16; 1 John 3:17). But stewardship also provides an incentive to grow in Christ. If we give sparingly, we will live cramped, emaciated lives; if we give generously, we live expansively and deeply (Luke 6:38).

In the end what God wants back is not an untouched creation or an intact (but unused) human ability; God wants a "return" on his investment. Stewardship is the way God gets such a return. It is not simply giving things away or keeping them safely in trust, but wisely investing them in contexts in which they will do some good and multiply. On the judgment day God will be asking individuals, families, churches and nations what we did with what we had. How well will we have managed God's household in the time between Christ's first and second coming?

References and Resources

J. Chrysostom, *On Wealth and Poverty,* trans. Catherine P. Roth (Crestwood, N.Y.: St. Vladimir's Seminary Press, 1984); Oscar E. Feucht, *Everyone a Minister* (St. Louis: Concordia, 1974); R. Foster, *Freedom of Simplicity* (New York: Harper & Row, 1989); D. J. Hall, *Stewardship of Life in the Kingdom of Death* (Grand Rapids: Eerdmans, 1988); L. T. Johnson, *Sharing Possessions: Mandate and Symbol of Faith* (London: SCM, 1981); M. MacGregor, *Your Money Matters* (Minneapolis: Bethany House, 1988); R. J. Sider, *Cry Justice: The Bible on Hunger and Poverty* (New York: Paulist, 1980); R. J. Sider,

Living More Simply: Biblical Principles and Practical Models (Downers Grove, Ill.: InterVarsity Press, 1980); R. J. Sider, *Rich Christians in a Hungry World* (Dallas: Word, 1990); C. J. H. Wright, *God's People in God's Land: Family, Land and Property in the Old Testament* (Grand Rapids: Eerdmans, 1990).

—R. Paul Stevens

STRESS, WORKPLACE

Stress is as necessary to life as eating and communicating. Without stress we would not be able to appreciate our limits or attain our objectives. Being under the right kind of pressure, whether self-induced or externally created, is integral to responding appropriately to the challenges of everyday life. To desire an existence that is stress-free is quite literally a death wish.

The Universality of Stress

In the Bible we find many of its key figures under stress at various points in their lives: Moses feeling overwhelmed by the number of things he has to do (Numbers 11), Jeremiah voicing his personal and vocational frustrations to God (Jeremiah 17) and Paul reconstructing the difficulties and anxieties he faced (2 Cor. 11). Most of these stressful experiences were constructive. Yet stress is a curse as well as a blessing, since it occurs in malignant as well as benign forms. It can be both constructive and destructive, opening up some possibilities in life and shutting down others. This negative side of stress is most devastating in modern Western societies.

Distinguishing between these two kinds of stress is relatively simple: if the situation generating stress requires no immediate physical response or if the stress response is greater than the need, then stress is inappropriate or wrong. This kind of stress is widely experienced and is more personally and socially injurious and causes more deaths than addictions to smoking, alcohol and drugs or the ravages of automobile accidents. About 30 percent of adults in the United States say that they experience high stress levels nearly every day; an even higher percentage reports high stress once or twice a week. This is stress in its pathological rather than healthy mode.

Stress is problematic to us when, instead of occurring intermittently in stretching or threatening situations, it becomes a recurring or habitual phenomenon caused by overstimulation and hyperactivity. Stress creates difficulties when it does not let up and when it is triggered by ordinary, everyday events. In our society this kind of stress has reached epidemic proportions. People in earlier times may have worked harder than we do and may have become more physically fatigued, but no generation has ever been as psychologically hyped up, exhausted or stressed out. Nervous breakdowns, burnout and stress-related illnesses and deaths are common. In the past it was only in extreme situations, such as mass warfare, that large numbers of people underwent severe stress. Now it is found in everyday situations and especially in the workplace.

Types and Degrees of Stress

The many general sources of stress have been documented: (1) continual busyness, the hectic pace of life and regulation by the clock; (2) constant noise, activity and movement, caused personally or by the immediate environment; (3) overly crowded and congested freeways, streets, shopping malls and other settings in which considerable time is spent; (4) long-term demanding or threatening circumstances that stretch people beyond their normal limits; (5) unrealistic expectations or anxiety-creating deadlines, leading to overwork and sometimes workaholism; (6) repeated shock, confusion or conflict in unfamiliar social and cultural situations; (7) chronic tension in family situations or relationships that creates ongoing anxiety. These things in themselves are not stresses; it is how they are perceived that induces stress. So an important distinction is generally drawn between the sources of potential stress and an individual's perception or interpretation of them, making these sources into stressors.

When we are stressed, our bodies pump more adrenaline to help us cope. If this continues beyond a reasonable time, we suffer from stress disease, and our performance becomes adversely affected. When this happens, not only our nerves but our whole bodies are stretched. Stress then seeks out a weak link in our system. Connections have been established between stress and exhaustion, depression, insomnia, migraines, ulcers, colitis, high blood pressure, asthma, allergies, alcoholism, heart disease and divorce. Chronic stress depletes both the brain's natural tranquilizers and the body's immune system, leading to a greater reliance on chemical tranquilizers, painkillers and antibiotics. The number of days lost to the workplace from all this and the indirect and direct cost to the individuals concerned are quite staggering.

Measuring devices like the Social Readjustment Rating Scale seek to quantify the amount of stress caused by various life events and then to analyze how vulnerable a person is to serious physical or psychological illness. At the top of the list of stressors are bereavement of a spouse or member of the family, divorce or marital separation, getting married and marital reconciliation, retiring or being fired, personal injury or illness. In the middle of the list are changing jobs or living conditions, taking out a heavy mortgage or facing forclosure, an outstanding personal achievement or trouble with the boss, a son's or daughter's leaving home. Near the bottom of the list is a change in eating habits, having a vacation or committing a minor violation of the law. When a person's score nears or overshoots 300 points, there is a 90 percent likelihood that he or she will experience some physical illness or psychological disturbance in the very near future.

Stress in the Workplace

One of the main settings in which stress occurs today is the workplace. For an increasing number of people a high level of abnormal as well as normal stress is created at work. Conditions, practices, structures, attitudes, expectations, relationships, changes and systems in the workplace often produce strains that are higher than elsewhere. Given the grave consequences of long-term abnormal stress, working can be a risky affair. Since work or the lack of it is now the dominant reality in Western life, its contribution to the amount and degree of stress in contemporary society must be carefully examined. It has been estimated that up to 50 percent of workplaces in the country are overly stress-producing. This includes many religious organizations and churches. It is little wonder that stress has become the greatest cause of job dissatisfaction and reduced productivity. Often complaints about conditions at work or about others in the workplace mask a deep stress over the character of the job itself. Sometimes this results in workers suffering from vague and undefinable sicknesses. Stress in the workplace can take many forms. Among the most serious forms of stress are the following.

Tensions with superiors. Bosses tend to generate stress if they love power, are overly ambitious, refuse to take responsibility for mistakes, cannot make decisions in a timely manner, do not maintain appropriate boundaries, tend to have unreal expectations of their employees and often display anger or fail to give affirmation. Superiors who have a need to control or intimidate are often uptight and overstressed themselves. Sometimes they try to minimize their own stress by provoking stress in others. Stresses further arise when employers do not give enough space for employees to use their full capabilities or expect more than some employees are capable of contributing. A supervisor's behavior toward subordinates is probably the single greatest contributor to stress in the workplace.

Problems with coworkers. This takes many forms. Examples include the clash of incompatible personalities and of conflicting beliefs or values, the lack of group cohesion and collaboration, failure on the part of some to pull their weight (especially when the performance of others is dependent on this), sexual harassment or abuse, racial prejudice or discrimination and even having unresponsive and emotionless colleagues. On the other hand, relating too intensively in the workplace or having too much concern for sexual and political correctness can also give rise to tensions. Tragically, this stress sometimes leads to violence in the workplace. Around one thousand people in the United States are killed at work by colleagues each year.

The atmosphere of the workplace. Organizational culture is largely shaped by workplace traditions and senior management. Workplace atmosphere is affected negatively by such internal factors as the inaccessibility of the ultimate decision makers, their lack of consultation with the rank and file, their inflexibility or incompetence, their being out of touch with current realities or unaware of the personal needs of the workers and their failure to establish adequate personnel policies or to provide proper staffing for an organization. Workplace atmosphere is also affected by external forces such as new technology, downsizing because of competition or the economic climate and the need for a more flexible and mobile work force. The attitudes and behaviors of workers themselves contribute to the atmosphere in such things as distrust of newcomers and outsiders, resistance to change or new ideas, an overly critical spirit or a passive-aggressive attitude toward the organization, fragmentation of the work force into competing interest groups or a tendency to find regular scapegoats for repeated workplace problems.

Personal struggles with work. Serious stress in the workplace is also caused by an employee's not fitting in a job, fear of unemployment, sidelining or demotion and attempts to strike a healthy balance between work and family or leisure. Boredom is also a major problem in the workplace.

As with the Social Readjustment Rating Scale, there are also instruments like the Job Stress Survey that measure occupational stress. People in different kinds of workplaces suffer from different kinds and levels of stress. Ranking highest in severity and occurrence is inadequate salary and lack of opportunity for advancement. After this comes problems related to superiors, such as those previously noted. Next comes problems relating to colleagues, such as others not doing their job properly. This is followed by matters relating to work conditions, such as meeting deadlines, excessive paperwork and inferior equipment.

What distinguishes stress in the workplace from stress elsewhere is its translation into dollars and cents. Given the central place financial reward plays in our society, this tends to heighten both the significance and level of stress there. Stress costs money not only in lost earnings and profits but in claims and medical costs. For example, around one-sixth of all workers' compensation claims now appear to be stress related, and over the last decade and a half such claims have risen exponentially. The stakes are high in the search for healthy responses to stressors.

Ways of Handling Stress Constructively

One unhealthy response is simply to resign oneself to it, but this is filled with physical and psychological risk. Others desperately seek to control the situation so as to minimize stress, but this often places others under unfair strain. There are more constructive ways of handling stress, and it is incumbent on those who have the greatest chance of making changes to find these. This places a heavy responsibility on boards of directors, senior management, employers, heads of departments, union officials and coaches. Here we will focus on what we as workers can do to improve the situation.

First, we should discern how much stress we are under. Symptoms we will look for include personal ones such as the use of substances to escape problems, overdependence on distractions, general sense of unhappiness, conflict with or avoidance of significant others. Emotional symptoms include tension and anxiety, restlessness and irritability, panic feelings or periodic depression, increased daydreaming and fantasizing, a general lack of responsiveness, including sexual responsiveness. Stress has health indications as well: high blood pressure, headaches, constant fatigue, sleep problems, ulcers, racing heart, muscle tension and aching and increased vulnerability to sickness or viruses.

Second, we should identify the source of the stress. This involves examining both external factors and our internal responses, the actions of others and our own perceptions of what is happening.

Third, we need to take responsibility for dealing with stress rather than expecting others to relieve us of stress. The two basic options here are fight or flight. Both are found in the biblical narratives. For example, Moses took up his leadership burden with God in prayer and was given a resolution to his problem; on the other hand, he ran from his God-given responsibility. Resistance can take several forms, among them thinking about the situation to get clarity on the key factors creating the stress, sounding out others by asking questions or sharing experiences that focus on your issues, owning up to your share in letting it get out of hand. The next stage is communicating this where it will do most good, generating discussion about the general issue of stress and setting individual or team priorities so that stressors can be minimized. Sometimes this involves saying no and seeing what the consequences are. A further stage is engaging in practices that will provide energy for this struggle until the situation improves: regular exercise, meditation and contemplation, listening to what our bodies are saying, eating a balanced diet and experimenting with ways to relax.

Sometimes, however, flight rather than fight is the best response. We find biblical examples of this even in the life of Jesus: stretched and exhausted by the number of people seeking his ministry, he withdrew into an isolated place for a time (Matthew 4:23; Matthew 5:2). This was not avoidance but a recognition that the problem was too overwhelming to be fought successfully in his present condition. Flight can take a variety of forms: asking to be demoted or moved sideways to a less stressful and more enjoyable position. It might also entail resigning from one's present position and seeking similar work in a less stressful workplace or another kind of work altogether. Sometimes people need a period of withdrawal, perhaps without pay, so that the whole situation can be reviewed in a less-harassed way and strength can be built up to fight or pursue a new path.

Whatever tactic is taken up, fight or flight, it is imperative that some action be taken. The alternatives are either eventual burnout (the last desperate plea from our whole system that "enough is enough") or physical breakdown (the whole system that has been pushed too far seizes up). In all this we need to recognize that we cannot control all the events of life. Our attempts to handle stress responsibly will be successful only to a point. What we can gain with God's and others' help is some control over our own feelings and a stronger sense of identity.

See also CONFLICT, WORKPLACE; OFFICE POLITICS; WORKPLACE

References and Resources

R. Crandall and P. L. Perewe, *Occupational Stress: A Handbook* (Washington, D.C.: Taylor & Francis, 1995); R. E. Ecker, *The Stress Myth: Why the Pressures of Life Don't Have to Get You Down* (Downers Grove, Ill.: InterVarsity Press, 1985); A. Hart, *The Crazy-Making Workplace* (Ann Arbor, Mich.: Servant, 1993); L. Levi, *Stress Sources: Management and Prediction* (New York: Liveright, 1967); J. Schor, *The Overworked American: The Unexpected Decline of Leisure* (New York: BasicBooks, 1991); F. C. Richardson, *Stress: Sanity and Survival* (London: Futura, 1979); J. C. Smith, *Understanding Stress and Coping (New York: Macmillan, 1992); P. Tournier, ed., Fatigue in Modern Society: Psychological, Medical, Biblical Insights* (Atlanta: John Knox, 1978).

—Robert Banks

STRIKES

Strikes have been with us for a long time. In the eighteenth century they were called *turnouts*. The word *strike* was first used in connection with a work stoppage involving British sailors who struck (that is, lowered) their sails to bring their ship to a halt. The term was eventually used in contexts other than nautical ones to describe a cessation of work by any group of employees.

The purpose of this article is to evaluate the strike on the basis of a Judeo-Christian understanding of justice and conflict resolution. To do so, we will first note the historical reasons that have made the strike dear to the hearts of labor unionists. A brief look at the prevalence of strikes will allow us to put them into perspective as a part of overall economic activity. Finally, ethical perspectives on strikes will be considered.

Strikes and the Rise of Unionism

Early Canadian and American unions incorporated some biblical principles into their methods and objectives (*see* Unions), but they did not oppose the use of the strike to further their aims. Gradually the union movement became more secular in its orientation. Whether unions leaned more in a Judeo-Christian or secular direction, employer response to their efforts was universally the same—fierce, even ferocious, resistance. Unions learned to respond in kind. In 1910, for example, trade unionists bombed the *Los Angeles Times* plant. In 1914 National Guardsmen opened fire on striking miners in Colorado, killing many.

It was a series of highly successful strikes against four major U.S. employers in the 1930s that brought labor unions into the mainstream of economic life in North America. In 1936 Congress passed the Wagner Act, which not only recognized the right of workers to organize but compelled employers to engage in collective bargaining with their unions. It also forbade any employer interference or domination in the formation or administration of unions. Similar Canadian legislation followed in 1944.

The lesson that union leaders learned, more than any other, from their history was this: strikes work—whether legal or illegal, quiet or violent, however costly in terms of dollars, reputations, even lives. No other method works better. To this day unions are convinced that this highly successful weapon must be retained to accomplish their objectives of furthering the economic and social interests of workers and the general betterment of society as they see it.

Strikes and the Economy

Advocates of the strike weapon will point out that as a percentage of working time, person-days lost to work stoppages are minuscule and pale in comparison to the impact of illness, absenteeism, involuntary unemployment and even weather. In 1989, for example, time lost to strikes in Canada was 0.18 percent of working time, whereas person-days lost to illness were more than five times that figure. Strike opponents, on the other hand, note that Canada and the United States are conflict-ridden compared to most of their international competitors and trading partners. In the period from 1960 to 1984, for instance, time lost from strikes in Canada was forty times that in Japan and five hundred times that in Germany and Sweden. These sharp contrasts have not altered greatly in recent years.

Industrial relations scholars admit that very little is known about the costs to society of strikes and lockouts, largely because of the lack of research on the issue. Strictly in terms of direct dollar costs, it could perhaps be argued that the economic impact of strikes is not as great as is often believed. But whatever the costs are, strike supporters argue that they are inevitable given the adversarial foundation of our industrial relations system. Any substitute for the adversary system, in their opinion, would be far more costly than strikes. How else can workers get management to take them seriously and to bargain in good faith?

Opponents counter that such reasoning ignores the experience of other highly successful industrial nations that run much more collaborative industrial relations systems than our own. They also point out that the prevalence of strikes has built up a backlash of bad feeling against the union movement. As one commentator said, "Strikes help some unions. That is not the same as saying that they help all workers; but the costs are borne by society as a whole" (Stewart, pp. 41-42).

Ethical Perspectives

Business ethicists recognize the dilemma that strikes pose. On the one hand, they can cause financial injuries to employers and employees, inconvenience and worse to consumers and at times significant economic problems in society. On the other hand, many feel that workers can often obtain justice only through this means. Given these assumptions, business ethicists William Shaw and Vincent Barry have argued that a strike is justified when three conditions are met: (1) just cause, which refers to job-related matters such as inadequate pay and dangerous conditions; (2) proper authorization, meaning that workers must make the decision to strike without coercion or intimidation; and (3) last resort, which means that all other measures have been tried.

A basic moral principle is that one should always use the least injurious means available to accomplish one's objectives. There are many alternatives to the strike, such as mediation and arbitration, that can achieve workers' objectives. These avenues should be exhausted before a strike is called (Shaw and Barry, pp. 280-81).

The Christian is faced with a quandary. One can deplore the abuse of the strike while at the same time accept that there could be arguments for its legitimacy if it was employed to achieve biblically just objectives, assuming that other methods had proven to be fruitless. As Christian businessperson Fred Catherwood points out,

> The Christian faith teaches us respect for the individual, and if society respects the individual, he must be protected from the possibility of exploitation by those who employ him. . . . The right to withhold labor is usually the only sanction available to the working man. . . . It is natural and right for a Christian to deplore the use of force to settle a dispute. (Catherwood, pp. 74, 76, 80)

John Redekop notes the incompatibility between the strike ethic and the love ethic: "How can a Christian justify doing something as part of a group which he cannot accept as correct individual action for himself?" (p. 14). Christian union leader Ed Vanderkloet maintains, "Most of us agree that industrial conflict is an ugly thing and that we should try to eliminate strikes. But that is not as easy as it sounds. In fact, it is next to impossible" (p. 31).

A strike is never wholly private in its effects. Other people beyond the direct participants are bound to suffer some harm. Unfortunately, it is not always possible to determine the nature and extent of the harm. If one could be convinced that for many strikes the harm suffered truly amounted to mere inconveniences or that only the deserving suffered (such as an evil employer), the moral judgment would be a relatively easy one. But in many cases that assessment would be very difficult to make. Thus, I feel that the considerations leading up to the decision to strike should go beyond what the ethicists suggested to include the following:

1. Is the dispute a grave matter addressing a genuinely unjust situation? (I appreciate the difficulty in assessing this and the temptation to make the assessment in a highly subjective manner.)

2. Have all other avenues for resolving the dispute been thoroughly explored? (Many dispute-resolution strategies have proven to be more effective than is commonly held.)

3. Will innocent bystanders be hurt?

4. Will the legitimate moral rights of others be violated?

Conclusions

Vanderkloet has noted that in medieval Europe trial by battle was the most common means of determining guilt and innocence and of settling disputes. The victor of the duel was assumed to be both morally and legally right. Gradually that system was discarded as people became more aware of the need for doing public justice. Now for virtually every kind of dispute other than industrial ones, our society has developed methods employing impartial judges, juries or umpires to settle them. Only in labor disputes do we still "slug it out on the picket line where ultimately the strongest wins" (Vanderkloet, p. 31).

The strike is to a large extent the major symptom of our adversarial industrial relations system here in North America. It is indeed a powerful instrument and has been used to good effect by organized labor in achieving its aims. But other international trading partners, including those lacking our Judeo-Christian heritage, have developed more just, collaborative industrial relations systems in which the use of the strike is a fraction of ours. Labor and management alike have tended to wave aside too easily the potential for alternative dispute-resolution strategies. The time has come for North Americans to decide whether the status quo represents either economic or ethical sense.

See also TRADES; UNIONS; WORK; WORKPLACE

References and Resources
F. Catherwood, *On the Job: The Christian 9 to 5* (Grand Rapids: Zondervan, 1983); J. H. Redekop, "Should Christian Teachers or Nurses Ever Strike?" (unpublished); W. H. Shaw and V. Barry, *Moral Issues in Business,* 5th ed. (Belmont, Calif.: Wadsworth Publishing, 1992); W. Stewart, *Strike* (Toronto: McClelland and Stewart, 1977); E. Vanderkloet, *In and Around the Workplace: Christian Directions in the World of Work* (Toronto: Christian Labour Association of Canada, 1992).

—John R. Sutherland

STRUCTURES

Life is full of visible and invisible structures all of which are fundamental to making sense of life in this world. There are structures obviously made by human beings (such as buildings and bridges), structures of living things (such as the bone structure of animals and the organization of a microscopic cell) and invisible structures (of such things as time, works of literature and the human psyche). In every aspect of everyday life—marriage, work, business, leisure, church, and social responsibility—we encounter structures for good or ill, often as a mixed blessing.

The word *structures* communicates two things: how the members of the whole are related to each other and how the whole achieves some purpose. The structure of a house expresses how the various building materials are put together so that the purpose of the architect is fulfilled. The structure of a poem describes how the words and lines are put together to create the impact intended by the poet. Structures help us to experience regularity, pattern, form and order. Without these there would be chaos, anarchy and confusion.

Intentional Order

The biblical account of creation describes God's bringing order out of chaos, the formless void mentioned in Genesis 1:2. God separated light from darkness (Genesis 1:4), the sky from the waters (Genesis 1:6-7), the sea from the land (Genesis 1:9) and the day from the night (Genesis 1:14), so bringing order to the formless void. In the ancient Near East the symbol of disorder was the sea (or the sea monster)—that unpredictable and uncontrollable domain whose saline substance could not be used by an agrarian society. But in a number of places in the Old Testament, Hebrew poets declare God's control over the sea. By setting a boundary for it, God made possible an ordered creation (Genesis 1:5-9; compare Job 38:8-11; Psalm 74:12-17; Psalm 93; Proverbs 8:29).

Living things were also created in a structured way: vegetation of all kinds appears with seeds to reproduce (Genesis 1:11-12); sea creatures, birds and land animals are all assigned their respective places to live and given the ability to reproduce (Genesis 1:20-25). Finally, human beings were made in God's image so that they might have stewardship over creation (Genesis 1:26-28). Genesis 2:1 summarizes the work: "Thus the heavens and the earth were finished, and *all their multitude*" (NRSV, emphasis ours)—this last phrase often being translated as "host" or "army." Like an army, the creation consists of a diverse collection of objects, properly arranged and organized. So creation is literally a *kosmos,* an ordered world, which, as the apostle Paul says, continues to be held together in Christ (Col. 1:17). But this world making, of which structures are so central, is not exclusively a divine work.

Genesis 2 suggests that part of the mandate God gave to Adam was also to bring order into the world. Adam was to take care of the garden (Genesis 2:15), an activity that involved creating and maintaining order. Adam was invited to name the animals (Genesis 2:19-20)—a work requiring insight into the nature of each one—thereby bringing order to the diversity among all the creatures. Part of the godlikeness of human beings is that people are invited to be cocreators with God, an activity that involves crafting structures.

To summarize, we live in a structured world; while God always remains free to do whatever he wants, there is an order to the world that God both creates and maintains. This structure is intelligible; we can discover something about this order by observing God's creation. Human activity involves creating structures, though not at the same level as God's creative activity.

Discerning Given Structures

Part of the human vocation is to discern and delight in the ordered way God has made the world in which we live and work. Even people who do not believe the biblical account of creation still assume the world is structured and that it is meaningful to ask questions about why things are the way they are.

Making the physical world intelligible. Scientific investigation would not be possible if the physical world were not structured (*see* Creation). Scientists try to explain the various patterns they observe in terms of laws. Johannes Kepler, for example, noted that planets travel in elliptical orbits. Isaac Newton then suggested that the reason for this was the gravitational force between a planet and the sun—an attractive force directly proportional to the product of their masses and inversely proportional to the square of the distance between them. This turned out to explain not only planetary orbits but also why apples fall to the ground. Newton's gravitational law helps us understand something about the structure of our world.

In chemistry Dmitri Mendeleev's periodic table of the elements demonstrates something of the internal structure of the hundred or so basic substances known to exist and explains family resemblances among them. In biology the process known as *photosynthesis,* whereby chlorophyll in a plant uses sunlight to combine carbon dioxide and water in the production of more complex compounds such as sugars, is another description of the structure of the world. Gregor Mendel's observations regarding the breeding of peas has given us insight into the structure of heredity.

A dramatically new approach to exploring structures in the world is emerging from the field of chaos theory. Here the focus of attention is on how very complex and apparently random systems—systems too complex to be explained by the relationships among the various parts (that is, by natural laws)—can in fact be the result of very simple and well-defined causes. The structure of such things as clouds, coastlines and trees are of particular interest.

The term *fractal* was introduced to denote structures whose pattern repeats itself at different levels of magnification. Blood vessels, for example, are fractal. Beginning with the aorta of the heart, the blood vessels continuously branch and divide until in the capillaries the blood cells flow through single file. This structure has several advantages: (1) it is a very efficient way of transporting a limited supply of blood to each cell in the body; (2) the volume taken up by the blood vessels is only 5 percent of the body; and (3) the amount of information needed to encode this structure in the DNA is relatively limited since the pattern simply repeats itself over and over again. It turns out that many naturally occurring structures can be more easily understood in terms of fractal rather than Euclidean geometry, which limits itself to shapes such as squares, triangles, circles and so on. Concerning the latter, James Gleick suggests that Euclidean shapes "fail to resonate with the way nature organizes itself or with the way human perception sees the world" (pp. 116-17). The German physicist Gert Eilenberger comments on why we see beauty in natural landscapes but not in cityscapes: "Our feeling for beauty is inspired by the harmonious arrangement of order *and disorder* as it occurs in natural objects—in clouds, trees, mountain ranges, or snow crystals" (quoted in Gleick, p. 117, emphasis ours).

The structure of the physical world is wonderful—literally. It evokes wonder, as it did for the psalmist: "O LORD, how manifold are your works! In wisdom you have made them all" (Psalm 104:24 NRSV). So the scientific exploration of structures in space is a holy occupation, but so is the study of structures in time.

248

Structured time. The regular movement of the earth structures our lives: days are divided into periods of light and darkness, a time to work and a time to rest. Years are divided into seasons, which are often celebrated in some way. In the biblical account of creation, the days are also gathered together into groups of seven with the seventh being a day of rest—a time to align oneself with the pattern God established in creation (Exodus 20:8-11) and to reflect on God's work in bringing about liberation (Deut. 5:12-15; *see* Leisure; Sabbath).

The Israelites, like most societies, celebrated various seasonal events (for example, new moon, harvest), but often combined these with the memory of significant events in their nation's history: Passover celebrated the exodus from Egypt at the time of the barley harvest; the Feast of Weeks (Pentecost), originally a celebration of the wheat harvest, later became a commemoration of God's giving of the law on Mt. Sinai; and the Feast of Tabernacles, coinciding with the olive harvest, was a celebration of God's preservation of the chosen people through the wilderness.

The teacher of Ecclesiastes, reflecting upon various rhythms of life, notes how various actions are appropriate at one time but not at another: at one time it is appropriate to weep, at another to laugh; at one time to tear, at another to sew (Eccles. 3:1-8). So to discern the appropriate action for each day of our lives, we need wisdom.

The moral structure of the universe. According to the Bible the wise person has insight into the created order. Certain patterns of behavior are compatible with the way God intended; others conflict with it. Although freedom is often thought to be an escape from all structure, it is found by living within the boundaries of created structures.

The purpose of legal and Wisdom literature in the Bible is to make these structures clear, to instruct people on the way God intended life to be lived. The Ten Commandments are like a fence marking out an area in a field within which life will thrive. Breaking the law is like crossing the fence into forbidden territory; it is self-destructive behavior. In the Wisdom literature the field is divided, not so much into right and wrong, but into wise and foolish. Not only in morality but even in artistic expression, there are given structures.

Structure and the arts. Artists find avenues of expression by creatively working with the structure and content of their media: poets and storywriters crafting words into stanzas and plots, sculptors using hammer and chisel to create form from a piece of stone (often finding the structure in the stone itself), musicians transforming vibrations of strings, reeds or wind cavities into melody, harmony and rhythm (*see* Music). While human creativity is involved in all artistic expression, artists must respect the implicit structures and forms of their media.

Social and political structures. We were also created to live in families and nations, these being ordained by God as fundamental social structures (Romans 13:1). These are not merely invented by humans but designed by the Creator as a social context for our good. Without them we would destroy ourselves in random promiscuous relationships (were there no family) and in anarchy (were there no government and no nation).

Politics is essential to the human vocation and a service rendered for the commonweal (the common good). These contextual structures define a sphere for human activity and give people a sense of identity. The sin of Babel (Genesis 11:1-9) was precisely the desire to create a homogenous, uniform world without national boundaries, without diversity as expressed in nations and people groups. God intended national structures to exist. "From one man he made every nation of men, that they should inhabit the whole earth; and he determined the times set for them and the exact places where they should live. God did this so that men would seek him and perhaps reach out for him and find him" (Acts 17:26-27).

Being World-Makers

But in all of the above areas, human beings are not only those who inherit an intentionally structured world that God could consider as "very good" (Genesis 1:31); human beings are also world-makers. Human creativity involves making human structures: in the physical realm (through architecture, technology, science), in time (through planning and sabbath), in morality (through developing life patterns to express love and justice), in the arts (through making new things, which is the heart of creativity) and in society (through the art of government and politics).

In *The Sacred Canopy* Peter Berger has helpfully outlined the dynamic process in which we shape our world and in which our world shapes us. This involves three movements: (1) through cultural expression we relate to the world around us; (2) at some point we begin to experience the world, which has been shaped by our actions, as an object distinct from ourselves; and (3) this world then has the capability of acting back upon us and shaping our lives.

An example of this process is the creation of a nation. The founding fathers draft a constitution outlining the ideals (for example, equality of all people, democracy, freedom of speech) on which the nation will be built. Then they proceed to put in place people, institutions and laws to ensure that these ideals will be realized. But at some point the nation takes on a life of its own and is no longer dependent on the support of its founders. Finally the ideals expressed by the founders and protected and promoted by various means influence the lives of the citizens.

Every day we experience the influence of a wide variety of social structures—the nation, workplace, families, churches and so on. Each has been shaped by human activity, and each in turn shapes the lives of those living under them. But in world-making we face a double problem: we do not feel free to "make our worlds" the way we believe we should, and what we make turns out to be a mixed blessing, sometimes even a curse.

Fallen Structures and the Powers

Every day we encounter unjust and unloving structures, principles of conformity (for example, professionalism), negative cultural expectations, laws without moral foundations, technology as master and not mere servant, intractable institutions. With the growing awareness among social scientists of the role of social structures in shaping behavior, emotions and actions—often a detrimental influence—many theologians have begun to ask how the Bible addresses this reality. One approach has been to see a double reference in the phrase in Paul's letters "principalities and powers" (or more literally, "rulers and authorities")—one on a human level, another on a cosmic or spiritual level.

The background to this is in the Jewish belief that God assigned various angelic beings to rule over each of the nations (Deut. 32:8-9; *Jub.* 15:31-32; compare Psalm 82, where God chastises the members of the heavenly council for not extending justice to the poor). This idea seems to be reflected in Daniel 10, where Michael, the angel overseeing the affairs of Israel (Daniel 12:1), is in conflict with the prince of Persia. Heavenly and earthly events paralleling and influencing each other (compare Rev. 12:1-12) is typical of apocalyptic literature.

The fact that Paul uses words such as *rulers* and *authorities* to refer to cosmic powers—words that normally denote earthly figures—and the fact that he uses such words more than others that clearly refer to spiritual beings (for example, *Satan* and *demons*) suggest that he has both earthly and heavenly realities in mind when he speaks of rulers and authorities. Thus, when he writes in Colossians that all rulers and authorities have been created in, through and for Christ (Col. 1:16); that Christ is the head of every ruler and authority (Col. 2:10); and that Christ, by means of the cross, disarmed, exposed and triumphed over the rulers and authorities (Col. 2:15); he is referring not only to spiritual realities but also to structures of human existence.

Paul further expounds the relationship between spiritual powers and earthly structures in Ephesians, where he points out that believers struggle against rulers and authorities (Ephes. 6:12). This, however, is the conclusion to his section on the ethical implications of the gospel in which he appeals for unity within the church (Ephes. 4:1-16), godly living in the midst of a pagan society (Ephes. 4:17-5:20), husbands and wives loving each other (Ephes. 5:21-33), children and fathers relating properly (Ephes. 6:1-4) and slaves and masters showing mutual respect (Ephes. 6:5-9). When Paul talks about "spiritual" battles, he has in mind the very concrete situations of life: marriage, family, work, church, society. It is in these structures that spiritual forces are at work.

A further insight comes from the New Testament about the power of sin. The word *sin* normally refers to an act contrary to God's will. But Paul also uses the word to refer to a power that enslaves people to a life of self-centered activity (Romans 5-8). The significance of choosing the word *sin* to refer to such a power (rather than *Satan* or *demons*) appears to be that Paul saw an interrelationship between the acts and the power. Clearly, the power promotes the acts, but it is also true that the acts feed the power.

Recall Berger's description of world-building. Once again we can see how this applies. We are world-builders, but we are sinful ones. Therefore, everything we build in our world—institutions, culture and so on—is at least to some degree infected by sin. As this world takes on a life of its own and shapes the lives of people, it will also promote sin. How are we to relate to fallen existing structures or to the task of creating new ones?

Grappling with Structures

There are four historic approaches to relating to structures as powers, each one involving a view of reality (metaphysics) and an approach to the human vocation: (1) exorcism and intercession (dealing with the demonic in society), (2) suffering powerlessness (bearing witness to the kingdom of God as a redeemed society and refusing to resist evil), (3) creative participation (taking our part, to function as regents and stewards, in all the institutions of the world) and (4) engaging in a just revolution (overthrowing the existing structures, with violence if necessary).

In the way of exorcism, the assumption is that our role is to continue the liberation of individuals from bondage to Satan by preaching and prayer. The powers are much more than social structures. The social structures are merely fronts for Satan's grand plan to woo people away from God.

The way of suffering powerlessness is patterned after the way of the cross. Many in the Anabaptist tradition take this approach. Our role is not to change society directly but rather to witness. When we do this, even at the loss of our own lives, we expose the fallen state of all human rule and reflect God's action in the cross and the coming kingdom. The powers have been colonized by Satan and can only be overthrown by God. When the world is off center, it would take a lever with a fulcrum outside the world to move it. Christians, according to this approach, believe that the lever to move the world is the wooden cross.

The way of creative participation assumes that our role is to be stewards on earth. According to the creation mandate we are called to order and husband all the dimensions of societal and creational life. The structures have been colonized by Satan (according to some) or merely reflect the fallen condition of human beings (according to others). But it is possible, indeed it is our vocation, to bring these structures into conformity to the rule of Christ. We do this through our daily work, social action and mission. The danger in taking this approach exclusively is to minimize the demonic and the nonhuman forces and personages that we encounter in our public discipleship.

The final option is the way of the cleansed temple with Jesus as the model revolutionary. It has been promoted actively by liberation theologians, both Catholic and Protestant. One such Christian revolutionary, Dom Helder Cmara, summarized the dilemma implicit in taking this approach with these searching words: "When I give people food, they call me a saint. When I ask why there is no food, they call me a communist" (quoted in Brown, p. 86).

Which approach is right? Indeed all, with the possible exception of the last, have strong support in Scripture and may be chosen in particular circumstances. The people of God as a whole must engage in a full-orbed approach. But discernment is needed.

Christ's complete victory over the principalities and powers, over Satan, sin and death, assures us that there is nowhere in the universe so demonized that a Christian might not be called to serve there. We fight a war that is already won. Therefore, as much as is now possible, Christians should Christianize the powers, to "peace" the powers through involvement in business, education, government, politics and social action, all the while knowing that the task of finally subjugating them is reserved for Christ alone (Ephes. 1:10; Phil. 2:10-11). We work on the problems of ignorance, pollution, food distribution, injustice, genetic engineering and the proliferation of violence and weaponry, knowing that this work is ministry and holy. In the short run our efforts may seem futile, but in the long run this work will be gloriously successful because we are cooperating with what Christ wants to do in renewing all creation. In this we must live with heaven-mindedness, knowing that Christ said, "All authority in heaven and on earth has been given to me" (Matthew 28:18). While the beast is master here for a moment (Rev. 13:1-18), all dimensions of social unity will be restored according to God's design. And in the New Jerusalem the redeemed principalities and powers will provide structure for our common life and work (Rev. 21:24).

See also ORGANIZATION; POWER; PRINCIPALITIES AND POWERS; SYSTEM

References and Resources

C. Arnold, *Ephesians: Power and Magic* (Cambridge: Cambridge University Press, 1989); P. L. Berger, *The Sacred Canopy: Elements of a Sociological Theory of Religion* (Garden City, N.Y.: Doubleday, 1967); H. Berkhof, *Christ and the Powers,* trans. J. H. Yoder (Scottdale, Penn.: Herald, 1962); R. M. Brown, *Spirituality and Liberation* (Philadelphia: Westminster, 1988); W. Carr, *Angels and Principalities: The Background, Meaning and Development of the Pauline Phrase "kai archai hai exousia"* (Cambridge: Cambridge University Press, 1981); J. Ellul, *The New Demons* (New York: Seabury, 1975); J. Gleick, *Chaos: Making a New Science* (New York: Penguin, 1987); H. Schlier, *Principalities and Powers in the New Testament* (New York: Herder & Herder, 1964); W. Wink, *Engaging the Powers: Discernment and Resistance in a World of Domination* (Minneapolis: Fortress, 1992); W. Wink, *Naming the Powers: The Language of Power in the New Testament* (Philadelphia: Fortress, 1984); W. Wink, *Unmasking the Powers: The Invisible Forces That Determine Human Existence* (Philadelphia: Fortress, 1986).

—Gerry Schoberg and R. Paul Stevens

SUCCESS

Any decent dictionary can define success for you in an unexceptionable way. *Success* is attaining a desired result. Thus, a successful building project is one in which the building gets built, and a successful builder is one who can complete such projects. The problem comes when you stop talking about specifics like buildings and builders and begin talking in general. What does it mean for a *person* to be a success? The question does not ask about success at something in particular, like constructing a building. Rather, it asks about success as a person.

Here the dictionary definitions are not so helpful. It is difficult for a mere dictionary to tell you the desired result of being a person so that you can check to see if you have attained it. Dictionaries do try, however, to express dominant cultural values. A typical desktop dictionary gives this as a second meaning: "the attainment of wealth, position, honor, or the like."

Cultural Understandings of Success

Such a view of success has two strong variants in Western cultures. The first is the "crass" vision of success. A commonly seen poster embodies this meaning. It shows a pile of cars, jewelery, houses, and money. At the bottom is the caption: "He who dies with the most toys wins." The poster is poking fun at the crass vision of success. But that understanding of success is around us and has its appeal. Yet when we actually think about living life compiling material goods, just so we can die at the end, it seems less compelling. The crass vision of success cannot seriously help determine whether a person has attained the desired result of life.

The second common variant of success avoids the excesses of the crass vision. It says that success in life means being materially comfortable and relatively independent. Attaining these goals allows you the possibility of attaining whatever other goals you might decide are worth pursuing. This vision is somewhat attractive. Being free from the immediate requirement of self-preservation and being safe, fed and warm do seem to be a good foundation for whatever particular success you might want to achieve. Yet there is a subtlety here. This common vision of success, for all its attractions, is what you might call vertical. It envisions success as being attained by an individual's climbing over adversity and attaining comfort. And the not-so-hidden assumption is that the measure of this success is still fundamentally economic. In the end this variant is not all that far from the crass vision of success.

Everyone wants to be successful, by which we mean attaining some set of life goals. But the economic description of success implicit even in the comfort-and-independence idea is far too limited to describe what we really mean by success. As a thought experiment, consider the following people who were undeniably successful in some sense but do not fit into the comfort-and-independence idea of success: Socrates, Jesus, Francis of Assisi, Søren Kierkegaard, Mahatma Gandhi, Martin Luther King

Jr. This list could be extended arbitrarily, but the point it makes is simple. Many people have been successful in a way we find meaningful without having been either comfortable or independent. Some of them deliberately sacrificed both comfort and independence to attain their success. Furthermore, some of them attained success that was outside the scope of their own lifetimes: they died as failures but were clearly successful nonetheless.

We should call the people on this list (and others who could easily be added to their number) the *uncomfortable succeeders*. They make it clear that success is both broader and deeper than the simple definition of comfort and independence would lead us to believe. Success seems to be inextricably linked with attaining goals that are deep within a person but also far broader than a single individual. Whatever success as a person is, it is neither simple nor, apparently, easily attained.

Success and Character

Stephen Covey claims to have uncovered two divergent themes in two centuries' worth of American literature on success. The first dominated for the 150 years or so, and he calls it "the character ethic." This approach "taught that there are basic principles of effective living, and that people can only experience true success and enduring happiness as they learn and integrate these principles into their basic character" (Covey, p. 18). The character ethic includes virtues like integrity, fidelity, patience, industry and simplicity, virtues that can be attained only through sacrificing a certain amount of comfort and independence.

The past fifty years has, by contrast, been dominated by a vision of success that Covey calls "the personality ethic." In this vision "success became a function of personality, of public image, of attitudes and behaviors, skills and techniques, that lubricate the process of human interaction" (Covey, p. 19). Various schools of positive thinking and other popular approaches counsel that manipulating your own personality to maintain a particular attitude, or to "win friends and influence people," is the correct approach to success.

Covey and others have found this latter approach, however dominant it has been for the past two generations, fundamentally flawed and superficial. It thinks of success as something *added to* a person (like comfort and independence) rather than something that *grows out of* a person. Success understood in terms of a character ethic sees it as something that comes from the gradual unfolding of the best of what a person can be. But although success is rooted in a person's becoming a good person, exemplifying the virtues of that life, success is not limited to a kind of personal evolution and attainment, however good it might be. The uncomfortable succeeders may perhaps have been virtuous individuals, but that is not the measure of their success. Rather, they were successful in that they were successful *for others* regardless of what they attained for themselves.

The uncomfortable succeeders, and many like them, are successful just because they are not driven to attain success in its own right. Rather, they are driven to serve others, to make them successful, and so become successful themselves in the process. Kierkegaard's way of saying this is that it must be approached by means of indirection. To be successful, you must not try to find success directly. Instead, by trying to attain a different goal like helping others succeed, you discover that (lo and behold!) success has found you.

A Biblical Vision of Success

If we come to the Bible with one of the common understandings of success, it will provide us no help at all. Indeed, some analytical concordances show no uses of the word *success* at all in English translations. This, in itself, does not mean that the concept of success is absent; rather, it may imply that many translators believed that the common sense of success was not a good match for what the biblical writers were trying to express.

If the biblical writers believe in success, they do not think it is at all wrapped up in comfort and independence. On the contrary, they are often exhorting those who will listen to seek other goals. Success, for them, is measured by the attainment of other goals for the sake of other people. As good an example as any of this inversion of the idea of success comes in the letter to the Philippians. Quoting what was apparently a common Christian song of the time, the letter says,

Let the same mind be in you that was in Christ Jesus,

who, though he was in the form of God,
     did not regard equality with God
     as something to be exploited,

but emptied himself,
     taking the form of a slave,
     being born in human likeness.

And being found in human form,
     he humbled himself
     and became obedient to the point of death—
     even death on a cross.

Therefore God also highly exalted him
     and gave him the name
     that is above every name,

so that at the name of Jesus
     every knee should bend,
     in heaven and on earth and under the earth,

and every tongue should confess
     that Jesus Christ is Lord,
     to the glory of God the Father. (Phil. 2:5-11 NRSV)

This is a remarkable vision of the path to success. First, it is highly centripetal in its orientation. Far from concentrating on the self and arranging things so its goals are met, the orientation is spinning outward as hard as possible. Everything here is other-directed; nothing is oriented to self-attainment. Second, the vision of success finds its fulfillment not in success but in another state entirely: servanthood. The servant has no guarantee of comfort nor independence (compare Phil. 4:10-13). Yet the way of the servant is, paradoxically, the way of success. In order to find success one cannot grasp after it but must accept and embrace its opposite. If you want with all your heart to be successful, that passion itself will make you fail; if you are willing to become a servant, you will find a different kind of success waiting for you there.

The uncomfortable succeeders all, in their own manners, went the way of the servant. Embracing service gave them the freedom not to have to succeed and so allowed them to do so. Jesus and the other uncomfortable succeeders knew their efforts were doomed from the point of view of success measurement. By not concerning themselves with attaining success, but instead concerning themselves with being servants, they allowed success to surprise them and overtake their activities.

For this very reason, because Jesus humbled himself, God gave Jesus the name above all other names. Those around us who seek directly for success find that it eludes them. All they have in its place are the ambition and self-involvement they used in their quest. The crass vision of success, according to which the one who has the most toys when he dies wins, has loftier neighbors, each of which is just as wrong. The goal may be the most friends or the most good deeds or the most converts or the most victories. In every case they are less crass than the materialistic version and no less wrong. All seek success directly and can be measured against their particular goals. All miss success, from the biblical point of view, because they are not willing to attain success on the way of the servant.

References and Resources

S. R. Covey, *The Seven Habits of Highly Successful People* (New York: Simon & Schuster, 1989).

—Hal Miller

SYSTEM

In everyday discourse we sometimes hear people say, "Blame it on the system!" or "You've got to know the system to get ahead." What do we mean by such language? And how are we to think in Christian terms about the experiences to which such talk refers?

A *system* is a number of things connected together as a whole. The whole is not a random happening but gives evidence of regularity and order in its organization and method, in its plan and operation. The human body is a system of systems, and within the body we can identify a skeletal system, a circulatory system, a nervous system and so on. A machine, like an automobile or computer, is a system. Most of us have some kind of stereo system at home, an integrated whole composed of various electronic components. Schools and colleges are usually thought of as parts of an educational system. Nature and the environment form an ecosystem of interdependent parts. A system may be rigid or flexible, enduring or evolving, formal or informal.

To understand any individual thing, we need to attend to the systems of which it is a part. It is not enough simply to isolate something for study and reflection; we must also see its roles and relations within its systems. In the academic, business and professional worlds, there are now specialists in systems engineering and systems analysis.

A Christian Approach to Systems

God's creation brought forth a kind of system. The individual parts of this created system (man and woman, animals, plants, the sun, moon, stars, etc.) each have a certain uniqueness, dignity, beauty and purpose (*see* Structures). But the individual parts are intended to flourish in relationships, not in isolation. As a whole, this created system displayed an equilibrium of freedom and order, innovation and constancy, individuality and community. The social system intended partnership and complementarity, meaningful work and rest. The broader ecosystem was characterized by beauty as well as utility.

The fall away from God and into sin brought disorder into God's created system. While the grace and providence of God have sustained the systems of our universe as a livable milieu, humankind's alienation from God is the fundamental cause of our problems in coping with the "systems questions" of our experience. Our social systems degenerated from partnership to competition, oppression and exploitation. Our ethical and moral systems replaced reliance on God's judgment of what is good with a quest to know and declare autonomously what is good and what is evil. In place of God's system of partnership, we soon had a rigid separation in the roles of man and woman, polygamy, a violent competition between brothers and the creation of systems of war. Systems of idolatry and religion replace the living relationship with God.

Christians should not reject the notion of systems per se but should adopt a critical and redemptive stance toward them. We cannot live without systems of some kind—but systems can be better or worse, and they can help or hinder our pursuit of God's purposes for life. Our intervention into the various systems of nature is part of the human task. What is necessary, especially from a Christian point of view, is that these interventions (to fight disease, increase food production, explore the universe, acquire sources of energy, etc.) ought to be undertaken with respect for the value and integrity of God's creation. As stewards and caretakers of God's creation and as responsible keepers of our brother's and sister's life, we must be careful not to add to the disorder of the world through our interventions (*see* New Reproductive

Technology). This is not an easy accomplishment in an era of great threats, great needs and a voracious appetite for technological development.

Our social systems present us with other challenges. Some of these systems, for example, families and households, tend to be informal. Traditions, habits and unarticulated expectations and assumptions often form an invisible system within which we carry out our tasks. Even so, such systems for child rearing, decision-making and other activities can be better or worse. We cannot make every decision *de novo*. We need continuity, stability, tradition. But we must reflect critically on these patterns and systems. Are they promoting the partnership, dignity, growth, beauty and goodness of each member as God's creation intended? Are they redemptive, reconciling, healing and life-giving as our Lord intends?

Businesses, churches, schools, community groups and political organizations also have informal systems: customs, habits and traditions for decision-making and action. But they also, more than family and friendship, create systems of formal structures and policies. The organizational structure (administrative hierarchy, bureaucracy, committees, job descriptions) might be thought of as the "skeleton" and "organs" of the system. Constitutions, laws, regulations, curricula, policy statements and employee handbooks describe the functional "circulatory system" in such social systems. Social systems, in short, have formal structures and processes as well as informal constraints.

The Challenge of Reforming Systems

We cannot live and work very well without such systems. No business or community or school will survive without adequate organization, without developing its system. Nevertheless, social systems can become unjust, repressive and even demonic. History gives us many examples of political structures whose laws were blatantly racist or discriminatory against women, religious and ethnic minorities, the landless or poor. Businesses, schools and churches have also been prone to systematic, structural and procedural evil and oppression.

Even when structural reforms have occurred, informal traditions and old-boy networks have kept many systems frozen to improvement. Reforming the system requires not only formal structural and procedural changes but changes in attitudes and values in the organizational culture. It is, of course, more difficult to reform the many than the few: the size and scale of organizations and systems present special problems. It is more difficult to reform the old and long-standing than the new and recent; old habits and traditions die hard. It is more difficult to reform the successful than the struggling; leaders and beneficiaries are resistant to upsetting the apple cart. It is difficult to bring about reforms without them being undergirded by powerful, shared values.

Part of the difficulty in reforming social systems arises because of the way responsibility is diffused in organizations. The "buck" gets passed around, and individuals find responsibility avoidable or unattainable: "It's not my fault." "That's the way we've always done things, and I can't change that." This resistance to change leads some to argue that at a fundamental level organizations and systems have been captivated by the principalities and powers of evil. Well-intentioned individuals seem incapacitated by a demonic system.

Christians will recall that Paul "used the system" when he appealed to Caesar (Acts 22:25-29; Acts 25:11). Peter urged subordination to human institutions and even to the economic system of slavery (1 Peter 2:13-25). On a personal level, however, Paul urged Philemon to set free his slave Onesimus (Philemon 8-16). The New Testament suggests that (1) where possible, we create new, transformed systems bearing witness to the creative and redemptive purposes of God; (2) we speak up on behalf of those oppressed, challenging the masters of the system to be accountable to God; (3) we encourage those who are struggling under the weight of the system; and (4) when caught within an oppressive system, we exercise faithful servant leadership, trusting God to use our faithful, alien presence to bring about divine purposes in due time.

In short, blaming our predicaments on "the system" may be true enough; evil and good are structural and systemic as well as personal. In fact it may be the system more than any individual's malice that is the source of our displeasure. But the assignment of blame hardly begins to describe the Christian calling in the world. Rather than seek objects to blame, we should look for causes to address and create redemptive alternatives that bear witness to the goodness of God.

As Paul did, we may "use the system" but never in a self-serving, world-compromising way. We want to be "wise as serpents and innocent as doves" (Matthew 10:16 NRSV), but this counsel to prudence must never justify an abandonment of our identity as the children of light, the citizens of God's kingdom, the ambassadors of the coming age of Jesus Christ. Because the weapons of our warfare are spiritual and because our battle with "the system" is not always with flesh and blood but rather with principalities and powers, with the cosmic powers of this present darkness, we must always be vigilant in prayer, and we must draw close to our fellow soldiers in the Christian community as we carry out our life in various systems (Ephes. 6:10-18).

See also AMBITION; FAILURE; PROFESSIONS/PROFESSIONALISM

References and Resources

L. von Bertalanffy, *General System Theory* (New York: Braziller, 1968); L. von Bertalanffy, *Perspectives on General System Theory: Scientific-Philosophical Studies* (New York: Braziller, 1975); P. Collins and R. Paul Stevens, *The Equipping Pastor: A Systems Approach to Empowering the People of God* (Washington, D.C.: Alban Institute, 1993); E. H. Friedman, *Generation to Generation: Family Process in Church and Synagogue* (New York: Guilford Press, 1985); A. W. Schaef and D. Fassel, *The Addictive Organization* (San Francisco: Harper & Row, 1988); E. H. Schein, *Organizational Culture and Leadership: A Dynamic View* (San Francisco: Jossey-Bass, 1991); P. Senge, *The Fifth Discipline: The Art and Practice of the Learning Organization* (New York: Doubleday, 1990).

—David W. Gill

TECHNOLOGY

In the popular mind *technology* usually means things like machines. Technology is what engineers give us: telephones, fax machines, automobiles, electric lights, water purification plants, compact disk players and so on. We live in a high-tech world—a world of computers and advanced technologies. While we might resist some aspects of modernity, it is very difficult to establish and live out a critical perspective on technology, the very thing we will explore in this article.

Defining Technology

Our word technology derives from the Greek roots *technē* and *logos*. As biology is the study of bios (biological life) and theology is the study of theos (God), so technology originally meant "the study of *technē*." *Technē* is the Greek word for an art, skill or craft—for a technique of making or doing something. In this basic sense, of course, we could say that birds have techniques for building nests, beavers have techniques for building dams, and flies have techniques for irritating us. Human beings also have always had techniques—various arts, skills and methods for meeting their needs and desires—for building houses, making clothing, raising and preparing food (*see* Meal Preparation). We have had other techniques for making decisions, governing ourselves, communicating with others, raising children and worshiping God.

Some of our techniques are handed on by our traditions. Others are imposed by authorities: "This is the way we do this; period!" But what distinguishes our human (from animal) techniques is our capacity to revise or replace our various techniques through the application of our rationality. Human techniques are not just a product of our instincts or traditions but of our reason. We do not merely submit to nature but create artificial means; we develop tools to more effectively achieve our ends or goals. The difference between science and technology is that while science aims to know and understand things, technology aims to change things, to have a practical effect, to be useful.

Today, of course, we use the word *technology* not just for "the study of techniques" but for "tools" and "techniques" themselves ("Do we have the technology to do this or that?"). This subtle change in language highlights the fact that our modern techniques are now virtually all linked with study (discourse, *logos*), with research and rational analysis. There remain, of course, techniques that are handed on by long-standing tradition, socialization, religious faith and even biological instinct. But such techniques are in retreat because of the demonstrable, measurable success, the efficiency, of our rational technologies.

Technology in the Modern World

For most of human history, nature has been the primary milieu in which human life, including human technical development, proceeded. Specific techniques assisted life in remarkable ways, but choices were conditioned primarily by nature. For example, the length of one's workday was determined by when the sun rose and set. The range of one's movement was typically confined to the distance one could walk or ride a horse. Learning was passed on from one person to another and depended on the presence of a living teacher.

Human life has also been conditioned by society and human culture. Traditions placed constraints on what people did. Values, embedded in customs and expressed in beliefs, constrained the development and use of techniques. Even if nature allowed the conditions for work, social or religious tradition might prevent you from working during certain times (for example, the institution of the sabbath day), at certain places (for example, sacred burial grounds or mountains) or in certain ways (for example, cruelty to animals, dietary prohibitions against pork, etc.). So too, the way one worked or played might be defined by social roles assigned to men and women, to old and young or to one social class or another.

But in the modern world, while neither nature nor human culture is a negligible factor, our primary milieu is technologically defined. We can work as long as our electrical power keeps the lights on and our computers running. We can travel as often and as far as our transportation technologies will take us. Our entertainment is for the most part technologically constructed. Social taboos against shopping or working on Sunday have disappeared. Socially determined roles for men and women, for old and young, have largely, though not entirely, disappeared. For the most part today, what we do, how we do it, where we do it, is determined by technology not by nature or social tradition. We live in a technological milieu.

How Technology Serves Us

For most of us most of the time, this change to a technological milieu is a good thing. Who would want to return to a time when the whims and constraints of nature were so confining? And who would want to return to a situation in which often irrational social traditions decided the possibilities of life for one's class or gender? In this sense technology has served and even liberated us.

Consider, for example, how technology has served us by creating tools that vastly extend our human powers: construction tools like hammers instead of rocks, then jack hammers instead of sledge hammers; medical tools like x-ray machines, prostheses and pharmaceuticals; transportation tools like planes, trains and automobiles; communication tools such as television, compact disc players, computers and fax machines. The list of technological tools is awesome. The ways these tools have served us is spectacular.

Technology has also served us by its development of methods. Technology is not just tools; it is a method of rational analysis, of quantification and measurement, of empirical testing, of innovation, of new ways of approaching problems. In the material world technology is the method of rationally analyzing how to move things from one place to another, how to multiply, divide, simplify or combine various elements and factors. As such, technology helps us break down a production and distribution process into its constituent parts and then restructure the process toward greater efficiency.

The method that works with automobile assembly lines and other material processes is also applied to human relations, as in the conduct of business meetings, the creation of effective advertising and the development of psychotherapy. Technology is the creation of better means, in fact, of the "one best means" in every field of human activity. Modern bureaucracy, for example, operates under the rule of technological method—even if in practice it often is far less efficient than we would like.

How Technology Masters Us

Modern technology is not only our servant but our master in some important ways. It frees us in some ways; in others it constrains us and sets our agenda. This mastery has four characteristics.

Technology is ambivalent. This means that specific technologies always have both positive and negative aspects. It is common to say that technology is neutral and only its use or its users are good or bad. But technology is not neutral, nor is it exclusively evil or good; it is both good and bad. Certainly you can say that, for example, a gun in the hands of a crook will be put to bad use, and a gun in the hands of a good person can be put to good use. But it is the technology itself that makes possible these uses. One cannot simply invent guns without weighing these outcomes and deciding whether to proceed. So too, the development of automobiles not only results in freedom to travel but also in pollution, in serious injuries to people and in anonymity that facilitates social breakdown. The possibilities of television are accompanied by the loss of human conversation and the capacity to entertain oneself in a spectator era.

Our lives and choices are mastered and increasingly determined by both the positive and negative impacts of technology. Every benefit is accompanied by a cost. Often the positive and negative impacts of a technology are not fully seen by their inventors. Monks who invented the clock in the Middle Ages to add precision to their daily prayers in service of God did not realize that it would end up being a major instrument in the service of mammon by regulating work. The inventor of the stethoscope did not foresee that physicians would lose their capacity to listen to patients as they increasingly relied on technical instruments interposed between them and human beings. Inventors of computer networks did not foresee that pornography would be the major content traveling on their information superhighway.

Technology has an almost deterministic force. Technological developments create technological problems that require further technological responses ad infinitum. There has been a qualitative shift from earlier eras in which specific tools and techniques were developed through the freely chosen creativity of human beings to meet specific, limited objectives. Technology now obeys its inner logic of development as rigorously as we used to think that nature obeyed its own laws. This necessity is especially visible in a larger view of the technological complex as a whole. "If it can be done, it will be done; indeed, it must be done": technology carries its own imperative to further development. Who today can oppose technological expansion and development?

Technology is universalistic. It invades every area of the world and every aspect of human existence. This is what Neil Postman calls "technopoly"—a monopoly over all human affairs. This includes the geographic universalization of technology. Every corner of the world is affected by technological intervention. Global development means technological development. Traditional ways of agriculture are replaced by technological ones. Traditional forms of governance must be replaced by bureaucracies. Those who resist are condemned to live at best as an underclass, at worst as the refuse dump of the globally dominant technological complex.

But technological universalism or technopoly also refers to the invasion of technology into every aspect of our lives. Politics and campaigning are technicized; sport and entertainment are dominated by technologies; public relations and fundraising obey technological laws; churches employ public relations techniques to build their memberships; even prayer and spirituality are analyzed and taught as a set of rational techniques for manipulating God and the self. Sexuality, the last domain of the truly wild and mysterious, has never been so technicized—not just in terms of reproductive or prophylactic technologies but in the technical analysis of the sex act itself. Our physical space is dominated by technological instruments; our psychic space is dominated by the method and values of technology: rationality, effectiveness, measurable success.

Technology serves as the sacred. The sacred or the divine is whatever occupies the very center of our existence, giving our lives unity, direction and meaning. The traditional gods have been toppled and replaced by technology. Traditional gods may receive lip service in church or in private conversation, but in practice, on Monday morning if not before, it is technology that is served. Technology is our hope for the future and for our present-day salvation. When something is omnipresent, omnipotent and not subject to criticism, when it inspires and compels our sacrifices and praise, it is serving as a god. But is technology an adequate god? Or is it a bogus pretender to divinity that needs to be demythologized and desacralized? Is the technogod ultimately a liberating, redeeming god or an enslaving one?

Another way to express this is by saying we have moved from technology to *technologism*. Adding that *ism* is a way of saying that technological thinking and values have become the foundation, the worldview, the criterion of all judgment. The potential goodness of technology is radically in question when it develops into technologism as an all-embracing intellectual, moral, cultural and spiritual identity.

The questions are these: Who or what is in control of our lives? Have we become mere tools of our tools? Have we made technology the god of our civilization? Gods always demand some kind of worship in return for the salvation, meaning and direction they offer. The worship demanded by technology has meant lives of frantic absorption into the latest technological development. Our lives are dominated by the products and the problems of technology. Our learning is dominated by the acquisition of technological literacy and competence.

We should evaluate this covenant with technology by asking what has been excluded. What has been lost is the value of the inefficient, the nonrational, the aesthetic, the spiritual and the traditional. Love and beauty, for example, are prostituted and lost when they are made to serve a technological calculus. Relationships with family members and colleagues are seriously distorted when rationality and efficiency are the criteria of value.

Four Basic Responses to Technology

Responses to this kind of critical questioning of modern technology usually take one of four forms.

Denial. Some will deny that there is a problem and protest that modern technology is more or less desirable and under control. This first response is partly a product of exhaustion. We simply do not have the time or energy to stop and take a critical look at the broader dimensions of what is happening to our human life. We are too busy. It is also true that our technological society provides innumerable distractions and opiates to its members. Denial is also a product of a lack of perspective. Most of our technologically trained population at large have little significant background in history, philosophy, theology and non-Western cultural attitudes. Yet these are precisely what we need for a critical perspective. We have much knowledge of a certain type, but little wisdom. Hence we tend to regard our Western technological perspective as the only legitimate one, though it is by no means the only perspective in the Western tradition, to say nothing of the rest of the world.

Love of technology. A second response allows that we have some serious dysfunctionality in our technological civilization, but we only need more and better technology to resolve these problems. This is the *technophile* response, the true believers. The priests and evangelists of technology want to get everyone on the information superhighway—with an integrated office system, linked to our home entertainment and work centers and to our portable cellular phone and powerbook computer. Thus the technological environment becomes essentially airtight, and everyone is technologically linked to everything at every moment. But where is this superhighway going?

Fear of technology. Opposite the technophiles are the third group, the *technophobes*. In the Industrial Revolution these were the Luddites, the band of protesters who wished to smash the machines and maintain a more balanced existence. The hippies of the sixties made a somewhat similar call, but romanticism and adolescent anger make a flimsy foundation for resistance, as the subsequent absorption of the sixties generation into the yuppies has demonstrated. Technological reactionaries are doomed to be the colorful feather in the cap of the technological giant: a dash of color on a giant who moves forward unimpeded.

Resistance and revolution. This response calls first for a profound awareness and critical analysis of our reality: the reality of the technological main currents under the surface of the ocean of our existence and the reality of our flesh-and-blood neighbors. For such awareness we must stop relying on *USA Today* and on *CNN*-type news bites—and invest our time in broader, deeper works of cultural criticism, including historical and multicultural perspectives that will give depth and breadth to our own analysis of social and cultural reality. Along with this we will need to turn off the distractions and carve out time to develop human relationships with people around our living and working areas. This means learning how to listen, how to be quiet, how to reflect deeply, how to care.

With this growing awareness, we need to resist, indeed, to refuse the necessity, universality and divinity of technology in our life and work, that is, "just saying no" to technology at decisive points. But gods do not easily vacate their thrones. To dethrone the old, we need to install a more appropriate one. To begin with, we can resist in the name of humanity. Our thinking, living, working and playing can revolve around the sacredness of human life, earth and universe in which, and with which, we flourish or come to grief. Concretely this means that people are not reducible to statistics, that intelligence is not reducible to IQ numbers or degrees held or genetic maps, that this living student or friend before me is sacred and is more important in his or her living wholeness and mystery than any rational calculation could ever account for. So we need to replace technologism with a robust humanism.

Christians, of course, would suggest that the strongest foundation on which to base such a humanism and to resist technologism is a theological one in which the transcendent God who created the universe and human beings is invited back into our sacred space. We would say that humanism is true and good because God has created humans in the divine image, whereas technological civilization tends to promote uniformity and reduce individuals to faceless atoms in a mass society. Biblical people would say that to mistreat or undervalue a person is to mistreat an irreplaceable child of God. To exploit and to abuse the earth and the universe are not merely a technological dysfunction but a serious sin against God and his creation.

Resisting technology as a pretender to the place of God in our lives can thus proceed from resistance to a revolution in values that rebuilds authentic individuality and community—a life in which we do not smash the machine, but we do question it, appraise it in reference to our human or religious values, and then sometimes say yes and sometimes no to its deployment as a servant in our lives.

266

The Impact of Technology on Theology and Religion

Without any doubt the development of certain technologies has served theology and the religious life in impressive ways. Communication techniques, most notably translation techniques and the printing press, have made possible a relatively inexpensive, massive diffusion of the Bible into the hands of the people, bringing new spiritual life to multitudes. It has also tended to move authority away from hierarchies and elites, who alone previously had access to Holy Scripture, into the hands of literate, popular masses. Better transportation has facilitated people's possibilities for gathering together for worship, witness, learning and service. Radio, television and other media have multiplied the potential exposure of large numbers of people to things theological and religious. Organizational, public relations and therapeutic techniques have contributed to the effectiveness of some aspects of religious life. Political techniques are now being used by various religious groups (for example, the "religious right") to increase their social impact, for better or worse.

But while noting the benefits, we must also ask how we respond to the lies, half-truths, manipulation and corruption that are technologically foisted on a gullible audience? Technology has vastly increased the potential impact of religious hucksterism and charlatanism. And how should we evaluate the impact of the technological medium on the life and message it is intended to serve? What is lost when the dynamic, personal character of the Christian gospel is replaced by the passive, depersonalized character of watching religious television (*see* Televangelism)? What is lost when pastoral searches, evangelistic campaigns, fundraising campaigns and pastoral care are primarily structured by technobusiness models and methods?

Technology as a worldview and intellectual paradigm tends to progressively put in question and then marginalize the traditional, inefficient, unquantifiable, nonrational and transcendent. Individual techniques and technologies need not necessarily have this exclusionary impact. But we live in the era of technologism, of the global technological ensemble, of technology as infrastructure and intellectual/spiritual paradigm.

Towards a Theology of Technology

Any theological critique of technology must return to the biblical sources. There we find that technology is an expression of divinely created human creativity and imagination, of doing and making good and helpful life-enhancing things. Technology and engineering are the expression of our human imagination and creativity in forming and transforming nature for practical purposes and uses. While there is plenty of biblical material emphasizing the spiritual and inward over the material and external, this is balanced by passages affirming the concrete, external world of things. For example, the Old Testament describes in detail the materials, dimensions and building techniques for Noah's ark, Moses' tabernacle and Solomon's temple. In a classic text, Moses says, "See, the LORD has chosen Bezalel . . . and he has filled him with the Spirit of God, with skill, ability, and knowledge in all kinds of crafts . . . to engage in all kinds of artistic craftsmanship" (Exodus 35:30-33).

A major problem arises, however, when we treat technology as sacred, when it moves to the center of our lives, receives our sacrifices, bestows meaning, direction and significance on what we do. The root problems are idolatry and autonomy. What should be carried out in a living relationship to God, subordinate to the character and plans of God, is now autonomous, subject to nothing except its own internal imperatives. Such technology carries with it no respect for nature, social tradition, religious authority, the absurd or the paradoxical, the weak and the unproductive. And yet all of the foregoing are part of the world God has created and wishes to redeem. So it is essential for us to develop a theology of technology.

God's creativity as the source of human theological imagination. Recall the accounts in Genesis 1-2. God created; God made the heavens and the earth. God gave shape, order and design to what was without form, filled what was void or empty and illuminated the darkness. What God made was described as "good," "useful" and "pleasing to the eye." What God made was diverse, complex and awesome in scope. It was orderly and bounded but also set free.

We human beings are made in the image and likeness of this creating God. So the first and basic source of our own creativity is this fact of our nature. But human creativity and technology are not just an exhibition of our nature—they are also a response to the command and invitation of God. It is the freedom of obeying God's Word that underlies technological activity in a biblical worldview. God commands us: "Be fruitful and multiply," "Fill the earth and subdue it," "Have dominion," "Till and keep the garden," "Name the animals." At its best our technological creativity continues to bear witness to God's creation when it combines innovation harmoniously with what already exists as good, when it contributes both beauty and utility to the world and when it allows both individual uniqueness and partnership/community to flourish.

Human creativity is bounded. Our technological and creative work is bounded in four ways. First, it is launched by the Word of God. Creation begins when God says, "Let there." Human work begins when God says, "Be fruitful . . . fill . . . subdue . . . till . . . keep . . . name." It doesn't begin out of idle curiosity, boredom, greed or lust for power. Second, it is bounded temporally by the sabbath: God rests on the seventh day and so do those made in God's image. There is a time to cease from technology. Third, it is bounded spatially in that there is a tree at the center of the garden that is not to be harvested for food; a limit is respected; it was a tree that could be harvested but must not be. There are limits that technology should not transgress. Finally, human creative work was bounded ethically in that the prohibited tree was the "ethics tree"—the tree of the knowledge of good and evil. Humans were to live and work in relationship to the God who sees and names the good; they were not to try to take this ethical knowledge for themselves outside of this relationship with God. All technology must be subjected to this fundamental ethical judgment of God.

Human technology now needs redemption. The Fall occurs when man and woman misuse their freedom, breech the boundaries and grab for the fruit of the ethics tree. The human situation changes dramatically. They are evicted from the garden and cannot go back. Technology is itself now fallen, sometimes perverse and violent, open to becoming idolatrous and autonomous.

Because of the Fall, the creativity motifs in a theology of technology must now be caught up within a theology of present and final redemption. Redemption means that in a fallen, broken world we are not able to act naively. Realism means we must take account always of the potential for deception and destruction in our work. Redemption means that our work (our technology) must aim at healing what is hurting, repairing what is broken, liberating what is in bondage, preserving what is degenerating, conserving what is disappearing. Creating, illuminating, ordering, filling, naming—these original motifs of creation continue, but the arena is no longer pure and innocent. Sacrifice, servanthood and humility will need to characterize a redemptive technology.

Human technology must keep the end in view. Technology is a development and perfection of means. But in our civilization the means have become ends in themselves and are developed without adequate attention to the proper ends of human life. Christian life is eschatological life: it is life lived in expectation of the coming end, the consummation of God's kingdom and purposes. The Holy Spirit is given as the pledge, the down payment, of our future inheritance. Christians lean toward the future (Romans 13:11-14). Thus, our technology needs a new, rigorous assessment of the true ends of human life. In the light of these ends, specific technologies can be assessed and evaluated. Our means must not be self-justifying. They must be justified by God's end, and then they must exhibit the character (not the contradiction) of that end.

Faithful Technology

Our challenge is to recover the notion of fidelity. The most important exercise of fidelity is toward God and his Word. After the Fall of Adam and Eve, God continues to speak to humankind. Often the word of God takes the form of questions: Where are you? What have you done? Where is your brother? Who do you say that I am? Faithful technology will hear God's commands and questions, seeking them not only as the starting point of our technological activity but as its boundary. It will aim to contribute to God's purposes for life in the world, trying to discern and respect appropriate limits and boundaries in space and time.

Fidelity to God means trying to hear God's ethical judgment on our projects instead of pronouncing our own and overcoming evil with the good. Fidelity to God means fidelity to our Creator and Redeemer. Faithful technology will not just be fruitful, fill, subdue, create, name, till and keep—but will go into all the world, love your neighbor, love your enemy, heal the sick, set free the captives, comfort the lonely, welcome the children.

Fidelity also must govern our relationships with others. Faithful technology will not subordinate people to technique. It will express faithfulness to partners, neighbors, friends, fellow humans. It will promote technology on a human scale. It will refuse to reduce people to technical categories, not try to adapt people to the requirements of technology. It will invite others to help rebuild the boundaries and discern and support good technological work.

Our modern choices with respect to technology are symbolically represented by the tower of Babel and Abraham's altars (Genesis 11-12). The technology of Babel intends to make a name for the self, make security for the self, breech all limits, choose and occupy its own chosen place. But the technology of Abraham builds an altar for God and lets God care for our reputation, protect and guide us to the place he chooses. As Christians we know we cannot go back to Eden. We must go forward either to Babylon, where Babel's project is fulfilled, or to the New Jerusalem, where Abraham's project is fulfilled. The afterlife is depicted in the form of a city, not a new garden, into which the nations bring their glory. We must pray and work that something of our own generation's technology might be worthy of a place in that city of God.

References and Resources

I. Barbour, *Ethics in an Age of Technology* (San Francisco: Harper Collins, 1993); D. J. Boorstin, *The Republic of Technology* (San Francisco: Harper & Row, 1978); J. Ellul, *The Presence of the Kingdom* (London: SCM Press, 1951); J. Ellul, *The Technological Society* (New York: Vintage Books, 1964); S. C. Florman, *The Existential Pleasures of Engineering* (New York: St. Martin, 1975); G. P. Grant, *Technology and Justice* (Toronto: Anansi, 1986); C. Mitcham, *Thinking Through Technology* (Chicago: University of Chicago Press, 1994); S. V. Monsma, ed., *Responsible Technology* (Grand Rapids: Eerdmans, 1986); N. Postman, *Technopoly: The Surrender of Culture to Technology* (New York: Vintage Books, 1992).

—David W. Gill

TRADES

At thirty-seven years of age, with two university degrees and a well-established professional career, I became a tradesman and apprenticed to a carpenter in the home renovation business. Most of my ministerial colleagues thought I had temporarily lost my moorings. But I had several good reasons. My wife and I were called to plant a new church, and without a salary being volunteered, we needed to support ourselves financially (*see* Financial Support; Tentmaking). Further, I liked to work with my hands and have a natural talent for making things out of wood. But finally I was convinced that I needed to see the work world of the ordinary Christian "from the bottom up." In the modern Western world professionals are at the apex of the occupational pyramid, business and craftspersons a notch down, with tradespeople and common laborers near the bottom. This is the case not only in so-called secular society but in the church, where leadership positions on boards are normally filled by professionals and executives. It has not always been so and certainly was not so in the Bible. But every day, as I hammered and sawed and ate my lunch with drywall tapers and electricians, sharing their worlds and their loves, I was being educated in what could be called a blue-collar or denim-jeans spirituality.

Trades, as distinguished from professions, are occupations that employ primarily manual skills learned mainly in the context of apprenticeship on the job and result in making things, normally for pay. In contrast, *crafts*—personal skills employed in an artistic and aesthetic manner—are ways of making things that are intrinsically beautiful whether or not they are useful or sold. A craft may be undertaken as a hobby for the sheer pleasure of enjoying oneself and God's creation or as a remunerated occupation, such as the work of a silversmith or perfumer. A trade may involve craftsmanship but not necessarily so, as in the case of the electrician.

Trades in the Bible and Beyond

In contrast to the hierarchy of occupations in the modern world, the Bible witnesses to a wide variety of ways of working without rating them on a scale of public importance or divine approval. For example, Deuteronomy prescribes that the king must not enrich himself through his position (Deut. 17:16) and must "not consider himself better than his brothers" (Deut. 17:20). In contrast to the view today that charismatic pastors and religious leaders are likely to be the most Spirit-filled persons, the only Old Testament saint who is specifically said to be "filled . . . with the Spirit of God" is a craftsman, Bezalel (Exodus 31:3). The rich diversity of occupations named in Scripture, more than two hundred in all, has been researched by Walter Duckat in *Beggar to King.* The entries under *C* alone are indicative of the significance given by the Bible to trades and crafts: calker, camel driver, candymaker, captain, caravan chief, carpenter, carpetmaker, cattleman, census taker, charioteer, cheese maker, choirmaster, chorister, circumciser, clothier, cook, coppersmith, counselor, counterfeiter (not an approved occupation!), cupbearer, custodian and customs clerk.

Duckat notes that the life of the Hebrews in the Bible was similar to a medieval village, being largely agricultural and fairly self-sufficient. Farming and shepherding were the fundamental occupations for men and homemaking for women, something which in ancient times included crafts such as weaving. But specialists emerged in due course and guilds of craftspeople, merchants and even guilds of prophets were formed for common economic and cultural benefits (Duckat, p. xv). This was the beginning of the modern trade unions. In biblical times people followed in the footsteps of their father or mother with little regard to *job satisfaction,* that relatively modern obsession.

By the time of Jesus and the birth of the church, there was a stunning contrast between the Greek view of trades and the Jewish. In the Jewish world it was a duty to have a trade. So Jesus was a carpenter and Paul a tentmaker. The Talmud said, "He who does not teach his son a trade is as if he teaches him robbery" (*Tosepta Qiddušin* 1:11). Duckat notes, "The Hebrews were virtually the only ancient people who preponderantly viewed work as dignifying rather than demeaning" (p. xxi). In contrast, the Greek world into which the church was also born held laboring in contempt. The work of tradespeople was for slaves. Citizens should occupy themselves with contemplation and politics. The tension between these two views is with us to this day and is manifested in the hierarchical arrangement of "valuable work" within the Western Christian mind, even though this was temporarily corrected by Luther (Hardy). The professional minister and missionary are on the top, those in people-helping professions next, then business and then, near the bottom, trades. Someone really serious about serving God leaves the trade world and "goes into the ministry" rather than the reverse.

Trades as a Reflection of Society

With industrialization the world recovered the dignity of trades once again with the worker as the engine of economic development. Karl Marx took this a step further and made manual work, including the trades, as the primary means of finding the meaning in life, without, of course, any reference to a supreme being. This lopsided view of work made an idol rather than a curse of work. It failed to recover work as part of one's calling, viewing it instead as the whole of one's calling. But with passing from the industrial society to the information society, trades have slipped once again, giving way to the omnipotent knowledge worker dealing everyday in computer bytes rather than two-by-fours and pneumatic nailers. Routine manual work on assembly lines is being replaced by robots, and most of the trades are desperately trying to project an image of expertise as almost everything from rug cleaning to garbage collection gets "professionalized."

Duckat notes that "how work is viewed in any society casts important light on the prevailing thinking, social structure, and values of that people" (p. xx). The thought can be extended. What kind of work is praised casts a revealing light on the mindset of the church and what it really values. Further, it shows what we think of God and whether we are a people who resemble their God.

The gods of antiquity, and especially those of the Greeks, spent their time in debauchery or pleasures. The Hindu gods occupied themselves with everlasting repose. But the God of the Bible is a worker, a craftsperson, a tradesperson—the maker of things and people. Robert Banks's rich discussion of the metaphors of God as worker shows that almost every human activity imaginable that is for the common good is something God does. So the Talmud credits God with the origination of all trades (*Midrash on Genesis* 24:7).

How can we demean trades and worship God at the same time? Does our attitude to work constitute a more direct way of "speaking rightly of God" (which is the heart of true theology; see Job 42:7) than our written theological tomes? If hymnology is sung theology (*see* Music, Christian), is work acted theology? So what can be done to recover the dignity of trades?

Recovering the Dignity of Trades

First, the church can become truly countercultural in treating every member of the body with equal dignity, refusing to estimate the value of people by degrees, income and social approval. This is part of empowering the whole people of God. Why do we interview visiting missionaries on Sunday and not tradespeople to find out how their faith makes a difference to everyday life? The relative absence of blue-collar workers in many churches is a simple reflection that they do not feel welcome or prized. But on a deeper level it is an indication that we are something less than the new humanity (Ephes. 2:15) characterized by a broken wall between formerly separated people. If people of the same "kind" gather together as they would anyway, Christian or not, Christ is not confessed. There is no new creation in evidence.

Second, we can help tradespeople revision their daily work as ministry. Tradespeople need to receive affirmation in ways other than good pay for their sometimes monotonous work. They are indispensable to the healthy functioning of society. A city can manage without a mayor, at least for a while, but not without its trash collectors. As with all other forms of human work, tradespeople serve God (and therefore are "ministers") by meeting a genuine human need, by making God's world work, by providing for themselves and their families with some to give to others and by doing what they do for Jesus (Ephes. 6:5-9). Through working as a carpenter for five years, I discovered that tradespeople have many advantages. At the end of the day they can usually see what they have done and say to themselves, in unison with their Creator, "It is good" (Genesis 1:31).

Third, we can explore the contemplative dimensions of being a tradesperson. I quickly discovered that at the end of a strenuous day I slept well. Manual work is healthy and is less likely to kill a person than a stressful profession: "The sleep of a laborer is sweet" (Eccles. 5:12). But there is more. While anyone doing business today must wrestle with the principalities and powers, manual work possibly allows one to reflect and pray more "on the job" than in other careers, certainly so when the tools are laid down. As Paul knew so well, working "night and day" as a tentmaker-cum-apostle—visiting people, teaching in a public hall, meeting with churches and sharing the gospel—was invigorating and often challenging. In contrast, most professionals are spent forces when they finally close the office door and often take work home with them, to the neglect of their families, before they attempt a fitful sleep.

A negative note on this subject was sounded by Ben Sira (Ecclesiasticus) in the second century B.C. "Conversation with animals and the noise of the hammer and the anvil are not conducive to wisdom" (Sirach 38:24-33), but this seems to be a criticism against work that consumed time that might be spent in the study of Torah. Indeed, most trades, with the exception of certain high-risk construction workers, allow for greater "leisure" on the job to reflect. An example would be the poems and songs written by David while a shepherd.

Finally, the life of a tradesperson is shot through with intimations of eternity and invitations to develop a denim-jean spirituality: forming things by hand, making the connection between bodily activity and mental creativity, creating something of benefit for others, working in teams, learning and teaching in an apprentice relationship life on life, talking with fellow workers about the stuff of everyday life (sports, food, family, play). Trades are like chores; they are not just opportunities to practice spiritual disciplines, but because of their somewhat tiresome nature and service role, they invite us Godward. Usually there is more laughter and play on a construction site than in a pastor's study. There might even be more prayer.

See also PROFESSIONS/PROFESSIONALISM; UNIONS; WORK

References and Resources

R. Banks, *God the Worker: Journeys into the Mind, Heart and Imagination of God* (Valley Forge, Penn.: Judson, 1994); R. Banks, *Redeeming the Routine: Bringing Theology to Life* (Wheaton: Victor Books, 1993); R. F. Capon, *An Offering of Uncles: The Priesthood of Adam and the Shape of the World* (New York: Crossroad, 1982); W. Duckat, *Beggar to King: All the Occupations of Biblical Times* (Garden City, N.Y.: Doubleday, 1968); L. Hardy, *The Fabric of This World* (Grand Rapids: Eerdmans, 1990); R. Hoppock, *Occupational Information: Where to Get It and How to Use It* (New York: McGraw-Hill, 1967); Jacob Neusner, trans., "Qiddushim," in *The Tosefta*, vol. 3 (New York: KTAV, 1979); Jacob Neusner, trans., *Genesis Rabbah, the Judaic Commentary to the Book of Genesis: A New American Translation*, vol. 1 (Atlanta: Scholars Press, 1985).

—R. Paul Stevens

UNEMPLOYMENT

Many images are evoked by the term *unemployment:* children in rags, soup kitchens, fat employers, government inaction and movies of the Great Depression when men walked hours in search of a day's work. In these images, depending on one's values and beliefs, the tendency is to want to blame someone or something, be it business, individuals or politicians. The fact is that many countries are plagued with high unemployment. In some countries the rate is as high as 12 percent, and in certain age groups, such as youth, it is 20 percent. In many countries on the African continent, where people struggle for basic survival, the category is not even considered.

In the early 1960s there were some who argued that the time was coming when the majority of people would not work; a minority would be employed and provide for the rest. What is happening? Is there a limit to the world's potential or need for work? Is the implication that a portion of the population is going to be chronically out of work? Or delightfully so?

Being unemployed is not simply being "out of work." When a company lays off, fires or downsizes, the persons affected may continue to work doing chores at home, doing volunteer service in church and community and looking for a new job—a form of work itself. Unemployment is the situation in which remuneration for one's labor is absent despite the desire and need for such pay. For people in the Western world, where identity is tied deeply to occupation, the experience is usually devastating; they have become nobodies. But on a personal level unemployment is a time for reassessment and deep spiritual work. On a societal and national level unemployment is a stewardship issue, since it reflects systemic sin and lack of social creativity in providing opportunities for all citizens to use their gifts and talents for the common good.

The Reality Today

Once unemployment was considered a major sin. Now it is often regarded as inevitable. Many blue-collar jobs were lost or moved to different labor markets. While there used to be a safe haven in white-collar jobs, suddenly there is downsizing and reengineering of the firm or corporation. New terms such as *underemployment* are now part of the vocabulary. What does this mean? What is one to do? Does the Bible have something to say about all this?

In some parts of the world unemployment reaches astronomic proportions, such as the 30 percent unemployed in the city of Nairobi. In many Third World cities people may spend up to seven years looking for their first job when they move to the city, since the rural farmlands are now decimated into ever smaller, unproductive units that cannot sustain a family. Unemployment in such areas is harder to define, since most people can provide some of their daily needs for food and shelter from the land unless there is drought, famine or war. Living as we do in a global village, the problem is not merely "their problem" but ours. Robert Kaplan draws a disturbing picture of the disparities between countries:

> Think of a stretch limo in the potholed streets of New York City, where homeless beggars live. Inside the limo are the air-conditioned post-industrial regions of North America, Europe, the emerging Pacific Rim, and a few other isolated places, with their trade summetry and computer-information highways. Outside is the rest of mankind, going in a completely different direction. (p. 60)

In the industrial and postindustrial nations unemployment has taken on a new face. Instead of lifelong tenure with a corporation, school system or government office, most people increasingly face a lifetime of scramble from job to job. Changes in the work world are taking place faster than people can cope. Workers today are faced with unsettling trends: from production to service, from generalist to specialist, from repetitive tasks to intervention (especially by means of the computer), from age-specific education to lifelong learning, from working with tangibles to working with intangibles, and from hard work to stressful work. But one of the most threatening trends is the change from a lifelong career to multiple short-term assignments. This means that most people will experience some form of unemployment in their lifetime, even if the period of transition is brief.

The banking industry is a classic case study (see Aley). Layoffs in this industry, primarily through attrition, are not likely to lead to employment in the same field but rather the use of one's experience of handling finances and people in a related field, usually at a lower salary. Vocational guidance once was the "what am I going to be when I grow up" dilemma of young people. It is now a lifelong discipline. We must also learn to see unemployment itself as a spiritual discipline.

Unemployment and Idleness

How shall we regard unemployment? It does occur in Scripture. Jesus pictures workers waiting to be hired as day laborers without commenting on the morality of the men waiting to be hired or those who did not get hired (Matthew 20:1). More commonly we find reference to the willfully unemployed or idle. This is clearly a sin (2 Thes. 3:10-13). Even in retirement, persons will continue to work doing chores and volunteering so long as they are able. For the independently wealthy or the recently retired, indulging perpetual idleness and leisure is spiritually dangerous (Proverbs 6:9, 10-11; Proverbs 10:5; Proverbs 19:15, 24; Proverbs 20:4).

While these texts are clear, surely there is a difference between sheer laziness and forced unemployment. If so, why do these texts not express it? One assumption is that there was no structural unemployment in Bible times. Another is that there was always work to be done. In an agrarian society of small farmers both assumptions were undoubtedly true. Most people were self-employed in a trade or worked as farmers in the context of an extended family structure in which kith and kin cared for each other, especially during times of famine, drought and economic difficulty. Also there were not carefully defined "jobs" as we know them, separate from the rest of life, but only "work" of various kinds in which everyone was involved, most of which was home-based and a family concern.

It is true that some people suffer unemployment because of poor performance and failure to keep learning in their job. These people may find in unemployment a challenge from God to work, to make a full-time job out of looking for work, to explore the reasons for their lack of really "getting into" their jobs or even their outright refusal to do more than the minimum required. Those suffering "outplacement," as it is euphemistically called, need to cultivate employment as an attitude. One key principle is to insist that the displaced person think of finding a job as being a job in itself.

One should have the same discipline in finding work as holding a regular job—starting time, ending time, dressing for work and so on. Maintaining a frame of mind of actively working to meet one's most important need—to be employed—is essential.

There are always alternatives and choices. My father (Stevens), a business executive, worked in the shipping room for a time when the company had to become "mean and lean." My father (Mestre) was working for a company which fell on hard times. His work was designing, but for several weeks he was assigned to clean up the factory, as it was the only work available. Effort, skill level and attitude are key factors. "Whatever you do, work at it with all your heart, as working for the Lord" (Col. 3:23). This is a text both for those looking for remunerated employment and for those who feel they are underemployed. But for many people the causes of unemployment are more complex. How are we to think and act when the whole economy is disrupted, when unemployment is clearly not the result of one's effort, attitude or performance?

Unemployment as a Structural Evil

When companies go bankrupt, when oversupply forces the government to reduce production until the situation has normalized, when the stock market in Japan crashes and the rest of the economic world suffers major reverses, when the economy of a country requires structural unemployment in order to sustain high salaries, we are dealing with a much more complex reality.

Echoing the view of many economists and sociologists, P. G. Schervitch argues that statistics of unemployment "elude any simple interpretation—the simple fact is that unemployment is not a unidimensional reality" (Schervitch, p. 2). Actually the redundant—people who lost their jobs because those jobs ceased to exist—represent only about one-quarter of the unemployed. Workers found their first jobs following redundancy surprisingly quickly. One-third found new jobs before becoming unemployed (Daniel, p. 3). Workers displaced by major redundancies tended to be more able and skilled, with good work records and substantial periods of service. They went straight to the head of the line. Those who suffered most were the less attractive job seekers, such as the longer-term unemployed already on the register, young people entering the job market for the first time and people returning to the labor market after a break for some reason (Daniel, p. 4).

How are we to respond to this? Part of our Christian ministry is not only to individual persons but to structures, organizations, nations and the principalities and powers. Those of us who are employed should help individual unemployed persons to take appropriate creative initiatives to seek work, retrain and become productive again. We must also address the systemic factors that make unemployment a social problem. As someone said, "There, to the displeasure of God, go all of us." God's will is that a nation thrive in providing opportunities for all of its citizens to use their gifts and talents for the common good.

The earliest extant Christian writings contain admonitions for Christian communities to provide employment for the newly converted. Thomas Aquinas took this matter farther by regarding the efforts of employers in opening up remunerated work on a grand scale as an act of virtuous magnanimity (Gossé, p. 8). The contemporary activist William Droel calls for public discipleship:

All workers—the employed, the unemployed, homemakers, volunteers, business leaders and students—are called to exercise their voting franchise, their lobbying ability, their collective strength in unions and professional associations, and their wits on the job to affect company policies, to advance legislation, and to fashion other mechanisms aimed at building an economy in which all willing workers find employment. Economic structures do not arise by themselves. People establish them, set them in motion, and administer them. Therefore, people who are right thinking and acting can form and improve them. (Gossé, pp. 8-9)

The Spirituality of the Unemployed

Undoubtedly, for the unemployed there are difficult temptations to be overcome: to slip into self-pity, to wallow in being victimized by "the system," to conclude they have lost their self-worth, to feel shamed before family, friends, neighbors and church. Like most others this crisis is both danger and opportunity. There is the opportunity of reaffirming our identities in terms of Whose we are rather than what we do. There is the invitation to rediscover how God has made us with talents and personalities fitting us for occupations, possibly several. There is the discipline of vocational guidance and the growth that can come from exploring what can be learned about ourselves from the painful process of being "outplaced."

Being unemployed can drive a wedge into our family, church relations and community as the hurt person vents anger and frustration on others, or feels unable to face people. Being unemployed can be the occasion for a root of bitterness to grow in our relationship with God for denying us meaningful and remunerated employment. But being unemployed can also become the means of strengthening our relationships with God and others as we seek the prayers, help and advice of those closest to us. This interior work, alongside the exterior work of looking for a job, can be pleasing to God and work done to God himself (Col. 3:23).

There are inevitably hard choices to be made if we are determined to find work. Should one relocate to a region where employment is increasing, or is unemployment insurance the safety net one needs? Is maintaining one's roots more important than being employed? Should we take any work just to be employed, even if we are unsuited or unmotivated? These are other questions that need to be considered in the context of a caring Christian community, such as a small group in the church. Few people can gain perspective on their unemployment without the support of a nurturing community. Some churches and communities sponsor support groups for the unemployed to meet and share their pilgrimage. Books, especially those dealing with grief and unemployment, can be of substantial help, as can a day retreat for prayer and reflection (Gossé, pp. 37-41). While we are looking for work we are working and doing some internal work that may prove to turn the tragedy of unemployment into a discovery of the sufficiency of God's grace. Meanwhile the employed may pray for the forgiveness of society's sins and in whatever context God has placed us—teacher, neighbor, citizen, businessperson, government employee—to do our own work in such a way that we not only thrive ourselves but equip others, so humanizing the world in line with God's intention.

See also BUSINESS ETHICS; CALLING; CAREER; FIRING; LOYALTY, WORKPLACE; NETWORKING; PART-TIME EMPLOYMENT; VOCATIONAL GUIDANCE

References and Resources
J. Aley, "Where the Laid-Off Workers Go," *Fortune,* October 30, 1995, 45-48; D. D. Daniel, *The Unemployed Flow* (London: PSI Publishing, 1990); J. Gossé, *The Spirituality of Work: Unemployed Workers,* (Chicago: ACTA Publications, 1993); R. D. Kaplan, "The Coming Anarchy," *Atlantic Monthly,* February 1994, 44-76; P. G. Schervitch, *The Structural Determinants of Unemployment* (New York: Academic Press, 1983).

—Michel Mestre and R. Paul Stevens

UNIONS

In response to a poll done by a Christian magazine, a retired clergyman who was also a long-time member of a union stated that "unions have done more to help the working[person] than our churches could ever do." But another pastor, who was also a former mechanic, was much less generous in his response: "Unions go to any extent to hold power" ("Christians on the Picket Line," p. 27). This diversity is typical of Christians today who, in spite of common principles and worldviews, see trade unions in various lights and make decisions concerning their involvement with unions accordingly. To help Christians deal with this conflict, this article will evaluate the modern-union worldview, which union leaders claim is characterized by justice, according to the biblical standard of justice.

Evolution of the Union Worldview

Unions are controversial bodies, as are the methods that they employ. The worldview of the labor movement itself is shaped by its history of dealings with employers, governments and the courts; its perceived mandate as an agent of social change and its acceptance of the adversary system as its best form of protection.

In the 1860s American unions began to organize Canadian workers. Some of these groups attempted to base their objectives and practices on Judeo-Christian principles. The Knights of Crispin, for instance, drew their name and inspiration from a third-century nobleman, Saint Crispin, who gave up his privileged position to work among the boot makers of France and Italy. That union soon folded but was succeeded by the Knights of Labor, founded in 1869 by Uriah Stevens, who studied for the Baptist ministry. The Knights of Labor saw as their task to "Make industrial and moral worth, not wealth, the true standard of individual and national greatness." In the 1880s the Knights were one of the two dominant grassroots movements among the working class in Ontario, the other being the Salvation Army. Each organization was an outlet for strong religious convictions of members of the laboring class of the day. The editor of the Knight's principal newspaper, for instance, took the view that "the doctrines of Jesus Christ the carpenter—who would have been called a tramp and a Communist had he lived in these days—if applied to the present conditions would solve the question satisfactorily" (Marks, pp. 103-4). The Knights of Labor eventually disappeared from the North American scene, to be supplanted by more secular counterparts.

While early union leaders could be characterized more as social reformers than militant organizers with fat contracts in view, as idealists with lofty visions and compassion for the truly exploited and as fighters for changes that the most right-wing among us today would support, no corresponding chord of Christian charity could be discerned among the employers whose abuses they addressed or the legislatures and courts that rushed to the owners' aid. Unions eventually learned to respond in kind.

The history of unionism in the nineteenth and through much of the twentieth century in North America is marked by fierce, even ferocious, resistance on the part of employers to any attempts by unions to interfere with their preferred style of management and employee relations. But in the mid-1930s in the U.S. a series of dramatic strikes against Ford and General Motors and against U.S. and Bethlehem Steel led to the arrival of trade unions as successful advocates for workers regarding wages, hours and working conditions. A boom in union membership ensued, although it has waned in recent years. It was only in 1936 in the U.S. and in 1944 in Canada that workers were finally granted the right to organize and bargain collectively without employer interference.

The Union Movement's View of Its Mandate

In describing its priorities and values, labor stakes out the moral high ground. In fact, many union leaders see themselves and their unions as taking the leadership in ensuring that justice is done in our society despite the best efforts of corporations and governments to subvert and exploit vulnerable individuals and groups. This concern goes well beyond bread-and-butter issues such as wages and working conditions. The Canadian Labour Congress (CLC), for instance, believes that such matters as child poverty, health care, education, equality of men and women, child care, unemployment and other political and social issues fall within its mandate (White, p. 38). Its definition of a morally just society, of course, does not necessarily employ a traditional Judeo-Christian understanding of morality. This is evident from CLC criticism of the largely Christian women's organization REAL (Realistic, Equal, Active, For Life) Women. The CLC attacked REAL Women because they "purport to represent the women of Canada although they wish to deny rights to lesbians, homosexuals, feminists, [and] pro-choice advocates" ("Canadian Labour Congress," p. 9).

280

Unions and Adversarialism

Beyond considerations of the proper mandate of the labor movement, trade unions see themselves as being in a disadvantaged position vis-à-vis the employer and the government. Unions fear that without the right to strike as protection from the arbitrary use of employer power, the individual worker is highly vulnerable to exploitation. The late Tommy Douglas, the first socialist to head a government in North America and a Baptist minister, defined the nature of the relationship of workers with their managers as follows: "The essence of industrial relations is conflict. It is a confrontation in which the workers through their collective power seek to wrest from the employer what they deem a fair share of the wealth they helped to create" (Douglas, p. 11). Industrial relations scholar Jack Barbash agrees: "Conflict in industrial relations, or more often the threat of it, far from being pathological or aberrant, is normal and even necessary. The principle is that the parties can be kept 'honest' only by countervailing checks and balances" (Barbash, p. 131).

Nevertheless, two schools of thought have developed in recent years within the union movement. One argues that the highly competitive international situation requires unions to work together with employers in a partnership that embraces teamwork, total quality management, even profit sharing and jointly managed retraining programs. The second and more dominant position rejects the notion of worker-initiated ways of improving the competitive capacity of employers. Such initiatives are viewed as ultimately requiring harder work for less pay and the concession of workplace rights.

A Biblical Critique of the Union Worldview

The early Christian influence on the labor movement has clearly waned to the point at which many Christians have a personal problem with any involvement with a union. Others have no difficulty with union membership and urge Christians to become more involved. What follows is an attempt to critique the union understanding of justice because it is on the basis of the pursuit of justice that unions chose many of their objectives and tactics.

Biblical justice. Biblical justice has a particular concern for those on the margins of society, the vulnerable and exploitable, and is not prepared to ignore them in the pursuit of some cause, however important to the person in a position of power (Jeremiah 22:13-17). The biblical understanding of justice includes an extra component beyond dispassionate fairness. It is often characterized as *love in action*. Words such as righteousness, love and compassion are often found together with justice in describing God's dealings with humanity (for example, Psalm 89:14; Jeremiah 9:24; Hosea 12:6; Luke 11:42). The biblical perspective on economic life is shot through with the idea of just relationships and objectives. Economic pursuits are never to include the exploitation of another's weakness or ignorance. Material goods are to be viewed as gifts from God and to be used in the development of a society characterized by economic justice and balance. Life is not one of self-indulgence or self-interest but of concern for raising up the vulnerable, enabling them to live a meaningful life, even at the expense of one's own self-interest.

Unions and justice. On the surface justice would appear to be a major preoccupation of labor unions, especially in their many pronouncements about their concern for the vulnerable members of society, whom they feel are open to exploitation by either big business, big government or the courts. But while the trade union movement has to a certain extent included notions of justice within its stated objectives, it has ignored a number of other instances in which it could be accused of unjust practices of its own. Justice in reality is reserved for the union members themselves, too often without sufficient regard for those who might be exploited or ignored while the union is pursuing its objectives. This could include a weak employer whose livelihood is sacrificed by a powerful national union pursuing a *master contract* for a total industry, which many smaller employers in that industry could not afford. Innocent third parties are frequently inconvenienced and even genuinely harmed by such job action as strikes by teachers, health-care workers, postal workers and so on.

So-called fairness that only benefits union members in accord with the majority of the union, while ignoring others who might not benefit or who in fact may lose as a result of union success, is not justice at all, at least not in the biblical sense. Such justice lacks its sister values of love and reconciliation. What we are really seeing is a form of utilitarianism; that is, that which benefits the greatest number, with the minority, who are affected by the union's actions but not benefiting from them, losing out.

Justice and worker independence. It is precisely in this area of biblical justice, however, that a strong case can be made for one of the union movement's most important contributions—worker independence. Workers, if they are to realistically expect just treatment at the hands of employers, need the kind of protection that unions provide.

The Bible is quite realistic with respect to the issue of exploitation. It takes for granted that individuals in a more powerful position will inevitably exploit those weaker or more vulnerable than themselves, even within the ranks of the church. Thus, while the authority of church leaders was to be acknowledged and respected by church members (1 Tim. 5:17; 1 Peter 5:2), church leaders had to be warned not to take advantage of their positions to enrich themselves or to abuse their authority (1 Peter 5:2-3). Similar warnings of abuse were issued to husbands vis-à-vis wives (Ephes. 5:21-28; Col. 3:18-19; 1 Peter 3:7), parents in their relationship with their children (2 Cor. 12:14; Ephes. 6:4; Col. 3:21) and masters as they supervised their employees or slaves (Ephes. 6:9; Col. 4:1). In the Judeo-Christian tradition those in a dependent or vulnerable position have the right to expect just treatment and to be protected from exploitation, and those in a position of authority are never to exercise that authority in a self-interested fashion, but with a view to accomplishing just objectives.

Recent studies in the United States have clearly shown that workers lacking union membership have experienced exploitation that might not have occurred with the protection unions provide. Trends identified by the respected *Business Week* journal have included productivity rising faster than the wages of the increasingly productive employees; real wages of workers actually falling, especially in industries experiencing deunionization; executive pay rising at a breathtaking clip; and owners of capital realizing gains on their investments triple that of wage increases during the same period (Bernstein, pp. 70-82). Consequently, even hard-line opponents of American labor such as Sen. Orrin Hatch (R-Utah) have said: "There are always going to be people who take advantage of workers. Unions even that out, to their credit. . . . If you didn't have unions, it would be very difficult for even enlightened employers to not take advantage of workers on wages and working conditions because of [competition from] rivals" (Bernstein, p. 70).

Conclusion

As I said at the beginning, unions are controversial bodies. Common criticisms cited are that unions abuse their right to strike and pursue their objectives without regard for their impact on vulnerable parties. Others praise union accomplishments when they parallel Christian objectives. From a Christian perspective one must be concerned with any organization that claims to pursue just goals either through unjust means or with a corrupted view of justice. Involvement in such organizations presents the challenge of assessing both union means and ends from a thoroughly biblical worldview and deciding how one will respond.

See also CONFLICT RESOLUTION; MANAGEMENT; ORGANIZATION; POWER; STRIKES; TECHNOLOGY; TRADES; WORK

References and Resources

J. Barbash, *The Elements of Industrial Relations* (Madison: University of Wisconsin Press, 1984); A. Bernstein, "Why America Needs Unions but Not the Kind It Has Now," *Business Week,* 23 May 1994, 70-82; "Canadian Labour Congress (CLC) Opposes REAL Women," *Reality* 10, no. 4 (1992) 9; "Christians on the Picket Line," *Faith Today* (September-October 1989) 27-32; T. C. Douglas, "Labor in a Free Society," in *Labor Problems in Christian Perspective,* ed. J. H. Redekop (Grand Rapids: Eerdmans, 1972) 11-13; L. Marks, "The Knights of Labor and the Salvation Army: Religion and Working Class Culture in Ontario," *Labour/Le Travail* 28 (1991) 89-127; R. White, "Labor's Political Goal: Defeat Corporate Agenda," *Canadian Speeches: Issues of the Day* 6, no. 5 (1992) 41.

—John R. Sutherland

VOCATIONAL GUIDANCE

Never before in history have so many people had the opportunity to change their lifestyles. Since many people no longer have to work "down in the mine," "take over their father's farm" or be "only a mother," they are faced with a myriad of choices. Because people bring to these choices fantasies and unconscious expectations, vocational decision-making today is less like fitting a peg into its proper hole and more like compressing an unruly spring into a container and wondering how long it will stay. It is an awkward and lifelong process, one substantially helped by being a Christian.

Definitions

Vocation is our divinely given life purpose embracing all dimensions of our human existence and the special dimensions of service Christians undertake in the church and world. *Vocational guidance* is the process of helping others, or receiving help oneself, to discover and persist in that life direction. It is more than finding the right job. It has a larger and deeper meaning: responding to God's purpose in marriage, singleness, family, neighborhood, church, political service and occupation. Vocational guidance is a modern concept that emerged principally from the Protestant Reformation. At a time when the rigid structures of society were breaking down, the idea of *calling* and the recovery of the dignity of work permitted people to make choices in occupations. Out of this the idea of vocational guidance was born.

Misunderstandings

The confusion surrounding this topic is illustrated by Barbara Zikmund. Vocation, she says, is presented as something that "(1) has little to do with our jobs, (2) has something to do with all jobs, (3) has more to do with certain jobs, (4) or has everything to do with on-the-job and off-the job existence. No wonder good Christians get confused" (Zikmund, p. 328). So we must start by clearing away several misunderstandings.

The idea of choosing a calling is an oxymoron. The word *vocation* is derived from the Latin *vocatio* which means "to call." So vocation and calling are identical in meaning. It would be a good thing if we used *calling* more often since it invites the questions, By whom? and For what? Basic to the idea of vocation is a divine, not a human, choice. God has issued a summons to his creatures. This summons is all-embracing and includes work, family, neighborhood, civic responsibility and the care of creation. The basic structure is found in Ephes. 4:1, where Paul urges all Christians (and not just church leaders) to "lead a life worthy of the calling to which you have been called" (RSV) and then in Ephes. 4-6 elaborates some of the contexts in which we are to live as called people: congregational life (Ephes. 4:1-16), marriage (Ephes. 5:21-33), home (Ephes. 6:1-4), workplace (Ephes. 6:5-9) and society (Ephes. 6:10-

18). Simply put, the Christian vocation is God's call to live for the praise of his glory (Ephes. 1:12, 14) and to serve God's purposes in every context of life. A career is chosen; a calling is accepted.

God does not have a wonderful plan for our lives. He has something far better—a wonderful purpose! For some Christians, concern "to be in the center of God's will" leads to guidance anxiety. A plan, like a blueprint, must be followed in slavish detail, but a purpose is like a fast-flowing stream that carries a boat along and incorporates even mistakes into its ultimate direction. God's primary concern, according to the Bible, is not that we fit like pegs in their proper slots but that we become people who love God, neighbors and God's creation. To participate in God's grand purpose of renewing everything in Christ means to oppose evil, to do the work of maintaining a city, to build community, to create systems that bring dignity and value to human life. So John Calvin counsels that believers should "choose those employments which yield the greatest advantage to their neighbors" (*Opera,* XLI, 300). This does not mean, however, going into the ministry or choosing a Christian service career or a "people" job.

Vocation is not the same as remunerated employment. Indeed, we do not need to have remunerated employment to have vocational contentment. Some fulfill their service to humankind through volunteer work instead of or outside their remunerated occupation. Work, occupations, careers and professions are important parts of our vocation in Christ, but they are not the whole. According to Scripture the first human couple was given three full-time jobs, not just one: first, to enjoy full-time communion with God; second, to build community on earth starting with the relationship of male and female and third, to take care of God's earth (Genesis 2:15) and develop God's creation as coworkers with God (Genesis 4:20-22). While sin marred this threefold human vocation, Christ has reclaimed us for this, and we enjoy substantial redemption until there is complete fulfillment of the human vocation in the New Jerusalem. So work in all its forms is much more than remunerated employment, though that employment may be located primarily in one of the three full-time jobs. Christians are required to seek gainful employment, to meet needs of their own (1 Thes. 4:12; 2 Thes. 3:12) and of others (Ephes. 4:28). But when we are technically unemployed or retired, we are still caught up in God's all-embracing summons.

Vocational decision-making is not a once-for-all event but a lifetime process. There is only one once-for-all vocational decision, and that is to yield to the gracious invitation of God in Christ and to welcome being caught up in his grand purpose. Within that purpose, life is full of adjustments, decisions, redirections, mistakes and even second chances. This has not always been recognized, as when vocation was identified with one's station in life. In fairness to Luther (who is often charged with promoting fixed callings understood as positions in life), he stressed the duties attendant on one's station as a means of fulfilling calling, not the location of that calling. Calvin and his followers developed this further: vocational living is using our gifts and talents within our callings—thereby opening the door to "changing jobs" to fulfill calling. In a modern mobile society we must grasp the heart of vocational living as a continuous process of discerning God's will and purpose.

Vocational guidance is not simply an individual matter.

Gifts and talents are discovered and affirmed communally, and roles and responsibilities are defined communally. While we should, as the Puritan William Perkins advised, explore our own affections, desires and gifts, we should also consult the advice of others because of our inherent tendency to be biased (p. 759). The Christian community should create an environment where people with a broad vision can encourage one another with the particularity of one's vocation (Fowler, pp. 115-25). Most people will find this possible in local churches, accountability groups and spiritual friendships.

A Short Theology of Vocational Guidance

Amid the confusion surrounding vocational decision-making, there is nothing quite as comforting or constructively helpful as good theology. This brief summary will include Christian identity, personal vocation, God as vocational director, the will of God, the providence of God and knowing ourselves.

Our vocation comes out of our identity, not the reverse. In the secular world people are defined by what they do: She is a doctor; he is a business person. Guidance counselors speak of helping people gain a "vocational identity." But the Christian approach is the exact reverse. Our fundamental identity is to become children of God through Christ. So instead of developing a vocational identity, we should seek an identity-formed vocation. Being precedes doing. First we are called to Someone to become somebody. Then we are called to do something for that Someone. Vocation flows out of our essential identity in Christ. On this note Augustine insightfully recommended that someone wanting to find out who a person was should not ask what that person *does* but what that person *loves*.

Personal vocation particularizes God's general call to all humanity and his special call to his people. Unfortunately most discussions of vocation focus on the relative importance of two "doing" mandates: the creation (or cultural) mandate (Genesis 1:27-29) and the Great Commission (Matthew 28:18-20). Large parts of the contemporary church regard the Great Commission as the only mandate now in force and relegate the creation mandate to pre-Christian existence. The Reformers and Puritans had a better grasp of the breadth of God's call, arguing that God had diversified all the ways we fulfill the cultural mandate into all the occupations that keep the world running: homemakers, blacksmiths, cobblers, teachers and farmers.

A contemporary refinement of the Reformed view is supplied by Klaus Bochmuehl (p. 34). He asks us to imagine a three-tiered wedding cake. The bottom (and largest) layer is the *human vocation* of communion with God, building community and cocreativity (Genesis 1-2). The second (and smaller) layer is the *Christian vocation* expressed in discipleship to Jesus, holiness in life and service in the world. This second layer is related to the first: becoming a Christian makes us more fully human (rather than angelic) and empowers us to fulfill the human vocation. Then we can imagine a third (even smaller) layer representing the *personal vocation*—that combination of human and Christian tasks to which a person is uniquely fitted by God and led by the Holy Spirit. Taken as a whole—all three layers of the wedding cake—we are not left guessing about who we are and what we are to do with our lives.

God is the ultimate vocational director. Robert Banks notes that God is also our vocational model dignifying all the ways God invites us to make the world work (p. 22). God is craftsperson, shepherd, weaver, farmer, architect, potter, host, homemaker, ruler and warrior, just to mention a few biblical metaphors. But God directs people providentially as he did with Adam and Eve in the garden, Ruth gleaning in the field of Boaz, David in the court of Saul, Ezekiel among the exiles and Peter fishing just where Jesus needed to borrow a boat. Human freedom is real but limited. God is the only one who does "whatever he pleases" (Psalm 115:3 NRSV). Our whole story, even parts that do not yet "make sense," is ordered and intended. Nothing can happen to us that cannot, by God's sovereignty, be turned into good (Romans 8:28).

God's will is not hard to find. Guidance is essentially a pagan concept. Outside the revelation of God to Israel and the church, people seek guidance by consulting mediums, casting spells and examining the entrails of animals and birds—all ancient equivalents to fortunetelling, reading the horoscope and looking for signs and portents. What Scripture offers is better than guidance; it offers the Guide. The Bible is more concerned with our relationship to the Guide than our being in "the center of his will," a concept not actually found in the Bible but promoted by popular Christianity. Perhaps 90 percent of our questions about what we are to do with our lives are answered by the teaching of Scripture. As Bochmuehl says, "If God does not call us to a particular task at a particular time, we must fall back on the creational and salvational tasks that have already been given: to sustain and to further physical and spiritual life in the family and in the community, in the neighborhood and in the nation" (p. 34).

Sometimes God will speak directly through an inner persuasion, a vision or a dream. Though normally it is bad advice to tell someone to do that for which he or she is disinclined or unqualified, Scripture witnesses to God's surprising and unwelcome summons, for example, to Moses, Jonah and Paul. Lee Hardy wisely comments, "When [God] does that, it is because he is about to give a special demonstration of his power. That is, he is about to perform a miracle—which is, by definition, a departure from the normal course of affairs" (p. 93). Lacking such supernatural direction, Christians are not powerless to move forward in their lives. They can do so confidently for good reason.

Vocational decisions are rarely irrevocable. We can trust God's providence in our lives. Calvin said God's hand is at the helm of both the universe and the life of the individual. Our lives are not a bundle of accidents. Family background, educational experiences and life experiences are a reflection of God's good purpose for our lives. Our personalities, spiritual gifts and talents have been given by God. This can be overemphasized, as it sometimes was by the Reformers. But we should not reduce the hope and comfort implicit in a high view of God's providence by looking for God's leading mainly in supernatural signs and wonders. Even mistakes get incorporated into God's overall purpose though our life path may be temporarily revised as a result. Joseph is a stunning example of God's providence. He was able to say to his brothers, "So then, it was not you who sent me here, but God" (Genesis 45:8) and "You intended to harm me, but God intended it for good" (Genesis 50:20). Since career decisions, for example, are rarely irrevocable, we are saved from paralyzing fear of ruining everything by one bad choice. So we can do the thing at hand. We can laugh at ourselves because God is God. Indeed laughter in face of a life decision may be an act of worship. Trusting in God's providence, however, is not an alternative to knowing ourselves.

Self-knowledge is an important part of our spirituality. A study by the Marketing and Research Corporation showed that three or four out of every five people are in the wrong jobs (Jones, p. 30). Ralph Mattson and Arthur Miller have devoted themselves to making links between the central motivational thrust and its primary vocational expression in the workplace. Their approach, now systemized in the SIMA test, assumes that (1) God has made us with the capacity to enjoy working and serving in a particular way; (2) what brings joy to us is a powerful indication of what God has designed us to be and do; (3) our central motivating pattern is consistent through life—the boy that nurses a wounded bird at five drives an ambulance at thirty-five.

Sophisticated and popular tests are now available to measure interests, natural aptitudes, values, personality type, learning style and life changes, and many of these tests have been made available in self-help workbooks, such as *Naturally Gifted: A Self-Discovery Workbook* (Jones). These tests are useful and helpful in understanding ourselves, though they seldom acknowledge that much of the world does not enjoy the luxury of occupational choice or the privilege of a fulfilling career.

In some circles, knowing ourselves, especially if it involves loving ourselves, is considered antithetical to denying ourselves—taking up the cross and following Jesus (Matthew 16:24). Sometimes it is. As John Stott reminds us, we are not commanded to love ourselves but our neighbor as much as we already love ourselves in a fallen state (Matthew 22:39; Mark 12:31). Further, love (*agapē*) in the New Testament implies self-sacrifice. Finally, self-love as a form of idolatry is the essence of sin in the last days (2 Tim. 3:2, 4; Stott, pp. 34-35).

Taking this warning seriously, we may nevertheless develop a biblical approach to self-affirmation. (1) We will never know ourselves as we really are apart from God's view of us, a view we gain primarily from Scripture and the inner affirmation of the Spirit. (2) It is safe and healthy to know ourselves when our primary focus is the glory of God and his will. (3) Neither self-confidence nor self-depreciation but true humility is the normal result of being in God's presence. C. S. Lewis put this aptly, "It is when I turn to Christ, when I give myself up to His personality that I first begin to have a real personality of my own" (p. 189). (4) Even our inabilities, flaws and weaknesses revealed to us in every vocational context become strengths for the person who lives by the grace of God (2 Cor. 4:7; 2 Cor. 11:30; 2 Cor. 12:9). (5) Loving, or better affirming, ourselves in the sense of accepting and respecting ourselves as God does may be distinguished from God-excluding self-absorption (*philautos,* "lovers of one's own self"; 2 Tim. 3:4). (6) Self-affirmation involves coming to a sane estimation of our own value and strengths (Romans 12:3) and agreeing with the priorities Scripture places on life purposes: maturity more than effectiveness, faithfulness more than success, character development more than skill development, being more than doing. Such God-inspired self-acceptance, unlike egotistical self-preoccupation, is marked by grace.

Since our capacity for self-deception is enormous, the process of knowing ourselves is lifelong. Action-oriented, task-oriented, high-energy people especially need spiritual disciplines to get in touch with themselves. The choice of a career, a marriage partner or even a role in the church frequently is infused with internal fantasies, a wished-for self that becomes a means of gaining a psychosocial identity. All of this points to the process of vocational guidance as being central, rather than auxiliary, to our life in God.

Vocational Guidance as a Spiritual Discipline

The process of lifelong vocational decision-making *is* a discipline. It is not only helped by the use of spiritual disciplines, such as meditation and journaling, but it directs us to God for some of the following reasons.

Vocational guidance is concerned with both entering in and continuing in a calling in worthy manner (Ephes. 4:1). Vocational life is littered with idols: the idols of gain (being in it for the money), glory (seeking position in the church for human approval) and instant ecstasy (getting a "fix" or "high" from making a sale). All too easily a challenging profession or an all-consuming role like mothering can feed our addictions and become idolatrous. *Idolatry* is defined simply as making something one's ultimate concern other than the One who is ultimate. The Puritan William Perkins reminds us that "walking worthy of one's calling" requires an ongoing process of sanctification of the worker and the works. He uses seventeenth-century examples of how not to walk worthy, examples that apply equally to today: for physicians, prescribing remedies without proper diagnosis; for booksellers, selling immodest and improper books; for the merchant and tradesman, having false weights and dressing up the wares so people are deceived; for the patron, making a public pledge of a large gift but following through with only part of it; and for the landlord, racking the rents (Perkins, p. 771).

The chief cause of a vocational mismatch is not being in the wrong location but yielding to the lust of the spirit. We should be living contentedly within our calling, but joy in service is not a matter of location as much as spirit. Drivenness is a symptom of something wrong inside. The lust of the spirit is the desire for something other than what God deems best for us. If we do not judge that the particular calling in which God has placed us is the best of all callings for us, we will yield to discontentment, as did Absalom, the sons of Zebedee and Cain (Perkins, p. 756).

To counteract this pernicious lust, Perkins offers several practical measures: (1) discerning the initiative of God in our lives so that even in times of crosses and calamities we may rest certain that God has placed us in this calling (p. 760); (2) repenting if necessary for the wrong reasons we entered a calling (be it marriage, career or ministry) but refusing to forsake our place and so continuing with diligence and good conscience (p. 762)—a strategy that is crucial for those who feel they entered marriage for the wrong reasons. Further, Perkins advises (3) seeking sanctification both of the worker and the work by the Word of God and prayer (p. 766); (4) resisting the temptation to covetousness by laboring to see our particular situations as a providence of God no matter how difficult it may be and by resolving in our hearts that God—not a perfect situation—is our portion (Psalm 16:6); (5) turning our affections from this world to better things by not seeking more in this world than we actually need and setting our mind on heaven (p. 770; compare Ephes. 1:18); (6) persisting in our calling by pruning our lives of ambition, envy of others placed in "better" callings, and impatience, all of which incline us to leave our calling when trouble comes. On this last measure Perkins uses a medical image from the days before anesthesia that is superbly graphic. He says we must continue in our callings as the surgeon who continues to cut his patient even through the patient is screaming a lot (Perkins, p. 773)!

Hardship is not an indication of our being in the wrong calling. Run through all the callings, Luther pleaded, and you will find that every earthly occupation has a cross. We can suffer for the sake of others and identify in some small way with the suffering of Christ right where we are. This is entirely in line with a faithful interpretation of 1 Cor. 7:20—"Each one should remain in the situation which he was in when God called him"—namely that change, while permissible, should not be undertaken as though it had spiritual significance. Paul is a classic case. Though he was being stoned, dragged out of cities and suffered privations, not least of which was his day and night handwork to support himself as a tentmaker, he knew he was doing God's will. Hardship can become a pruning experience, even a means of grace. Being in the will of God does not guarantee health, wealth and a creative, fulfilling career. Discovering that nothing in this world will ultimately satisfy us, as C. S. Lewis once pointed out, is a powerful hint that we were made for another life and another world. In the end what counts is that we are found in Christ.

We are accountable in the last day for what we have done with our lives. The supreme motivating factor in walking worthy of one's calling is the fact that we must all give account on the day of judgment for what we have done in our callings. Perkins asks,

"How then can we give a good account of ourselves before God on that day? We must calculate our blessings, weigh all that was defective and then cleave to the surety of Christ, his death being all the satisfaction God needs" (p. 779). This strongly biblical note (Matthew 25:19) is conspicuously missing in most Christian treatments of vocational guidance, as is the next.

We must walk by faith not sight. Walking by faith means that we cannot find the explanation of our lives in the circumstances in which we find ourselves but only by faith in God. This involves the daily discipline of seeking God's face, finding our satisfaction in God, affirming our acceptance in Christ—rather than finding the joy of our life in how well things are going. At the root of this—as Luther so wisely discerned—is our actual heart-level experience of the gospel.

A person who has gospel confidence, Luther stated, is like a man who feels completely comfortable and secure in the mutual love between his wife and himself. Such a person does not have to weigh which act or deed might bring about the maximum positive response: "For such a man there is no distinction in works. He does the great and the important as gladly as the small and the unimportant, and vice versa. Moreover, he does them all in a glad, peaceful, and confident heart, and is an absolute willing companion to the woman" (Luther, pp. 26-27). But if the man is insecure in his or her love, he will calculate and offer the largest and most impressive deed to gain what he thinks he can obtain by works. So too the person insecure in his or her relationship with God may choose to win approval by works, works that might include going into the monastery (in Luther's day) and going into the ministry (in our day). Without the foundation of divine approval, vocational decision-making will normally become a means of inventing personal meaning and satisfaction—a form of self-salvation for the unbeliever—or an attempt to win God's approval in the case of the believer.

In summary, we should regard the Christian life and service as a comprehensive and liberating summons of God. We already know what God's will in broad terms is for our life! Finding the best job is a minor part of this. We should do the thing at hand for God's glory until clearly led by God. We should affirm God's providence in our life. We are not a bundle of accidents, and even occupational—and other—mistakes can be incorporated into God's purpose for our life. This means we can live wholeheartedly and exuberantly in the present, not with our eye on the next (and more fulfilling) assignment. The heart of Christian vocation, and therefore the essence of vocational guidance, is not choosing to do something, but responding to the call to belong to Someone and because of that, to serve God and our neighbor wholeheartedly.

See also CALLING; GUIDANCE; MINISTRY; SERVICE, WORKPLACE; SPIRITUAL DISCIPLINES; TALENTS; WORK

References and Resources
R. Banks, "The Place of Work in the Divine Economy: God as Vocational Director and Model," in *Faith Goes to Work: Reflections from the Marketplace,* ed. R. Banks (Washington, D.C.: The Alban Institute, 1993) 18-29; K. Bockmuehl, "Recovering Vocation Today," *Crux* 24, no. 3 (September 1988) 25-35; J. Calvin, *Institutes of the Christian Religion,* 2 vols., ed. J. T. McNeill, trans. F. L. Battles (Philadelphia: Westminster, 1960); W. Dumbrell, "Creation, Covenant and Work," *Crux* 24, no. 3 (September 1988) 14-24; J. W. Fowler, *Becoming Adult, Becoming Christian: Adult Development and Christian Faith* (San Francisco: Harper & Row, 1984); L. Hardy, *The Fabric of This World: Inquiries into Calling, Career and Choice, and the Design of Human Work* (Grand Rapids: Eerdmans, 1990); G. Jones and R. Jones, *Naturally Gifted: A Self-Discovery Workbook* (Downers Grove, Ill.: InterVarsity Press, 1993); M. Kolden, "Luther on Vocation," *Word and World* 3, no. 4 (1983) 382-90; C. S. Lewis, *Mere Christianity* (New York: Macmillan, 1952); M. Luther, *Treatise on Good Works,* vol. 44 of *Luther's Works,* trans. W. A. Lambert, ed. J. Atkinson, (Philadelphia: Fortress, 1966); R. T. Mattson and A. F. Miller, *Finding a Job You Can Love* (New York: Thomas Nelson, 1982); W. Perkins, *The Works of That Famous Minister of Christ in the University of Cambridge* (London: John Legatt, 1626); J. R. W. Stott, "Must I Really Love Myself?" *Christianity Today,* 5 May 1978, 34-35; B. B. Zikmund, "Christian Vocation—In Context," *Theology Today* 36, no. 3 (1979) 328-37.

—R. Paul Stevens

VOLUNTEER WORK

Volunteers are ordinary people who have chosen to become involved in providing a needed service, solving a problem or advancing a worthy cause, without thought of payment other than personal satisfaction. The history of volunteering is filled with people who set off on their own to create programs when no one else has had the vision—or the willingness—to act. As we will see, volunteerism has its roots not only in human altruism but in the divine mandate to love one's neighbor. Further, it is implicit in the Christian gospel that those who have received the free gift of salvation will, in turn, give their service without obligation of recompense.

How Volunteerism Began

From the beginning of human experience, as modern sociology and anthropology show, human beings have striven to share and to cooperate just to survive in the face of hostile environments and strangers. As we read the pages of history, we find countless instances of individual effort to help others and promote the common good. These acts of kindness and goodwill are based on the Judeo-Christian principles of love, justice and mercy. The command given to the Israelites by God through Moses to love your neighbor as yourself (Leviticus 19:18) was quoted by Jesus (Matthew 22:39). Some of the Pharisees limited the meaning of the term *neighbor* but Rabbi Nahmanides took a wider view when he said, "One should place no limitations upon the love of neighbor, but instead a person should love to do an abundance of good for his fellow being as he does for himself." In telling the story of the good Samaritan,

Jesus made it abundantly clear that *neighbor* means not merely "one who lives nearby" but "anyone with whom one comes in contact." Jesus' teaching has encouraged, even mandated, that we all are to be volunteers and reach out to those who need help. Further, the experience of acceptance by God and the gift of new life in Christ are a powerful motivation to serve others voluntarily, without restraint, obligation or demand for payment. Jesus said, "It is more blessed to give than to receive" (Acts 20:35), a principle that Paul embodied in his practice of tentmaking.

How Volunteerism Developed

People have always come together to get jobs done. Sharing equipment and labor at barn raisings or harvest, caring for a sick neighbor or friend, lending money to help through a tough spot or being willing to listen are examples of ways people have endeavored to fulfill Jesus' mandate. The more primitive the society or the more remote the community is from civilization, the greater will be the need to rally around one another in time of crises or stress.

"Modern associational forms of voluntary effort were stimulated by the Reformation's endorsement of freedom of association; they flowered with the urbanization of society during the industrial revolution, and experienced greater expansion during the twentieth century" (Manser and Cass, p. 19). The organizations that were formed as the result of these influences fulfill an incredible variety of purposes, some to serve the individual needs of their members, such as service clubs, Boy Scouts, Girl Guides and so on, and others to offer services to individuals and communities, for example, hospital auxiliaries, Red Cross, United Way and so on. Most often it was the voluntary effort of ordinary citizens, often working though their religious or cultural institutions, that led to the establishment of orphanages and homes for the aged as well as health and welfare agencies. Evangelical Christians have been especially prominent in the creation of such institutions.

A few examples will give some idea as to how widespread and diverse are the projects undertaken by volunteers: in Israel volunteers work closely with the military to provide grief counseling for families of soldiers killed in combat; in Ecuador volunteers run some of the major cemeteries and provide basic supplies, such as blankets, for hospitals; in Sri Lanka volunteers build wells.

Volunteerism Today

The need for voluntary action is as great today as it ever was, possibly even greater in our fast-paced, mobile society in which so many demands are placed on the family and the community. While the direct effects of volunteer work are felt at the individual or community level, the combined action of many millions of ordinary citizens from every region of the country has had a profound impact on virtually every aspect of society and has, in fact, fostered its growth and development. At the present time, informal volunteer work goes on every day as people occasionally help out neighbors, friends and others in a personal and spontaneous manner. More formal volunteer work is carried out within an organization or agency and is planned in advance.

Recent surveys have dispelled a number of widely held myths regarding volunteerism. One belief is that the great majority of volunteers are women, most likely middle-aged or older. Also there is the myth that they are from the more affluent strata of society and can afford to give away their time freely. According to a public opinion survey conducted in 1991, 71 percent of Canadian adults had done volunteer work at some point in their lives. According to a 1993 survey the volunteers were 33 percent male and 67 percent female, but this would not include all men who run sports programs as coaches and referees. Over 60 percent of volunteers were under 30 years of age, and 33 percent were unemployed. Only 12 percent were listed as being homemakers. It is quite evident that the traditional profile of a volunteer has changed radically over the years.

Agencies and organizations using volunteers have had to become increasingly adaptable and more effective in managing a very valuable and often very scarce resource. The formula for successful volunteering appears to go something like this: provide opportunities for personal achievement, allow volunteers to make new discoveries about themselves and others and enable them to feel that they are forming social bonds and strengthening the community. Mix this with appropriate training, feedback and recognition, and you will have volunteers who feel energized by the assignment, see it as a fun endeavor and will complete it feeling better than when they started.

Some of the benefits volunteers bring to an organization are personal attention to one-to-one relationships; closer contact with the community; objectivity in the delivery of service; credibility, as volunteers have fewer vested interests; specialized skills, knowledge and contacts; refreshed energy; new ideas; a reservoir from which to recruit new paid staff; an opportunity to mix generations and cultures; a flexible transition stage for new services; freedom from experimentation; humanizing of services; consumer input and education. Yet these benefits are not without cost: there is considerable expense in paid-staff time and resources to organize and support an effective volunteer program. Nevertheless, the benefits the volunteer brings to the organization usually exceed these costs many times over.

Managing Volunteers

It is critical to consider the purpose of the volunteer program, how you plan to use the volunteers and to do everything possible to make the program work for volunteers, staff and organization. It is important to prepare the administration and staff of your organization for the introduction of the volunteer program as it is essential to have a positive attitude on their part and their full support. It is also necessary to have someone assigned to manage the program, whether presently on staff or newly hired. Many organizations today have job descriptions for their volunteers so that they have a clear understanding of what is expected of them.

The majority of volunteers expect to be treated with dignity and respect, to be given periodic evaluations of their work and to receive recognition of their contributions to the group. They may even expect and need to have out-of-pocket expenses such as bus fare, lunch money and even baby-sitter costs to make it possible for them to offer their time and services. Contrary to what is often said, "You cannot expect reliability from a volunteer but only from paid staff," volunteers that have a clear job description and are held accountable can be as reliable as those who serve for remuneration.

Those who manage volunteers need to understand the many possible motivations behind voluntary service, not all of which are purely altruistic. One pamphlet put out by a group called Parlay International listed forty-one reasons why people volunteer, including the following: to feel needed; to share a skill; to get to know a community; to demonstrate commitment to a cause or belief; to gain leadership skills; to act out a fantasy; to do your civic duty; because of pressure from a friend or relative; to keep busy for recognition; to repay a debt; to donate your professional skills; because there is no one else to do it; to have an impact; to learn something new; to fill up some free time; to help a friend or relative; for escape; to become an "insider"; because of guilt; to be challenged; to be a watchdog; to feel proud; to make new friends; to explore a career; to help someone; as therapy (Parlay International, 1350.009).

In the church volunteering expresses the heart of Christian ministry. As a spiritual discipline volunteering provides an arena for personal transformation and growth as we learn the blessing of giving without material reward and sometimes without intangible rewards.

See also SERVICE, WORKPLACE; WEALTH; OWNERSHIP; POWER; PRINCIPALITIES AND POWERS; STEWARDSHIP

References and Resources

W. H. Brackney, *Christian Voluntarism: Theology and Praxis* (Grand Rapids: Eerdmans, 1997); S. Ellis, *Focus on Volunteering* (Emeryville, Calif.: Parlay International, 1992); G. Manser and R. H. Cass, *Volunteerism at the Crossroads* (New York: Family Service Association of America, 1976); J. Lautenschlager, *Volunteering: A Traditional Canadian Value* (Ottawa: Voluntary Action Directorate, 1993); *Volunteers: How to Find Them, How to Keep Them* (Vancouver: Vancouver Volunteer Centre, 1990); Volunteer Centre of Ottawa—Carleton, *Why People Volunteer* (Ottawa: Voluntary Action Directorate, 1992).

—Ruth Oliver

WEALTH

Hardly anyone wants to be poor; most people would like to be rich. Wealth brings power, standing in the community, increased leisure and freedom from worry—so it is thought. Not surprisingly, in the richest part of the world many Christians are preaching a "prosperity gospel"—that faithfulness to Jesus will lead to personal wealth. Tragically, this distorted message is now taking root in some of the poorest countries of the world. Is wealth a sign of God's blessing? Is money the main measure of wealth? Why does money "talk"? Does the Bible endorse wealth, promote it or exclude it? How are we to respond in spirit and action? Our souls hang on our answers to these questions.

Wealth as Power

Principalities and powers form an invisible background to our life in this world. One of those powers is money. *Mammon,* as it is sometimes called, comes from an Aramaic word, *amen,* which means firmness or stability. It is not surprising that a common English phrase is "the almighty dollar."

As an alternative god, mammon inspires devotion, induces guilt, claims to give us security and seems omnipresent—a godlike thing (Foster, p. 28). It is invested with spiritual power that can enslave us, replacing single-minded love for God and neighbor with buying-selling relationships in which even the soul can be bought (Rev. 18:11-13). So money, wicked "mammon" (Luke 16:9 KJV), is a form or appearance of another power (Ephes. 1:21; Ellul, pp. 76-77, 81, 93). "The rich rule over the poor, and the borrower is servant to the lender" (Proverbs 22:7). Joseph, the righteous and Jesus are sold (Amos 2:6).

Money is not the only form of wealth, and not the first one named in Scripture. In ancient societies of Old Testament times, real wealth was associated with land. Even today in many Third World countries, land is the only permanent possession. Crops, cattle and houses could be destroyed by calamity, but the land will remain. So will the family. In God's threefold promise to the descendants of Abraham (presence of God, peoplehood and a place to belong) the land figures prominently. Poised on the edge of Canaan, Israel was promised a good land to gain wealth. "Remember the LORD your God . . . gives you the ability to produce wealth" (Deut. 8:18). Land belonged to God but was trusted to families. When the land had been mortgaged or sold to pay debts, the Jubilee year (Leviticus 25) was the instrument of returning land to the original families.

How this applies to Christians today is a sensitive question. The meaning of "in the land" to Israel has now been encompassed by the phrase "in Christ" through which both Jews and Gentiles become joint heirs (Ephes. 3:6). This includes economic sharing and justice but does not literally mean a common piece of geography (*see* Stewardship). So we are already seeing that Scripture appears to be ambiguous on this subject.

There are two voices of Scripture: one blessing the rich, the other cursing; one declaring that wealth is a sign of God's redemptive love to make us flourish on earth, the other declaring that wicked mammon (Luke 16:9), usually gained at the expense of the poor, is an alternative god (*see* Money). We need to look at each of these in turn.

296

Wealth as Blessing

The idea that wealth is a sign of God's blessing(Deut. 30:9; Proverbs 22:4) is illustrated by the lives of Abraham, Job and Solomon. In contrast to those who praised the Lord because they were rich (Zech. 11:5) but were soon to be judged, it is noteworthy that each of these exemplars depended on God rather than their wealth (Genesis 13:8-18; Job 1:21). The wise person in Proverbs is essentially a better-off person with servants—equivalent to our modern household machines—neither fabulously wealthy nor living in grinding poverty. Some wealth is a good thing; too much or too little would be alienating from God (Proverbs 30:9). So the wise person prays, "Give me neither poverty nor riches, but give me only my daily bread" (Proverbs 30:8).

The prosperity gospel now being preached worldwide is not satisfied with a comfortable existence or merely praying for our daily bread. We can critique it on at least three grounds. First, it encourages perverted motives: focusing on profitability. Second, it misinterprets God's deepest concerns for us: material well-being rather than total well-being. Third, it misinterprets God's promises to Israel as immediately applicable to Christians without being fulfilled and transfigured in Christ (compare 1 Tim. 6:3-10). Nevertheless, the Old Testament clearly presents wealth as a means of God's grace.

Wealth as Sacrament

The Old Testament affirms that God is the true owner, proprietor and giver of wealth (1 Samuel 2:7-8; Proverbs 3:16; Eccles. 5:19; Hosea 2:8). We are merely stewards (Proverbs 3:9). But the fact that God gives wealth, indiscriminately it seems, produces what Jacques Ellul calls "the scandal of wealth." God sometimes gives wealth to the wicked (Job 21:7-21; Psalm 73:12-13). Why would God do this if wealth were a sign of being blessed? Contrary to the common argument that wealth is the result of "our hard-earned labor" or "our faithfulness," the Old Testament takes a more sacramental view.

Wealth is a free gift of God, a sign of God's grace given generously and without merit. Further, wealth points to the final consummation when our wealth will be taken into the Holy City (Isaiah 60:3; Rev. 21:24-26; see Ellul, p. 66). It is a gross and dangerous oversimplification to say the Old Testament endorses wealth as the blessing of God and the New Testament proclaims it is a curse.

Wealth as Temptation

Even the Old Testament warns that the pursuit of wealth for its own sake is vain and harmful, leading to self-destructive autonomy (Psalm 49:6-7; Proverbs 23:4-5; Proverbs 28:20; Proverbs 30:8-9; Hosea 12:8). Proverbs 10:15, for example, "The wealth of the rich is their fortified city," is illuminated by Proverbs 18:11, "They imagine it an unscalable wall." Wealth is an *illusionary* security. Wealth will not satisfy (Psalm 49:6-7; Eccles. 5:10). Several points need to be made here.

First, no one is made right with God (justified) by the fair acquisition of wealth (Proverbs 13:11) or by dispersing it on behalf of the poor. In the absence of a "principle" or "doctrine" about money, we are called to find our justification not in our use of money but in our relationship to God. We are accepted by faith through grace.

Second, instead of becoming stewards of wealth for the benefit of the poor (Proverbs 31:5, 8-9), we are tempted to use what wealth we have to dominate others (Amos 2:6)—a subject taken up by John Chrysostom in his sermons on Luke 16. Just as the brothers of Joseph enjoyed their fine meal and did not "grieve over the ruin of Joseph" (Amos 6:6; Genesis 37:25), very few wealthy people have been able to resist becoming desensitized to the poor.

Third, especially reprehensible is yielding to the temptation to enlist God's Word to serve our lust for wealth (2 Kings 5:20-27; Micah 3:11), to "baptize" greed, a matter symbolized in the commercialized temple which Jesus cleansed.

When we turn to the New Testament we discover that "Jesus Christ strips wealth of the sacramental character that we have recognized in the Old Testament" (Matthew 6:24; Luke 6:30; Luke 12:33; Ellul, p. 70). The rich fool trusts in his barns and investments and is not ready to meet God, nor is known by God. The rich already have their comfort (Luke 6:24); they have nothing to look forward to. The rich young man must give everything away and follow Jesus. True wealth is not the accumulation of houses, farms, jewels and money but something more.

Though these passages seem to argue for an antiwealth New Testament ethic, it is not that simple. Jesus affirmed the extravagant and wasteful display of love when the woman poured perfume on him head: "She has done a beautiful thing to me" (Mark 14:1-11). And Jesus himself accepted the generous financial support of women with means (Luke 8:3). How are we to resolve this tension?

Heavenly Wealth

Unquestionably many of Jesus' negative statements about the rich and the wealthy are addressed to the spiritual malady fed by material abundance. "Be on your guard against all kinds of greed; a man's life does not consist in the abundance of his possessions" (Luke 12:15; compare James 5:1-6). As an alternative god wealth must be repudiated, if necessary by giving it all away (compare Luke 16:13). Ultimate security and blessing cannot be found in the accumulation of things (compare Matthew 6:19).

At this point Scripture gives us a harmonious, though disturbing, single message. Possessions are solely and simply a matter of stewardship, not ownership, and this life's assets are to be used with a heavenly orientation. What are these heavenly treasures, and how do they relate to everyday wealth, or the lack of it?

We gain an important paradigmatic perspective on this question from the Old Testament. There the inheritance received by Israel through the promise was a threefold blessing: the presence of God ("I will be with you"), the people ("you will be my people; I will be your God") and a place to belong ("the land will be yours").

As noted above, what we are given "in Christ" more than fulfills the promises made to Abraham and his descendants. God is with us in an empowering way through the Spirit. What greater treasure can there be than to belong to God and be known by him? In Christ we experience peoplehood, a new family with hundreds of brothers and sisters, fathers and mothers, children and lands (Matthew 19:29; Mark 10:29-30; *see* Church-Family). The promise of a place is fulfilled doubly: first in true fellowship here on earth through a full sharing of life with other believers, and second in the place which Christ has prepared for us (John 14:2) in the new heaven and new earth, the city of God (Hebrews 11:13-16). Presence, peoplehood and a place—these are true wealth for the Christian. Money in the bank, ownership certificates of bonds and title deeds to properties are only an optional extra to this wealth. But what are we to do with the temporal wealth God has entrusted to us?

Stewards of Wealth

Stewardship is much more than giving money to the church or to charities. It is caring for God's creation, managing God's household, bringing God's justice. Old Testament social legislation pointed to the coming (and present) kingdom of God with principles that were economically gracious: the provision for the gleaning of the poor by not harvesting everything one could (Ruth); the provision of the sabbath for the land and for indebted people; the cancellation of debts with Israelites and resident aliens in the seventh year—thus stressing neighbor love (Deut. 15:1-6); the command to lend without interest to one's neighbor (Deut. 15:7-11); the release of Israelite slaves on the seventh year (Deut. 15:12-18); the provision of Jubilee, by which the hopelessly indebted could start again (Leviticus 25); the command that kings and leaders must not enrich themselves by that leadership but should live simply as brother-leaders (Deut. 17:16-20).

While these commands are not to be slavishly followed under the circumstances of the new covenant, they reflect a minimum standard for economic life for people "in Christ." Christian stewardship cares for the earth, releases debts, empowers the poor, brings dignity to the marginalized and equalizes opportunity. But there is also direct giving.

Probably no other single factor indicates our true spirituality more than what we do with the wealth we have and in what spirit we share it. Christian giving is marked by hilarity (Luke 6:38; 2 Cor. 9:7) that takes us beyond a calculated tithe and reflects the generosity of God. The Lord might well ask in this area as in others, "What more do you do than the pagans who know not God? And why?"

First, we are to invest primarily in people, especially the poor. The only treasure we can take from this life to the next is the relationships we have made through Jesus (Luke 16:9). The treasures in heaven are relationships that have been formed through the gracious use of money, the investment of the things of this life in a world without end, often in the context of everyday work.

Second, we are to give wisely and carefully. It was John Wesley who advised: "Gain all you can, save all you can, give all you can." But the giving must take us beyond merely relieving the symptoms of people's distress through giving alms. Almsgiving may be a perversion of giving, because, as Ellul (p. 112) shows, it binds the recipient in an obligatory relationship, demands gratitude and does not usually address the reasons behind the person's poverty. So individuals and churches should invest in people and causes grappling with the systemic powers that hold people in bondage to a cycle of poverty. There may be no greater area of discernment needed for the Christian in everyday life than to decide when, where and how to give money away.

Third, some form of voluntary impoverishment is required of all followers of Jesus. It is not sufficient to say, as many do, "The rich young ruler was a special case" (see Matthew 19:16-30). We are all in need of profaning the false god of Mammon and relativizing wealth in this life as something less than full treasure in heaven. There are several dimensions of voluntary impoverishment. We start by relinquishing ownership to God. We practice continuous thanksgiving, which is the only way to become content whatever our circumstances (Phil. 4:12-13). We should pay our taxes with a generous heart, knowing that some of this is being used to provide services and care for the poor and disadvantaged. We should give directly to the poor with no strings attached as personally as possible (Luke 16:9; Stevens, pp. 159-65). We should give to God's global work (2 Cor. 8-9). Finally we should be ready, if so commanded by Christ, to sell all.

Christian people do not have a monopoly on giving, any more than they have a monopoly on gifts of teaching and administration or showing mercy. What makes giving a spiritual ministry, as Paul notes in Romans 12:7-8, is an extra anointing that God gives to people who are harmonizing themselves with God's Spirit. Then those who show mercy do it "cheerfully," and those contributing to the needs of others "generously." Throughout the New Testament it is the interiority of the matter that is emphasized: freedom from manipulation and covetousness, motivated by true love for God and neighbor. As Jacques Ellul notes, "Ultimately, we follow what we have loved most intensely either into eternity or into death" (Matthew 6:21; Ellul, p. 83).

References and Resources

J. M. Bassler, *Asking for Money in the New Testament* (Nashville: Abingdon, 1991); J. Chrysostom, *On Wealth and Poverty*, trans. C. P. Roth (Crestwood, N.Y.: St. Vladimir's Seminary Press, 1984); J. Ellul, *Money and Power*, trans. L. Neff (Downers Grove, Ill.: InterVarsity Press, 1984); R. Foster, *Money, Sex and Power* (San Francisco: Harper & Row, 1985); D. J. Hall, *Stewardship of Life in the Kingdom of Death* (Grand Rapids: Eerdmans, 1988); J. C. Haughey, *The Holy Use of Money: Personal Finances in the Light of the Christian Faith* (New York: Doubleday, 1986); L. T. Johnson, *Sharing Possessions: Mandate and Symbol of Faith* (London: SCM Press, 1981); R. J. Sider, *Rich Christians in an Age of Hunger* (Dallas: Word, 1990); R. P.

Stevens, *Disciplines of the Hungry Heart* (Wheaton, Ill: Harold Shaw, 1993); C. J. H. Wright, *God's People in God's Land: Family, Land and Property in the Old Testament* (Grand Rapids: Eerdmans, 1990).

—R. Paul Stevens

WHISTLE-BLOWING

Whistle-blowing can be defined as an employee's disclosing to the public illegal, immoral or unethical behavior of an employer or organization that is likely to result in harm to others. Whistle-blowing should not be done without serious reflection on the part of the prospective whistle-blower. It presents a moral conflict of loyalty—between one's employer and/or colleagues and the prevention of harm to third parties. Whistle-blowers, by calling attention to possible wrongdoing within their organizations, are the subjects of much controversy. Some see them as disgruntled employees who are tattletales, squealers and snitches. Others see them as noble characters or heroes who are willing to put themselves at risk to expose organizational practices that are wasteful, fraudulent or harmful to the public safety.

Purposes of Whistle-blowing

In an ideal organizational world whistle-blowing would be unnecessary. However, in those situations in which management has a myopic fixation on maximizing the bottom line at any cost, whistle-blowing may be needed. Some of the areas whistle-blowers have called attention to in recent years include price fixing, fraud, unsafe products, widespread embezzlement, insider trading and dumping of toxic waste. Frequently, these whistle-blowers have courageously put themselves at risk in the pursuit of bringing pressure on an organization to correct its wrongs.

Some whistle-blowers' actions, however, are ethically suspect. These individuals act out of selfish or egoistic reasons. Sometimes whistle-blowing suits are instituted by employees with an ax to grind. They may be blowing the whistle with the intent of getting even with the organization for recent decisions that affected them adversely or with the hope of getting a big financial payoff (for example, under the False Claims Act whistle-blowers can receive up to 25 percent of any money recovered by the government).

A Cost-Benefit Analysis of Whistle-blowing

The costs of whistle-blowing are high for both the company and the whistle-blower. Whether it wins or loses, the company "gets a black eye." It spends considerable time and money defending itself, and regardless of the outcome its reputation may be tarnished.

The potential costs to the whistle-blower are especially noteworthy. Unfortunately, many firms not only discourage but actually punish whistle-blowing. Other than outright dismissal, retaliation often includes demotion, false complaints about job performance, relocation or reassignment, investigation of finances and personal life, and harassment of family and friends. Even if the whistle-blower ultimately wins, the costs can still be considerable: attorney fees, money spent for living expenses while the case drags on, mental anguish and possible ostracism by former coworkers.

Criteria for Whistle-blowing

To approach whistle-blowing from both a moral and rational perspective, certain criteria should be met:

1. The purpose of the whistle-blowing should have a moral base. The public interest should be the prime concern (for example, the desire to expose unnecessary harm, a violation of human rights or conduct counter to the defined purpose of the organization).

2. What is being protested should be of major importance, be carefully analyzed and be specifically articulated. Whistle-blowing requires that the wrongdoing is a *serious* breach of ethics (for example, a company engaged in the upcoming release of a product that does serious harm to individuals or society in general).

3. The prospective whistle-blower should have compelling evidence to substantiate the facts of the protest. It is also important for the employee to have tangible documentation of the practice or defect.

4. Before the whistle is blown, all internal avenues for change within the organization should be exhausted. The employee should report this concern or complaint to his or her immediate superior to provide an opportunity for rectifying the situation. If no appropriate action is taken, the employee should take the matter up the organizational hierarchy. Before he or she goes public, the resources for remedy within the company must be exhausted.

5. The whistle-blower should be above reproach. Specifically, the whistle-blower should not benefit from revealing the information. Whistle-blowing should be an act of conscience—it should not be done principally from a selfish or vindictive orientation. To check for possible personal bias, the employee should seek considerable objective advice and then have the courage to personally accept responsibility for providing the information.

Some Final Thoughts

Sadly, legitimate whistle-blowing comes about too often because bureaucratic management blinds itself to shoddy products, environmental danger and questionable practices in order to maximize profit. Whistle-blowing may provide a signal that the organization is not performing well, has poor management or both.

It seems tenable to assume that three of the salient obligations that organizational members owe to the public it serves or to which it sells are truthfulness, noninjury and fairness. Therefore, when these crucial concomitants are willfully dashed, whistle-blowing may be necessary to bring this breach of trust to the public.

To avoid the costs of whistle-blowing for both the company and employee, some progressive organizations are attempting to provide ways for employees to report concerns and complaints. Some constructive avenues allowing employees to share their concerns include open-door policies, ombudspersons, confidential questionnaires and hot lines. While this is an encouraging sign, it would be naive to believe that there no longer will be a need for whistle-blowing.

Paul Tillich in *The Courage to Be* suggests that following one's conscience and defying unethical and unreasonable authority is an act that entails considerable risk and great courage. As Christians we must not see our relationship with our employer as one of unilateral blind loyalty. Our ultimate responsibility and loyalty are owed to the Lord. We also have a responsibility to our neighbors, other employees, customers and the general public (Matthew 22:34-40).

See also BUSINESS ETHICS; LOYALTY, WORKPLACE; ORGANIZATIONAL CULTURE AND CHANGE

References and Resources

S. Bok, *Secrets* (New York: Random House, 1983); N. Bowie, *Business Ethics* (Englewood Cliffs, N.J.: Prentice-Hall, 1982); G. F. Cavenagh, *American Business Values* (Englewood Cliffs, N.J.: Prentice-Hall, 1990); J. Richardson, ed., *Annual Editions: Business Ethics 95/96* (Sluice Dock, Guilford, Conn.: Dushkin, 1995); W. H. Shaw and V. Barry, *Moral Issues in Business* (Belmont, Calif.: Wadsworth, 1992); P. Tillich, *The Courage to Be* (New Haven, Conn.: Yale University Press, 1950).

—John E. Richardson

WORK

Work, whether in its presence or absence, is a pervasive part of everyday life. One of the first things we want to know about people is what they do. The waking time of most adults is taken up with work, and a person's passing is often noted in terms of their workplace achievements. Work and worth, industry and identity, are very closely related in contemporary culture. This article deals with work in this modern context. It will examine (1) a wider definition of work, (2) a biblically integrated view of work, (3) the disintegration of work and faith, (4) reintegrating spirituality and work and (5) redirecting Sunday towards Monday.

A Wider Definition of Work

Over the last two centuries work has become equated with a job.

This is a seismic shift in our understanding of ourselves, our world and even our God. It has had earthquakelike effects on people's emotional, family, social and spiritual life. The tremors have been felt hardest by the overworked, the unemployed, housewives, the forcibly retired and the attention-deprived children.

Despite society's materialistic definition of work as what we are paid to do, work can include any positive productive activity. A helpful, wider Christian definition of work is this: "Work is the expenditure of energy (manual or mental or both) in the service of others, which brings fulfillment to the worker, benefit to the community and glory to God" (Stott, p. 162). On that definition many people in socially destructive jobs, for example, in a cigarette or armaments factory, might not be working. On the other hand, the unemployed person cleaning up the streets and recycling a cart full of soda cans, volunteers working for schools and churches or parents changing diapers or cooking meals are working. We need to revalue these tasks for both men and women by recognizing fundamental activities that keep the world going, even though they are unpaid and economically invisible.

But does this wider view of work have biblical backing? Unlike today, in biblical times work was not a separate sphere of life. Work was integrated with the home (which was usually the workplace) and worship (through sacrifice from God's gifts and one's produce). People were not primarily valued or identified in terms of their jobs as they are today. We need to develop a more integrated biblical view of work that does justice to the value of other vital activities and relationships.

A Biblically Integrated View of Work

There are several ways of developing a biblical approach to work. One is to do a concordance study of the word. Another is a creed-based approach in terms of God as Creator, Reconciler and Re-Creator—Father, Son and Holy Spirit (Preece). Here I will identify broad perspectives and principles that can help us place work within a scriptural framework of relationships—to God, humanity and the earth (Wright, pp. 89-90, 100).

God's work. The God of the Bible is a worker, in contrast to the ancient Near Eastern gods, who slept while their human slaves labored. Sadly, many of us forget that before we get up on Monday morning, God has already been at work: "He who keeps Israel will neither slumber nor sleep" (Psalm 121:4 NRSV). Jesus said, "My Father is still working, and I also am working" (John 5:17 NRSV). The sabbath is a reminder that we live by God's work, not our own (Genesis 2:3; Matthew 11:28; Hebrews 4).

Exploring the wide-ranging biblical imagery of divine work can give us a greater sense of being junior partners in God's work of creation, preservation and redemption. For example, God is an architect and a builder (Proverbs 8:27-31), a doctor-healer (Mark 2:12, 17), a teacher (Matthew 7:28-29), a weaver (Psalm 139:13-16), a gardener/farmer (Genesis 2:8-9; Genesis 3:8; John 15:1-8), a shepherd (Psalm 23; John 10), a potter/craftworker (Jeremiah 18:1-9; Romans 9:19-21) and a homemaker (Luke 15:8; Banks). By seeing our work in the light of God's work, we can see God's hand in our everyday tasks. Unless we do so, we will underestimate the importance of God's work and either worship our work or think it worthless. But work can be an expression of worship or communion with God. It should not be confused with or replace our corporate worship, but it is an everyday offering of our whole selves, bodies and minds, to God (Romans 12:1-2). "Render service with enthusiasm, as to the Lord and not to men and women" (Ephes. 6:7 NRSV).

Human work and human relationships. Work is not only to provide for ourselves (2 Thes. 3:10-13) and our families (1 Tim. 5:8) but also "to have something to share with the needy" (Ephes. 4:28 NRSV). So work is one of the basic ways we fulfill our social responsibilities. Many things we make at work also provide the stage in which people can interact, for example, telephones and furniture. Making hand-held video games largely does not. From a biblical view one question we can ask of our work is whether it furthers relationships or not.

While we should distinguish ourselves from what we do, we should not divorce the two. Being and doing flow into each other. A mother working in a shop does not stop being a mother while she is at work. Her homegrown experiences and skills are valuable (even if unrecognized) in her paid employment, and her experience on the job will be reflected at home.

The author of Ecclesiastes provides a balance between being and doing by emphasizing relationships. He has a word of warning for both the envious workaholic and the lazy shirkaholic who neglect relationships and lead meaningless lives. The alternative is that "two are better than one, because they have a good reward for their toil. For if they fall, one will lift up the other; but woe to one who is alone and falls and does not have another to help. . . . A threefold cord is not quickly broken" (Eccles. 4:9-12 NRSV). So, after communion with God "community building is every person's second full-time job" (Stevens, pp. 15-16).

The same writer provides a commentary on the fallen or cursed dimension of work or toil (see also Genesis 3:17-19). Work done out of mere ambition and selfishness and work neglected out of laziness are both vain. Even work with good motives will often be ignored or wasted. We all die, and our work will not last; it is transient. While we have opportunity, we should simply enjoy working, as well as the food and drink it puts on the table, as a gift from God. It is best to have modest expectations of work and not try to build lasting monuments (Eccles. 2:18-26; Stevens, pp. 4-5).

Our groaning as we toil is part of creation's groaning, longing for liberation from the vanity to which it was subjected by God in hope (Romans 8:20-23). But *under the risen Son,* work done for God and others is not in vain, even if society may not value it. In the new heavens and new earth "my chosen shall long enjoy the work of their hands. They shall not labor in vain" (Isaiah 65:22-23 NRSV). "Therefore, my beloved, be steadfast, immovable, always excelling in the work of the Lord, because you know that in the Lord your labor is not in vain" (1 Cor. 15:58 NRSV).

Caring for the earth. According to Genesis 1:28 (NRSV), as those made in God's image, we are to "be fruitful and multiply, and fill the earth and subdue it." This is balanced by the direction in Genesis 2:15, in which Adam is to till and keep the garden, or serve and preserve it. This has not only agricultural but also cultural dimensions, as Adam's naming the animals shows. As God's representatives we are to care for the earth (*see* Ecology) and each other in the productive realm of work and the reproductive realm of family. Women are involved in both realms. The wise woman of Proverbs 31 is involved in providing food, land and clothing, planting vines, trading and caring for the poor. Her work was publicly recognized, bringing her praise in the city gates (Proverbs 31:10-31). This needs to be heard in a world in which women are often paid less in jobs and work a second shift at home and in which many people receive no recognition for unpaid work done well.

In the divine economy, work is evaluated according to the way it fosters or retards relationships—between ourselves and God, our companions and the earthly resources we are called to develop.

The Disintegration of Work and Faith

Given the Bible's integrated view of spirituality and work, how did these two come apart, so that even many Christians do not feel the connection?

Historical reasons. In the Greek world work was seen as a necessity or curse for slaves to perform. The truly free and human pursuits were politics and philosophy: "Work was called 'unleisure,'. . . *ergon or ponos,* a burden and toil" (Stevens, p. 26). During the fifth century B.C. some cities issued a decree prohibiting their citizens from engaging in work!

This Greek influence appears in the apocryphal Wisdom book Ecclesiasticus, which, though more respectful of the trades than the Greeks or the Egyptians, exalts the scribe over the tradesperson, contemplation and leisure over material action. Only the one who is free from toil can become wise. Workers have to concentrate on their work rather than the wonders and mysteries of the world. The merchant or businessperson "can hardly remain without fault" (Sirach 26:29) for "between buying and selling sin is wedged" (Sirach 27:2).

Sadly, this is still the way many Christians see trades and business. In the hierarchy of vocations clergy and missionaries (our equivalent of Ecclesiasticus' scribes of Bible scholars) are still near the top; the caring professions (for example, social workers and doctors) are next, while business people and trades come last. Working with things such as technology, money and administration is often seen as inferior both by those who stress soul-winning and those who stress social activism. This stems from the division between spirituality and work, head and hand, wisdom and skill, people and things, which is not present in the more creation-centered canonical Wisdom literature (compare Proverbs 31) nor in the cultural mandate to rule the earth responsibly (Genesis 1:26-28). Tradespeople and business people do not have to be social workers or evangelists to serve God at work.

Under the influence of Greek dualism the early church and the Middle Ages reinforced the distinction between spirituality and work. As a result the story of Mary and Martha (Luke 10:38-42) was reinterpreted to exalt the contemplative over the active life.

Martin Luther reacted against the medieval disparagement of ordinary work in favor of the work of priests or monks. He reclaimed the idea of vocation, or divine calling, for the ordinary Christians as homemakers, paid workers or citizens. Luther saw all of these as providential ways in which Christians could serve their neighbor and worship God. The tools of one's workshop were constant reminders to do this: "In making shoes the cobbler serves God, obeys his calling from God, quite as much as the preacher of the Word." Luther could say, "God himself will milk the cows through him whose vocation it is!"

Unfortunately, around the time of the later Puritans (mid-17th century), the notion of vocation became secularized and narrowed down to the job. It became increasingly individualistic, losing the sense of worshiping God and serving the common good (*see* Calling). Through Benjamin Franklin (a Deist, not a Christian), the Protestant work ethic became popularized through such maxims as "Early to bed and early to rise makes a man healthy, wealthy, and wise" and "Time is money." Through the concept of a career, work increasingly became a means to the end of status and security rather than a means to the end of serving God and supporting self and others, which becomes a joy in itself.

For all its gains in living standards, the Industrial Revolution separated the spheres of work, home and church, institutionalizing working for a wage (something previously regarded as degrading compared with self-employment). Despite its considerable difficulties preindustrial life had a greater sense of integration between work, home and church. All were within sight of one another, and the church was the connecting link to the whole of life.

Contemporary reasons. Today many people are split between the Sunday and Monday, or private and public, areas of their lives. In a highly specialized society we play different roles according to different rules with different parts of our personalities, and our lives slowly disintegrate. Our name is truly "Legion."

Many of the pastoral and spiritual crises people face are a direct result of this disintegration of work, home and church. The absent-father syndrome has now been extended to include the absent-mother, as both parents struggle to keep jobs as well as maintain marriages and families. There is often a direct clash between escalating demands on people by family, education, career and church that can be crippling unless an integrative spirituality sensitive to life stages is taught, modeled and nurtured.

Surveys indicate that in far-flung commuter suburbs low church attendance was due not to people there being less religious but to the long hours spent at, or going to and from, work. Some people want to attend church and small groups but have too little time and energy. The church's mainly female pool of volunteer labor is shrinking rapidly as the personal, social and financial rewards of working prove more attractive (although there are recent signs of a move back from this). In failing to shape and develop a spirituality for the workplace and neglecting to challenge its dehumanizing structures, the church has by default been (mis)shaped by it.

Reintegrating Spirituality and Work

To maintain spiritual integrity, we need a spirituality that integrates, not separates, our faith and work. The individualistic "Protestant prayer ethic," which gets the leftovers from the Protestant work ethic, fails to provide this. Under the pressures of modern work many Christians feel isolated and unsupported in the workplace and find it difficult to pray and reflect in a way that integrates their church and work lives. Some theological guidelines for developing a corporate spirituality of work follow.

Reemphasizing the importance of the church scattered as well as the church gathered. Both the vocational (the church scattered) and the worship (the church gathered) activities of Christians are important. On Sunday the latter equip and mobilize the scattered people of God for their mission and ministry on Monday. But also needed are small committed groups in which people can honestly share their struggles in faith, home and work.

We also need mission groups as well as Christian peers and mentors in the workplace. Without this our professional group unconsciously becomes our church, determining major life decisions concerning where to live, what car to drive, how to dress, where to school our children. This then determines our de facto spirituality, which is then used to justify our professional lifestyle.

Recapturing a sense of vocation. From the Bible and the Protestant Reformation emerges the understanding that all Christians have a ministry and vocation to serve in the working world, an understanding modeled on Christ as prophet, priest and king. This does not pit preaching or evangelism against ordinary work but sees kingdom work as healing creation and the Great Commission (Matthew 28:19-20) as fulfilling the creation commission (Genesis 1:26-28). So we do not unethically evangelize on the boss's time, trying to justify our job to the full-time preachers, but work, live and speak in a way that represents the rule of Christ over the whole of creation, including the working world.

Recapturing the idea of the "mixed life." We must not abandon Christian people to the totalitarian demands of many workplaces and the Martha life of unreflective activism. Nor should we forfeit the workplace and adopt the monastic, contemplative Mary life. The fourteenth-century monk Walter Hilton wrote letters to an English man of affairs, involved in commercial and political life, who wanted to enter contemplative life in a religious community. In his *Letters to a Layman* Hilton wisely counseled a third way, a mixed life combining the activity of Martha with the reflectiveness of Mary (Stevens, pp. xiv-xv). Such a spirituality needs to be consciously modeled and taught.

Reconnecting wisdom, virtue and skill. Developing a spirituality of competence and compassion is needed to overcome the split between Mary and Martha. Work is a major way we can cultivate and develop Christian virtues (Galatians 5) and attitudes (Matthew 5:1-13). It can develop either the fruit of the Spirit, making us patient, gentle and self-controlled, or the opposite fruits of the flesh. These virtues do not spring up in a vacuum but emerge through much practice and, above all, grace. The "supernatural" virtues of faith, hope and love have particular significance for a spirituality of work. Paul commends the Thessalonians for their "work produced by faith, . . . labor prompted by love, and . . . endurance inspired by hope in our Lord Jesus Christ" (1 Thes. 1:3). We carry these characteristics, and work characterized by them, all the way to heaven. This idea is captured in a painting of the Second Coming by Swiss artist Paul Robert in Neuchatel, Switzerland. It portrays the people rising to meet Christ, bearing the fruits of their callings: doctors having healed people, architects having built beautiful buildings and so on—each one eager to render an account to Christ of his or her work.

Redirecting Sunday Toward Monday

If we are to overcome the perceived gap between Sunday and Monday, the church will have to shift its pastoral and mission priorities toward Monday. Today the primary place where men and women meet others is the workplace. Evangelism in the marketplace was common in the New Testament (Acts 16:16-19; Acts 17:17; Acts 19:9-10, 23-29). While we should not be evangelizing on the boss's time, a truly integrated life and a willingness to speak in a wise and timely way tailored to the needs of others (Col. 4:5-6) will attract questions and interest that can be explored during breaks and lunchtime and before or after work.

As Scripture imaginatively used workplace terminology to express aspects of the gospel message, so should we in sharing our faith. In early Christian times the terms *sacrifice* (of the work of one's hands), *redemption* (of slaves) and *debts* (of money) all had strong workplace connections. Moreover, teaching topics and illustrations should include work-related ones. Paul spoke at length of master-slave relationships (Ephes. 6:5-9; Col. 3:22-4:1). In 2 Tim. 2:1-7 he draws from a range of working illustrations (athlete, farmer, soldier) for single-mindedness.

Corporate worship opportunities should be related to working life. Workers' testimonies—drawn from homemaking, volunteer work or the market-place—can be a great encouragement to others and can be included in services during announcements, the offering (when we give the products of our work back to God) or at the conclusion of the service when we hear the call to mission. Prayers for people's working lives should be a regular part of intercession. Church rolls or address lists might include work roles to enable members to make connections and offer appropriate prayers. Special services, such as a faith-and-work Sunday or urban harvest festival with people bringing symbols of their work, are also a useful way of encouraging a more integrated spirituality.

Pastoral care should be extended to the workplace. Preventive pastoral care will often involve standing for justice with God's people and providing emotional and financial support if they face loss of employment for taking a Christian stand on an issue. Moreover, mutual confession, counseling and discipline need to be restored and related to workplace struggles and sins. Puritan manuals often dealt with issues of conscience in the workplace. Pastors, leaders' groups, church counseling ministries and small groups could provide appropriate supportive and accountable contexts.

The gap between Sunday and Monday can be narrowed further by creatively bridging the physical distance between churches and the workplace. The New Testament church met in homes that often had workplaces in the front room on the street. Masters and slaves shared the same living space and social life. While we cannot turn back the clock, we should bring our work, home and church life as close together as possible. We can use occasional fringe-work activities over meals or beverages to build relationships. Opening our homes in hospitality to fellow workers can lead to a new level of relationship. Where possible, church buildings should be located near the commercial center rather than be lost in suburban back streets.

These wide-ranging suggestions can begin to turn the tide of a war that has seen the workplace forfeited rather than lost. Together they can enable a greater integration of faith and work, Sunday and Monday, spirituality and activity.

References and Resources

R. J. Banks, *God the Worker* (Valley Forge, Penn.: Judson, 1994); R. J. Banks and G. R. Preece, *Getting the Job Done Right* (Wheaton: Victor Books, 1992); L. Hardy, *The Fabric of This World* (Grand Rapids: Eerdmans, 1990); G. R. Preece, "The Threefold Call," in *Faith Goes to Work,* ed. R. J. Banks (Washington D.C.: Alban Institute, 1993) 160-71; J. B. Schor, *The Overworked American* (New York: Basic, 1991); P. Stevens, *Disciplines of the Hungry Heart* (Wheaton: Harold Shaw, 1993); J. Stott, *Issues Facing Christians Today* (Basingstoke, U.K.: Marshalls, 1984); M. Volf, *Work in the Spirit: Toward a Theology of Work* (New York: Oxford University Press, 1991); C. J. H. Wright, *An Eye for an Eye* (Downers Grove, Ill.: InterVarsity Press, 1983).

—Gordon Preece

WORK ETHIC, PROTESTANT

We hear frequent mention of the *Protestant work ethic,* sometimes positively but more often negatively. Except in some scholarly circles the phrase does not have a precise meaning, and even there not everyone is in full agreement. Generally it refers to some of the following attitudes and behavior: (1) believing that work gives meaning to life; (2) having a strong sense of duty to one's work; (3) believing in the necessity of hard work and of giving work (even before the family) the best of one's time; (4) believing that work contributes to the moral worth of the individual and to the health of the social order; (5) viewing wealth as a major goal in life; (6) viewing leisure as earned by work and as preparation for work; (7) viewing success in work as resulting primarily from the amount of personal effort; (8) viewing wealth that accrues from work as a sign of God's favor. Though writers might single out one or two of these characteristics for special attention, everyone seems to be confident that he or she knows what the term means.

Individual reactions to the term and what it stands for tend to be all positive or all negative. Some regret the passing or weakening of this traditional understanding of work and would like to see it reinstated. Others regard the gradual demise of the Protestant work ethic as liberating, for it raises the possibility of a more open and flexible approach to work that is better suited to people's personal makeup and to current economic realities. An early depiction of conflict between these two attitudes is in the well-known play *Death of a Salesman* by Arthur Miller. Later examples may be found in such popular sitcoms as *All in the Family* and *Till Death Do Us Part*. As we shall see, present understandings of the Protestant work ethic contain a strange blend of authentic and inauthentic elements. It is by telling the story of how a focus on the Protestant work ethic arose that we can begin to distinguish between them.

Major Interpretations of the Protestant Work Ethic

In the middle of the nineteenth century, Karl Marx insisted that the modern middle-class ethic owed its existence to material factors, such as the spread of capitalist forces of production and the division and exploitation of labor. Shortly after the turn of the twentieth century, sociologist Max Weber acknowledged the role of these factors but argued that the root of the work ethic lay further back in religious beliefs about calling, election and work stemming from John Calvin. These beliefs were further developed by such later Puritans as William Perkins and Richard Baxter and came to concrete expression in the approach of people like Benjamin Franklin. The unforeseen consequences of the Protestant perspective included a heightened sense of moral obligation to work, the conviction that a person's election by God was authenticated by his or her achievements at work and the perceived importance of living thriftily off the proceeds from work, with the remainder being saved, invested or given away. R. H. Tawney popularized a modified version of Weber's thesis. He argued that since the understanding of calling and pockets of capitalism had emerged before the Reformation, the work ethic was not a purely Protestant phenomenon. Also, it was not until the latter, largely post-Puritan, part of the seventeenth century that it developed the strong emphasis on individual success, rather than social obligations, which we associate with it. From this point on, though more closely connected with Nonconformists and Methodists, the work ethic took hold. So Puritanism was only partially responsible for it. Since Tawney wrote, other historians have suggested that the story is even more complex. For example, even where Protestantism held sway, there were significant differences between regions in their attitudes toward work. Even climatic conditions appear to have played a part.

Key Criticisms of the Main Interpretations

There are good grounds for arguing that what most people have in mind when they refer to the "Protestant work ethic" would be more accurately described as the "post-Protestant work ethic." Calvin, following Luther, wrote in a time when ordinary work (when compared with monastic work) was devalued, and he was attempting to give work a new dignity before God, not insist on its centrality. In any case, his emphasis was on diligence in work and its usefulness to others, not on a preoccupation with work or on its personal significance. Calvin insisted on the importance of each person's finding a place through work for his or her God-given gifts (or talents, a word whose meaning owes much to his influence) and of work as embodying and expressing the mutual dependence of people on each other, that is, as a concrete expression of human fellowship, solidarity and community. This also led Calvin to discern a connection between the general order of work in society and the provision of social justice to those in need.

Weber lumped together the views of Calvin and later Puritans, but Calvin's followers began to move beyond his views in subtle ways. For example, many developed a greater interest in the use of time at work and in the link between fruitful work and the doctrine of divine assurance. After the Restoration, when Puritanism again became a minority position, certain Nonconformists and eighteenth-century Methodists (on whom Tawney places the major weight) gave greater attention to the importance of getting the most financially that a person can through work, though with a view to saving and responsibly investing it or giving it away (*see* Stewardship). Many also experienced solid work and its fruits as granting them upward social mobility, for which they were devoutly thankful to God.

The crucial differences in the development of the work ethic took place after this, occurring chiefly in the nominally religious, or early post-Protestant, attitudes that developed in the early days of the Industrial Revolution. In that period many people were gradually moving away from full dependence on the sufficiency of Christ's work for their salvation and sanctification. Requiring some other ground on which to justify themselves—before God, before others and sometimes most of all before themselves—they began to look around for a replacement. The burgeoning and increasingly dynamic field of work was nearest at hand, at least for the emerging middle class. So work began to become invested with new significance.

In pre-Reformation days many people had sought to justify themselves and gain acceptance with God and others through religious works. This road was largely closed to Protestants, but their ordinary work was still available to them as a substitute. As this happened, work moved into a more central place, being viewed less as a context for serving others than as a context for human achievement and less as a divine calling than as a personal career. Work increasingly became the place where most of one's time and energy was invested, throwing out of balance the relationship between work, family and leisure. The degree of success in one's work, rather than a person's full acceptance by God, increasingly determined a person's status in the eyes of others. All of these attitudes are in basic conflict with the Protestant understanding of the gospel and vision of the Christian life.

Conclusion

In view of these criticisms, we cannot unreservedly regret the weakening of what is called the Protestant work ethic. Over the last two centuries it has become at best encrusted with, and at worst transformed into, something different from what it was originally. Also not everything said about the ethic by earlier Protestants was equally valid. For example, if Luther too rigidly tied people's work to their existing station in life rather than to the particular gifts God had given them to use, later Puritans too rigidly identified people's God-given vocation with work, at the expense of people's other involvements and responsibilities. Frequently, with some illustrious exceptions including Calvin and many early Puritans, the vocation of rest alongside the vocation of work was not given its proper emphasis.

Even if we need to correct the earlier Protestant understanding of work and identify the secularized distortions that later crept in, the work ethic still preserves some genuine Protestant values. Among these we should include the virtue and dignity of work; the sanctity of all legitimate types of work; the importance of responsible work rather than slovenly work or idleness; the outcome of proper work—whether successful or not—as proceeding from a service to God and society. Other aspects of the original Protestant understanding of work need to be reclaimed: for example, its view of our work as part of our divine calling or vocation rather than as a personal career or just a job; its recognition of service to others, rather than self-fulfillment or even our own gifts, as the main guide to our choice and conduct of work; its assurance that God is well able to supply such fulfillment if we put the purposes of the kingdom above our personal preferences (compare Matthew 6:33); its refusal to regard work as what gives us our basic identity or meaning; its essentially communal, rather than individual,character; and its recognition of leisure as the foundation of work rather than requiring work for its justification. Taking all these characteristics into account, we can say, with the social commentator Daniel Yankelovich, that in some respects the work ethic is not so much overvalued as undervalued by too many people today. In other respects, far too much is made of it, and workaholic tendencies should be challenged wherever they arise.

References and Resources

S. N. Eisenstadt, *The Protestant Ethic and Modernization* (New York: Basic, 1968); A. Homes, "Wanted: A Work Ethic for Today," *The Reformed Journal* 28 (October 1978) 17-20; M. J. Kitch, ed., *Capitalism and the Reformation* (New York: Longman, 1967); H. Lehmann and G. Roth, *Weber's Protestant Ethic: Origins, Evidence, Contexts* (Cambridge: Cambridge University Press, 1995); P. Marshall et al., *Labor of Love: Essays on Work* (Toronto: Wedge, 1980); L. Ryken, *Work and Leisure in Christian Perspective* (Portland, Ore.: Multnomah, 1987); R. H. Tawney, *Religion and the Rise of Capitalism: A Historical Study* (London: Pelican, 1938); M. Weber, *The Protestant Ethic and the Spirit of Capitalism:*

The Relationship Between Religion and the Economic and Social Life in Modern Culture (New York: Scribner's, 1958).

—Robert Banks

WORKPLACE

Alongside work itself, workplaces are undergoing significant changes today. There was a time, as during the biblical and classical periods, when work was largely undertaken in the field or open country, home or street, in small-scale factories or fishing enterprises. By late medieval and early modern times, open markets and guild-based businesses became more important. In the wake of the revolutions in industry and technology large mechanized factories and bureaucratized offices came into being, and even farming, ranching and fishing became big business. Now the context in which work takes places is changing substantially again.

In considering the workplace, I am thinking of the architecture and layout, the conditions and procedures, the dynamics and ethos, of the spaces in which we work. This whole environment should receive as much thoughtful Christian attention as what we do in it. Yet if work itself has often received little Christian reflection, this is even truer of the workplace. A main reason for this is that in many forms of Christianity, there is a dualistic tendency that separates the spiritual and the material, persons and structures, the relational and cultural. Since the workplace is in part a physical context, in part a set of structures and in part an institutional culture, it easily falls victim to this dualistic way of looking at reality. Yet the total environment of the workplace is important, partly because as a human creation it tells us something about ourselves, our attitudes and values and partly because our workplaces shape us, the work we do and the relationships we form at work.

The Changing Nature of the Workplace

Among the changes occurring in workplaces today, three-quarters of which are still small businesses, the following are particularly noteworthy. The majority of workplaces are becoming technologized. Nearly three-quarters of all jobs today require at least some elementary word-processing skills. Increasingly office work, retail work and even factory work are being mechanized and computerized. Though this replaces some monotonous jobs, it also tends to reduce the personal element in the workplace and creates a new class of mechanized workers who require special training or reeducation.

Another noticeable trend is the integration of smaller business enterprises into larger ones, or the more intentional collaboration of large and small businesses. The first is taking place even as many firms downsize and large public corporations are being broken up into more competitive units: this means we now have blended workplaces as well as blended families.

In most places the workplace is rapidly becoming more multicultural and international. While affirmative-action practices have had their impact, the growing pluralism in modern societies has generated its own organic changes. In some sectors of the marketplace, links or business between firms in different countries is also forcing their work forces to be more cross-cultural.

With the breakdown in family life and neighborhood community, workplaces have increasingly assumed some of the character of both. As a number of television sitcoms illustrate, many people now look to their workplaces for a sense of belonging, for quality relationships and for the experience of community. Sadly, sometimes Christians encounter these more in their workplaces than in their churches. At the same time, workplaces have become more volatile contexts with respect to charges of sexual harassment and personal discrimination. Anxiety has also increased about the incidence of workers with AIDS. Violence is also increasing as highly disgruntled and disturbed individuals are taking out their frustrations and pathologies on others in the workplace. Concern about injury, assault and even murder in the workplace is growing.

Other changes can be mentioned. For example, for a small but growing proportion of people, the home is once again becoming their workplace, largely because of the personal computer. In some cases this allows people to work in a different state or part of the country from where their company or firm is located. At present, approximately 4 percent of the population already work from home, and some predict that this will ultimately rise to around 20 percent. Others challenge this, arguing that most people will not want to give up the social benefits of working with others and that many jobs will require a mix of home- and office-based activity.

A Christian Perspective on the Workplace

All environments, whether human or divine, appealing or appalling, shape us in some degree or other. They affect what we are seeking to do and how we do it, our personal reactions and our relationships with others. We are built by the Creator in such a way that we are influenced not only by our bodies but by our physical surroundings. Because of this, we should become more aware of the changes that are occurring in the workplace. The more responsible our position, the more obligation we have to know and interpret such changes to others around us. But we need to evaluate as well as understand the changes in our workplaces. What are their positive and negative effects? How do we decide what has the character of one and what has the character of the other? We can look at these under the headings of architecture and layout, conditions and procedures, ethos and culture.

The architecture and layout of a workplace raise questions about the atmosphere in which work is done, the comfort level of employees, the connection with the rhythms of the day or the natural world, the accessibility of leaders and the quality of communication with colleagues. It is important to create a setting that is as spacious and comfortable as possible. If, as is the case, most people are now spending more time at work than in any other activity, including sleep, they should perform their tasks in conditions that are as congenial and conducive as possible. It is also important to create a setting that enhances the capacity for spontaneous as well as organized contact to happen between people. This is especially important for people whose work would be enhanced by it or, because of the repetitive nature of their jobs, would simply be made more enjoyable and less monotonous. Both lead to greater productivity and loyalty. With workplaces becoming more technologized, care must be exercised lest they become as machine oriented as older mechanized factories did in the past. How to avoid the office becoming a kind of electronic assembly line is a real issue. Training people to use computers properly and exhibiting a concern for possible physical repercussions are useful as far as they go, but more attention needs to be given to the social consequences of the new technology and its effect upon people's attitudes and general ways of thinking.

The conditions and procedures in workplaces are also important. It is still sadly the case that the majority of hours lost to the workplace is due to accidents—not to people taking illegitimate sick leave or wasting time on the job. Safety is still an important issue in the workplace, and we should have far more of it. Procedures also need to be developed to deal with the increasing possibility of violence in the workplace. Workers need to be informed about and prepared for the forms this takes, to learn how to handle it when it arises and to be helped to manage stress and debrief after it takes place. On a different note, while gains were made earlier in the century by applying time-and-motion-study techniques to the workplace, these did not always take into account the differences between humans and machines. The detailed timing of operations in some plants, financial institutions and fast-food outlets places workers under an extraordinary strain. After a while ongoing attempts to *kaizan,* that is, to increase time-and-motion efficiency of particular operations, become impractical or counterproductive. Too many workplaces are like a prison. This is not to say that everything should have a flexible character; ultimately that would be as frustrating and restrictive as its opposite.

While procedures for helping workplaces deal more responsibly with issues of harassment and discrimination are now fairly well in place, more organic ways of raising awareness and creating an inclusive culture still lag behind. So too does educating people into the differences between people of different ethnic groups or nationalities, so that, where appropriate, workplaces can develop a genuinely crosscultural way of operating. The dynamics and ethos of a workplace are crucial to its functioning well, mainly because they are vital to the well-being of its members. At work, as in all areas of life, being comes before doing, a fact that has often been forgotten. On the other hand, things can go too far in the opposite direction. Regarding the workplace as a surrogate family or community mistakes its proper purpose. If the workplace should never be an impersonal Fordian assembly line or Kafkaesque bureaucratic maze, nor should it be a kind of living room or community space. It is primarily a task-oriented, not person-oriented, affair. People are taken seriously because they are first and foremost persons, not functions, and because they perform tasks better when their personhood is respected, affirmed and developed. Some degree of community naturally arises as this is done, but it is not the main purpose of the workplace. The trick is to strike the right balance in the workplace between care for the task and care for the person.

A Christian perspective on the workplace cannot be summed up under any one phrase, such as enhancing its attractiveness or making it more congenial, improving its safety or bringing greater justice into it, making it more humane or helping it to become more caring and compassionate. Any of these may be relevant at one time or another, often one more than another, sometimes several at once. All are important and at different times may have priority. The main thing is to have a good understanding of the total environment in which we are operating, along with a sharp sense of what is the most pressing concern at the present.

References and Resources

J. F. Coates, J. Jarratt and J. B. Mahaffie, *Future Work: Seven Critical Forces Reshaping Work and the Workforce in North America* (San Francisco: Jossey-Bass, 1990); R. Flannery, *Violence in the Workplace* (New York: Crossroad, 1995); J. Renesch, ed., *New Traditions in Business: Spirit and Leadership in the 21st Century* (San Francisco: Berrett-Koehler, 1992).

—Robert Banks

Printed in the United States
105473LV00003B/94-102/A

9 781573 832946